Wireless Home Networking For Dummies®

Wireless LAN Technologies

Wireless LAN Technology	Frequency	Max. Speed	Compatibility	Available?
802.11b (Wi-Fi)	2.4 GHz	11 Mbps	802.11g	Now
802.11a (Wi-Fi5)	5 GHz	54 Mbps	none	Now
802.11g	2.4Ghz	54 Mbps	802.11b (at 11 Mbps)	Now

Wireless Home Network Equipment Requirements

Stuff You Need	Quantity You Need
Broadband DSL or cable modem connection	One
Wireless LAN access point (AP)	One (or maybe more if you've got a big house)
Cat 5e patch cable*	Two: One short one (to connect AP to broadband modem) and one 100-ft one (for troubleshooting and emergencies)
Wireless LAN network adapters	One per computer
Wireless Ethernet bridge	One per other networked device with Ethernet port (for example, Xbox)
Home network router	One (optional; usually included in access point)
Wireless repeater	One or more (optional)

* Make sure that your broadband router, AP, and other gear comes with a Cat 5e patch cable, or be sure to buy one separately on top of the cable you'll need to connect the AP to the broadband router (if your AP doesn't come with a cable).

Wireless LAN Glossary

802.11: The general standard, developed by the IEEE, for wireless local area networks. Within the 802.11 standard, there are various substandards, including 802.11b (11 Mbps using the 2.4 GHz spectrum), 802.11a (54 Mbps using the 5 GHz spectrum), and 802.11g (54 Mbps using the 2.4 GHz spectrum).

access point (AP): A wireless LAN base station that connects a wired network (like the wired Ethernet connection on a broadband modem) to the wireless network. The AP contains a radio transceiver (which transmits and receives radio signals), and most APs contain a router which reads the addresses within data packets and can direct them to the appropriate networked computer.

Bluetooth: A standard system for wireless personal area networks (or PANs). Bluetooth provides speeds of up to 723 Kbps at short ranges (typically less than 10 meters). PAN technologies, like Bluetooth, are complementary to LAN technologies (like 802.11), and are typically used to connect peripheral devices together (like keyboards to computers, or wireless headsets to mobile phones).

For Dummies: Bestselling Book Series for Beginners

Wireless Home Networking For Dummies®

Cheat Sheet

Ethernet: A standard data communications protocol enabling computers and computer peripheral devices such as printers to interface with one another and across networks for the exchange of information. The most common variation of Ethernet found in home networks is the 10 Mbps 10BaseT variant, but dozens of other variations exist with speeds up to 1000 Mbps.

IP address: The "phone number" of the Internet, the IP address is used to identify computers and devices connected to the Internet, and allows traffic to be routed across the Internet. In most wireless home networks, there are two IP addresses: a *public* IP address (used by your modem and access point or router) that identifies your network to other computers on the Internet, and a set of *private* IP addresses used only within your network. Your access point (or separate router, if you have one) translates between your public and private IP addresses to send data to the right computer within your network.

LAN (local area network): A computer data communications network used within a limited physical location, like a house.

network adapter (also Network Interface Card, or NIC): A device that connects to an internal bus in a PC, which provides an interface between the computer or device and the LAN. For wireless networks, network adapters typically connect to the PC Card bus, or the USB bus of the device being networked.

Network Address Translation (NAT): A process performed within your access point (or separate router, if you use one) to route, or direct, data from your network's public IP address to the appropriate computer or devices within your network using a private IP address.

Service Set Identifier (SSID): Also referred to as ESSID, Network Name, Service Area, and other terms, this is the name that identifies a specific wireless LAN. In order to connect to a network, a device must "know" the SSID of the network.

wireless LAN repeater: A device which extends the range of a wireless LAN by receiving signals from an access point (and other devices on a wireless LAN) and retransmitting them. A wireless LAN repeater is often placed in a separate part of the house and is used to allow devices that are too far from the access point to "get onto" the wireless LAN.

wireless Ethernet bridge: A device which connects to an Ethernet port on a networked device (like a PC, game console, or networked audio system), and provides network adapter functionality for that device.

Wired Equivalent Privacy (WEP): The encryption system used by wireless LANs to provide security on the network. WEP uses an encryption *key* (which can be 40 or 108 bits long — these are often referred to as 64 and 128 bit keys, due to some extra bits used in the WEP system) to encrypt data flowing across the network. Without the WEP encryption key, unauthorized users see only garbled data, and are unable to read what is being sent across the network.

Copyright © 2003 Wiley Publishing, Inc.
All rights reserved.

Item 3910-8.

For more information about Wiley Publishing, call 1-800-762-2974.

For Dummies: Bestselling Book Series for Beginners

Wireless Home Networking

FOR

DUMMIES®

Wireless Home Networking
FOR DUMMIES®

by Danny Briere, Walter R. Bruce III,
and Pat Hurley

WILEY

Wiley Publishing, Inc.

Wireless Home Networking For Dummies®

Published by
Wiley Publishing, Inc.
909 Third Avenue
New York, NY 10022
www.wiley.com

For general information on our other products and services or to obtain technical support, please contact our Customer Care Department within the U.S. at 800-762-2974, outside the U.S. at 317-572-3993, or fax 317-572-4002.

Wiley also publishes its books in a variety of electronic formats. Some content that appears in print may not be available in electronic books.

Library of Congress Control Number: 2003101860

ISBN: 0-7645-3910-8

Manufactured in the United States of America

10 9 8 7 6 5 4

1B/SR/QV/QT/IN

About the Authors

Danny Briere founded TeleChoice, Inc., a telecommunications consulting company, in 1985 and now serves as CEO of the company. Widely known throughout the telecommunications and networking industry, Danny has written more than 1,000 articles about telecommunications topics and has authored or edited eight books, including *Internet Telephony For Dummies*, *Smart Homes For Dummies,* 2nd Edition, and *Home Theater For Dummies*. He is frequently quoted by leading publications on telecommunications and technology topics and can often be seen on major TV networks providing analysis on the latest communications news and breakthroughs. Danny lives in Mansfield Center, Connecticut, with his wife and four children.

Walter R. Bruce III is a writer and consultant who is an avid wireless network user and who has been programming and using computers since the late 1960s (that's right, he's old). For more than a dozen years, Walter has been training computer users and writing and publishing books about computer technology. He has written many internationally published books on a variety of computer operating system, database, telecommunication, and networking topics. As a publishing professional, he has also directed the publication of hundreds of computer-related books for three successful publishing companies. Walter holds an undergraduate degree in mathematics as well as a law degree. Walter installed his first network in 1985 in the Pentagon while working for the Judge Advocate General of the United States Air Force. He was practicing law in the USAF when he discovered his affinity for teaching people how to use computers. For several years, he has directed Novell Press, the official publisher of books about Novell networking technology. Walter currently lives with his family in the Silicon Valley area of northern California.

Pat Hurley is a consultant with TeleChoice, Inc., specializing in emerging telecommunications technologies including all the latest access and home technologies: wireless LANs, DSL, cable modems, satellite services, and home networking services. Pat frequently consults with the leading telecommunications carriers, equipment vendors, consumer goods manufacturers, and other players in the telecommunications and consumer electronics industries. Pat is the co-author of *Internet Telephony For Dummies*, *Smart Homes For Dummies,* 2nd Edition, and *Home Theater For Dummies.* He lives in San Diego, California, with his wife and two smelly dogs.

Dedication

To Mom and Dad, you've always been there for us. We can't thank you enough.

—Walt

Authors' Acknowledgments

Danny wants to thank his wife, Holly, and kids, for their infinite patience while he and Pat wrestled with this book toward the finish line. He agrees that the wireless Webcam in the shower was not a good idea. (Just kidding.) He also wants to thank his sister, Michelle, for all her hard work over the years that has made it possible to continue to survive in this crazy business environment — we could not have made it without her. He also wants to note that he got his pot rack (see *Smart Homes for Dummies,* 2nd Edition for details). Now if we can only talk her into the 42-inch Samsung HDTV that he wants.

Walt would like to thank all the staff at Wiley for the incredible hours of work that go into the publication of every book — especially this one. There are many people whose work is essential to each book's publication but who seem to go unnoticed and unthanked. So let me say thank you to Andy Cummings, to Melody Layne for having the confidence in us to write this book, and to Nicole Sholly for her invaluable project management. Thanks also to Teresa Artman for her crisp copy editing, to Michael Williams for his invaluable technical review, and to all the unnamed people at Wiley who buy the paper, hire the printer, design and produce the cover, hire and manage the proofreader and indexer, design and implement marketing plans and promotions, sell the book to the retailer, pay the bills (especially the royalties), and perform all the other unnamed but still necessary tasks to keep a major publisher in business. Finally, I want to thank my family — Terry, Rich, Rob, Heather, Heidi, Monty, and Tahj (yes, I have a big family) — for putting up with me for all these years. You're the greatest.

Pat, as always, thanks his wife, Christine, for providing her impeccable "Can I write this wisecrack and not get in trouble?" judgment, and for her ability to restrain her desire to knock him over the head with a big frying pan when deadlines and late-night writing intrude on the domestic tranquility. He also wants to thank her for letting him hog the computers *and* the sofa while writing.

Danny and Pat want to thank the following people and organizations for their support in writing this book: Jeff Denenholz at X10 who has been a huge supporter for all our books (buy X10 stuff so that Jeff looks good); Doug Fay at ConnectPR for Siemens/Efficient Networks and D'Andre Ladson at Siemens/Efficient Networks; Doug Hagan at NETGEAR; Fred Bargetzi at Crestron; Shawn Gusz at G-NET Canada (still waiting to try Auroras in our cars!); Karen Sohl at Linksys; Keith Smith at Siemon; Mark Shapiro at Davis Marin for Proxim/ORiNOCO; Michael Scott at D-Link; Brad Kayton at Prismiq (best of luck with the venture!); Bryan McLeod at Intrigue Technologies; Craig Slawson at CorAccess (good luck too!); and others who helped get content correct for the readers.

Really extra special thanks go to Ed Ferris, IT Manager at TeleChoice, who by all rights should have been a co-author on this book (and only wasn't because the covers had already printed) for all the process and technical editing that he performed on the book. Ed, you'll be on the cover next edition if we have any say in the matter.

Thanks also to our acquisition editor, Melody Layne, who by now knows every product that will be wirelessly enabled from here to eternity, and to our project editor, Nicole Sholly, who probably hates being an editor at this point but nonetheless let us rant about the problems when they occurred (which they did constantly, continually, and drastically). Melody was a true champ keeping her faith up in Pat and Danny while they continually rewrote text in this book to make it more accurate and timely.

Publisher's Acknowledgments

We're proud of this book; please send us your comments through our online registration form located at www.dummies.com/register/.

Some of the people who helped bring this book to market include the following:

Acquisitions, Editorial, and Media Development

Associate Project Editor: Nicole Sholly

Acquisitions Editor: Melody Layne

Senior Copy Editor: Teresa Artman

Technical Editor: Michael Williams

Editorial Manager: Kevin Kirschner

Permissions Editor: Carmen Krikorian

Media Development Manager: Laura VanWinkle

Media Development Supervisor: Richard Graves

Editorial Assistant: Amanda Foxworth

Cartoons: Rich Tennant www.the5thwave.com

Production

Project Coordinator: Dale White

Layout and Graphics: Jennifer Click, Seth Conley, Kelly Emkow, Stephanie D. Jumper, Tiffany Muth, Jackie Nicholas, Lynsey Osborn, Brent Savage, Rashell Smith, Ron Terry

Proofreaders: John Greenough, Angel Perez Carl Pierce, TECHBOOKS Production Services

Indexer: TECHBOOKS Production Services

Publishing and Editorial for Technology Dummies

    Richard Swadley, Vice President and Executive Group Publisher

    Andy Cummings, Vice President and Publisher

    Mary C. Corder, Editorial Director

Publishing for Consumer Dummies

    Diane Graves Steele, Vice President and Publisher

    Joyce Pepple, Acquisitions Director

Composition Services

    Gerry Fahey, Vice President of Production Services

    Debbie Stailey, Director of Composition Services

Contents at a Glance

Introduction *1*

Part 1: Wireless Networking Fundamentals *5*

Chapter 1: Introducing Wireless Home Networking 7

Chapter 2: From a to g and b-yond 25

Chapter 3: Bluetooth, HPNA, and HomePlug 47

Part 11: Making Plans *63*

Chapter 4: Planning a Wireless Home Network 65

Chapter 5: Choosing Wireless Home Networking Equipment 87

Part 111: Installing a Wireless Network *103*

Chapter 6: Installing Wireless Access Points in Windows 105

Chapter 7: Setting Up Your Windows PCs for Wireless Networking 117

Chapter 8: Setting Up a Wireless Mac Network 135

Chapter 9: Setting Up Internet Sharing 163

Chapter 10: Securing Your Wireless Home Network 183

Part 1V: Using a Wireless Network *201*

Chapter 11: Putting Your Wireless Home Network To Work 203

Chapter 12: Gaming over a Wireless Home Network 225

Chapter 13: Networking Your Entertainment Center 245

Chapter 14: Other Cool Things You Can Network 261

Chapter 15: Using a Bluetooth Network 277

Chapter 16: Going Wireless Away from Home 291

Part V: The Part of Tens *303*

Chapter 17: Ten FAQs about Wireless Home Networks 305

Chapter 18: Ten Ways to Troubleshoot Wireless LAN Performance 313

Chapter 19: More Than Ten Devices You'll Connect to Your
Wireless Network in the Future 325

Chapter 20: Top Ten Sources for More Information 337

Index *345*

Table of Contents

Introduction *1*

About This Book 1
System Requirements 2
How This Book Is Organized 2
    Part I: Wireless Networking Fundamentals 2
    Part II: Making Plans 2
    Part III: Installing a Wireless Network 3
    Part IV: Using a Wireless Network 3
    Part V: The Part of Tens 3
Icons Used in This Book 3
Where to Go from Here 4

Part 1: Wireless Networking Fundamentals *5*

Chapter 1: Introducing Wireless Home Networking *7*

Nothing but Net(work): Why You Need (Or Want) One 8
    File sharing 8
    Printer and peripheral sharing 9
    Internet connection sharing 10
    Home arcades and wireless to go 12
Wired versus Wireless 13
    Installing wired home networks 13
    Installing wireless home networks 15
Picking a Wireless Standard 16
Planning Your Wireless Home Network 19
Choosing Wireless Networking Equipment 20

Chapter 2: From a to g and b-yond *25*

Networking Buzzwords That You Need to Know 26
    Workstations and servers 26
    Network infrastructure 28
    Network interface adapters 31
Get the (Access) Point? 35
Your Wireless Network's Power Station — the Antenna 38
Industry Standards 40

Chapter 3: Bluetooth, HPNA, and HomePlug *47*

Who or What Is Bluetooth? 48
Wi-Fi versus Bluetooth 49
Piconets, Masters, and Slaves 50

Integrating Bluetooth in Your Wireless Network 53
  Wirelessly synching your PDAs 54
  Wireless printing and data transfer 56
Integrating HPNA and HomePlug with Your Wireless
  Home Network 57
Home Phoning (ET Got It Backward!) 58
Network Power(line)! 59

Part II: Making Plans 63

Chapter 4: Planning a Wireless Home Network 65

Deciding What Is Connected to the Network 66
  Counting network devices 66
  Choosing wired or wireless 67
  Choosing a wireless technology 68
  Choosing an access point 69
  Deciding where to install the AP 71
  Adding printers 76
  Adding entertainment and more 78
Connecting to the Internet 79
Budgeting for Your Wireless Network 84
  Pricing access points 84
  Pricing wireless network adapters 85
  A sample budget 85
Planning Security 86

Chapter 5: Choosing Wireless Home Networking Equipment 87

Selecting Access Points 87
Certification and Standards Support 88
Compatibility and Form Factor 89
Bundled Functionality: Servers, Gateways, Routers, and Switches 90
  DHCP servers 91
  Gateways, NAT, and cable/DSL routers 91
  Switches 93
  Print servers 93
Operational Features 94
Security 95
Range and Coverage Issues 97
Manageability 97
  Web-based configuration 97
  Software programming 98
  Telnetting to your device 99
  Upgradeable firmware 99
Price 100
Warranties 100
Customer and Technical Support 101

Part III: Installing a Wireless Network 103

Chapter 6: Installing Wireless Access Points in Windows 105
Before Getting Started, Get Prepared 105
Setting Up the Access Point 107
    Preparing to install a wireless AP 107
    Installing the AP 108
    Configuring AP parameters 111
Changing the AP Configuration 115

Chapter 7: Setting Up Your Windows PCs for Wireless Networking 117
Setting Up Wireless Network Interface Adapters 117
    Installing device drivers and client software 118
    PC Cards and mini-PCI cards 120
    Compact Flash cards 122
    PCI and ISA cards 124
    USB adapters 125
Modifying Wireless Network Adapters 126
Synchronizing and Internet Access 127
Wireless Zero Configuration with XP 129
    Easy installation 129
    Automatic network connections 130
Tracking Your Network's Performance 132

Chapter 8: Setting Up a Wireless Mac Network 135
Apple AirPort Hardware 135
    Pick an AirPort Card, any card 136
    "Come in, AirPort Base Station, over . . ." 139
Apple AirPort Software Updates 141
    AirPort 2.0 software 141
    AirPort 2.0.4 software 142
    AirPort 2.0.5 software 142
    AirPort 2.1.1 software 143
OS 9 Wireless Networks 144
    Installing AirPort software on Mac OS 9 145
    Upgrading AirPort Base Station firmware on OS 9 146
    Configuring the AirPort Base Station on OS 9 148
    Adding a computer to your AirPort network on OS 9 151
OS X Wireless Networks 152
    Installing the AirPort software on OS X 153
    Upgrading AirPort Base Station firmware on OS X 154
    Configuring the AirPort Base Station on OS X 155
    Adding another computer to your AirPort network on OS X 158
Adding a Non-Apple Computer to Your AirPort Network 159
Connecting to Non-Apple-Based Wireless Networks 161

Chapter 9: Setting Up Internet Sharing **163**

Deciding How to Share Your Internet Connection 163
    Connection sharing 164
    Routers and gateways 164
    Sharing dialup Internet connections 166
Obtaining an IP Address Automatically 167
    Windows 9x 169
    Windows 2000 170
    Windows XP 172
    Mac OS 173
Setting Up Internet Connection Sharing 175
    Windows 98 SE and Windows Me 176
    Windows 2000 178
    Windows XP 180
    Mac OS X v. 10.2 (Jaguar) 181

Chapter 10: Securing Your Wireless Home Network **183**

Assessing the Risks 184
    General Internet security 185
    Airlink security 186
Introducing Wired Equivalent Privacy (WEP) 187
    How about a bit more about WEP? 188
    What's wrong with WEP? 189
Clamping Down on Your Wireless Home Network's Security 190
    Getting rid of the defaults 191
    Enabling WEP 192
    Closing your network 195
Looking into the Crystal Ball 197
    Waiting for WPA 197
    The future: 802.11i 198

Part 1V: Using a Wireless Network *201*

Chapter 11: Putting Your Wireless Home Network To Work **203**

A Networking Review 204
    Basic networking terminology 204
    Setting up a workgroup 205
Will You Be My Neighbor? 206
Sharing — I Can Do That! 210
    Enabling file sharing on Windows 95/98/Me 211
    Sharing a document or folder on Windows 95/98/Me 211
    Enabling sharing on Windows 2000/XP 213
    Setting permissions 214
    Accessing shared files 216

Be Economical: Share Those Peripherals 216
 Setting up a print server 216
 Sharing other peripherals 221
Sharing between Macs and Windows-based PCs 221

Chapter 12: Gaming over a Wireless Home Network 225

PC Gaming Hardware Requirements 227
Networking Requirements for PC Gaming 228
Getting Your Gaming Console on our Wireless Home Network 229
 Console online gaming services and equipment 230
 Console wireless networking equipment 234
Dealing with Router Configurations 237
 Getting an IP address 238
 Dealing with port forwarding 239
Setting Up a Demilitarized Zone (DMZ) 243

Chapter 13 Networking Your Entertainment Center 245

Wirelessly Enabling Your Home Entertainment System 246
Wireless Home Entertainment Gear 249
Expanding Your Home Entertainment Center
 with Wireless Adapters 251
The Home Media Player 255
The Home Theater PC 257
Internet Content for Your Media Players and HTPCs 259

Chapter 14: Other Cool Things You Can Network 261

Making a Connection to Your Car 262
 Your car's path to wireless enlightenment 262
 Synching your car stereo with home 264
 Getting online with your own car PC 266
 Picking wireless gear for your car 267
Look Ma, I'm on TV — Video Monitoring over Wireless LANs 268
Controlling Your Home over Your Wireless LAN 270
 Using your PDA as a remote control 271
 Whole home 802.11-based IR coverage 272
 See me, feel me, hear me, touch me 273
Sit, Ubu, Sit . . . Speak! 275

Chapter 15: Using a Bluetooth Network 277

Discovering Bluetooth Basics 278
Bluetooth Mobile Phones 281
Bluetooth PDAs 282
Other Bluetooth Devices 285
 Printers 285
 Digital cameras 286
 Keyboards and meeses (that's plural for mouse!) 287
 Bluetooth adapters 288

Chapter 16: Going Wireless Away from Home ... **291**

Discovering Public Hot Spots 292
    Freenets and open access points 294
    For-pay services 295
Using T-Mobile Hot Spots 298
Using Wayport Hot Spots 299
Using Boingo Hot Spots 299
Tools for Finding Hot Spots 300
    Netstumbler.com 301
    Boingo 302

Part V: The Part of Tens *303*

Chapter 17: Ten FAQs about Wireless Home Networks 305

Chapter 18: Ten Ways to Troubleshoot Wireless LAN Performance 313

Check the Obvious 314
Move the Access Point 315
Move the Antenna(s) 316
Change Channels 316
Check for Dual-Band Interference 317
Check for New Obstacles 317
Install Another Antenna 318
Add a Signal Booster 318
Add an AP 320
Add a Repeater or Bridge 322
Check Your Cordless Phone Frequencies 323

Chapter 19: More Than Ten Devices You'll Connect to Your Wireless Network in the Future 325

Your Bath 326
Your Car 326
Your Exercise Gear 328
Your Home Appliances 329
Your Musical Instruments 330
Your Pets 331
Your Phones 331
Your Robots 332
Your Wearing Apparel 334

Chapter 20: Top Ten Sources for More Information 337

CNET.com 338
802.11 Planet 338
Broadband Wireless Exchange Magazine 338

80211b.weblogger.com 339

PC Magazine 339

Electronic House Magazine 340

Home Automation Magazine 340

Practically Networked 341

ExtremeTech.com 341

Network World 341

Other Cool Sites 342

Index..*345*

Introduction

· ·

*W*elcome to *Wireless Home Networking For Dummies*. Wireless networking for personal computers is not really a new idea; it's been around for at least five years. The emergence of an industry standard, however, has caused the use of wireless networking technology to explode.

One of the most appealing things about the current crop of wireless networking equipment is the ease with which you can set up a home network, but its reasonable price might be the most attractive aspect of all. Setting up a wireless home network can be both inexpensive and easy. In some cases, it's almost as simple as opening the box and plugging in the equipment; however, you can avoid many gotchas by doing a little reading beforehand. That's where this book comes in handy.

About This Book

If you're thinking of purchasing a wireless computer network and installing it in your home, this is the book for you. Even if you've already purchased the equipment for a wireless network, this book will help you install and configure the network. What's more, this book helps you get the most out of your investment after it's up and running.

With this book in hand, you'll have all the information that you need to know about the following topics (and more):

- ✔ Planning your wireless home network
- ✔ Evaluating and selecting wireless networking equipment for installation in your home
- ✔ Installing and configuring wireless networking equipment in your home
- ✔ Sharing an Internet connection over your wireless network
- ✔ Sharing files, printers, and other peripherals over your wireless network
- ✔ Playing computer games over your wireless network
- ✔ Connecting your audio-visual gear to your wireless network
- ✔ Securing your wireless network against prying eyes
- ✔ Discovering devices that you'll be able to connect to your wireless home network in the future

System Requirements

Virtually any personal computer can be added to a wireless home network, but some computers are easier to add than others. This book focuses on building wireless networks that connect PCs running the Windows operating system (Windows 95 or later) or the Mac OS (Mac OS 9 or later). Wireless networking is also popular among Linux users, but we don't cover Linux in this book.

Because wireless networking is a relatively new phenomenon, the newest versions of Windows and Mac OS do the best job of helping you quickly and painlessly set up a wireless network. However, because the primary reason for networking your home computers is to make it possible for all the computers (and peripherals) in your house to communicate, this book gives you information about connecting computers that run older versions of Windows and the two most widely used versions of Mac OS, as well as connecting those that run the newest versions of these two operating systems.

How This Book Is Organized

This book is organized into several chapters that are grouped into five parts. The chapters are presented in a logical order — flowing from planning to installing to using your wireless home network — but feel free to use the book as a reference and read the chapters in any order that you want.

Part 1: Wireless Networking Fundamentals

The first part of the book is a primer on networking and on wireless networking. If you've never used a networked computer — much less attempted to install a network — this part of the book provides background information and techno-geek lingo that you need to feel comfortable. Chapter 1 presents general networking concepts; Chapter 2 discusses the most popular wireless networking technology and familiarizes you with wireless networking terminology; and Chapter 3 introduces you to several popular alternatives to wireless networking.

Part 11: Making Plans

The second part of the book helps you plan for installing your wireless home network. Chapter 4 helps you decide what you will be connecting to the network and where to install wireless networking equipment in your home, and Chapter 5 provides guidance on making buying decisions.

Part III: Installing a Wireless Network

Part III discusses how to install a wireless network in your home and get it up and running. Whether your computers are Apple Macintosh running Mac OS 9 or X (Chapter 8) or are PCs running a Windows 95 or later operating system (Chapters 6 and 7), this part of the book explains how to install and configure your wireless networking equipment. In addition, this part includes a chapter that explains how to use your wireless home network to share a single Internet connection (Chapter 9). The last chapter in this part covers securing your wireless home network (Chapter 10).

Part IV: Using a Wireless Network

After you get your wireless home network installed and running, you'll certainly want to use it. Part IV starts by showing you the basics of putting the wireless network to good use: sharing files, folders, printers, and other peripherals (Chapter 11). We spend some time discussing other cool things that you can do over a wireless network, including playing multi-user computer games (Chapter 12), connecting your audio-visual equipment (Chapter 13), and operating various types of smart home conveniences (Chapter 14).

Bluetooth-enabled devices are becoming more prevalent these days, so you won't want to miss Chapter 15 or Chapter 16, for that matter, where we describe how to use wireless networking to connect to the Internet through wireless *hot spots* in coffee shops, hotels, airports, and other public places. How cool is that?

Part V: The Part of Tens

Part V provides four top-ten lists that we think you'll find interesting — ten frequently asked questions about wireless home networking (Chapter 17); ten troubleshooting tips for improving your wireless home network's performance (Chapter 18); ten devices to connect to your wireless home network . . . sometime in the future (Chapter 19); and the top ten sources for more information about wireless networking (Chapter 20).

Icons Used in This Book

All of us these days are hyper-busy people, with no time to waste. To help you find the especially useful nuggets of information in this book, we've marked the information with little icons in the margin. The following icons are used in this book:

As you can probably guess, the Tip icon calls your attention to information that will save you time or maybe even money. If your time is really crunched, you might try just skimming through the book and reading the tips.

The little bomb in the margin should alert you to pay close attention and tread softly. You don't want to waste time or money fixing a problem that could have been avoided in the first place.

This icon is your clue that you should take special note of the advice that you find there . . . or that this paragraph reinforces information that has been provided elsewhere in the book. Bottom line: You will accomplish the task more effectively if you remember this information.

Face it, computers and wireless networks are high-tech toys — we mean _tools_ — that make use of some pretty complicated technology. For the most part, however, you don't need to know how it all works. The Technical Stuff icon identifies the paragraphs that you can simply skip if you're in a hurry or you just don't care to know.

Where to Go from Here

Where you should go next in this book depends on where you are in the process of planning, buying, installing, configuring, and/or using your wireless home network. If networking in general and wireless networking in particular are totally new to you, we recommend that you start at the beginning with Part I. When you feel comfortable with networking terminology, or you just get bored with the lingo, move on to the chapters about planning your network and selecting equipment in Part II. If you already have your equipment in hand, head to Part III to get it installed — and secured (unless you _like_ the idea of your neighbor or even a hacker being able to access your network).

The wireless industry is changing fast. We'll provide regular updates on this book at www.dummies.com/extras so that you can see what changes, as it changes, on a chapter by chapter basis.

Happy wireless networking!

Part I
Wireless Networking Fundamentals

The 5th Wave   By Rich Tennant

"If it works, it works. I've just never
seen network cabling connected with
Chinese handcuffs before."

In this part . . .

If you've never used a networked computer or you're installing a network in your home for the first time, this part of the book provides all the background info and down-and-dirty basics that will have you in the swing of things in no time. Here you find general networking concepts, the most popular wireless networking technology, wireless networking terminology, and several popular alternatives to wireless networking.

Chapter 1

Introducing Wireless Home Networking

In This Chapter

▶ Jump-starting your wireless revolution at home

▶ Comparing wired and wireless networks — and why wireless wins!

▶ Planning for your home wireless network

*W*elcome to the Wireless Age! Nope, we're not talking about your grandfather's radio — we're talking about just about everything under the sun. Truly. What's not going wireless? Wanna say your refrigerator? Wrong — it is. How about your stereo? Yup, that too. Watches, keychains, baby video monitors, high-end projectors . . . even your thermometer is going wireless and going digital. It's not just about computers anymore! Your entire world is going wireless, and in buying this book, you're determined not to get left behind. Kudos to you!

A driving force behind the growing popularity of wireless networking is its very reasonable cost: You can save money by not running network wiring all over your house, spending less on Internet connections, sharing peripherals such as printers and scanners, and using your PC to drive other applications around your home, like your home entertainment center. This book helps you spend your money wisely by helping you decide what you need to buy and helping you choose between the products that are on the market. Not only are wireless networks less expensive than more traditional wired networks, but wireless networks are also much easier to install. An important goal of this book is to provide you the skinny on how to install a wireless network in your home.

Whether you've got one computer or several, there are several good reasons to want a personal computer network that until recently just didn't exist. The plummeting cost of wireless technologies, combined with the fast-paced technical development, has meant that more and more manufacturers are getting on the home networking bandwagon. That means that more applications around your house are going to try to ride your wireless backbone — talking amongst themselves and to the Internet. So wireless is here to stay and is critical for any future-proofed home.

Nothing but Net (work): Why You Need (Or Want) One

Wireless home networking is not just about linking computers and the Internet with each other. Although that is important — nay, critical — in today's network-focused environment, it's not the whole enchilada. Of the many benefits for wireless in the home, most have one thing in common: sharing. When you connect the computers in your house through a network, you can share files, printers, scanners, and high-speed Internet connections between them. In addition, you can play multi-user games over your network, access public wireless networks while away from home, check wireless cameras, or even enjoy your MP3s in your stereo system from work (really!).

Reading *Wireless Home Networking For Dummies* will help you understand how to create a whole home wireless network to reach the nooks and crannies of your house. Wireless home networks don't have to be all about your PC. The big initial reason why people have wanted to put a wireless network in their home has been to "unwire" the PC, especially laptops, to enable more freedom of access in the home. But just about every major consumer goods manufacturer is hard at work wirelessly enabling their devices so that they, too, can talk to other devices in the home.

Along these lines, we encourage you to think of your home wireless network as another utility network in your house. Just like electricity. Just like water. Instead of having outlets or spigots, your connection is in the air floating around your head. If you have a device that has the right protocols and passwords — and is in range — it can log onto this wireless *backbone* in your home. Over this backbone can ride data, running between computers and the Internet; MP3s, going from your stereo to your car; videos, from the Internet to your TV set; and more. As you find more and more consumer devices sporting wireless interfaces, you can be happy that you've got a home wireless network for them to log onto and link to your other devices and network connections . . . and your PC!

File sharing

As you probably know, computer *files* are created any time that you use a computer. If you use a word processing program such as Microsoft Word to write a document, Word saves the document on your computer's hard drive as an electronic file. Similarly, if you balance your checkbook by using Intuit Quicken, this software saves your financial data onto the computer's drive in an electronic file.

A computer network lets you share those electronic files between two or more computers. For example, you can create a Word document on your computer, and your spouse, roommate, child, sibling, or whoever can pull the same document up on his/her computer screen over the network. With the right programs, you can even view the same documents at the same time!

But here's where you get into semantics — what's a computer? Your car has more computing and networking capability than the early moon rockets. Your stereo is increasingly looking like a computer with a black matte finish. Even your refrigerator and microwave are getting on-board computing capabilities — and they all have files and information that needs to be shared.

The old way of moving files between computers and computing devices involved copying the files to a floppy disk and then carrying the disk to the other computer. Computer geeks call this method of copying/transferring files the *SneakerNet* approach. In contrast, copying files between computers is easy to do over a home network with no need for floppy disks (or sneakers). It's almost as simple as copying files from your computer's hard drive to a floppy disk.

What's interesting is that more computers and devices are getting used to talking to one another over networks in an automated fashion. A common application is *synchronization*, where two devices will talk to one another and make the appropriate updates to each other's stored information so that they are current with one another. Rockford Corporation (`www.omnifimedia.com`), for instance, offers MP3 servers for cars that have wireless connectivity built in so that when your car returns home, it can "talk" to your home wireless network and computers and add any new CDs to its hard drives that your spouse might have added while you were gone. So you always have your music at your fingertips — literally.

Printer and peripheral sharing

Businesses with computer networks have discovered a major benefit: sharing printers. Companies invest in high-speed, high-capacity printers that are shared by many employees. Sometimes an entire department shares a single printer or perhaps a cluster of printers co-located in an area of the office set aside for printers, copy machines, and fax machines.

Just like in a business network, all the computers on your home network can share the printers on your network. The cost-benefit of shared printers in a home network is certainly not as dramatic as it would be for a business, but the opportunity to save money by sharing printers is clearly one of the real benefits of setting up a home network. Figure 1-1 depicts a network through which three personal computers can share the same printer.

Other peripherals, such as extra storage for your computers or for all those MP3s that someone in the household might be downloading, also are great to share. Anything connected to your PCs or which has a network port (we talk about these in great detail throughout the book) can be shared anywhere on your wireless network.

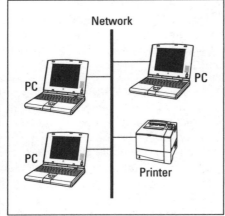

Figure 1-1:
Share and share alike: Share one printer via your home network.

Internet connection sharing

Another driving reason behind many homeowners' interest in home networking is a desire to share an Internet connection. As the Internet becomes a critical part of day-to-day living — from kids doing their homework to managing your bank account — it's only natural that more than one person in the household wants to get online at the same time. And with the sudden interest in *broadband connections* (cable, digital subscriber line (DSL), and satellite modems) for Internet connections, we can guess that the demand at home has only soared.

High-speed *(broadband)* Internet service is very appealing. Not only is the connection to the Internet up to 50 times or more faster than a dialup connection, with sharing enabled over your wireless network, all the computers connected to the network can access the Internet at one time through the same broadband service for one monthly fee (roughly $50 a month or even less in some areas). And you can surf and talk on the phone at the same time. No more having your dialup connection tie up your phone line!

Modem types

Your wireless network helps you distribute information throughout the home. It's agnostic as to how you access your outside-of-home networks, like the Internet. Whether you use a dialup connection or broadband, your wireless home network will be applicable.

- ✔ **Dialup modem:** A device that connects to the Internet by dialing an Internet service provider (ISP), such as America Online (AOL) or EarthLink, over a standard phone line.

- ✔ **Cable modem:** Modems that connect to the Internet through the same cable as cable TV. Cable modems connect to the Internet at much higher speeds than dialup modems and can be left connected to the Internet all day, every day.

- ✔ **DSL modem:** Digital subscriber line modems do use your phone line, but they permit the phone to be free for other purposes — voice calls, faxes, and so on — even while the DSL modem is in use. DSL modems also connect to the Internet at much higher speeds than dialup modems and can be left connected 24x7.

- ✔ **Satellite modem:** Satellite modems tie into your satellite dish and give you two-way communications even if you're in the middle of the woods. Although they're typically not as fast as cable modems and DSL links, they are better than dialup and available just about anywhere in the continental United States.

Phone jacks versus a network

Most homes built in the last 20 years have a phone jack (outlet) in the wall in every room in the house where you'd likely use your computer. Consequently, connecting your computer to the Internet via a dialup modem over a telephone line doesn't require a network. You simply run a phone line from your computer's modem to the phone jack in the wall and you're in business.

However, without a network or Internet connection sharing turned on at the computer, the connection cannot be shared between computers; only one computer can use a given phone line at any given time. Not good.

With a wireless home network, we can help you extend that modem connection throughout the home. The same is true with your broadband modem — it can be shared throughout the home.

Sure, you could have more than one cable or DSL modem in your house, but don't bother. Because of their speed (bandwidth), cable and DSL modems can easily handle the Internet traffic generated by many individual computers, just like a 50-lane interstate can handle lots of cars at once. Use a network to connect multiple computers to a cable modem or DSL modem to share an Internet connection.

When configuring your PCs on a network, you can buy equipment that lets you connect multiple computers to a regular or high-speed modem through the phone lines — or even through the power lines — in your house. The most popular method for connecting computers to a broadband modem, however, is to use a network technology known as Ethernet. *Ethernet* is an industry standard protocol used in virtually every corporation and institution; consequently, Ethernet equipment is plentiful and inexpensive. What's more, Ethernet equipment sends data around the network at much faster speeds than phone-line or power-line networking equipment. Figure 1-2 illustrates a network that enables three personal computers to connect to the Internet through a DSL or cable modem (works the same for a satellite or dialup modem).

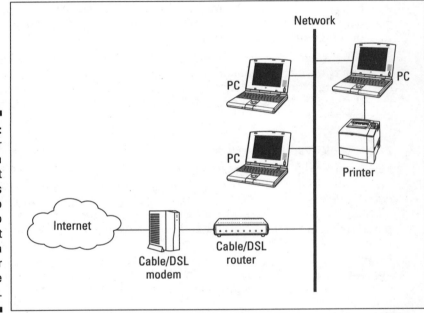

Figure 1-2:
Internet for all: Set up a network that enables many PCs to connect to the Internet through a DSL or cable modem.

Refer to Chapter 4 for more about planning and budgeting for your network and to Chapter 5 for help in selecting your wireless networking equipment.

Home arcades and wireless to go

If you aren't convinced yet that a home wireless network is for you, we have five last points that just might change your mind. Check out these:

✔ **Multi-user games over the network:** If you're into video games, multiplayer card games, or role-playing games, you might find multi-user games over the network or even over the Internet fascinating. Chapter 12 discusses how to use your wireless network to play multi-user games.

✔ **Audio anywhere in the household:** Why spend money on CDs and keep them stacked next to your stereo? Load them on your PC and make them wirelessly available to your stereo, your car, your MP3 player that you take jogging, and lots more. Check out Chapter 13 for more info on how to use your wireless network to send audio and video signals around the house.

✔ **Phone (your Mom's) home:** With some new wireless phone capabilities, you can get rid of the static of your cordless phone and move digital over your home wireless network, thus saving money on calls by using less-expensive, Internet-based phone calling options.

✔ **Check your home wireless cam:** You can check out your house from anywhere in the house — or in the world — with new wireless cameras that hop on your home network and broadcast images privately or publicly over the Internet. Want to see whether your kids are tearing apart the house while you're working in your office downstairs? Just call up your wireless-networked camera and check them out. (In our generation, we always said that "Mom had eyes in the back of her head;" this generation will probably think that Mom is omniscient!)

✔ **Wireless on-the-go:** This is great for those with a portable computer. Many airports, hotels, malls, and coffee shops have installed public wireless networks that enable you via hot spots to connect to the Internet (for a small fee, of course). Refer to Chapter 16 for more about using wireless networking while away from home.

Wired versus Wireless

Ethernet is the most-often used method of connecting personal computers together to form a network because it's fast and its equipment is relatively inexpensive. In addition, Ethernet can be transmitted over several types of network cable or sent through the air by using wireless networking equipment. Many new computers have an Ethernet connection built in, ready for you to plug in a network cable. The most popular wireless networking equipment transmits a form of Ethernet.

Installing wired home networks

Even though we're talking mostly about wireless networks in this book and how great they are, we'd be misleading you if we told you that wireless was the only way to go. Wireless and wired homes each have advantages.

Wired homes are

- ✔ **Faster:** Wired lines can reach 1000 Mbps in speed, whereas wireless homes tend to be in the 10 Mbps and soon 100 Mbps range. Both wireless and wired technologies are getting faster and faster, but wired will always be ahead.

- ✔ **More reliable:** Wireless signals are prone to interference and fluctuations; wired connections typically are more stable and reliable.

- ✔ **More secure:** You don't have to worry about your signals traveling through the air and being intercepted by snoopers, like with unsecured wireless systems.

- ✔ **Economical over the long term:** The incremental cost of adding Cat 5e voice and data cabling and RG-6 coaxial cabling into your house — over a 30-year mortgage — will be almost nothing each month.

- ✔ **Salable:** More and more homebuyers are not only looking for well-wired homes but are discounting homes without the infrastructure. As good as wireless is, it is not affixed to the house and is carried with you when you leave. Most new homes have structure wiring in the walls.

If you're building a new home or renovating an old one, we absolutely recommend that you consider running the latest wiring in the walls to each of your rooms. That doesn't mean that you won't have a wireless network in your home — you will. It just will be different than if you were wholly reliant on wireless for your networking.

If you choose to use network cable, it should ideally be installed in the walls, just like electrical and phone wiring. Network jacks (outlets) are installed in the walls in rooms where you would expect to use a computer. Connecting your computer to a wired network is just as easy as plugging a phone into a phone jack — after the wiring is in place, that is.

Without question, the most economical time to install network cable in a home is during the home's initial construction. In upscale neighborhoods, especially in communities near high-tech businesses, builders often wire new homes with network cable as a matter of course. In most cases, however, installation of network cable in a new home is an option or upgrade that's installed only if the new owner orders it and pays a premium. Installing a structured wiring solution for a home can cost at least $2,000–$3,000, and that's for starters.

Although certainly possible, installation of network cable in an existing home is much more difficult and expensive than installing cable during construction. If you hire an electrician to run the cable, you can easily spend thousands of dollars to do what would have cost a few hundred dollars during your home's construction. If you're comfortable drilling holes in your walls and crawling around in attics and crawl spaces, you can install the cabling yourself for the cost of the cable and outlets.

The reality is that no home will ever be purely wireless or wireline (wired). Each approach has benefits and costs, and they will coexist in any house. If you're building a new house, most experts tell you to spend the extra money on a structured wiring solution because it adds value to your house and you can better manage all the wiring in your home. We agree. But no wiring solution can be everywhere that you want it to be. Thus, wireless is a great complement to your home, which is why we advocate a whole home wireless network for your entire home to use.

Installing wireless home networks

If you're networking an existing home or are renting your home, wireless has fabulous benefits:

- ✔ **Portable:** You can take your computing device anywhere in the house and be on the network. Even if you have a huge house, you can interconnect wireless access points to have a whole home wireless network.

- ✔ **Flexible:** You're not limited to where a jack is on the wall; you can network anywhere.

- ✔ **Cost effective:** You can start wireless networking for a couple of hundred dollars. Your wiring contractor can't do much with that!

- ✔ **Clean:** You won't have to tear down walls or trip over wires when they come out from underneath the carpeting.

What's more, there's really no difference how you use your networked computer, whether it's connected to the network by a cable or by a wireless networking device. Whether you're sharing files, a printer, your entertainment system, or the Internet over the network, the procedures are the same on a wireless network as on a wired network. In fact, you can mix wired and wireless network equipment on the same network with no change in how you use a computer on the network.

Time for the fine print. We'd be remiss if we weren't candid and mention any potential drawbacks to wireless networks compared with wired networks. The possible drawbacks fall into four categories:

- ✔ **Data speed:** Wireless networking equipment does transmit data at slower speeds than wired networking equipment. Wired networks are already networking at gigabit speeds, although the fastest wireless networking standards (in the best situations) tops out at 54 Mbps. (Some vendors have proprietary extensions that will take the speed higher, but even these top out at a little more than 100 Mbps in the best scenarios.) But for almost all the uses that we can think of now, this is plenty fast. Your Internet connection probably doesn't exceed a few Mbps in speed, so your wireless connection should be more than fast enough.

✔ **Radio signal range:** Wireless signals fade when you move away from the source. Some homes, especially older homes, might be built from materials that tend to block the radio signals used by wireless networking equipment, causing even faster signal degradation. If your home has plaster walls that contain a wire mesh, the wireless networking equipment's radio signal might not reach all points in your home. Most modern construction, however, uses drywall materials that reduce the radio signal only slightly. As a result, most homeowners can reach all points in their home with one centralized wireless *access point* (also called a *base station*) and one wireless device in or attached to each personal computer. And if you need better coverage, you can just add another access point — we show you how in Chapter 18.

✔ **Radio signal interference:** The most common type of wireless networking technology uses a radio frequency that's also used by other home devices, such as microwave ovens and portable telephones. Some home wireless network users, as a consequence, experience network problems (the network slows down or the signal is dropped) caused by radio signal interference.

✔ **Security:** The radio signal from a wireless network doesn't stop at the outside wall of your home. A neighbor or even a total stranger could access your network from an adjoining property or from the street unless you implement some type of security technology to prevent unauthorized access. To prevent unauthorized access, you can safeguard yourself with security technology that comes standard with the most popular home wireless networking technology. However, it's not bulletproof, and it certainly won't work if you don't turn it on. For more on wireless security, go to Chapter 10.

For our money, wireless networks compare favorably with wired networks for most homeowners who didn't have network wiring installed when the house was built.

Picking a Wireless Standard

The good news about wireless networks is that there are multiple flavors, each with their own advantages and disadvantages. The bad news is that trying to decide which version to get when buying a system can get confusing.

The good news is that very rapidly, the dropping prices of the wireless systems and fast-paced development is creating dual- and tri-mode systems on the market that can speak many different wireless languages.

Here are the three major wireless systems on the market today:

- ✔ **IEEE 802.11a:** Wireless networks that use the Institute for Electrical and Electronics Engineers (IEEE) 802.11a standard use the 5 GHz radio frequency band. Equipment of this type is among the fastest wireless networking equipment widely available to consumers.

- ✔ **IEEE 802.11b:** Home wireless networks that use the IEEE 802.11b standard use the 2.4 GHz radio band. This is the most popular standard in terms of numbers of installed networks and numbers of users.

- ✔ **IEEE 802.11g:** The last and newest member of the 802.11 wireless family, IEEE 802.11g is coming to market as this book goes to press. In fact, only a draft of the IEEE 802.11g specification has been approved with the finalized specs due by mid-2003. In many ways, 802.11g offers the best of both worlds — backward compatibility with IEEE 802.11b networks (it, too, operates over the 2.4 GHz radio frequency band) and the speed of 802.11a networks.

Note: Equipment that's based on the IEEE 802.11a standard does not interoperate with equipment based on the IEEE 802.11b standard. Several manufacturers sell equipment, however, that supports *both* standards — the best of all worlds. And if you really want to hedge your bets, keep your eyes peeled for the new wave of dual-mode, tri-standard IEEE 802.11a/b/g wireless networking equipment that's on the streets.

Both IEEE 802.11a and IEEE 802.11b can carry the Wi-Fi logo — a trademark that's short for *wireless fidelity* — that's licensed for use by the Wi-Fi Alliance trade group, based on equipment that passes interoperability testing. (802.11g will, too, when the standard is finalized and interoperability testing can begin.)

The terms surrounding wireless networking can get complex. First off, the order of lettering isn't really right because 802.11*b* was approved and hit the market before 802.11*a*. Also, you'll see the term *Wi-Fi* used a lot. (In fact, we thought about calling this book *Wi-Fi For Dummies* because it's used so much.) Wi-Fi refers to the collective group of 802.11 specifications: 802.11a, b, and g. You might sometimes see this group also called *802.11x* networking, where x can equal a, b, or g. To make matters more confusing, a higher-level parent standard called 802.11 predates 802.11a, b, and g and is also used to talk about the group of the three standards. Technically, it's a standards group over several other emerging specifications as well. For simplicity in this book, we're going to use 802.11 and Wi-Fi synonymously to talk about the three standards as a group. We could have used 802.11x, but we just wanted to save a lot of x's (for our wives).

The differences between these three standards fall into five main categories:

- **Data speed:** IEEE 802.11a and IEEE 802.11g networks are almost ten times faster than IEEE 802.1b networks. However, IEEE 802.11b networks are almost ten times faster than the fastest broadband Internet connection. Unless you expect to routinely share very large files over your network, you probably wouldn't be able to notice the difference in speed between these two standards.

- **Price:** IEEE 802.11a and g networking equipment is typically more expensive than similar IEEE 802.11b equipment, but the price differential might be temporary. IEEE 802.11b equipment has been on the market for a longer period of time than 802.11a and g with dozens of products in the marketplace. As a result, IEEE 802.11b will probably be the least expensive version of Wi-Fi for some period of time. However if the first IEEE 802.11g products out the door are any indication, the price differential between 802.11g and 802.11b will be negligible very soon.

- **Radio signal range:** IEEE 802.11a wireless networks tend to have a shorter maximum signal range than IEEE 802.11b and g networks. The actual distances vary depending on the size construction of your home. In most modern homes, however, all three of the competing standards should provide adequate range.

- **Radio signal interference:** The radio frequency band used by both IEEE 802.11b and IEEE 802.11g equipment is also used by other home devices, such as microwave ovens and portable telephones, resulting sometimes in network problems caused by radio signal interference. Very few other types of devices currently use the radio frequency band employed by the IEEE 802.11a standard.

- **Interoperability:** Because IEEE 802.11a and IEEE 802.11b/g use different frequency bands, they aren't able to communicate over the same radio. Several manufacturers, however, have already released products that can operate with both IEEE 802.11a and IEEE 802.11b/g equipment simultaneously. By contrast, IEEE 802.11g equipment is designed to be backward compatible with IEEE 802.11b equipment — both operating on the same frequency band — but in early tests of the first IEEE 802.11g products, actual interoperability was often problematic. Nevertheless, it will only be a matter of time before IEEE 802.11g is fully adopted, and multi-standard (802.11 a/b/g) wireless networking equipment will be the norm.

Think of dual-mode, multi-standard devices as being in the same vein as AM/FM radios. AM and FM stations transmit their signals in different ways, but hardly anyone buys a radio that's only AM anymore because almost all the receiving units are AM/FM. The user selects which band he or she wants to listen to at any particular time. With an 802.11a/b/g device, you can also pick the band that you want to transmit and receive in.

The Intel Centrino chip

You might start hearing the term *Centrino* with respect to wireless products. No, this isn't a new atomic particle but Intel's new wireless-enabled chip — the chip that will bring wireless connectivity to most laptops on the planet. Representing Intel's best technology for mobile PCs, the Intel Centrino mobile technology includes a new mobile processor, related chipsets, and 802.11 wireless network functions that have been optimized, tested, and validated to work together. If you're in the market for a laptop, you'll be confronted with a flood of advertising regarding the Centrino chipset. With Intel Inside and wireless at that, you can expect that when your children's friends come to your home for a sleepover, they'll be able to wirelessly connect their laptops back to their own homes so that they can say good night to Mommy.

We expect that 802.11a/b/g products — all-in-one devices — will be the standard device that's deployed in most home networks. This enables the home network to be able to communicate with the protocols that it senses. We think, however, that it's going to be some time before this is a really seamless activity. There are lots of issues of dealing with multiple protocols in the same wireless area, and these are growing pains that will be worked through over time.

For most home networks, IEEE 802.11b wireless networks are the best choice because they're the least expensive, offer the best signal range, and provide more than adequate data speed. It's a great way to get started. However, the prices for the faster (and compatible) 802.11g products are dropping so fast that we urge you to look at upgrading to the faster g standardized products. If you find that 802.11a is best for you, that's okay, too. The reality is, however, that the combined 802.11a/b/g units "future-proof" you the best and are likely what will be on the shelves almost exclusively within a few years. So you can take either fork in the wireless road. Buy low-cost 802.11b units now and upgrade to a nice 802.11 a/b/g unit in a few years when costs have come down and all the kinks are worked out. Or, buy one of the a/b/g units now and upgrade your firmware every once in a while to take advantage of bug fixes and new functionality.

Planning Your Wireless Home Network

Installing and setting up a wireless home network can be very ridiculously easy. In some cases, after you unpack and install the equipment, you're up and running in a matter of minutes. To assure yourself that you don't have a negative experience, however, you should do a little planning. The issues that you'll need to consider during the planning stage include the following:

- Which of your computers will you connect to the network (and will you be connecting Macs and PCs or just one or the other)?

- Will all the computers be connected via wireless connections, or will one or more computers be connected by a network cable to the network?

- Which wireless technology — IEEE 802.11a, IEEE 802.11b, or IEEE 802.11g — will you use? (Or will you use all of them?)

- Which type of wireless adapter will you use to connect each computer to the network?

- How many printers will you connect to the network?

- How will each printer be connected to the network — by connecting it to a computer on the network or by connecting it to a print server?

- Will you connect the network to the Internet through a broadband connection (cable or DSL) or dialup? If so, will you share the Internet connection through a cable/DSL/satellite/dialup router or by using Internet connection-sharing software?

- What other devices might you want to include in your initial wireless network? Do you plan on listening to MP3s on your stereo? How about downloading movies from the Internet (instead of running out in the rain to the movie rental store!)?

- How much money should you budget for your wireless network?

- What do you need to do to plan for adequate security to assure the privacy of the information stored on the computers connected to your network?

We discuss all these issues and the entire planning process in more detail in Chapter 4.

Choosing Wireless Networking Equipment

For those of us big kids who are enamored with technology, shopping for high-tech toys can be therapeutic. Whether you're a closet geek or (cough) normal, a critical step in building a useful wireless home network is choosing the proper equipment.

Connecting to your wireless home network via your PDA

One of the few areas of personal computing where Microsoft and Windows has not been the dominant software is the area of handheld computers. The PDA devices from Palm became the first big success story in handheld computers in the early '90s and have maintained their leadership position ever since. Handhelds from Hewlett-Packard (formerly Compaq) and other manufacturers based on Microsoft's Pocket PC 2002 are finally giving Palm a run for its money. Even though Pocket PCs are still (on the average) more expensive than Palm PDAs, they boast computing power more akin to a full-sized PC, running scaled-down versions of the most popular Windows-based application software.

Handheld computers, such as computers that run the Windows Pocket PC 2002 operating system (and later versions of the Microsoft operating system for handheld computers), are perfect candidates for wireless network connectivity. By definition, handheld computers are highly portable.

Here are a couple of reasons why going wireless with Pocket PC 2002 might be worth the trouble. You will be able to

✔ **Wirelessly synchronize** your address book, calendar, inbox, and so forth on your Pocket PC with your desktop computer from anywhere in your house without needing to plug into the docking station.

✔ **Access the Internet** from your Pocket PC, both over your wireless home network and at wireless hot spots, such as in Starbucks coffee shops and in many airports and hotels.

✔ **Connect to other Pocket PC devices.** For example, mobile businesspeople can exchange files or even electronic business cards via a wireless connection.

✔ **Download MP3 files** to play on your Pocket PC.

The thought of being able to access your e-mail or browse the Internet on your HP iPAQ while sipping a latté in Starbucks is compelling. After you get your Pocket PC set up with a wireless connection, synchronizing your calendar and phone list becomes a snap. But you'll need a CF card to do it. See Chapter 2 for more details about this new category of wireless network adapter. Chapter 7 walks you through installing wireless network adapters and getting your PDA ready for Internet access.

Before you can decide which equipment to buy, take a look at Chapter 4 for more about planning a wireless home network. And read Chapter 5 for a more detailed discussion of the different types of wireless networking equipment. Here's a quick list of what you'll need:

✔ **Access point:** At the top of the list will be at least one wireless *access point* (AP), also sometimes called a *base station*. An AP acts like a wireless switchboard that connects wireless devices on the network to each other and to the rest of the network. You gotta have one of these to create a wireless home network. They range in price from about $100 to $300, with prices quickly coming down. You can get APs from many leading vendors in the marketplace, including Apple (www.apple.com), D-Link (www.d-link.com), Linksys (www.linksys.com), NETGEAR (www.netgear.com), and Siemens/Efficient Networks (www.speedstream.com). We give you a long list of vendors in Chapter 20, so check that out when you go to buy your AP.

For wireless home networks, the best AP value is often an AP that's bundled with other features. The most popular APs for home use also come with one or more of the following features:

- **Network hub or switch:** A *hub* connects wired PCs to the network. A *switch* is a "smarter" version of a hub that speeds up network traffic. (We talk more about the differences between hubs and switches in Chapter 2.)

- **DHCP server:** A *Dynamic Host Configuration Protocol* (DHCP) server assigns network addresses to each computer on the network; these addresses are required for the computers to communicate.

- **Network router:** A *router* enables multiple computers to share a single Internet connection. The network connects each computer to the router, and the router is connected to the Internet through a broadband modem.

- **Print server:** Use a *print server* to add printers directly to the network instead of attaching a printer to each computer on the network.

In Figure 1-3, you can see an AP that also bundles in a network router, switch, and DHCP server.

✔ **Network interface adapters:** As we mention earlier in this chapter, home networks use a communication method *(protocol)* known as *Ethernet.* The communication that takes place between the components of your computer, however, does not use the Ethernet protocol. As a result, for computers on the network to communicate through the Ethernet protocol, each of the computers must translate between their internal communication protocol and Ethernet. The device that handles this translation is a *network interface adapter,* and each computer on the network needs one. Prices for network interface adapters are typically much less than $50, and most new computers come with one at no additional cost.

A network interface adapter that installs inside a computer is usually called a *network interface card* (NIC). Many computer manufacturers now include an Ethernet NIC with each personal computer as a standard feature.

Figure 1-3:
Look for an AP that bundles a network router, switch, and DHCP server.

✔ **Wireless network interface adapter:** To wirelessly connect a computer to the network, you must obtain a wireless network interface adapter for each computer. Prices range between $50 and $150. A few portable computers now even come with a wireless network interface built in. These are very easy to use; most are adapters that just plug in.

The four most common types of wireless network interface adapters are

• **PC Card:** This type of adapter is often used in laptop computers because most laptops have one or two PC Card slots. Figure 1-4 shows a PC Card wireless network interface adapter.

Figure 1-4:
A PC Card wireless network interface adapter.

- **CF card:** A *Compact Flash* (CF) card adapter is smaller in size than a PC Card adapter and enables you to link a Pocket PC or other palm-sized computer to your network. Many high-end personal digital assistants (PDAs) now even come with wireless capability built-in, obviating the need for a wireless adapter.

- **USB:** A *Universal Serial Bus* (USB) adapter connects to one of your computer's USB ports; these USB ports have been available in most computers built in the last four or five years.

- **ISA or PCI adapter:** If your computer doesn't have a PC Card slot, CF card slot, or USB port, you have to either install a network interface card or a USB card (for a USB wireless network interface adapter) in one of the computer's internal peripheral expansion receptacles (slots). The expansion slots in older PCs are Industry Standard Architecture (ISA) slots. The internal expansion slots in newer PCs and Apple Macintosh computers follow the Peripheral Component Interconnect (PCI) standard.

More and more PDAs, laptops, and other devices are shipping with wireless already onboard so you wouldn't need an adapter of any sort. It just comes with the wireless installed in the device. We tell you how to get your wireless-enabled devices onto your wireless backbone in Part II of this book.

Chapter 2

From a to g and b-yond

In This Chapter

▶ Learning your a, b, g's

▶ Networking terms you've got to know

*U*ntil very recently, networked computers were connected only by wire: a special-purpose network cabling. This type of wiring has yet to become a standard item in new homes. And the cost of installing network cabling after a house is already built is understandably much higher than doing so during initial construction. By contrast, the cost of installing a wireless network in a particular home is a fraction of the cost of wiring the same residence — and a lot less hassle. As a result, because more and more people are beginning to see the benefits of having a computer network at home, they are turning to wireless networks in growing numbers. Many of us can no longer recall life without wireless phones; similarly, wireless computer networking is fast becoming the standard way to network a home.

But that's not to say that it's easy. Face it — life can sometimes seem a bit complicated. The average Joe or Jane can't even order a cup of Java anymore without having to choose between an endless array of options . . . regular, decaf, half-caf, mocha, cappuccino, latté, low fat, no fat, foam, no foam, and so on. Of course, after you get the hang of the lingo, you can order coffee like a pro. And that's where this chapter comes in — to help you get used to the networking lingo slung about when you're planning, purchasing, installing, and using your wireless network.

Like so much alphabet soup, the prevalent wireless network technologies go by names like 802.11a, 802.11b, and 802.11g, employ devices such as APs and PC Cards, and make use of technologies with cryptic abbreviations (TCP/IP, DHCP, NAT, WEP, and WPA). Whether you're shopping for, installing, or configuring a wireless network, you'll undoubtedly run across some or all of these not-so-familiar terms and more. This chapter is your handy guide to this smorgasbord of networking and wireless networking terminology.

If you're not the least bit interested in buzzwords, you can safely skip this chapter for now and go right to the chapters that cover planning, purchasing, installing, and using your wireless network. You can always refer to this chapter anytime that you run into some wireless networking terminology that throws you. But if you like knowing a little bit about the language that the locals speak before visiting a new place, read on.

Networking Buzzwords That You Need to Know

A computer *network* comprises computers or network-accessible devices — and sometimes other peripheral devices such as printers — connected in a way that they transmit data between participants. Computer networks have been commonplace in offices for nearly 20 years, but with the advent of reasonably priced wireless networks, computer networks are becoming increasingly common in homes. Now we mere mortals can share printers, share the Internet, play multi-player video games, and stream video like the corporate gods have been doing for years.

A computer network that connects devices in a particular physical location, such as in a home or in a single office site, is sometimes called a *local area network* (LAN). Conversely, the network outside your home that connects you to the Internet and beyond is called a *wide area network* (WAN).

In a nutshell, computer networks help people and devices share *information* (files and e-mail) and expensive *resources* (printers and Internet connections) more efficiently.

Workstations and servers

Each computer in your home that's attached to a network is a *workstation*, also sometimes referred to as a *client* computer. The Windows operating system (OS) refers to the computers residing together on the same local area network as a *workgroup*. A Windows-based computer network enables the workstations in a workgroup to share files and printers that are visible through the *Network Neighborhood* (or *My Network Places*). Home networks based on the Apple Macintosh OS offer the same capability. On a Mac, all the computers on the network are called a network *neighborhood*.

Some networks also have *servers,* which are special-purpose computers or other devices that provide one or more services to other computers and devices on a network. Examples of typical servers include

✔ **File server:** A *file server* makes storage space on hard disks or some other type of storage device available to workstations on the network. Home networks seldom have a file server because each computer typically has enough storage space to store the files created on that computer. Common in-home applications of a file server today are consumer devices such as Yamaha's MusicCast (www.yamaha.com; $2,000) or Turtle Beach Systems' AudioTron (www.turtlebeach.com; $269) MP3 servers that enable you to play your MP3s over your stereo wirelessly.

✔ **Print server:** A *print server* is a computer or other device that makes it possible for the computers on the network to share one or more printers. You won't commonly find a print server in a home network, but some wireless networking equipment comes with a print server feature built in, which turns out to be very handy.

✔ **E-mail server:** An *e-mail server* is a computer that provides a system for sending e-mail to users on the network. You might never see an e-mail server on a home network. Most often, home users send e-mail through a third-party service, such as America Online (AOL), EarthLink, MSN Hotmail, Yahoo!, and so on.

✔ **DHCP server:** Every computer on a network, even a home network, must have its own unique network address in order to communicate with the other computers on the network. A *Dynamic Host Configuration Protocol* (DHCP) server automatically assigns a network address to every computer on a network. You most often find DHCP servers in another device like a router or an AP.

There are many types of client computers — network-aware devices — that you can find on your network, too. Some examples include

✔ **Gaming consoles:** Microsoft's Xbox (www.xbox.com), Sony PlayStation 2 (www.playstation.com), and Nintendo's GameCube (www.nintendo.com) have adapters for network connections or multi-player gaming and talking to other players while gaming. Cool! Read more about online gaming in Chapter 12.

✔ **Wireless network cameras:** Panasonic's KX-HCM250 and KX-HCM270 Network Cameras (www.panasonic.com/consumer_electronics/gate/cameras.asp) enable you to not only view your home from when away but also pan, tilt, scan, zoom, and so on your way around the home. Now *that's* a nanny-cam.

✔ **MP3 players:** Yamaha's MusicCAST interactive wireless home music network system (www.yamaha.com) enables you to use wireless technology to stream music files throughout your home. The system uses a main server (about $2,000), which stores your CDs in the MP3 (or other) electronic format, and a series of receivers or clients (about $800) in remote rooms for playing back music. You can have one in each room — if you can afford it!

Most consumer manufacturers are trying to network-enable their devices, so expect to see everything from your washer and dryer to your vacuum cleaner network-enabled at some point. Why? Because after such appliances are on a network, they can be monitored for breakdowns, software upgrades, and so forth without you having to manually monitor them.

Network infrastructure

Workstations must be electronically interconnected in order to communicate. The equipment over which the *network traffic* (electronic signals) travels between computers on the network is the *network infrastructure*.

Network hubs

In a typical office network, a strand of wiring similar to phone cable is run from each computer to a central location, such as a phone closet, where each wire is connected to a network hub. The *network hub*, similar conceptually to the hub of a wheel, receives signals transmitted by each computer on the network and sends the signals out to all other computers on the network.

Figure 2-1 illustrates a network with a star-shaped *topology* (the physical design of a network). Other network topologies include *ring* and *bus*. Home networks typically use a star topology because it's the simplest to install and troubleshoot.

Figure 2-1:
It's all in the stars: A typical network star-shaped topology.

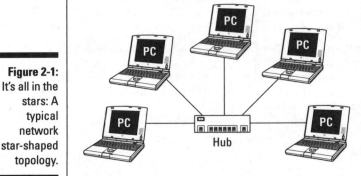

Bridges

A network *bridge* provides a pathway for network traffic between networks or segments of networks. A device that connects a wireless network segment to a wired network segment is a type of network bridge. In larger networks, network bridges are sometimes used to connect networks on different floors in the same building or in different buildings. In a wireless home network, the device that manages the wireless network, an *access point*, often acts as a bridge between a wireless segment of the network and a wired segment.

Hubs and switches

Networks transmit data in bundles called *packets*. Along with the raw information that's being transmitted, each packet also contains the network address of the computer that sent it and the network address of the recipient computer. Network hubs send packets indiscriminately to all ports of all computers connected to the hub.

A special type of hub called a *switched hub* examines each packet, determines the addressee and port, and forwards the packet only to the computer and port to which it is addressed. Most often, switched hubs are just called *switches*. A *switch* reads the addressee information in each packet and sends the packet directly to the segment of the network to which the addressee is connected. Packets that aren't addressed to a particular network segment are never transmitted over that segment, and the switch acts as a filter to eliminate unnecessary network traffic. Switches make more efficient use of the available transmission bandwidth than standard hubs and therefore offer higher aggregate throughput to the devices on the switched network.

Routers

Over a large network and on the Internet, a *router* is analogous to a super-efficient postal service — reading the addressee information in each data packet and communicating with other routers over the network or Internet to determine the best route for each packet to take. Routers can be a standalone device, but more often, home networks use a device known as a *cable/(digital subscriber line) DSL router.* This type of router — which marries a cable or DSL modem and a router — uses a capability called *Network Address Translation* (NAT) to enable all the computers on a home network to share a single Internet address on the cable or DSL network. Such routers also exist for satellite and dialup connections. Generically, these are called *WAN routers* because they have access to your *wide area network* connection, whether it's broadband or dialup.

So your local area network, or LAN, in your home connects to your wide area network, or WAN, which takes signals out of the home.

Transmission Control Protocol/Internet Protocol (TCP/IP) is the most common protocol for transmitting packets around a network. Every computer on a TCP/IP network must have its own *IP address*, which is a 32-bit numeric address that's written as four numbers separated by periods (for example, 192.168.1.100). Each number can have a value from 0 (zero) to 254. The Internet transmits packets by using the TCP/IP protocol. When you use the Internet, the Internet service provider (ISP), such as AOL or EarthLink, assigns a unique TCP/IP number to your computer. For the period of time that your computer is connected, your computer "leases" this unique address and uses it like a postal address to send and receive information over the Internet to and from other computers.

A WAN router with the Network Address Translation (NAT) feature also helps to protect the data on your computers from intruders. The NAT feature acts as a protection because it hides the real network addresses of networked computers from computers outside the network. (For more details on NAT, see Chapter 9.) Many WAN routers also have additional security features that more actively prevent intruders from gaining unauthorized access to your network through the Internet. This type of protection is sometimes described generically as a *firewall*. Good firewall software usually offers a suite of tools that not only block unauthorized access but also help you to detect and monitor suspicious computer activity. In addition, these tools also provide you ways to safely permit computers on your network to access the Internet.

Internet gateways

In some cases, you can get a device that really does it all — a *wireless Internet gateway*. These devices combine all the features of an access point, a router, and a broadband modem (typically cable or DSL). Some wireless Internet gateways even include a print server (that enables you to connect a printer directly to the gateway and use it from any networked PC), a dialup modem, and even some Ethernet ports for computers and devices that connect to your network using wires.

For example, the Cayman Systems 3500 Series Smart Gateways (www. netopia.com) include a built-in DSL modem, a router, a wireless access point, and other networking features such as a firewall and an easy-to-use graphical user interface (GUI) for configuring and setting up the gateway.

There aren't a lot of these devices on the market; you can't buy many of them off-the-shelf, but you can get them directly from your broadband service provider.

TIP

The term *gateway* gets used a lot by different folks with different ideas about what such a device is. Although our definition is the most common (and, in our opinion, correct), you might see some vendors selling devices that they call Internet gateways that don't have all the functions that we describe. For example, some access points and routers that don't have built-in broadband modems are also called gateways. We don't consider these to be Internet gateways because they actually link to the WAN modem. They are more of a modem gateway, but no one uses that term — it just is not as catchy as an Internet gateway. We call them *wireless gateways* to keep everyone honest. So keep these subtle differences in mind when you're shopping.

Network interface adapters

Wireless networking is based on radio signals. Each computer or *station* on a wireless network has its own radio that sends and receives data over the network. Like in wired networks, a station can be a *client* or a *server*. Most stations on a home wireless network are desktop personal computers with a wireless network adapter, but they could also be a portable device, such as a laptop or a PDA.

Each workstation on the network has a network interface card or adapter that links the workstation to the network (we discuss these in Chapter 1). This is true for wireless and *wireline* (wired) networks. In some instances, such as where the wireless functionality is embedded in the device, the network interface adapter is merely internal and pre-installed in the machine. In other instances, these are internal and external adapters that are either ordered with your workstation or device, or which you add during the installation process. We describe these options in the following sections.

Figure 2-2 shows an external wireless networking adapter that is designed for attachment to a computer's Universal Serial Bus (USB) port, and Figure 2-3 shows an internal wireless networking adapter designed for installation in a desktop computer.

Figure 2-2:
A wireless network adapter that attaches to a computer's USB port.

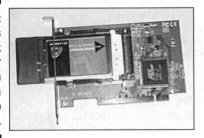

Figure 2-3:
A wireless
network
adapter for
installation
inside a
desktop
computer.

PC Cards

When you want to add wireless networking capability to a laptop computer, your first choice for a wireless network interface should probably be a Personal Computer Memory Card International Association (PCMIA) card (also called a PC Card; shown in Figure 2-4). Nearly all Windows and some Mac notebook/laptops have PCMCIA ports that are compatible with these cards. (An AirPort card is a special type of PC Card. In Chapter 8, we tell you more about the AirPort card and how to set up a wireless Mac network.)

Figure 2-4:
A PC Card
wireless
network
adapter.

All wireless PC Cards must have an antenna so that the built-in radio can communicate with an access point. Most have a built-in patch antenna that's enclosed in a plastic casing that protrudes from the PC while the card is fully inserted. At least one manufacturer offers a retractable antenna that's less likely to get damaged when not in use.

PCI adapters

Nearly all desktop PCs have at least one Peripheral Component Interconnect (PCI) slot. This PCI slot is used to install all sorts of add-in cards, including network connectivity. Most wireless NIC manufacturers offer a wireless PCI adapter — a version of their product that can be installed in a PCI slot (see Figure 2-5).

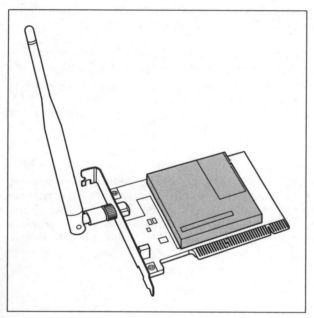

Figure 2-5:
A wireless
PCI adapter.

Some wireless PCI adapters are cards that adapt a PC Card for use in a PCI slot. The newest designs, however, use a mini-PCI Card that's mounted on a full-size PCI Card with a removable dipole antenna attached to the back of the card.

USB adapters

The USB standard has over the last several years become the most widely used method of connecting peripherals to a personal computer. First popularized in the Apple iMac, USB supports a data transfer rate many times faster than a typical network connection and is, therefore, a good candidate for connecting an external wireless network adapter to either a laptop or a desktop computer. Several wireless networking hardware vendors offer USB wireless network adapters. They are easy to connect, transport, and reposition in order to get better reception.

Most computers built in the last two or three years have at least one (and usually two) USB port(s). If your computer has a USB port and you purchased a wireless USB network interface adapter, see Chapter 7 for more on setting up that adapter.

USB wireless NICs are sometimes a better choice than PC Cards or PCI cards because you can more easily move the device around to get a better signal, kinda like adjusting the rabbit ears on an old TV. If a computer doesn't have a PC Card slot but does have a USB port, you either need to install a PCI adapter or select a USB wireless network adapter.

Note that there are two forms of USB adapters: ones that have cables and ones that don't. The cabled USB adapters allow for positioning of the antenna; the non-cabled ones directly connect in a fixed way into the back of your computer, and are designed for economy of size. You might hear either of these form factors referred to as *dongles*. (See Chapter 5 for more about form factors.)

CF cards

With the growing popularity of handheld personal digital assistant (PDA) computers, the newest category of wireless network adapters uses a Compact Flash (CF) interface to enable connection to PDAs. With a Compact Flash card, such as that from SMC shown in Figure 2-6, you can connect a Pocket PC to a wireless home network. (For more about PDAs and how they can enhance your wireless home network experience, check out Chapter 1.)

Figure 2-6: A Compact Flash card wireless network interface card.

CF cards are small, 1½"-wide electronic modules that you insert into a CF card slot. The CF card slot where you insert the card is an 1½" slot in the top edge of the Pocket PC. Compact Flash refers to the technology used to store software or other data on the device. Many users employ CF cards to expand the memory in their Pocket PCs and for many other PDA add-ons.

Most Pocket PC manufacturers provide either standard or optional support for add-on cards built to the Compact Flash form factor. D-Link, for example, makes the DCF-660W model (`www.dlink.com/products/wireless/dcf660w`; $99.99) that works with Compaq, HP, Casio, Sharp, and other PDAs. As times goes by, more and more PDAs will have wireless natively onboard; the top-of-the-line HP Pocket PC h5400 series includes integrated support for IEEE 802.11b wireless networking, as well as for Bluetooth, for instance.

Although Pocket PCs are typically more expensive than Palm PDAs (see the nearby sidebar, "Wi-Fi network adapters and the Palm OS"), they boast computing power more akin to a full-sized PC, and they are perfect candidates for wireless network connectivity. You can use them for data synchronization, Internet access, and connecting with other Pocket PCs.

Get the (Access) Point?

Let's talk some more about the central pivot point in your wireless network: the access point. Somewhat similar in function to a network hub, an *access point* in a wireless network is a special type of wireless station that receives radio transmissions from other stations on the wireless and forwards them to the rest of the network. An access point can be a standalone device or a computer that contains a wireless network adapter along with special access point management software. Most home networks use a standalone AP, such as shown in Figure 2-7.

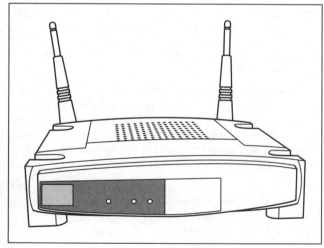

Figure 2-7:
A stand-
alone
access
point.

Wi-Fi network adapters and the Palm OS

Wi-Fi network adapters for handhelds using the Palm operating system (OS) are less widely available today than are those for Pocket PCs. The one module that we see most often used is the Xircom Wireless LAN Module for Palm (www.intel.com/ network/connectivity/products/ xirpwe1130.htm). Unlike the CF cards that we talk about in this chapter, this module is a *sled.* That is, you slide the Palm handheld into it, much like how you might slide it into its cradle for syncing with your PC or Mac.

Only time and the marketplace will determine whether 802.11-based technology, Bluetooth, or some yet unidentified technology will become the dominant method of connecting PDAs and other small devices to local area networks. The list of potential applications of wireless technology to handheld electronic devices is virtually limitless.

Because many homes and businesses use wireless networking, a method is needed to distinguish one wireless network from another. Otherwise, your neighbor might accidentally send a page to the printer on your network. (That could be fun, or that could be a little scary.) Three parameters that can be used to uniquely identify each segment of a wireless network:

✔ **Network name:** When you set up your wireless network, you should assign a unique name to the network. Some manufacturers refer to the network name by one of its technical monikers — *Service Set Identifier* (SSID) or perhaps *Extended Service Set Identifier* (ESSID). This can be confusing and comes up most often if you're using equipment from different manufacturers. Rest assured, however, that network name, SSID, and ESSID all mean the same thing.

If the AP manufacturer assigns a network name at the factory, it will assign the same name to every AP that it manufactures. Consequently, you should assign a different network name to avoid confusion with other APs that might be nearby (like your neighbor's). *Note:* All stations and the AP on a given wireless network must have the same network name to ensure that they can communicate.

Assigning a unique network name is good practice but don't think of the network name as a security feature. Most APs broadcast their network name, so it's easy for a hacker to change the network name on his computer to match yours. Changing the network name from the factory setting to a new name just reduces the chance that you and your neighbor accidentally have wireless networks with the same network name.

✔ **Channel:** When you set up your wireless network, you have the option of selecting a radio channel. All stations and the access point must broadcast on the same radio channel in order to communicate. Multiple radio channels are available for use by wireless networks. The number of channels available varies according to the type of wireless network that you're using and the country in which you install the wireless network. Wireless stations normally scan all available channels looking for a signal from an AP. When a station detects an AP signal, the station negotiates a connection to the AP.

✔ **Encryption key:** Because it's relatively easy for a hacker to determine a wireless network's name and the channel on which it's broadcasting, every wireless network should be protected by a secret encryption key unless the network is intended for use by the general public. Only someone who knows the secret key code will be able to connect to the wireless network.

The most popular wireless network technology, *Wi-Fi*, uses the Wired Equivalent Privacy (WEP) encryption protocol. This technology uses the RC4 encryption algorithm and a private key phrase or series of characters to encrypt all data transmitted over the wireless network. For this type of security to work, all stations must have the private key. Any station without this key cannot get on the network. A new encryption protocol that will replace WEP has recently been announced. This new protocol, Wi-Fi Protected Access (WPA), will soon be available built in to all new Wi-Fi equipment and as a free upgrade from most Wi-Fi equipment manufacturers . . . probably by the time you're reading this book.

You'll commonly find AP functionality bundled into the same device as several separate but related functions. For instance, some APs perform the functions of a router, a switched hub, and a DHCP server as well as normal AP functions. Similar devices might even throw in a print server. This Swiss Army knife-like approach is often a real bargain for use in a home wireless network.

Wireless networking devices can operate in one of two modes: *infrastructure mode* or *ad hoc mode*. The next two sections describe the difference between these two modes.

Infrastructure mode

When a wireless station (such as a PC or a Mac) communicates with other computers or devices through an AP, the wireless station is operating in *infrastructure mode*. The station uses the network infrastructure to reach another computer or a device rather than communicate directly with the other computer or device. Figure 2-8 shows a network that consists of a wireless network segment with two wireless personal computers, and a wired network segment with three computers. These five computers communicate through the AP and the network infrastructure. The wireless computers in this network are communicating in infrastructure mode.

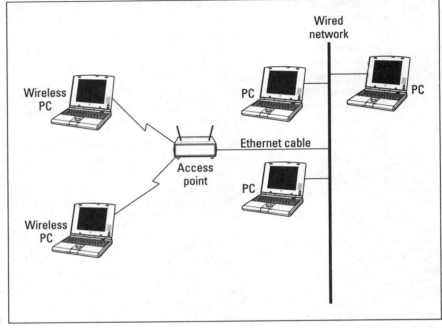

Figure 2-8:
The two
wireless
computers
in this
network
commun-
icate
through the
AP in
infrastruc-
ture mode.

Ad hoc mode

Whenever two wireless stations are close enough to communicate with each other, they are capable of establishing an *ad hoc network:* that is, a wireless network that doesn't use an AP. Theoretically, you could create a home network out of wireless stations without the need for an AP. It's more practical, however, to use an AP; an AP is more effective because it facilitates communication between many stations at once (as many as 30 stations simultaneously in a single wireless network segment). In addition, an AP can create a connection or *bridge* between a wireless network segment and a wired segment.

Ad hoc mode isn't often used in wireless home networks, but it could be used on occasion to connect two computers together to transfer files where there is no AP in the vicinity to create a wireless infrastructure.

Your Wireless Network's Power Station — the Antenna

The main interface between your access point or network interface card and the network is the antenna. Signals generated and received by your wireless gear is dependent on a high quality antenna interface. To be smart in wireless networking, you need to know the basics about antennas. If you know how they work, you can better optimize your network.

Access point antennas vary from manufacturer to manufacturer. Many APs have a single external antenna about five inches in length. This type of antenna is a *dipole* antenna. Some APs have two external dipole antennas. Dual external antenna models should provide better signal coverage throughout the house. APs with dual antennas might transmit from only one of the antennas but receive through both antennas by sampling the signal and using whichever antenna is getting the strongest signal — a *diversity antenna system*.

Typical omnidirectional dipole antennas attach to the AP with a connector that enables you to position the antenna at many different angles; however, omnidirectional dipole radio antennas send and receive best in the vertical position.

The range and coverage of a Wi-Fi wireless AP used indoors is determined by the following factors:

- **AP transmission output power:** This is the power output of the AP's radio, usually referred to as *transmission power* or *TX power*. Higher power output produces a longer range. Wi-Fi APs transmit at a power output of less than 30 dBm (one watt). Government agencies around the world regulate the maximum power output allowed. APs for home use generally have power outputs in the range 13 dBm (20 mW) to 15 dBm (31.6 mW). The higher the power rating, the stronger the signal and the better range your wireless network will have. Some wireless networking equipment manufacturers offer add-on amplifiers that boost the standard signal of the AP to achieve a longer range. We talk about boosters in Chapter 18. (For more on TX power, see the sidebar, "TX power output and antenna gain.")

- **Antenna gain:** The AP's antenna and the antenna(s) on the other device(s) on the network improve the capability of the devices to send and receive radio signals. This type of signal improvement is *gain*. Antenna specifications vary depending on vendor, type, and materials. Adding a higher gain antenna at either end of the connection can increase the effective range.

- **Antenna type:** Radio antennas both send and receive signals. Different types of antennas transmit signals in different patterns or shapes. The most common type of antenna used in wireless home networks, the dipole antenna, is described as *omnidirectional* because it transmits its signal in all directions equally. In fact, the signal from a dipole antenna radiates 360° in the horizontal plane and 75° in the vertical plane, creating a doughnut-shaped pattern. Consequently, the area directly above or below the antenna gets a very weak signal.

Some types of antenna focus the signal in a particular direction and are referred to as *directional antennas*. In special applications where you want an AP to send its signal only in a specific direction, you could replace the omnidirectional antenna with a directional antenna. In a home, omnidirectional is usually the best choice, but that also depends on the shape of the home; some antennas are better for brownstones and multifloor buildings because they have a more spherical signal footprint rather than the standard flat-ish one.

✔ **Receive sensitivity:** The *receive sensitivity* of an AP or other wireless networking device is a measurement of how strong a signal is required from another radio before the device can make a reliable connection and receive data.

✔ **Signal attenuation:** A radio signal can get weaker as a result of interference caused by other radio signals because of objects that lie in the radio wave path between radios and because of the distance between the radios. The reduction in signal is *attenuation*. Read through Chapter 6 for a discussion of how to plan the installation of your wireless network to deal with signal attenuation.

In order to replace or add an antenna to an AP or other wireless device, you need to have a place to plug it in — as obvious a statement as that is, many antennas are not detachable, and you can't add another antenna. Some access points use reverse TNC connectors that let optional antennas be used in 802.11b/g products, but there's a minor trend away from using detachable antennas in 802.11a products because of potential conflict in the frequency channels allocated to 802.11a. This potentially thwarts misuse, but also robs those deploying access points of their ability to choose optimal antennas.

Industry Standards

One of the most significant factors that has led to the explosive growth of personal computers and their impact on our daily lives has been the emergence of industry standards. Although many millions of personal computers are in use today around the world, only three families of operating system software run virtually all these computers: Windows, Mac OS, and Unix (including Linux). Most personal computers that are used in the home employ one of the Microsoft Windows operating systems or one of the Apple Macintosh operating systems. The existence of this huge installed base of potential customers has enabled hundreds of hardware and software companies to thrive by producing products that interoperate with one or more of these industry standard operating systems.

Computer hardware manufacturers recognize the benefits of building their products to industry standards. To encourage the adoption and growth of wireless networking, many companies that are otherwise competitors have worked together to develop a family of wireless networking industry standards that build on and interoperate with existing networking standards. As a result, reasonably priced wireless networking equipment is widely available from many manufacturers. Feel safe buying equipment from any of these manufacturers because they're all designed to work together, with one important caveat. The current three major flavors of this wireless networking technology for LAN applications are IEEE 802.11a, 802.11b, and 802.11g. You just have to pick the flavor that best fits your needs and budget. (***Note:*** There are other wireless standards for other applications in the home, like Bluetooth for short range communications. We talk about these in Chapter 3 and elsewhere where their discussion is appropriate.)

The Institute for Electrical and Electronics Engineers

The *Institute for Electrical and Electronics Engineers* (IEEE) is a standards-making industry group that has for many years been developing industry standards that affect the electrical products that we use in our homes and businesses every day. At present, the IEEE 802.11b standard is the overwhelming market leader in terms of deployed wireless networking products. Products that comply with this standard weren't the first wireless networking technology on the market . . . but they are now, by far, the dominant market installed base. As you will soon see, the 802.11a and g products are coming on strong.

TECHNICAL STUFF

TX power output and antenna gain

TX power output is measured in milliwatts (mW) but is also often expressed by using dBm units of measurement. (*dBm* measures, in decibels, a radio's amount of power.) The FCC permits an AP to have a maximum power output of 1,000 mW (1 watt), which is the same as 30 dBm. Wi-Fi APs typically have maximum output power of 100 mW (20 dBm) or less. APs for home use generally have power outputs in the range 13 dBm (20 mW) to 15 dBm (31.6 mW). The higher the power rating, the stronger the signal and the better range that your wireless network will have.

Antenna gain is usually expressed in dBi units (which indicate, also in decibels, the amount of gain an antenna has). An antenna with a 4 dBi gain increases the output power (the effective isotropic radiated power, or EIRP) of the radio by 4 dBm. The FCC permits IEEE 802.11 radios a maximum EIRP of 36 dBm when the device is using an omnidirectional antenna. The antennas included with home wireless networking equipment are typically omnidirectional detachable dipole antennas with gains of from 2 dBi to 5 dBi. Some manufacturers offer optional high-gain antennas. (***Note:*** The maximum EIRP output permitted in Japan is 100 mW; and the maximum output in Europe is only 10 mW.)

The Wi-Fi Alliance

In 1999, several leading wireless networking companies formed the Wireless Ethernet Compatibility Alliance (WECA), a nonprofit organization (www.weca.net). This group has recently renamed itself the Wi-Fi Alliance and is now a voluntary organization of over 200 companies that make or support wireless networking products. The Wi-Fi Alliances' primary purpose is to certify that IEEE 802.11 products from different vendors will *interoperate* (work together). These companies recognize the value of building a high level of consumer confidence in the interoperability of wireless networking products.

The Wi-Fi Alliance organization has established a test suite that defines how member products will be tested by an independent test lab. Products that pass these tests are entitled to display the Wi-Fi trademark, which is a seal of interoperability. Although there is no technical requirement in the IEEE specifications stating that a product must pass these tests, Wi-Fi certification encourages consumer confidence that products from different vendors will work together.

The Wi-Fi interoperability tests are designed to ensure that hardware from different vendors can successfully establish a communication session with an acceptable level of functionality. The test plan includes a list of necessary features. The features themselves are defined in detail in the IEEE 802.11 standards, but the test plan specifies an expected implementation.

IEEE 802.11b: The defending champ

In 1990, the IEEE adopted a document entitled "IEEE Standards for Local and Metropolitan Area Networks" that provided an overview of the networking technology standards used in virtually all computer networks in prevalent use today. The great majority of computer networks use one or more of the standards included in IEEE 802; the most widely adopted is IEEE 802.3, which covers Ethernet.

IEEE 802.11 is the section that defines wireless networking standards and is often called *wireless Ethernet*. The first edition of the IEEE 802.11 standard, adopted in 1997, specified two wireless networking protocols that can transmit at either one or two megabits per second (Mbps) using the 2.4 GHz radio frequency band, broken into 14 5-MHz channels (11 in the United States). IEEE 802.11b-1999 was a supplement to IEEE 802.11 that added subsections to IEEE 802.11 that specify the protocol used by Wi-Fi-certified wireless networking devices.

The IEEE 802.11b protocol is backward compatible with the IEEE 802.11 protocols adopted in 1997, using the same 2.4 GHz band and channels as the slower protocol. The primary improvement of the IEEE 802.11b protocol is a technique that enables data transmission at either 5.5 Mbps or 11 Mbps.

Because 11 Mbps is as fast as standard Ethernet (10 Mbps) and is faster than most broadband Internet connections, it is quite adequate for use in most home networks. However, 11 Mbps is still a bit slow for transmission of DVD-quality streaming video.

Several vendors offer IEEE 802.11b products with a "turbo" setting that provides data transmission speeds up to 22 Mbps, double the normal maximum rate. Be aware that this feature is *proprietary,* which means that it might only work with other wireless networking equipment from the same manufacturer.

IEEE 802.11a: Fast, faster, and fastest

IEEE adopted 802.11a-1999 at the same time that it adopted 802.11b. IEEE 802.11a specifies a wireless protocol that operates at higher frequencies than the IEEE 802.11b protocol and uses a variety of techniques to provide data transmission rates of 6, 9, 12, 18, 24, 36, 48, and 54 Mbps. 802.11a has 12 non-overlapping channels in the United States and Canada, but most deployed products use only 8 of these channels.

Some wireless networking vendors offer proprietary enhancements to IEEE 802.11a-compliant products that double the top speed to over 100 Mbps.

An increasing number of products based on the IEEE 802.11a standard has reached the market. In addition to the higher transmission speeds, IEEE 802.11a offers the following advantages over IEEE 802.11b:

- ✔ **Capacity:** 802.11a has about four times as many available channels, resulting in about eight times the network capacity: that is, the number of wireless stations that can be connected to the AP at one time and still be able to communicate. This isn't a significant advantage for a wireless home network because you'll almost certainly never use all the network capacity available with a single access point (approximately 30 stations simultaneously).

- ✔ **Less competition:** Portable phones, Bluetooth, and residential microwave ovens use portions of the same 2.4 GHz radio frequency band used by 802.11b, which sometimes results in interference. By contrast, very few devices other than IEEE 802.11a devices use the 5 GHz radio frequency band.

- ✔ **Improved throughput:** Tests show as much as four to five times the data link rate and throughput of 802.11b in a typical office environment. *Throughput* is the amount of data that can be transferred over the connection in a given period of time. (See the sidebar elsewhere in this chapter, "Gauging your network's throughput.")

When does a + b = g?

The last of the IEEE standards-based products to hit the street is 802.11g, and these products are selling like hotcakes. Although the g standard is still being finalized as we write — it's expected to be final in mid-2003 and will enter interoperability testing soon thereafter — the appeal of 802.11g is so great that many vendors aren't waiting for the final standard to be adopted before they release their first products based on this technology. Instead, they will offer upgrades via firmware downloads when the final software is complete.

IEEE 802.11g is intended to be backward compatible with 802.11b wireless networking technology but still delivers the same transmission speeds as 802.11a — up to 54 Mbps — thus, effectively combining the best of both worlds. The 802.11g products are expected to outsell a and b products in the next few years.

IEEE 802.11g equipment offers a nice upgrade path to people who have already invested in IEEE 802.11b equipment. The first products released carry prices that are only marginally more expensive than plain-old IEEE 802.11b. Tests of these products have uncovered some interoperability problems with IEEE 802.11b equipment, but these problems are certain to be ironed out by the time products are released on the final standard.

If you plan to do streaming video over your network, you should seriously consider purchasing IEEE 802.11a equipment or IEEE 802.11g equipment. Otherwise, IEEE 802.11b products should be more than adequate for your wireless home network and are probably available at bargain prices. However, if you're one to hedge your bets, consider purchasing an access point that supports multiple standards — dual-mode, tri-standard a/b/g products are available. Only time and the marketplace will determine whether IEEE 802.11a will survive or be pushed out by IEEE 802.11g. We think that they'll coexist. It is a virtual certainty that IEEE 802.11b's current position as the dominant standard will give way to one or both of the faster standards. We predict that IEEE 802.11g will represent the majority of all wireless shipments within the next few years.

The ISM bands

Here we talk about frequency bands used by the various standards in detail. In 1985, the Federal Communication Commission (FCC) made changes to the radio spectrum regulation and assigned three bands designated as the industrial, scientific, and medical (ISM) bands. These frequency bands are

- 902 MHz–928 MHz: a 26 MHz bandwidth
- 2.4 GHz–2.4835 GHz: an 83.5 MHz bandwidth
- 5.15–5.35 GHz and 5.725 GHz–5.825 GHz: a 300 MHz bandwidth

Gauging your network's throughput

Wi-Fi standards call for different speeds, up to 11 Mbps for 802.11b and up to 54 Mbps for 802.11a and g. Radios attempt to communicate at the highest speed. If they encounter too many errors (dropped bits), the radios will step down to the next fastest speed, repeating the process until a strong connection is achieved. So although we talk about 802.11g, for instance, being up to 54 Mbps in speed, the reality is that unless you're very close to the AP, you're not likely to get that maximum rate. Signal fade and interference will cut into your speeds, and the negotiated rate between the two devices will drop.

And that just represents the speed. The actual throughput is another, but related, matter. *Throughput* represents the actual rate at which the validated data flows from one point to another. It might take some retransmissions for that to occur, so your throughput will be less than the negotiated speed of the connection. It might not be unusual for you to get only 20–30 Mbps on your 54 Mbps connection or 4–5 Mbps on your 11 Mbps connection. In fact, that's rather normal.

The FCC also opened up some additional frequencies known as Unlicensed National Information Infrastructure (U-NII), in the lower reaches of the five GHz frequencies.

The purpose of the FCC change was to encourage the development and use of wireless networking technology. The new regulation permits a user to operate radio equipment that transmits a signal within each of these three ISM bands without obtaining an FCC license, within certain guidelines.

Wireless networks use radio waves to send data around the network. IEEE 802.11a uses part of the U-NII frequencies, and IEEE 802.11b and g use the ISM 2.4 GHz band.

An important concept when talking about frequencies is the idea of overlapping and non-overlapping channels. As we discuss in Chapter 18, signals from other APs can cause interference and poor performance of your wireless network. This specifically happens when the APs' signals are transmitting on the same (or sometimes nearby) channels. Recall that the standards call for a number of channels within a specified frequency range.

Take 802.11b, for example: Its frequency range is between 2.4 GHz and 2.4835 GHz, and it's broken up into 14 equally sized channels (although only 11 can be used in the United States — any equipment sold for use here will only allow you to access these 11 channels). The problem is that these are defined in a way such that many of the channels overlap with one another — and with 802.11b, there are only three non-overlapping channels. Thus, you wouldn't want to have channels 10 and 11 operating side by side because you'd get signal degradation. You want non-interfering, non-overlapping channels. So you find that people tend to use Channels 1, 6, and 11, or something similar. 802.11a doesn't have this problem because its eight channels, in the 5 GHz frequency band, don't overlap; therefore, you can use contiguous channels. As with 802.11b and g, however, you don't want to be on the same channel.

Chapter 3

Bluetooth, HPNA, and HomePlug

● ●

In This Chapter

▶ Understanding the Bluetooth standard

▶ Data networking with HPNA

▶ Plugging in with HomePlug

● ●

*G*etting the most from computer technology is all about selecting the best and most dominant technology standards. The most dominant technology for home wireless networks today clearly is the Wireless Fidelity (Wi-Fi) family of technologies defined by the IEEE 802.11a, 802.11b, and 802.11g standards (which we describe in Chapter 2).

But Wi-Fi isn't the only game in town. You'll run into other home networking standards when you buy and install your Wi-Fi gear — standards that will make it easier to get Wi-Fi where you want it.

This chapter briefly describes the Bluetooth wireless technology that either complements or competes with Wi-Fi, depending on your application. Even if you intend to purchase and use only Wi-Fi wireless networking equipment, you should still be aware of Bluetooth. Who knows? — it might even come in handy for you.

We also talk about two key wired home networking standards (oops, did we say a dreaded word . . . *wired?*): Home Phone Networking Alliance (HPNA), the standard for networking over your installed phone wiring in your home; and HomePlug, the standard for networking over your electrical power cables in your home. As surprising as it might seem, you can actually connect your computers, access points, and other devices together over these in-wall cables. What's more, many APs come with these interfaces onboard to make it easier for you to install that AP wherever you want it. Isn't that nice? You betcha.

Who or What Is Bluetooth?

One of the most often talked about wireless standards, besides Wi-Fi, is *Bluetooth*. The Bluetooth wireless technology, named for the tenth-century Danish King Harald Blatand "Bluetooth," was invented by the L.M. Ericsson company of Sweden in 1994. King Harald helped unite his part of the world during a conflict around 960 AD. Ericsson intended for Bluetooth technology to unite the mobile world. In 1998, Ericsson, IBM, Intel, Nokia, and Toshiba founded the Bluetooth Special Interest Group (SIG), Inc. to develop an open specification for always-on, short-range wireless connectivity based on Ericsson's Bluetooth technology. Their specification was publicly released on July 26, 1999. The Bluetooth SIG now includes 3Com, Agere, Ericsson, IBM, Intel, Microsoft, Motorola, Nokia, Toshiba, and nearly 2,000 other companies. Dozens of Bluetooth-enabled products are already on the market, with many more on the way.

Sometimes a network of devices communicating via Bluetooth is described as a *personal area network* (PAN) to distinguish it from a network of computers often called a *local area network* (LAN). In March 2002, the Institute for Electrical and Electronics Engineers (IEEE) approved IEEE 802.15.1, a standard for wireless PANs (WPANs), which was adapted from portions of the Bluetooth wireless specification. IEEE 802.15.1 is fully compliant with the Bluetooth v1.1 specification. As IEEE worked toward the 802.15 standard, the Bluetooth SIG simultaneously has been working on Bluetooth Version 3.0. Any new Bluetooth standard will likely also become an updated IEEE 802.15 standard. (Read more at the Bluetooth Web site at www.bluetooth.com.)

The following is a small sampling of existing Bluetooth products:

- ✔ Microsoft Wireless IntelliMouse Explorer for Bluetooth (a wireless mouse)
- ✔ Microsoft Wireless Optical Desktop for Bluetooth (wireless multimedia center keyboard and mouse)
- ✔ Sony digital video camera recorder
- ✔ HP Deskjet 995c printer
- ✔ HP iPAQ H5450 Pocket PC with Bluetooth (and Wi-Fi) onboard
- ✔ Ericsson Bluetooth Phone Adapter
- ✔ Motorola Bluetooth Handsfree Car Kit
- ✔ Belkin Bluetooth Universal Serial Bus (USB) Adapter

Although originally intended as a wireless replacement for cables, Bluetooth is being applied to make it possible for a wide range of devices to communicate with each other wirelessly with minimal user intervention. The technology is designed to be low-cost and low-power to appeal to a broad audience and to conserve a device's battery life.

The projected growth plans for Bluetooth are phenomenal. It is expected that the number of devices enabled with Bluetooth will jump from near nothing in 2000 to nearly 1.4 billion units (yup, *billion* with a *b*) in 2005, according to industry analyst firm In-Stat/MDR.

Wi-Fi versus Bluetooth

Wi-Fi and Bluetooth are designed to coexist in the network, and although they certainly have overlapping applications, each has its distinct zones of advantage.

The biggest differences between Wi-Fi and Bluetooth are

- **Distance:** Bluetooth is lower powered, which means its signal can only go short distances (up to 30 feet). 802.11 technologies can cover your home, and in some cases more, depending on the antenna that you use. *Note:* New software for Bluetooth devices is enabling the creation of mesh networks in the home, where interconnected Bluetooth devices can create a large mesh network that can be interconnected to the Internet — thereby creating a network similar to an 802.11b network in the home, for instance.

- **Application:** Bluetooth is designed as a replacement of cables: that is, trying to get rid of that huge tangle of cables that link your mouse, printer, monitor, scanner, and other devices on your desk and around your home. In fact, the first Bluetooth device was a Bluetooth headset, eliminating that annoying cable to the telephone that got in the way of typing. New cars are also becoming outfitted with Bluetooth so that you can use your cell phone in your car, with your car's stereo speakers and an onboard microphone serving as your hands-free capability. Pretty neat, huh?

Wi-Fi (IEEE 802.11a, 802.11b, and 802.11g) and Bluetooth are similar in certain respects: They both enable wireless communication between electronic devices but are more complementary than direct competitors. Wi-Fi technology is most often used to create a wireless network of personal computers that can be located anywhere in a home or business. Bluetooth devices usually communicate with other Bluetooth devices in relatively close proximity.

The easiest way to distinguish Wi-Fi from Bluetooth is to focus on what each replaces:

- **Wi-Fi is wireless Ethernet.** Wi-Fi is a wireless version of the Ethernet communication protocol and is intended to replace networking cable that would otherwise be run through walls and ceilings to connect computers in multiple rooms or even multiple floors of a building.

- **Bluetooth replaces peripheral cables.** Bluetooth wireless technology operates at short distances — usually about 10 meters — most often replaces cables that connect peripheral devices, such as a printer, keyboard, mouse, or personal digital assistant (PDA) to your computer.

- **Bluetooth replaces IrDA.** Bluetooth can also be used to replace another wireless technology — Infrared Data Association (IrDA) wireless technology — that's already found in most laptop computers, PDAs, and even many printers. Although IR signals are very secure and aren't bothered with radio frequency (RF) interference, IrDA's usefulness is hindered by infrared's requirement for line-of-sight proximity of devices. Just like how your TV's remote control must be pointed directly at your TV to work, the infrared ports on two PDAs must be lined up to trade data, and your laptop has to be "pointing" at the printer to print over the infrared connection. Because Bluetooth uses radio waves rather than light waves, line-of-sight proximity is not required.

Like Wi-Fi, Bluetooth offers wireless access to LANs, including Internet access. Bluetooth devices can potentially access the Public Switched Telephone Network (PSTN: you know, the phone system) and mobile telephone networks. Bluetooth should be able to thrive alongside Wi-Fi by making possible such innovative solutions as a hands-free mobile phone headset, print-to-fax, and automatic PDA, laptop, and cell phone/address book synchronization.

Piconets, Masters, and Slaves

Communication between Bluetooth devices is similar in concept to the ad hoc mode of Wi-Fi wireless networks (which we describe in Chapter 2). A Bluetooth device automatically and spontaneously forms informal WPANs, called *piconets,* with from one to seven other Bluetooth devices that have the same Bluetooth profile. Piconets get their name from merging the prefix *pico* (probably from the Italian word *piccolo* [small]) and *net*work. A capability called *unconscious connectivity* enables these devices to connect and disconnect almost without any user intervention.

A particular Bluetooth device can be a member of any number of piconets at any moment in time (see Figure 3-1). Each piconet has one *master*, the device that first initiates the connection. Other participants in a piconet are *slaves*.

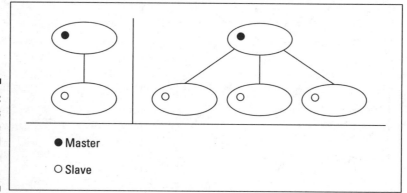

Figure 3-1:
Piconets
have one
master and
at least one
slave.

● Master

○ Slave

The three types of Bluetooth connections are

- ✔ **Data-only:** When communicating data, a master can manage connections with up to seven slaves.

- ✔ **Voice-only:** When the Bluetooth piconet is used for voice communication (for example, a wireless phone connection), the master can handle no more than three slaves.

- ✔ **Data and voice:** A piconet transmitting both data and voice can exist between only two Bluetooth devices at a time.

Each Bluetooth device can, in full compliance with the Bluetooth standard, join more than one piconet at a time. A group of more than one piconet with one or more devices in common is a *scatternet*. Figure 3-2 depicts a scatternet made up of several piconets.

The amount of information sent in each packet over a Bluetooth connection and the type of error correction used determine the data rate that a connection can deliver. Bluetooth devices can send data over a piconet by using 16 different types of packets. Sending more information in each packet (that is, sending longer packets) causes a faster data rate. Conversely, more robust error correction causes a slower data rate. Any application that uses a Bluetooth connection will determine the type of packet used and, therefore, the data rate.

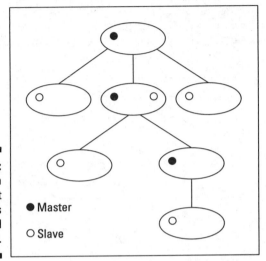

Figure 3-2:
A Bluetooth
scatternet
comprises
several
piconets.

● Master

○ Slave

In order to maintain the security of the data that you send over a Bluetooth link, the Bluetooth standard includes several layers of security. First, the two Bluetooth devices that are connecting use a process called *authentication* to identify each other. After the authentication process is done (sometimes called *pairing* in the Bluetooth world), the devices can begin sharing information. The data being sent across the radio link is *encrypted* (scrambled) so that only other authenticated devices have the key that can *decrypt* (unscramble) the data.

Both Wi-Fi (the IEEE 802.11b and g versions) and Bluetooth use the 2.4 GHz frequency radio band, but note the significant differences in how these technologies use the band. Bluetooth radios transmit a signal strength that complies with transmission regulations in most countries and is designed to connect at distances from 10 centimeters to 10 meters through walls and other obstacles — although like any radio wave, Bluetooth transmissions can be weakened by certain kinds of construction material, such as steel or heavy concrete. Although Bluetooth devices can employ a transmission power that produces a range in excess of 100 meters, you can assume that most Bluetooth devices are designed for use within 10 meters of other compatible devices, which is fine for the applications for which Bluetooth is intended, such as replacing short run cables.

To make full use of the 2.4 GHz frequency radio band and to reduce the likelihood of interference, Bluetooth uses a transmission protocol that hops 1,600 times per second between 79 discrete 1 MHz-wide channels from 2.402 GHz to 2.484 GHz. Each piconet establishes its own random hopping pattern so that you can have many piconets in the same vicinity without mutual interference. If interference does occur, each piconet switches to a different channel and tries again. Even though Wi-Fi (IEEE 802.11b/g) and Bluetooth both use the 2.4 GHz band, both protocols use hopping schemes that should result in little, if any, mutual interference.

Integrating Bluetooth in Your Wireless Network

Products that are the first to take advantage of Bluetooth technology include the following:

- Mobile phones
- Cordless phones
- PDAs
- Bluetooth adapters for PCs
- Bluetooth hands-free car kits
- Video cameras
- Refrigerators
- Microwaves
- Data projectors
- Scanners
- Printers

You can get a great idea of all the various ways that Bluetooth can be used in your network by going to the official Bluetooth products Web site at www. bluetooth.com/tech/products.asp. We also go into great detail about some of the more common ways that you'll use Bluetooth in Chapter 15.

One of the more interesting and promising applications of Bluetooth technology is for cell phones. Bring your Bluetooth-enabled phone home and dock it in a power station near your PC, and it will instantly log onto your home wireless network via a Bluetooth connection to a nearby PC or Bluetooth access point. Phones that function as PDAs can update their address books and sync data from the PC. All your events, to-do lists, grocery lists, and birthday reminders can be kept current just by bringing your Bluetooth-enabled product in range. There are even Bluetooth headsets for your Bluetooth phones — getting rid of that wireless headset hassle.

Bluetooth technology is advancing into the arena of autos, too. The Bluetooth SIG formed the Car Profile Working Group in December 1999, in response to interest by the automotive industry. This working group has defined how Bluetooth wireless technology will enable hands-free use of mobile phones in automobiles. Microsoft is using Bluetooth-driven products in car dashboards to enable the car to access your cell phone service for downloading digital music and live traffic updates.

The Microsoft Pocket PC 2002 operating system supports both Bluetooth and IEEE 802.11b through add-on adapters. The initial release of Windows XP offered native driver support for IEEE 801.11b but not Bluetooth. Microsoft cited the lack of commercially available Bluetooth devices as the main reason for not including the necessary Host Controller Interface (HCI) device drivers out of the box. Subsequently, Microsoft has added Bluetooth support to Windows XP through a software update. Mac OS v. 10.2 (Jaguar) also has integrated support for Bluetooth.

Wirelessly synching your PDAs

Bluetooth is onboard inside PDAs, like the HP iPAQ Pocket PC H5450 (www. hp.com; $699) that has both 802.11b and Bluetooth inside. Now that's really cool. (We won't mention that the H5450 also has a thermal biometric fingerprint reader that authenticates the owner's unique fingerprint, allowing access with a simple fingerprint swipe. That would probably be too cool for you to handle.)

If you have a PDA, you can get clip-on devices, like the BlueM from TDK Systems Europe (www.tdksys.com/products/intro.asp?id=2). Use the BlueM with your Palm handheld to communicate with other Bluetooth-enabled devices, including PCs, notebooks, printers, and other handhelds that are within range. This one-ounce device has a thin, sled design and slides onto the back of the Palm m500, m505, and m125 handhelds, as well as IBM C500 devices, connecting via the docking port on the bottom of the PDA.

For example, if you have your Bluetooth-enabled PDA in your pocket and walk into the room where your Bluetooth-enabled PC is located, the two will automatically synchronize your calendar, your e-mail, and your to-do list — with *no* intervention on your part. Or, if your cell phone is Bluetooth enabled, you can transfer your contact list wirelessly from your Bluetooth-enabled PC to the phone's address list. (That'd cut down on those expensive directory assistance calls, wouldn't it?)

Also now available are Bluetooth Compact Flash card adapters that can be used in Pocket PC-driven PDAs to add Bluetooth capability (see Figure 3-3).

Figure 3-3:
Use a Bluetooth Compact-Flash card in some PDAs.

Toshiba and other manufacturers have released Bluetooth PC Cards that add the Bluetooth wireless technology to any PC with a PC Card slot. Other adapters are available that plug into a USB port, making it possible to easily add Bluetooth capability to any desktop or laptop PC (see Figure 3-4). Prices for these adapters range widely — from as low as about $50 to as much as $170.

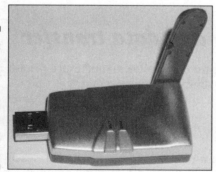

Figure 3-4:
Use a USB adapter to add Bluetooth capability to a desktop or laptop PC.

Ultra-cool Ultra Wideband (UWB) is coming

With all the innovation happening in the Wi-Fi and Bluetooth area, more neat stuff is on the way. *Ultra Wideband* (UWB) is a revolutionary wireless technology for transmitting digital data over a wide spectrum of frequency bands with very low power. It can transmit data at very high rates (for wireless LAN applications in the home). Within the power limit allowed under current FCC regulations, Ultra Wideband also has the ability to carry signals through doors and other obstacles that tend to reflect signals at more limited bandwidths and a higher power. At higher power levels, UWB signals can travel to significantly greater ranges.

Ultra wideband radiobroadcasts digital pulses (instead of traditional sine waves) that are timed very precisely on a signal across a very wide spectrum at the same time. Transmitter and receiver are coordinated to send and receive pulses with an accuracy of trillionths of a second! Not only does UWB enable high data rates, but it also does so without suffering the effects of multipath interference. *Multipath* is the propagation phenomenon that results in signals reaching the receiving antenna by two or more paths, usually because of reflections of the transmitted signal off walls or mirrors or the like. Because UWB has the ability to *time-gate* (that is, prescribe the precise time when it is supposed to receive the data), the receiver allows it to ignore signals arriving outside a prescribed time interval, such as signals caused by multipath reflections.

UWB is still in the early stages, but it is coming on strong. UWB is simpler, cheaper, less power-hungry, and 100 times faster than Bluetooth. What more could you want? UWB communication devices could be used to wirelessly distribute services such as phone, cable, and computer networking throughout a building or home. For now, it's still on the drawing boards, so just know that more cool stuff is on the horizon.

You can find out more about UWB at the official UWB Working Group Web site: www.uwb.org.

Wireless printing and data transfer

Hewlett-Packard and other printer companies manufacture printers that have built-in Bluetooth wireless capability, enabling a computer that also has Bluetooth wireless capability to print sans printer cables. Other examples are a wireless keyboard and a wireless mouse from Microsoft that both use Bluetooth technology to replace their traditional cables.

Another great use of Bluetooth wireless technology is to wirelessly transfer your digital photographs from your Bluetooth-enabled digital camera to your Bluetooth-enabled PC or Bluetooth-enabled printer . . . or even directly to your Bluetooth-enabled PDA. The newest wave of PDAs from several manufacturers includes wireless-enhanced models that include both Bluetooth and Wi-Fi built in. Wouldn't it be cool to carry your family photo album around on your Palm or iPAQ to show off at the office?

HomeRF

You might run into products that have the HomeRF logo. The HomeRF standard, which was sponsored by the Home Radio Frequency Working Group (HomeRF WG), was launched in March 1998, and died at the end of 2002, largely because of the widespread popularity of Wi-Fi. HomeRF was designed to be a wireless standard optimized for the consumer markets. Wi-Fi was initially used primarily in the corporate environment. Over time, Wi-Fi moved into the consumer space faster and with more success than ever envisioned, ultimately pulling the market from the HomeRF products. If you run into a HomeRF product, recognize that these are mostly gone from the shelves, and we don't recommend that you buy them because of Wi-Fi interoperability reasons.

Integrating HPNA and HomePlug with Your Wireless Home Network

Wireless networking is great — so great that we wrote a book about it. But in many instances, wireless is but one way to do what you want; and often, wireless solutions need a hand from *wireline* (that is, wired) solutions to give you a solid, reliable connection into your home network.

A common application of wireline and wireless networking is a remote AP that you want to link back into your home network. Suppose that your cable modem is in the office in the basement, and that's where you have your AP as well. Now suppose that you want wireless access to your PC for your TV, stereo, and laptop surfing in the master bedroom on the third floor. Chances are your AP's signal isn't going to be strong enough for that application up there. So how do you link one AP to the other?

You could install a wired Ethernet solution, which would entail running new Cat 5e cables through your walls up to your bedroom. Pretty messy if you ask us, but this approach certainly will provide up to 100 Mbps if you need it.

A more practical way to get your cable modem up to the third floor is to run an HPNA or HomePlug link between the two points. Think of this as one long extension cord between your router or AP in the basement and your AP in your bedroom. HPNA, as we discuss shortly, does this over your standard phone lines; HomePlug does it over electrical lines. Although the effective throughput won't match 54 Mbps, it will likely exceed the speed of your Internet connection. So if that's your primary goal, these are great, clean, and very easy options for you. Check out the next two sections for more.

Home Phoning (ET Got It Backward!)

Using your home phone lines to network devices together is (you guessed it) *phoneline networking*. This is a fairly mature technology having grown up about the same time as the digital subscriber line (DSL) industry, around the mid-1990s. Phoneline networking standards have been developed by an industry group called HomePNA or sometimes just HPNA (Home Phoneline Networking Association; www.homepna.org).

You'll find several types of HPNA available:

- **HPNA 1.0:** The first HPNA standard operates at a slower speed (1.3 Mbps) and is disappearing from the shelves.

- **HPNA 2.0:** Much faster than 1.0, the 2.0 version can reach speeds similar to those of an Ethernet LAN. It's advertised as 10 Mbps, but the maximum speed is actually 16 Mbps. This version is backward compatible with HPNA 1.0.

- **HPNA 3.0:** A 3.0 version of the standard that will allow much higher speeds is in the works. The goal is to reach speeds of up to 128 Mbps initially, with later versions reaching 240 Mbps — enough speed to carry even high-definition video signals. These were not available as we write but are coming soon, so check stores for which version is available when.

Although the newer 2.0 products can talk to older 1.0 ones, having even one HPNA 1.0 device connected to your phone lines slows *all* the HPNA 2.0 devices down to 1.3 Mbps. Make sure that all of yours are 2.0 if you want that technology. (We hate it when we buy five of something only to go home and find that one of the boxes is an older version — yech!). The new 3.0 version will have improved backward compatibility so that HPNA 3.0 devices (when they show up) won't be slowed down just because older HPNA endpoints are connected to the phone lines.

HomePNA products are available in several different form factors. You will likely encounter them in two major ways:

- **Built into the AP, router, or other device:** These are installed in peripheral or entertainment devices (such as Internet-enabled stereos) right from the factory.

- **A standalone adapter:** There are HomePNA Ethernet and USB adapters that are external devices that connect to a computer's Ethernet or USB ports by using a cable. You can also get internal Network Interface Card (NIC) adapters in PC Card and Peripheral Component Interconnect (PCI) Card formats for laptop and desktop machines.

The typical HomePNA interface has a regular RJ-11 phone jack that you plug into your nearest outlet. The HomePNA system operates on different frequencies than analog or DSL telephone services, so you can simultaneously use a single phone line for your computer LAN and for all the other things you currently use it for (making phone calls, sending and receiving faxes, or connecting to the Internet).

To connect your HomePNA endpoints (the computers or audio systems or other devices using HomePNA in your home) back onto your Internet connection, you need to connect the HomePNA network through your router to your Internet connection. The good news here is that HomePNA is built in to many home routers, such as those from NETGEAR (www.netgear.com), Linksys (www.linksys.com), and 2Wire (www.2wire.com), so if you think that you might want to use HomePNA, choose your router accordingly.

Network Power (line)!

Companies have been talking about powerline networking for some time, but only recently have they really gotten it right. In 2002, several networking companies (including Siemens/Efficient Networks [www.speedstream.com], Linksys, NETGEAR, and D-Link [www.d-link.com]) began releasing high-speed powerline networking products based on a standard known as HomePlug (www.homeplug.org).

The powerline networking concept takes a little getting used to. Most of us are used to plugging an AC adapter or electrical cable into the wall and then another Ethernet cable into some other networking outlet for the power and data connections. With HomePlug, those two cables are reduced to one — the power cable! That electrical cord *is* your LAN connection, — along with all the rest of the electrical cabling in your house. Cool, huh? To connect to your computer, you run an Ethernet cable from the HomePlug device (router, AP, and so on) to your computer, hub, or switch.

Networking on power lines is no easy task. Power lines are noisy, electrically speaking, with surges in voltage level and electrical interferences introduced by all sorts of devices both within and external to the home. The state of the electrical network in a home is constantly changing as well when devices are plugged in and turned on. Because of this, the HomePlug standard adopts a sophisticated and adaptive *signal processing algorithm,* which is a technique used to convert data into electrical signals on the power wiring. Because HomePlug uses higher frequency signals, the technology can avoid some of the most common sources of noise on the power line.

The current version of HomePlug can offer up to 14 Mbps networking over the power line — faster than 802.11b or HomePNA but slower than 802.11g or a and the higher-speed, wired Ethernet solutions. Besides the speed, HomePlug offers other benefits:

✓ **Ubiquity:** Power outlets are all over your house and are more plentiful than phone jacks and Ethernet outlets. With HomePlug, every one of the dozens (or even hundreds) of power outlets in the house becomes a data-networking jack.

✓ **Integrated:** HomePlug can be built right into many networked appliances. The almost legendary Internet refrigerator that we discuss in several places in this book is a great concept, but even we don't have a Cat 5e outlet in the dark nook behind our fridges. However, we do have a power outlet, and so do you.

✓ **Encrypted:** HomePlug has a built-in encryption system. Because power signals can bleed back into the local power network and because you might not want to share your LAN with your neighbors, you can turn on HomePlug's encryption. In that way, only devices that have your password can be on the network.

Like the wireless systems that we describe previously, most HomePlug systems come with encryption turned off by default. We recommend that you get your network up and running first . . . and then turn on encryption after you've proven to yourself that your network is working.

The most common application for HomePlug is as an Ethernet or a USB bridge. These devices look and act a lot like the external USB Wi-Fi NICs that we discuss earlier. You'll need two of them: one to connect to an Ethernet port on your router (or any LAN jack in your home) and another to plug into the wall outlet where you need LAN access.

The bridge typically has a power cord on one side of the box and an Ethernet or USB connector on the other. Plug the power cord into any wall outlet, plug the Ethernet or USB into the computer or other networked devices, and you have a connection. Pat has been using a NETGEAR Powerline Ethernet bridge like this for a spot in his house that has neither Ethernet nor good wireless coverage, and he loves it. Danny has a Siemens/Efficient Networks SpeedStream router connecting his office (where the cable modem is) to a SpeedStream adapter in the kids' computing area (where all the screaming is). Figure 3-5 shows a typical use of HomePlug bridges.

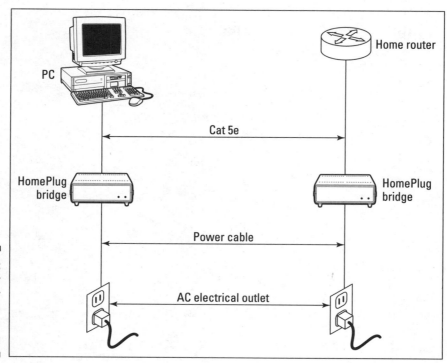

Figure 3-5:
Plug your
computer
into the
wall — and
that's all.

Powerline networking through HomePlug is a great complement to a wireless network, but we probably would never use it to replace our wireless LANs. Use it where you need it. HomePlug is quick, cheap (bridges cost about $80 each, with prices dropping rapidly), and perfect for networking on demand.

We hinted at this already, but we'll just come right out and say it. We think that HomePlug will have a huge effect in the non-computer market — stereos, TVs, gaming machines, Internet fridges, and other pieces of electronic equipment that might benefit from an Internet connection. And when HomePlug becomes incorporated into new generations of appliances, you'll need just a power cord to make it work.

Part II
Making Plans

The 5th Wave   By Rich Tennant

"...and Bobby here found a way to extend our data transmission an additional 3000 meters using coax cable. How'd you do that, Bobby—repeaters?"

In this part . . .

This part of the book helps you plan for installing your wireless home network — from deciding what you'll connect to the network, to making buying decisions, to planning the actual installation of wireless networking equipment in your home.

Chapter 4

Planning a Wireless Home Network

In This Chapter

▶ Determining what to connect to your network and where to put it

▶ Putting together a wireless home network budget

▶ Connecting to the Internet

▶ Planning for security

*W*e're sure you've heard the sage advice that, "One who does not plan is doomed to failure." On the other hand, management guru and author Peter Drucker says, "Plans are only good intentions unless they immediately degenerate into hard work." Because you're going to be spending your hard-earned money to buy the equipment necessary for your wireless network, we assume that you want to do a little planning before you actually start building your network. But if you prefer to shoot first and aim later, feel free to skip this chapter and also Chapter 5.

In this chapter, we show you how to plan a wireless home network — from selecting a wireless technology to deciding what things to connect and where to connect them to budgeting. You'll also find out about other issues that you should consider when planning your home network, including connecting to the Internet; sharing printers, other peripherals, and fun, non-computer devices; and security. When you're ready to begin buying the wireless home networking parts (if you haven't done so already), head to Chapter 5 where we give some detailed advice about buying exactly the equipment that you need. In Part III, we show you how to set up and install your wireless home network.

Deciding What Is Connected to the Network

Believe it or not, some techno-geeks have a computer in every room of their house. We have some close friends that fit into that category. You probably don't own as many computers as we do, but you might own more than one, and we're guessing that you have at least one printer and probably other peripherals as well. You're wirelessly networking your home for a reason, no matter whether it's to share that cool, new color ink jet printer (or scanner or digital video recorder), or to play your computer-based MP3s on your new wide-screen TV, or to give every computer in the house always-on access to the Internet. Whatever the reason, the first thing that you must do when planning a wireless home network is to determine what you want connected to the network.

Counting network devices

When deciding how many computers or other network-aware devices that you want to connect to your network, you can easily get your answer by counting all the computers and networkable devices that you own — if you have the dough to buy the necessary parts, that is. Fortunately, the prices for wireless networking equipment have dropped enough that cost probably won't deter you. If someone in your house regularly uses a particular computer to access the Internet and/or to print information, that computer should probably be connected to your network. Bottom line: You'll almost certainly connect to your network each of your computers that you use regularly.

Don't forget about your personal digital assistant (PDA), if you're lucky enough to own one of those little gems. Wireless adapters are available that fit into the Compact Flash slot in a typical PDA that enable you to connect your palm-sized computer to your home network. (Hop to Chapter 3 for the lowdown on different types of wireless connectivity.)

And if you're an audiophile or just like to have fun, you should consider adding your home digital entertainment system to your network so that you can share MP3 files, play video games, and watch DVDs from anywhere in your house, wirelessly! (These cool gadgets are covered in Chapters 11 through 13.)

Choosing wired or wireless

You must decide whether you will connect each computer and network-aware device wirelessly to the network or perhaps connect one or more by a wired connection. At first glance, this decision might seem obvious. You'd expect us to always recommend using *wireless* because this is a book about *wireless* networks; however, using both a wired and a wireless connection can sometimes make the most sense.

Wireless network devices and wired network devices can be used on the same network. Both talk to the network and to each other using a protocol known as Ethernet. (You should be getting used to that term by now if you've been reading from the start of the book. If not, read through Chapters 1 and 2 for more about networking technology.)

The obvious and primary benefit of connecting to a network wirelessly is that you eliminate wires running all over the place. But if two devices are sitting on the same desk or table — or are within a few feet of each other — connecting them wirelessly might be pointless. You can get Ethernet cables for $5 or less; an equivalent wireless capability for two devices might top $100 when everything is said and done. Keep in mind, however, that your computer must have a wired network adapter installed to be able to make a wired connection to the network. Fortunately, wired network adapters are dirt cheap these days. Many new computers come with one installed as a standard feature (at no additional charge).

Figure 4-1 shows a simple drawing of a network that connects a wireless PC to a wired PC through two network devices: an access point (AP) and a hub or switch. (Recall that your *AP* connects wireless devices to the rest of the wired network. A network *hub* or *switch* is often used to connect PCs to the network by a wired connection. In Chapter 1, we describe the purpose of and differences between APs and hubs and switches.) If you think that it seems absurd to need two network devices to connect two computers, you're not alone. Hardware manufacturers have addressed this issue by creating APs that have a built-in switch. See the "Choosing an access point" section later in this chapter for more about these multi-function APs.

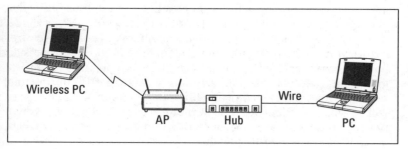

Figure 4-1: A network can use both wireless and wired connections.

Wireless PC

AP   Hub   Wire   PC

Choosing a wireless technology

After you decide that you want to connect a PC to the network wirelessly, choose a wireless technology to use. As we discuss extensively in Chapter 2, the three leading wireless technologies used to connect a computer to a home network are most often referred to by their technical names: Institute of Electrical and Electronics Engineers (IEEE) 802.11a, IEEE 802.11b, and IEEE 802.11g. The marketing name for the first two technologies is *Wi-Fi*, which is a brand name coined by a wireless trade group. Wi-Fi is supposed to denote *wir*eless *fi*delity. Apparently, some marketing guru seems to think that people still remember the term *Hi-Fi*, which means *hi*gh *fi*delity. We don't know about you, but we haven't heard that term used by normal humans since Wally told the Beaver to leave his Hi-Fi alone.

The discussion of wireless technology quickly degenerates into a sea of acronyms and techno-speak. If you need a refresher on all this alphabet soup — or to begin from square one — Chapter 2 is a primer on jargon, abbreviations, and other nuts-and-bolts issues.

For home users, the three most important practical differences between IEEE 802.11a, IEEE 802.11b, and IEEE 802.11g networks are speed, price, and compatibility:

- **IEEE 802.11a** equipment is typically more expensive than similar IEEE 802.11b equipment but is at least five times faster.

- **IEEE 802.11g** is as fast as IEEE 802.11a but is almost as cheap as IEEE 802.11b.

- **IEEE 802.11a and IEEE 802.11b** are *not* compatible.

- **IEEE 802.11b and IEEE 802.11g** *are* compatible.

Because 802.11g is compatible with 802.11b, an AP that includes 802.11g should work with any 802.11b device as well (at the lower 11 Mbps speed of 802.11b). Thus, you don't have to look for a dual-mode 802.11b-and-802.11g AP.

If your primary reason for networking the computers in your house is to enable Internet sharing, IEEE 802.11b is more than fast enough because your Internet connection probably won't exceed the 11 Mbps of the 802.11b connection anytime soon; it probably hovers in the sub-1 Mbps range. However, if you don't mind spending a little extra money (in some cases, very little extra), you can be ready for anything that the home electronics and broadband Internet services providers can throw at you. And, if you're a gamer and into graphics-intensive, multi-user intergalactic battles or dream of watching real-time streaming video over a broadband connection, your need for speed will be worth shelling out the extra bucks to get it. Finally, if you plan on having any servers at home, such as a home server for your DVDs, then you'll want the higher bandwidth.

If you want to hedge your bets, look for an AP that can handle both IEEE 802.11a and IEEE 802.11b/g technology standards. Linksys, NETGEAR, D-Link, and several other leading manufacturers of wireless home networking equipment already offer a/b/g dual-mode, tri-standard wireless devices.

Choosing an access point

The most important and typically most expensive device in a wireless network is the access point (AP; also sometimes called a base station). An AP acts like a wireless switchboard that connects wireless devices on the network to each other and to the rest of the wired network; it's required to create a wireless home network. Figure 4-2 depicts three PCs connected wirelessly to each other through an AP.

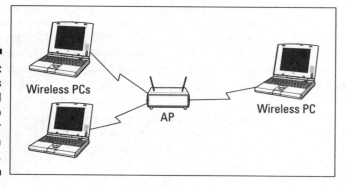

Figure 4-2: Three PCs connected wirelessly to each other through an AP.

Wireless PCs

AP

Wireless PC

Choosing an AP that performs several additional network-oriented services might also be economical for you. The most popular APs for use in home networks are those that can do one or more of the following:

✔ **Connect wired PCs:** A *switch* is an enhanced version of a hub that operates more efficiently and quickly than a simple hub. By building a switch inside the AP, you can use the one device to connect PCs to your network by using either wired network adapters or wireless adapters. We cover hubs and switches in more detail in Chapter 1.

✔ **Assign network addresses:** Every computer on a network or on the Internet has its own address: its Internet Protocol (IP) address. Computers on the Internet communicate — forwarding e-mail, Web pages, and the like — by sending data back and forth from IP address to IP address. A *Dynamic Host Configuration Protocol* (DHCP) server dynamically assigns private IP addresses to the computers on your home network so that they can communicate. You could use a software utility in

Windows (or Mac OS) to manually assign an IP address to each computer, but that process is tedious and much less flexible than automatic address assignment.

✓ **Connect to the Internet:** With a *cable/digital subscriber line (DSL) router* between a broadband modem and your home network, all computers on the network can access the Internet directly. An AP combined with a DHCP and cable/DSL router is sometimes called a *wireless Internet gateway.* (See the "Connecting to the Internet" section later in this chapter for more about the Network Address Translation [NAT] feature that makes Internet sharing possible and for more on Internet connectivity.)

✓ **Add a print server:** A *print server* enables you to connect a printer directly to the network rather than connecting it to one of the computers on the network. See the "Adding printers" section later in this chapter.

✓ **Connect in many ways:** The most common method of connecting an AP to your computer or to the wired portion of your network is through an Ethernet port, but other options may be much easier to install if your house isn't wired with Ethernet cable. If you've created a HomePNA wired network by using the phone lines in your home, look for an AP that has a HomePNA port. Similarly, if you have set up a HomePlug wired network using the power lines in your home, shop for an AP with HomePlug connectivity. (For more on HomePNA and HomePlug, skip to Chapter 3.)

Access points with HomePlug built into them are very handy when you want to add a second AP to your network in a remote part of the house (somewhere that doesn't get good coverage from your main AP). With HomePlug, you can plug a small device (like Siemens' SpeedStream 2521 [www.speedstream.com]) into the wall and have an instant extra access point with no special connections at all. (You'll need to have HomePlug in your main AP or router to make this work, of course.)

✓ **Provide firewall security:** A *firewall* is a device that basically keeps the bad guys off your network and out of your computers. We talk a lot more about firewalls in Chapter 10, but basically, a firewall might be included in your access point to provide network security.

✓ **Be combined with a modem:** If you're a cable Internet or DSL subscriber, you might be able to use your own modem instead of leasing one from your Internet service provider (ISP). In that case, consider purchasing a modem that's also a wireless AP. A cable or DSL modem combined with a wireless Internet gateway is the ultimate solution in terms of installation convenience and equipment cost savings.

Deciding where to install the AP

If you've ever experienced a dreaded dead zone while talking on a cellular phone, you know how frustrating that can be. Similarly, you should strive to install your wireless network in a way that eliminates dead wireless network zones in your house. Ideally, you determine the best placement of your AP so that no spot in your house is left uncovered; but, if that isn't possible for some reason, you should at least find out where, if anywhere, the dead zones in your house are to optimize your signal coverage.

To achieve optimum signal coverage, the best place to install an AP is near the center of your home. Think about where you will place the AP when you make your buying decision. All APs can sit on a shelf or table, but some APs can also be mounted to a wall or ceiling. When making your AP selection, ensure that it can be installed where it works best for the configuration of your house as well as keep the AP out of reach of your little ones or curious pets.

The position of the access point is critical because your entire signal foot-print emanates from the AP in a known way, centered from on the AP's antenna(s). Sometimes not enough consideration is given to the positioning of the access point because they so often work pretty well out of the box, just sitting on a table.

 Other people install it wrong in the first place. For instance, probably one of the worst manufacturing decisions ever done to access points was to put mounting brackets on them. People get the impression that you should then — duh — mount them on the wall. That's great except for the fact that, depending on the antenna you have, you might just kill most of your through-put. You see, when an antenna is flush up against a wall, as is typical in a wall mount situation, the signals of the antenna reflect off the wall back at the antenna, causing interference, and driving down throughput precipitously. Yech. (But you see, customers WANT their wall mount brackets, so product managers at wireless LAN companies decided they had to give it to them.) The best mounting is actually six or more inches off the wall.

The vertical orientation of the mounting point is important as well. Generally, you have more interference lower to the ground. If you did a cross section of your house in one-foot intervals, when you get higher and higher, you'd see less on your map. Thus, signals from an access point located on a shelf low to the ground are going to find more to run into than the ones that are mounted higher. Although this might sound like common sense, consider that most DSL and cable modems are installed by technicians who are used to installing phone and cable TV lines. How many of these are generally located five feet off the floor? They're not; they tend to be along the floorboards and low to the ground or in the basement. So it's not surprising that a combined DSL access point router would be plugged in low to the ground, too.

See where we are going with this? You don't care where your cable modem is, but you should care where your AP functionality is located. And if you have an integrated product, you're probably tempted to swap out the cable modem for the cable modem access point. Simply moving that unit higher will do a world of good.

Moving an AP out of the line of sight of microwaves, cordless phones, refrigerators, and so on is a good idea, too. Mounting the AP in the laundry room off the kitchen does not make a great deal of sense if you will primarily use the AP in rooms on the other side of the kitchen. In general, passing through commonly used interferers (all those metal appliances) like that is not a smart move.

Wireless interference in the home

Probably the single biggest threat to your home network is interference in the home. The Federal Communications Commission (FCC) set aside certain unlicensed frequencies that could be used for low-power wireless applications. In specific frequency bands, manufacturers can make (and you can use) equipment that doesn't require a license from the FCC for the user to operate. This is different from, say, buying a 50,000-watt radio transmitter and blasting it over your favorite FM radio frequency band, which would be a major no-no because those bands are licensed for certain power levels.

As a result, all sorts of companies have created products (including cordless phones, wireless radio frequency [RF] remote controls, wireless speakers, TV set extenders, and walkie-talkies) that make use of these frequency bands. If you have a lot of wireless devices already in your home, there is a good chance that they might use some of the same frequency bands that your home wireless network uses.

Another form of wireless interference comes from devices that emit energy in the same bands, such as microwave ovens. If you have a cordless phone with its base station near a microwave and you notice that the voice quality degrades every time that you use the

microwave, that's because the micro(radio)-waves are in the same radiation band as your cordless phone. Motors, refrigerators, and other home consumer devices do the same thing.

So what's the answer? The good news is that you can deal with almost all of these by knowing what to look for and being smart about where you place your equipment. If your access point is in the back office and you want to frequently work in the living room with your laptop — but your kitchen is in the middle — you might want to look at adding a second access point in the living room and link it with the office via any of a number of alternative connections options (which we talk about in Chapter 3) that are immune to the microwave problems that we mention earlier.

Remember these specific things to look for when shopping. You'll see cordless phones operating primarily in the 900 MHz, 2.4 GHz, and 5 GHz frequencies. The 900 MHz phones pose no problems, but the 2.4 GHz and 5 GHz phones will interfere with your wireless network signals. Just know that cordless phones and home wireless networks really don't like each other very much.

Factors that affect signal strength

Many variables affect whether you get an adequate signal at any given point in your house, including the following factors:

- **Distance from the AP:** The further away from the AP, the weaker the signal. Wi-Fi 802.11b standards, for instance, promise a maximum operating range of 100 feet at 11 Mbps to 300 feet at 1 Mbps. Indoors, a realistic range at 11 Mbps is about 60 feet. When 802.11a and 802.11g networks become more prevalent, their maximum range may vary. Range differs from vendor to vendor as well.

- **The power of the transmitter:** Wi-Fi APs transmit at a power output of less than 30 dBm (one watt).

- **The directivity or gain of the antennas attached to the AP and to wireless network adapters:** Different antennas are designed to provide different radiation patterns. That's a fancy way of saying that some are designed to send radio waves in all directions equally, yet others concentrate their strength in certain directions. We talk more about this in Chapter 6, but the thing to keep in mind here is that different brands and models of access points have different kinds of antennas designed for different applications. Check out the specifications of the ones that you're looking at before you buy them.

- **The construction materials used in the walls, floors, and ceilings:** Some construction materials are relatively transparent to radio signals, but other materials, such as marble, brick, water, paper, bulletproof glass, concrete, and especially metal, tend to reflect some of the signal, thus reducing signal strength.

- **Your house plan:** The physical layout of your house might determine not only where it's practical to position an AP, but it also might affect signal strength because the position of walls, the number of floors, brick fireplaces, basements, and so on can partially or even completely block the wireless networks radio signal.

- **Client locations:** Reception is affected by the distance from the AP to the rooms in your house where someone will need wireless network access.

- **Stationary physical objects:** Objects that are permanently installed in your home, such as metal doors, heating ducts, and brick fireplaces can block some or all of the signal to particular spots in your house.

- **Movable physical objects:** Other types of objects, including furniture, appliances, plants, and even people can also block enough of the signal to cause the network to slow down or even to lose a good connection.

- **APs:** Interference can also be caused by the presence of other APs. In other words, if you've got a big house (too big for a single AP to cover), you have to keep in mind that in parts of the house — like in the area that's pretty much directly in between the two APs — you'll find that the radio waves from each AP can interfere with the other. Check out the following section for more information regarding this phenomenon.

You should attempt to keep a direct line between APs, residential gateways, and the wireless devices on your network. A wall that is 1.5 feet thick, at a 45° angle, appears to be almost 3 feet thick. At a 2° angle, it looks over 42 feet thick. Try to make sure that the AP and wireless adapters are positioned so that the signal will travel straight through a wall or ceiling for better reception.

RF interference

Nowadays, many devices that once required wires are now wireless, and this is becoming more prevalent all the time. Some wireless devices use infrared technology, but many wireless devices, including your wireless network, communicate by using radio frequency (RF) waves. As a consequence, the network can be disrupted by RF interference from other devices sharing the same frequencies used by your wireless network.

Among the devices most likely to interfere with IEEE 802.11b and IEEE 802.11g networks are microwave ovens and cordless telephones that use the 2.4 GHz band. The best way to avoid this interference is to place APs and computers with wireless adapters at least six feet away from the microwave and the base station of any portable phone that uses the 2.4 GHz band.

Bluetooth devices also use the 2.4 GHz band, but the hop pattern of the Bluetooth modulation protocol all but ensures that any interference will be short enough in duration to be negligible.

Because there are relatively few devices that are trying to share the 5 GHz frequencies used by IEEE 802.11a, your network is less likely to experience RF interference if it's using IEEE 802.11a.

You should also try to keep all electric motors and electrical devices that generate RF noise through their normal operation, such as monitors, refrigerators, electric motors, and Universal Power Supply (UPS) units at least three and preferably six feet away from a wireless network device.

Signal obstacles

Wireless technologies are susceptible to physical obstacles. When you decide where best to place your AP(s), refer to Table 4-1, which lists obstacles that can affect the strength of your wireless signals. The table lists common household obstacles (although often overlooked) as well as the degree to which the obstacle is a hindrance to your wireless network signals.

Table 4-1	Relative Attenuation of RF Obstacles	
Obstruction	*Degree of Attenuation*	*Example*
Open space	Low	Backyard
Wood	Low	Inner wall; door; floor
Plaster	Low	Inner wall (older plaster is lower than newer plaster)
Synthetic materials	Low	Partitions; home theater treatments
Cinder block	Low	Inner wall; outer wall
Asbestos	Low	Ceiling (older buildings)
Glass	Low	Non-tinted window
Wire mesh in glass	Medium	Door; window
Metal tinted glass	Medium	Tinted window
Human body	Medium	Groupings of people (dinner table)
Water	Medium	Damp wood; aquarium; in-home water treatments
Bricks	Medium	Inner wall; outer wall; floor
Marble	Medium	Inner wall; outer wall; floor
Ceramic (metal content or backing)	High	Ceramic tile; ceiling; floor
Paper	High	Stack of paper stock, such as newspaper piles
Concrete	High	Floor; outer wall; support pillar
Bulletproof glass	High	Windows; door
Silvering	Very high	Mirror
Metal	Very high	Inner wall; air conditioning; filing cabinets; reinforced concrete walls and floors

*Source: Intel (*www.intel.com/network/connectivity/solutions/wireless/ deploy_site.htm*); TeleChoice*

The RF doughnut

The shape of the radio signal that will be transmitted to the rooms in your home is determined by the type of antenna that you've attached to the AP. The standard antenna on any AP is an *omnidirectional* antenna, which broadcasts its signal in a spherical shape. The signal pattern that radiates from a typical omnidirectional dipole antenna is shaped like a fat doughnut with a tiny hole in the middle. The hole is directly above and below the antenna.

The signal goes from the antenna to the floor above and the floor below, as well as to the floor on which the AP is located. If your house has multiple floors, try the second floor first. Most AP manufacturers claim a range of 100 feet indoors (at 11 Mbps for IEEE 802.11b or at 54 Mbps for IEEE 802.11a and IEEE 802.11g). To be conservative, assume a range of 60 feet laterally and one floor above or below the AP. Keep in mind that the signal at the edges of the "doughnut" and on the floors below or above the AP will be weaker than the signal nearer the center and on the same floor as the AP.

Because of this signal pattern, you should try to place the AP as close to the very center of your house as is practically possible. Use a drawing of your house plan to locate the center of the house. This spot will be your first trial AP location.

Draw a circle with a 60-foot radius on your house plan, using the trial AP location as the center of the circle. If your entire house falls inside the circle, one AP will probably do the job. Conversely, if some portion of the house is outside the circle, coverage might be weaker in that area. You'll need to experiment to determine whether you get an adequate signal there.

If you determine that one AP will not cover your house, you need to decide how best to place two APs (or even three, as necessary). The design of your house will determine the best placement. For a one-level design, start at one end of the house and determine the best location for a 60-foot radius circle that will cover all the way to the walls. The center of this circle is the location of the first AP. Then move toward the other end of the house, drawing 60-foot radius circles until the house is covered. The center of each circle will be a trial location of an AP. If possible, don't leave any area in the house uncovered. And especially don't forget your garage; before long, you'll be synchronizing your wireless network with your car, including sending digital movies and MP3 files. (See Chapter 14 for more about connecting to your car.)

You might want to consider reading Chapter 18 on troubleshooting before you finish your planning. There are some good tips in that chapter about setting up and tweaking your network.

Adding printers

In addition to your computer(s), you might also want to connect your printer(s) to the network. Next to sharing an Internet connection, printer sharing is perhaps the biggest cost-savings reason for building a network of home computers. Rather than buying a printer for every PC, everyone in the house can share one printer. Or maybe you have one color ink jet printer and one black-and-white laser printer. If both printers are connected to the network, all computers on the network can potentially print to either printer. Or perhaps you just want to sit by the pool with your wireless laptop and still be able to print to the printer up in your bedroom; it's easy with a network-attached printer.

You can also share other peripherals, such as network-aware scanners and fax machines. Leading manufacturers of digital imaging equipment (like Hewlett-Packard) offer feature-rich, multiple-function peripherals that combine an ink jet or laser printer with a scanner, copier, telephone, answering machine, and fax machine all-in-one device. If you want to share such a device over your network, make sure that you buy one that comes with network server software.

Here are two ways to share printers over a wired or wireless network:

- ✔ **Connect to a computer:** The easiest and cheapest way to connect a printer to the network is to connect a printer to one of the computers on the network. Windows enables you to share any printer connected to any Windows computer on the network. (For more on this, read Chapter 11.) The computer to which the printer is connected has to be running for any other computers on the network to use the printer. Similarly, if you're using Apple computers, any computer connected to the network can print to a printer that's connected to one of the computers on the network.

- ✔ **Print server:** Another way to add a printer is through a print server. Several hardware manufacturers produce print server devices that enable you to connect one or more printers directly to the network. Some of these devices connect via a network cable, and others are wireless. Many high-end printers even have print server options that install inside the printer cabinet. For home use, standalone network print servers are a bit pricey. Surprisingly, some manufacturers bundle a print server with their cable/DSL router at little or no additional cost. If you shop around, you can probably find a wireless AP, cable/DSL router, and print server bundled in one device for less than the cost of some standalone print servers.

You should be able to get your home network printer connections for free. Obviously, it won't cost anything to connect a printer to a computer that's already connected to the network. Several manufacturers also include a print server for free with other network devices. If you don't need one of those devices, just connect the printer that you want to share to one of the computers on your home network.

Figure 4-3 depicts a home network with one printer connected to one of the PCs on the network and another printer connected to a wireless Internet *gateway,* which is a device that bundles a wireless AP and a cable/DSL router into a single unit. In this case, the wireless Internet gateway also has a connection for a printer and acts as a print server. Read through Chapters 1 and 5 for more information about these devices, what they do, and how to choose between them.

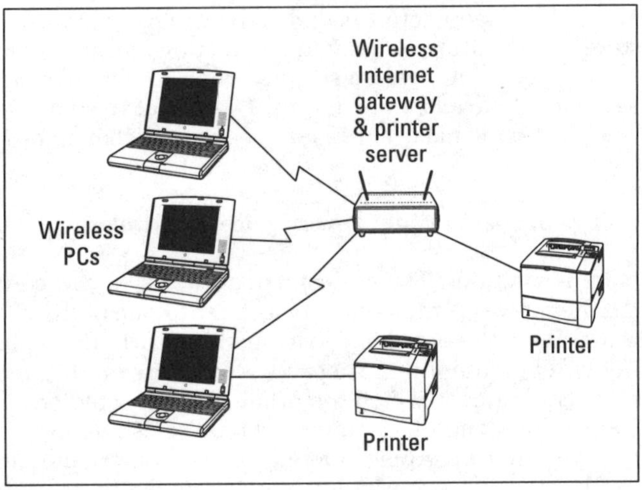

Figure 4-3:
A wireless home network with wireless Internet gateway and bundled print server.

Connecting your printer to the wireless Internet gateway device is advantageous because a print server permits the printer to stand alone on the network, untethered from any specific computer. When you want to print to a printer that's connected directly to a computer on the network, that computer must be present and turned on; and, in many cases, you must have a user account and appropriate permission to access the shared printer. A print server makes its printers always available to any computer on the network — even from poolside.

Adding entertainment and more

When you're planning your wireless network, don't forget to plan to add a few gadgets for fun and relaxation. The wildly popular video-game consoles from Sony, Microsoft, and Nintendo all offer network connectivity and Internet connectively as well. Don't forget to consult with the gamers in your household when planning where you will need network coverage in your home. And don't forget to take a look at Chapter 12 for the skinny about connecting your favorite console to your wireless network, as well as info on network-based, multi-user PC gaming.

An increasing number of consumer electronics devices, such as digital home entertainment systems, are network aware. Feature-packed home media servers can store thousands of your favorite MP3s and digital videos and make them available over the network to all the computers in your house. Several even include optional wireless networking connectivity. Connecting the sound and video from your PC to your home theater is even possible — really. Imagine surfing the Internet on a wide-screen TV! Jump to Chapter 13 for the details about connecting your A/V gear to your wireless home network.

Some of the coolest home electronic technology in recent years enables you to control the lights, heating, cooling, security system, home entertainment system, pool, and so on, right from your computer. Equally exciting technology enables you to use a home network to set up a highly affordable home video monitoring system. By hooking these systems to your wireless network and hooking the network to the Internet, you can make it possible to monitor and control your home's utilities and systems, even while away from home. Check out Chapter 14 for more about these smart home technologies as well as additional cool things that you can network, such as connecting to your car or using your network to connect to the world.

Connecting to the Internet

When you get right down to it, the reason why most people build a wireless network in their home is to share their Internet connection with multiple computers or devices that they've got around the house. That's why we did it — and we bet that's why you're doing it. We've reached the point in our lives where a computer that's not constantly connected to a network and to the Internet is just about useless. We're not really even exaggerating too much here. Even things that you do locally (use a spreadsheet program, for example) can be enhanced by an Internet connection; in that spreadsheet program, you can link to the Internet to do real-time currency conversions.

What a wireless network brings to the table is true whole-home Internet access. Particularly when combined with an always-on Internet connection (which we discuss in just a second) — but even with a regular dialup modem connection — a wireless network lets you access the Internet from just about every nook and cranny of the house. Take the laptop out to the back patio, let a visitor connect from the guest room, or do some work in bed. Whatever you want to do and wherever you want to do it, a wireless network can support you.

A wireless home network (or any home network, for that matter) provides one key element. It uses a *NAT router* (we describe this later in this section) to provide Internet access to multiple devices over a single Internet connection coming into the home. With a NAT router (which will typically be built into your access point or in a separate home network router), you cannot only connect more than one computer to the Internet, but you can simultaneously connect multiple computers (and other devices like game consoles) to the Internet over a single connection. The NAT router has the brains to figure out which Web page or e-mail or online gaming information is going to which *client* (PC/device) on the network.

Not surprisingly, in order to take advantage of this Internet-from-anywhere access in your home, you'll need some sort of Internet service and modem. We're not going to get into great detail about this topic, but we do want to make sure that you keep it in mind when you plan your network.

Most people access the Internet from a home computer in these ways:

- Dialup telephone connection
- Digital subscriber line (DSL)
- Cable Internet
- Satellite broadband

DSL, cable, and satellite Internet service are often called *broadband* Internet service, which is a term that gets defined differently by just about everyone in the industry. For our purposes, we define it as a connection that's faster than a dialup modem connection (sometimes called *narrowband*) and which is always on. That is, you don't have to use a dialer to get connected, but instead you have a persistent connection that's available immediately without any set-up steps necessary for the users (at least after the first time you've set up your connection).

Broadband Internet service providers are busily wiring neighborhoods all over the United States, but none of the services are available everywhere. (Satellite is available almost everywhere, but like satellite TV, you need to meet certain criteria such as having a view to the south: that is, facing the satellites, which orbit over the equator.) Where it is available, however, growing numbers of families are experiencing the benefits of always-on and very fast Internet connectivity.

In some areas of the country, wireless systems are beginning to become available as a means of connecting to the Internet. Most of these systems use special radio systems proprietary to their manufacturers. That is, you buy a transceiver and an antenna and hook it up on your roof or in a window. But a few are actually using modified versions of Wi-Fi to provide Internet access to people's homes. In either case, you'll have some sort of modem device that connects to your AP via a standard Ethernet cable, just like you'd use for a DSL or cable modem connection.

For the purpose of this discussion of home wireless networks, DSL and cable Internet are equivalent. If you can get both at your house, shop around for price and talk to your neighbors about their experiences. You might also check out www.broadbandreports.com, which is a Web site where customers of a variety of broadband services discuss and compare their experiences. As soon as you splurge for a DSL or cable Internet connection, the PC that happens to be situated nearest the spot where the installer placed the DSL or cable modem is at a distinct advantage because it will be the easiest computer to connect to the modem — and therefore to the Internet. Most DSL and cable modems connect to the PC through a wired network adapter card. The best way, therefore, to connect any computer in the home to the Internet is through a home network.

You have two ways to share an Internet connection over a home network:

- **Software-based Internet connection sharing:** Windows 98 (and later versions of Windows) and Mac OS X enable sharing of an Internet connection. Each computer in the network must be set up to connect to the Internet through the computer that's connected to the broadband modem. The disadvantage with this system is that you can't turn off or remove the computer that's connected to the modem without disconnecting all computers from the Internet. In other words, the computer that's connected to the modem must be on for other networked computers to access the Internet through it.

- **Cable/DSL router:** By connecting a cable/DSL router between the broadband modem and your home network, all computers on the network can access the Internet without going through another computer. The Internet connection no longer depends on any computer on the network. Cable/DSL routers are also DHCP servers and typically include switches. In fact, the AP and/or the modem can also include a built-in router that provides instant Internet sharing all in one device.

Read through Chapter 9 for the details on how to set up Internet sharing.

Given the fact that you can buy a router (either as part of an access point or a separate router) for well under $100 these days (and prices continue to plummet), we think that it's really a false economy to skip the router and use a software-based Internet connection sharing setup. In our minds, at least, the advantage of the software-based approach (*very* slightly less money up front) is outweighed by the disadvantages (requiring the PC to always be on, lower reliability, and lower performance).

Both software-based Internet connection sharing and cable/DSL routers enable all the computers in your home network to share the same network (IP) address on the Internet. This capability uses *network address translation* (NAT). A device that uses the NAT feature is often called a *NAT router*. The NAT feature communicates with each computer on the network by using a private IP address assigned to that local computer, but the router uses a single public IP address in data that it sends to computers on the Internet. In other words, no matter how many computers you have in your house sharing the Internet, they look like only one computer to all the other computers on the Internet.

Whenever your computer is connected to the Internet, beware the potential that some malicious hacker will try to attack your computer with a virus or try to break into your computer to trash your hard drive or steal your personal information. Because NAT technology hides your computer behind the NAT server, it adds a measure of protection against hackers, but you shouldn't rely on it solely for protection against malicious users. You should also consider purchasing full-featured firewall software that actively looks for and blocks hacking attempts, unless the AP or router that you purchase provides that added protection. We talk about these items in more detail in Chapter 10.

As we recommend earlier in the section "Choosing an access point," try to choose an AP that also performs several other network-oriented services. Figure 4-4 depicts a wireless home network using an AP that also provides DHCP, NAT, a printer server, and switched hub functions in a single stand-alone unit. This wireless Internet gateway device then connects to the DSL or cable modem, which in turn connects to the Internet. Such a configuration provides you with connectivity, sharing, and a little peace of mind, too.

If you already have a wired network and you've purchased a cable/DSL router Internet gateway device without the AP function, you don't have to replace the existing device. Just purchase a wireless access point. Figure 4-5 depicts the network design of a typical wired home network with an AP and wireless stations added. Each PC in the wired network is connected to the cable/DSL router, which is also a switch. By connecting the AP to the router, the AP acts as a bridge between the wireless network segment and the existing wired network.

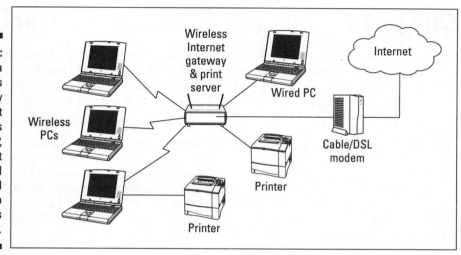

Figure 4-4:
Go for a
wireless
gateway
that
combines
AP, DHCP,
NAT, a print
server, and
switched
hub
functions
into one unit.

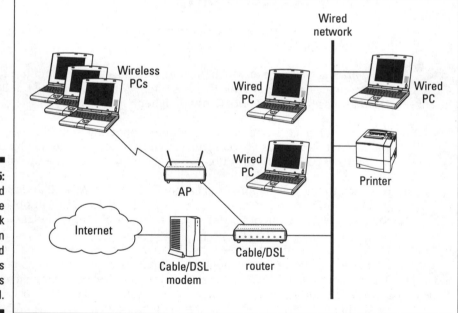

Figure 4-5:
A wired
home
network
with an
AP and
wireless
stations
added.

Budgeting for Your Wireless Network

Assuming that you already own at least one computer (and probably more) and one or more printers that you intend to add to the network, we do not include the cost of computers and printers in this section. In addition, the cost of subscribing to an ISP is not included in the following networking cost estimates.

Wireless networking hardware — essentially APs and wireless network adapters — is available at a wide range of prices. With a little planning, you won't be tempted to bite on the first product that you see. You can use the following guidelines when budgeting for an AP and wireless network adapters. Keep in mind, however, that the prices for this equipment will certainly change over time, perhaps rapidly. Don't use this information as a substitute for due diligence and market research on your part.

Pricing access points

At the time of this writing, wireless access points for home use range in price from about $75 (street price) to around $200.

Street price is the price at which you can purchase the product from a retail outlet, such as a computer-electronics retail store or an online retailer. The dreaded *suggested retail price* is often higher.

Multifunction access points that facilitate connecting multiple computers to the Internet — *wireless Internet gateways* if they contain modem functionality, and *wireless gateways* if they don't — range in price from about $100 to $300.

You need to budget roughly $100 for an IEEE 802.11b AP and about $120 for an IEEE 802.11g (draft) AP. An IEEE 802.11a AP will run $150, but prices are coming down. Add about $50 for a dual-mode (a/b or a/g) model.

The price differentials between the cheapest APs and the more expensive models will generally correspond to differences in features. For example, APs that support the IEEE 802.11a wireless standard are more expensive than similar APs that support only the much slower IEEE 802.11b standard. Similarly, an AP that is also a cable/DSL router costs more than an AP from the same manufacturer that doesn't include the router feature. You can also expect to pay a little bit more for the most popular brand names, such as Linksys and Microsoft. You don't need to buy the most expensive AP in order to get adequate performance.

You might run across APs from well-known companies such as Cisco and 3COM that are significantly more expensive than the devices typically purchased for home use. These "industrial-strength" products include advanced features and come with management software that enable corporate IT departments to efficiently and securely deploy enterprise-level wireless networks. The underlying technology, including the speed and the range of the wireless radios used, are essentially the same as those used in the economically priced APs used in most wireless home networks; but the additional features and capabilities of these enterprise-level products save IT personnel countless hours and headaches rolling out dozens of APs in a large wireless network.

Pricing wireless network adapters

Wireless network adapters range in price from $25 to $125, depending on whether you purchase IEEE 802.11a, b, or g technology and whether you purchase a PC Card, USB, or internal variety.

Like APs, wireless network adapters that support the IEEE 802.11a standard are somewhat more expensive than their IEEE 802.11g counterparts. An 802.11a/b/g card will cost around $75–$150. NETGEAR's WAG511 tri-standard card had a street price of $80 as we went to press. Wow!

A sample budget

If your plan involves a cable Internet connection, a laptop computer, and a home desktop computer that you want to connect via an IEEE 802.11b home wireless network, Table 4-2 shows a reasonable hardware budget.

Table 4-2	Hypothetical IEEE 802.11b Wireless Home Network Budget	
Item	*Price Range*	*Quantity Needed*
Access point	$75–$200	1
Wireless network adapters	$25–$100	2
Network cable	$10–$20	1
Cable or DSL modem (optional)	$75–$100	1

Planning Security

Any network can be attacked by a persistent hacker, but a well-defended network will discourage most hackers sufficiently to keep your data safe. However, it's easier for a hacker to gain access to a wireless network through the air than to gain physical access to a wired network, making wireless networks more vulnerable to attack, even home networks. Because a Wi-Fi signal is a radio signal, it keeps going and going and going, like ripples in a pond in a weaker and weaker form, until it hits something solid enough to stop it. Anyone with a portable PC, wireless network adapter, and an external antenna in a van driving by or even in your neighbor's house next door has a reasonable chance of accessing your wireless network. (Such skullduggery is known as *war driving.*) So you must plan for security. We give you all the down-and-dirty details in Chapter 10, but here are some key things to keep in mind:

✔ **Internet security:** Any Internet connection — especially always-on broadband connections, but dialup connections, too — can be vulnerable to attacks arriving from the Internet. In order to keep your PCs safe from the bad folks (who might be thousands of miles away), you should turn on any firewall features available in your AP or router. Some fancier APs or routers include a highly effective kind of firewall (a stateful packet inspection [SPI] firewall), but even just the basic firewall provided by any NAT router can be quite effective. You should also consider installing antivirus software as well as personal firewall software on each PC or Mac on your network for an extra level of protection.

✔ **Airlink security:** This is a special need of a wireless home network. Wired networks can be made secure by what's known as *physical security.* That is, you literally lock your doors and windows, and no one can plug into your wired network. In the wireless world, physical security is impossible (you can't wrangle those radio waves and keep them in the house), so you need to implement airlink security. You can't keep the radio waves from getting out of the house, but you can make it very hard for someone to do anything with them (like read the data that they contain). Similarly, you can use airlink security to keep others from getting onto your access point and freeloading on your Internet connection. The primary means of providing airlink security today — and new advances are on the way — is Wired Equivalent Privacy (WEP). You absolutely should use WEP (and do a few other tricks that we discuss in Chapter 10) to preserve the integrity of your wireless home network.

Chapter 5

Choosing Wireless Home Networking Equipment

In This Chapter

▶ Understanding the buying criteria for your wireless equipment

▶ Selecting access points

▶ Selecting a wireless networking adapter

▶ Understanding gateways and routers

*W*hen you're building something — in this case, a wireless home network — the time comes when you have to make up your mind what building supplies to buy. At a minimum, to set up a wireless home network, you need an access point (AP) and a wireless networking adapter for each computer or other network-enabled device that you want to have on the network. This chapter helps you evaluate and choose among the growing number of APs and wireless networking adapters on the market.

The advice in this chapter applies equally to PCs and Macs. You can use any access point for a Mac as long as it has a Web interface (that is, it doesn't require a PC program to configure it). That having been said, if you have a Mac, you might want to consider using Apple's system because it's easier to set up and use. On the network adapter/client side of the link, AirPort cards are definitely easier for a Mac owner.

Selecting Access Points

The heart of each wireless home network is the access point (AP), which is also known as a base station. Depending on the manufacturer and included features, the price of an AP suitable for home use ranges from about $75 to $200. Differences exist from model to model, but even the lowest priced units are surprisingly capable.

For most wireless home networks, the most important requirements for a wireless access point are as follows (sort of in order of importance):

- ✔ Certification and standards support
- ✔ Compatibility and form factor
- ✔ Bundled server and router functionality
- ✔ Operational features
- ✔ Security
- ✔ Performance (range and coverage) issues
- ✔ Manageability
- ✔ Price
- ✔ Warranties
- ✔ Customer and technical support

With the exception of pricing (which we cover in Chapter 4), we explore the selection of access point products in depth in terms of these requirements throughout the following sections.

In Chapter 4, we describe how to plan the installation of a home wireless network, including how to use your AP to determine the best location in your house as well as the number of APs that you'll need. If you can determine a location that gives an adequate signal throughout your entire house, your AP obviously is adequate. If some areas of your home aren't covered, you'll either need one or more additional APs or a more powerful AP (and we tell you how to do that in Chapter 18). Fortunately, most residences can be covered by the signal from a single AP.

Certification and Standards Support

We talk in Chapter 2 about the Wi-Fi Alliance and its certification process for devices. At a minimum, you should ensure that your devices are Wi-Fi certified. To the degree that you're buying pre-standard items (as was the case in early 2003, when pre-standard 802.11g products were shipping before certification testing had been started), understand from the vendor how future changes are implemented (for example, firmware upgrades, as we describe later in the chapter in the sidebar, "Performing firmware updates").

A key part of standards support is *multi-mode support:* that is, the ability to support more than one standard in a device, such as supporting 802.11a/b/g in the same device. This can be accomplished in several ways:

✔ **PC Card slot:** The device could have a Personal Computer Memory Card International Association (PCMCIA) card slot that can accept different cards for each mode or a single card that is multi-mode.

✔ **Onboard support:** The device can natively support the different standards onboard. In most cases, this is accomplished by actually having one chip each for 802.11a and g. A good example of this is the NETGEAR WAG511 Dual Band Wireless PC Card (www.netgear.com; $150), which is the first card that supports 802.11a/b/g.

Note: You'll run into some confusion in terms. Some companies call this *dual-mode*, others say *dual-band*, and still others use *multi-mode* or *multi-band*. These all kinda mean the same thing. Because the 802.11g standard is backward compatible to 802.11b, they are technically supporting both a and g. What seems to make the most sense is *dual-band, tri-mode*, which means that the AP operates in the 2.4 and 5 GHz frequency bands, in any of the three standards modes.

Like we write in Chapter 2, we see the industry converging toward supporting all standards in one device . . . and that device being smart enough to sense and simultaneously support transmissions in multiple bands. The current level of technology is not sophisticated enough to deftly manage this yet — current products tend to support one at a time — but this is an area where the technology is changing fast. To keep current, read product reviews because good reviewers can tell you when devices make inroads in better supporting these technologies simultaneously. In Chapter 20, we give you some good sites to check out.

Compatibility and Form Factor

When choosing an AP, make sure that it (and its setup program) is compatible with your existing components, check its form factor, and determine whether wall-mountability and outdoor use are important to you.

Hardware and software platform: Make sure that the device that you're buying supports the hardware and software platform that you have. Certain wireless devices only support Macs or only support PCs. And some devices only support certain versions of software.

Setup program and your operating system: Make sure that the setup program for the AP that you plan to buy will run on your computer's operating system and the next version of that operating system (if it's available). Setup programs will run only on the type of computer for which they were written. A setup program designed to run on Windows, for example, won't run on the Mac OS, and vice versa. Luckily, as we note later in this chapter, most vendors are moving towards browser-based configuration programs, which are a lot easier to support than standalone configuration utilities.

As a general rule, if you're using Windows 98 or 2000 (or Mac OS 9), make sure that the devices that you buy will work up through Windows XP (and Mac OS X). This will ensure your ability to use this wireless equipment in the future if you upgrade parts of your network and will also help you get the most value from your investment.

Form factor: Also, make sure the *form factor* (that is, the shape and form of the device, like whether it's external or a card) is what you're looking for. For example, don't assume that if you have a tower PC, you should install a PCI card. It's nice to have the more external and portable form factors, such as a Universal Serial Bus (USB) adapter because you can take it off if you need to borrow it for something/someone else.

USB is supported by Windows 98 and later versions. Windows 95 does not support USB ports. USB comes in two versions: USB 1.1 and USB 2.0. If your computer has a USB 1.1 port, it has a maximum data transfer speed of 12 Mbps. USB 2.0 ports can transfer data at 480 Mbps, which is 40 times faster than USB 1.1. If you plan to connect an IEEE 802.11a or IEEE 802.11g device to a USB port, it must be USB 2.0.

Many brands of PC Cards include antennas that are enclosed in a casing that is thicker than the rest of the card. The card still fits in the PC Card slot, but the antenna can block the other slot. For most users, this shouldn't pose a serious problem; however, several manufacturers offer wireless PC Cards that have antenna casings no thicker than the rest of the card. If you actively use both of your PC Card slots, make sure that the form of the PC Card that you're buying won't impede using your other card slot.

Even better, all cards should come from the same company that manufactured the AP that you select to ensure maximum interoperability and to take full advantage of any extended features that the AP offers.

Wall-mountability: If you plan on wall-mounting your device, make sure that the unit is wall mountable because many are not.

Outdoor versus indoor use: Finally, some devices are designed for outdoor — not indoor — use. If you're thinking about installing this outside, look for devices hardened for environmental extremes.

Bundled Functionality: Servers, Gateways, Routers, and Switches

Wireless APs are readily available that perform only the AP function; but for home use, APs that bundle additional features are much more popular for good reason. In most cases, you should shop for an AP that's also a network router and a network switch — a wireless gateway like we define in Chapter 2. To efficiently connect multiple computers and to easily share an Internet connection, you need devices to perform all these functions, and purchasing one multi-purpose device is the most economical way to accomplish that.

DHCP servers

To create an easy-to-use home network, your network should have a Dynamic Host Configuration Protocol (DHCP) server. A *DHCP server* dynamically assigns an IP address to each computer or other device in your network. This function relieves you from having to keep track of all the devices on the network and assign addresses to each one manually.

Network addresses are necessary for the computers and other devices on your network to communicate. Because most networks today use a set of protocols (Transmission Control Protocol/Internet Protocol, or TCP/IP) with network addresses (Internet Protocol [IP] addresses), we refer to network addresses as *IP addresses* in this book. In fact, the Internet uses the TCP/IP protocols, and every computer that is connected to the Internet must be identified by an IP address.

When your computer is connected to the Internet, your Internet Service Provider (ISP), such as America Online (AOL) or EarthLink, has assigned your computer an IP address. However, even when your computer isn't connected to the Internet, it needs an IP address to communicate with other computers on your home network.

The DHCP server can be a standalone device, but it's typically a service provided either by a computer on the network or by a network router. The DHCP server maintains a database of all the current DHCP clients — the computers and other devices to which it has assigned IP addresses — issuing new addresses as each device's software requests an address.

Windows, Macintosh, and most other types of computers — as well as network devices — can automatically communicate over the network with a DHCP server to request the server to issue an IP address.

Gateways, NAT, and cable/DSL routers

A *wireless gateway* is a wireless AP that enables multiple computers to share the same IP address on the Internet. This fact would seem to be a contradiction because every computer on the Internet needs its own IP address. The magic that makes an Internet gateway possible is Network Address Translation (NAT). Most access points that you buy today are wireless gateways.

When your wireless network needs some order

Your home network comprises many parts. If you're smart, you've consolidated these as much as possible because having fewer devices means easier installation and troubleshooting. But suppose that you have a cable modem, a router, a switch, and an access point — not an unusual situation if you grew your network over time. Now suppose that the power goes out. Each of these devices will reset at different rates. The switch will probably come back fairly quickly because it's a simple device. The cable modem will probably take the longest to re-sync with the network, and the AP and router will come back up probably somewhere in-between.

The problem that you, as a client of the DHCP server (which is likely in the router in this instance), have is that not all the elements are in place for a clean IP assignment to flow back to your system. For instance, the router needs to know the WAN IP address in order for you to have a good connection to the Internet. If the cable modem hasn't renegotiated its connection, it cannot provide that to the router. If the AP comes back online before the router, it cannot get its DHCP from the router to provide connectivity to the client. Different devices react differently when something is not as it should be on start up.

Our advice: If you have a problem with your connectivity that you didn't have before the electricity went out and came back on, follow these simple steps. Turn everything off, start at the farthest point from the client, and work back toward the client, letting each device get its full startup cycle complete before moving to the next device in line — ending with rebooting your PC or other wirelessly enabled device.

A device that typically provides the NAT service to a home network is called a cable/digital subscriber line (DSL) router or broadband router. (Note that you can also purchase a broadband modem that doubles as a router, but the typical modem is not a router.) Cable/DSL routers used in home networks also provide the DHCP service. The router communicates with each computer or other device on your home network via private IP addresses — the IP addresses assigned by the DHCP server. (See the earlier section "DHCP servers.") However, the router uses a single IP address — the one assigned by your ISP's DHCP server — in packets of data intended for the Internet.

In addition to providing a method of sharing an Internet connection, the NAT service provided by a broadband router also adds a measure of security because the computers on your network aren't directly exposed to the Internet. The only computer visible to the Internet is the broadband router. This protection can also be a disadvantage for certain types of Internet gaming and computer-to-computer file transfer applications. If you find that you need to use one of these applications, look for a router with features called *DMZ* (for *demilitarized zone*) and *port forwarding* that expose just enough of your system to the Internet to play Internet games and transfer files. (Read more about this in Chapter 12.)

A *wireless Internet gateway* is an AP that's bundled with a cable/DSL modem/router. By hooking this single device to a cable connection or DSL line, you can share an Internet connection with all the computers connected to the network, wirelessly. By definition, all wireless Internet gateway devices also include several wired Ethernet ports that enable you to add wired devices to your network as well as wireless devices.

Switches

Wireless gateway devices available from nearly any manufacturer include from one to eight Ethernet ports with which you can connect computers or other devices via Ethernet cables. These gateway devices are not only wireless APs but are also wired switches that efficiently enable all the computers on your network to communicate either wirelessly or over Ethernet cables.

As we discuss in Chapter 2, there is a huge difference in performance between a switch and a hub. Just because a device says that it has four ports or eight ports doesn't mean that it's one or the other — it could be either. Look for words like *switched LAN ports* for an embedded switch in the device.

Even though you might intend to create a wireless home network, sometimes you might want to attach a device to the network through a more traditional network cable. For example, we highly recommend that you configure an AP for the first time with the AP attached by a network cable directly to your computer. At times, it might also be convenient to connect one of the other computers in your home directly to your AP.

Print servers

A few multifunction Internet gateways add a feature that enables you to add a printer to the network: a print server. Next to sharing an Internet connection, printer sharing is the most cost-effective reason to network home computers because everyone in the house can share one printer. Wireless print servers have become a lot more economical in the past few years. However, when the print server is included with the Internet gateway device, it's suddenly very cost effective.

The disadvantage of using the print server bundled with the AP, however, is apparent if you locate your AP in a room or location other than where you'd like to place your printer. Consider a standalone print server device if you want to have your printer wirelessly enabled but not near your AP.

Operational Features

Most APs share a common listing of features, and most of them do not vary from one device to the next. Here are some unique, onboard features that we look for when buying wireless devices . . . and you should, too. Among these are

- **Wired Ethernet port:** Okay, this seems basic, but having a port like this will save you time. We will tell you time and again to install your AP first on your wired network (as opposed to trying to configure the AP via a wireless client card connection) and then add on the wireless layer (like the aforementioned client card). You will save yourself a lot of grief if you can get your AP configured on a direct connect to your PC because you reduce the things that can go wrong when you add in the wireless clients. *Note:* On some APs, like the Mac AirPort, directly connecting for setup is not an option.

- **Auto channel select:** Some access points, such as some from ORiNOCO (www.proxim.com), offer an automatic channel selection feature, which is cool. For instance, the ORiNOCO AP-2000 Access Point selects its own frequency channel, based on interference situation, bandwidth usage, and adjacent channel use, by using its Auto Channel Select feature. This is beneficial when first deploying your AP-2000 or adding an AP-2000 unit in an existing environment. For instance, for the 5 GHz radio card (used for 802.11a), the default channel is 52–5.260 GHz. When a second AP-2000 unit is turned on in the vicinity of the currently active AP-2000 device, the Auto Channel Select feature changes the frequency channel of the second unit so that no interference exists between the units. Multiple AP-2000 units can be turned on simultaneously to establish proper channel selection. That's pretty nice because as you can read in Chapter 6 and in the troubleshooting areas of Chapter 18, channel selection can try your patience. (You might wonder why it's necessary to pay more for more business-class access points — this is a good reason.)

- **Power over Ethernet (PoE):** Because every AP is powered by electricity (where's Mr. Obvious when you need him?), you should also consider whether the location that you choose for an AP is located near an electrical outlet. High-end access points, intended for use in large enterprises and institutions, offer a feature known as Power over Ethernet (PoE). PoE enables electrical power to be sent to the AP over an Ethernet networking cable so that the AP doesn't have to be plugged into an electrical outlet. Modern residential electrical codes in most cities, however, require outlets every eight feet along walls, so unless you live in an older home, power outlets shouldn't be a real issue. But if you're putting it on the ceiling, running one cable sure is easier than two!

- **Detachable antennas:** In most cases, the antenna or antennas that come installed on an AP are adequate to give you good signal coverage throughout your house. However, your house might be large enough or be configured such that signal coverage of a particular AP could be significantly improved by replacing a stock antenna with an upgraded version. Also, if your AP has an internal antenna and you decide that the signal strength and coverage in your house are inadequate, an external antenna jack allows you to add one or two external antennas. Several manufacturers sell optional antennas that extend the range of the standard antennas; they attach to the AP to supplement or replace the existing antennas.

The FCC requires that antenna and radio be certified as a system. Adding a third-party, non-FCC-certified antenna to your AP violates the FCC regulations and runs the risk of causing interference with other radio devices such as certain portable telephones.

✔ **Uplink port:** APs equipped with internal three- and four-port hub/ switch devices are also coming with a built-in, extra uplink port. The *uplink port* — also called the crossover port, output, X, bridge, and so on — is used to add on even more wired ports to your network by uplinking the AP with another hub or switch. This special port is normally an extra connection next to the last available wired port on the device, but it can look like a regular Ethernet jack (with a little toggle switch next to it). You want an uplink port — especially if you have an integral router/DSL/cable modem — so that you can add more ports to your network while it grows. (And it will grow.)

Security

Unless you work for the government or handle sensitive data on your computer, you probably aren't overly concerned about the privacy of the information stored on your home network. Usually it's not an issue, anyway, because someone would have to break into your house to access your network. But if you have a wireless network, the radio signals transmitted by your wireless network don't automatically stop at the outside walls of your house. In fact, a neighbor or even someone driving by on the street in front of your house can use a computer and a wireless networking adapter to grab information right off your computer, including deleting your files, inserting viruses, using your computer to send spam, and so on — unless you take steps to protect your network.

The security technology that comes standard with all Wi-Fi equipment is Wired Equivalent Privacy (WEP). Perhaps the most well-publicized aspect of Wi-Fi wireless networking is the fact that the WEP security feature of Wi-Fi networks can be *hacked* (broken into electronically). Hackers have successfully retrieved secret WEP keys used to encrypt data on Wi-Fi networks. With these keys, the hacker can decrypt the packets of data transmitted over a wireless network. The significance of this problem might have been overblown in the media because changing keys regularly greatly reduces the risk of a successful WEP attack. Nonetheless, many business and government agencies have prohibited implementation of wireless networks that rely only on WEP to protect the privacy of data.

In October 2002, the Wi-Fi Alliance announced a new, replacement security technology for WEP: Wi-Fi Protected Access (WPA). WPA is based on an IEEE standards effort that's not yet fully adopted. This technology, which makes cracking a network's encryption key much more difficult, is designed to work in the products on the market today and is expected to first appear in Wi-Fi certified products during the first quarter of 2003. Most vendors are expected to offer free firmware and software updates for Wi-Fi certified products currently in use.

Although WEP isn't as secure as WPA, you take a much greater security risk if you don't use WEP at all. See Chapter 10 for a full discussion of how to set up basic security for your wireless home network.

In addition to encryption features such as WEP (or WPA), many AP manufacturers have added a variety of security features often described loosely as *firewall protection.* One of the most common security features is typically described as a *MAC filter* because it enables you to set up a list of Media Access Control (MAC) addresses that are permitted to access the network. (The manufacturer of each networking device assigns a unique MAC address to the device at the factory.) A MAC filter can prevent network access by devices not on a predetermined list of MAC addresses.

Don't depend on the MAC filter feature as the sole form of security for your wireless home network. A determined hacker can discover the MAC address of one of your computers and then use software to masquerade as that MAC address. The AP would permit the hacker to join the network. This is a *spoof attack.*

Other useful firewall features to look for when buying an AP include

- **Network Address Translation** (NAT), which we discuss earlier in this chapter
- **Virtual Private Network** (VPN) pass-through that allows wireless network users secure access to corporate networks
- **Monitoring software** that logs and alerts you to computers from the Internet attempting to access your network
- **Utilities** that enable you to log content that's transmitted over the network as well as to block access to given Web sites

We talk a lot more about security in Chapter 10. We encourage you to read Chapter 10 so that you'll be well prepared for the process when you're ready to install your equipment.

Range and Coverage Issues

An AP's functional *range* (the maximum distance from the access point at which a device on the wireless network can receive a useable signal) and *coverage* (the breadth of areas in your home where you have an adequate radio signal) are important criteria when selecting an AP. Wi-Fi equipment is designed to have a range of up to 100 meters when used outdoors without any obstructions between the two radios. Coverage depends on the type of antenna used.

Just like it's hard to know how good a book is until you read it, it's hard to know how good an AP is until you install it. Buying an AP is definitely the type of thing for which you do your research ahead of time and hope that you make the right choice. Buying ten APs and returning the nine that you don't want is simply impractical. (Well, maybe not impractical, but rather rude.) The key range and coverage issues, such as power output, antenna gain, or receive sensitivity (which we cover in Chapter 2) aren't well labeled on retail boxes. Nor are these issues truly comparable among devices, either, because of the same lack of consistent information. Because many of these devices are manufactured by using the same chipsets, performance usually doesn't vary extensively from one AP to another. However, that is a broad generalization, and some APs do perform badly. Our advice: Read the reviews and be forewarned!

In Chapter 2, we tell you about the differences in range between 802.11b/g systems and 802.11a systems, with the latter having slightly less range, all other things being equal. Of the many good reasons to go for 802.11a systems, a big one is the lack of interference in the 5 GHz frequency range. And if you have range issues, we help you figure out how to boost that range (and your throughput) in Chapter 18.

Manageability

When it comes to installing, setting up, and maintaining your wireless network, you'll rely a lot on your device's user interface, so check reviews for this aspect of the product. In the next sections, we discuss the many different ways to control and manage your devices.

Web-based configuration

APs, wireless clients, and other wireless devices from all vendors ship with several utility software programs that help you set up and configure the device. An important selling feature of any wireless device is its setup process. The ideal setup procedure can be accomplished quickly and efficiently. Most available APs and devices can be configured either through the wired Ethernet port or through a USB port.

The best setup program varieties enable you to configure the device by connecting through the Ethernet port and accessing an embedded set of Web (HyperText Markup Language; HTML) pages. Look for an AP with one of these. This type of setup program — often described as *Web-based* — can be run from any computer that's connected to the device's Ethernet port and that has a Web browser. Whether you're using Windows, the Mac OS, or Linux, you'll be able to access any device that uses a Web-based configuration program.

Software programming

When shopping for an AP, look for one with an automated setup process. Several AP manufacturers provide setup software that walks you step by step through the entire process of setting up the AP and connecting to your network. The Windows variety of automated setup programs are typically called *wizards*. If you're new to wireless technology, a setup wizard or other variety of automated setup program will help you get up and running with minimum effort.

Versions of Windows starting with Windows XP and versions of the Mac OS starting with Mac OS 9 are more wireless aware than earlier versions of these operating systems. Automated setup programs are typically quick and easy to use when written to run on either Windows XP or Mac OS 9 or later.

Performing firmware updates

Most firmware updates come in the form of a downloadable program that you run on a computer connected to the AP (or other device) by a cable (usually Ethernet but sometimes USB). Make sure that you carefully read and follow the instructions that accompany the downloadable file. Updating the firmware incorrectly can lead to real headaches. Here are a few tips:

✔ Make sure that you make a backup of your current firmware before performing the update.

✔ Never turn off the computer or the AP while the firmware update is in progress.

✔ If something does go wrong, look through the AP documentation for instructions on how to reset the modem back to its factory settings.

Even if an AP comes with a setup wizard, it will also ship with configuration software that permits you to manually configure all the available AP settings. For maximum flexibility, this configuration software should be Web based (see the preceding section).

Telnetting to your device

When all else fails, you can rely on some good old, stand-by backdoors in computing. With your computer, it's the command prompt interface. With your wireless device, it's telnetting, which sounds very Scandinavian but isn't even close. *Telnet* is a terminal emulation program for TCP/IP networks such as the Internet; a *terminal emulation program* emulates what you would see if you were sitting at a terminal attached to the device that you want to manage. The Telnet program runs on your computer and links your PC to a device on the network: in this case, your AP. You can then enter commands through the Telnet program, and they will be executed as if you were entering them directly into the AP or through the manufacturer's Web-based program.

To start a Telnet session, you enter the IP address of the device and log in by entering a valid username and password. You will then be presented with a screen that is decidedly old-fashioned, but you can get the job done here. In order to telnet to a device, you might have to connect with it via a serial interface cable or a null modem cable like a cross-over Ethernet cable (an Ethernet cable with certain wires reversed). Danny recently had to use Telnet to manage a dialup router that he had just purchased on eBay because the software provided with the router wouldn't support XP . . . but he could get in via telnetting.

Windows ships with a free Telnet program: HyperTerminal. If you find that your software won't work and you need to get to the device, ask Technical Support whether you can telnet to the device (and leave the skis at home).

Upgradeable firmware

Wireless networking technology is still evolving. As a result, many features of Wi-Fi access points are implemented in updateable chips known as *firmware*. Before you decide which AP to buy, determine whether you'll be able to get feature updates and fixes from the vendor and whether you can perform the updates by upgrading the firmware (see the nearby sidebar "Performing firmware updates" for some pointers). Check also for updated management software to match up with the new or improved features included in the updated firmware.

You might feel that frequent firmware updates are evidence of faulty product design. Acknowledging that wireless technology will continue to be improved, buying a product that can be upgraded to keep pace with these changes without the need to purchase new equipment can save you money in the long run.

Price

Although we can't say much directly about price (except that the least expensive item is rarely the one that you want), we should mention other things that can add to the price of an item. Check out which cables are provided (yes, wireless devices need cables, too!). In an effort to trim costs, some (not many) companies don't provide an Ethernet cable for your AP (which you need for initial setup).

Also, before you buy, check out some of the online price comparison sites, like CNET (`shopper.cnet.com`) or Yahoo! Shopping (`shopping.yahoo.com`). Internet specials pop up all the time.

Warranties

There's nothing worse than a device that dies one day after the warranty expires. The good news is that because most of these devices are solid state, they work for a long time unless you abuse them by dropping them on the floor or something drastic. In our experience, if your device is going to fail for build reasons, it will do so within the first 30 days or so.

You'll encounter a rather large variance among vendors of warranty schedules. Some are only one-year long, but some are lifetime in length. Most are limited in some fashion, like covering parts and labor but not shipping.

When purchasing from a store, be sure to ask about its return policy for the first month or so. A lot of stores give you 14 days to return items, and after that, purchases have to be returned to the manufacturer directly, which is a huge pain in the rumpus, as Pat would say. If you only have 14 days, get the device installed quickly so that you can find any problems right away.

Extended service warranties are also often available through computer retailers. (We never buy these because by the time that the period of the extended warranty expires, they're simply not worth their price given the plummeting cost of the items.) If you purchase one of these warranties, however, make sure that you have a clear understanding of the types of problems covered as well as how and when you can contact the service provider if problems arise. As we mention above, if you don't purchase a warranty, you'll probably need to contact the product manufacturer for support and warranty service instead of the store or online outlet where you purchased the product.

Customer and Technical Support

Good technical support is one of those things that you don't appreciate until you can't get it. For support, check whether the manufacturer has toll-free or direct dial numbers for support as well as its hours of availability. Ticklish technical problems seem to occur at the most inopportune times — nights, weekends, holidays. If you're like us, you usually install this stuff late at night and on weekends. (We refuse to buy anything from anyone with only 9 a.m.–5 p.m., M–F hours for technical support.) Traditionally, only the high-end (that is to say, expensive) hardware products came with 24x7 technical support; however, an increasing number of consumer-priced computer products, including wireless home networking products, offer toll-free, around-the-clock, technical phone support.

Part III
Installing a Wireless Network

The 5th Wave   By Rich Tennant

"We take network security very seriously here."

In this part . . .

Now comes the work: installing a wireless network in your home and getting it up and running. Whether you're a Mac OS 9 or X user or have PCs running a Windows 95 or later operating system, this part of the book explains how to install and configure your wireless networking equipment. No doubt you're also interested in sharing a single Internet connection and, of course, making your home network as secure as possible. This part covers these topics as well.

Chapter 6

Installing Wireless Access Points in Windows

● ●

In This Chapter

▶ Installing a wireless network access point (AP)

▶ Modifying AP configuration

● ●

*I*n this chapter, we describe the installation and configuration of your wireless home network's access point. We explain how to set up and configure the access point so that it's ready to communicate with any and all wireless devices in your home network. In Chapter 7, we describe the process for installing and configuring wireless network adapters.

Note: Chapters 6 and 7 deal solely with Windows-based PCs. For specifics on setting up and installing wireless home networking devices on a Mac, see Chapter 8.

Before Getting Started, Get Prepared

Setting up an AP does have some complicated steps where things can go wrong. You want to reduce the variables to as few as possible to make debugging any problems as easy as possible. So don't try to do lots of different things all at once, like buy a new PC, install XP, add a router, add an AP, and wireless clients . . . all at the same time. (Go ahead and laugh, but a lot of people try this.) We recommend that you do the following:

1. **Get your PC set up first on a standalone basis.**

   If you have a new computer system, you probably shouldn't need much setup because it should be preconfigured when you buy it. If you have an older system, make sure that no major software problems exist before you begin. If you have to install a new operating system (OS), do it now. Bottom line: Get the PC working on its own fine so that you have no problems when you add on functionality.

2. **Add in your dialup or broadband Internet connection for that one PC.**

   Ensure that everything is working on your wired connection first. If you have a broadband modem, get it working on a direct connect to your PC first. If you're using a dialup connection, again — get that tested from your PC so you know that the account is active and works. Make sure that you can surf the Web (go to a number of sites that you know work) to ascertain that the information is current (as opposed to coming from your cache memory storage from prior visits to the site).

3. **Choose (and do) which of the following makes sense for your configuration.**

   a. **If you're sharing a broadband or dialup connection with a router, add in your home network routing option.**

      This will entail shifting your connection from your PC to your router, and your router will have instructions for doing that. After that is working, make sure that you can add another PC or other device, if you have one. Make sure that it can connect to the Internet, as well, and that the two devices can see each other on the local area network. This establishes that your logical connectivity among all your devices and the Internet is working. Because many of you reading this book are going to be installing an AP on an existing broadband or dialup network, we're covering the AP installation first; we cover the installation of the router and your Internet sharing in Chapter 9.

   b. **If you plan to use this machine as the gateway to the Internet (as opposed to a router), turn on Internet sharing on your host PC.**

      Get that going and working, testing that with other connected devices. Again, check out Chapter 9 for info on this.

4. **Now try adding wireless to the equation: Install your wireless AP and wireless NICs and disconnect the wired cable from each to see whether they work — one at a time is always simpler.**

   By now, any problems that occur can be isolated to your wireless connection. If you need to fall back on dialing into or logging onto your manufacturer's Web site, you can always plug the wired connection in and do so.

If your AP is in an all-in-one cable modem/router/AP combo, that's okay. Think about turning on the elements one at a time. If a wizard forces you to do it all at once, go ahead and follow the wizard's steps; just recognize that if all goes wrong, you can reset the device to the factory settings and start over (extreme, but usually saves time).

Setting Up the Access Point

Before you install and set up a wireless network interface adapter in one of your computers, you should first set up the wireless access point (also sometimes called a *base station*) that will facilitate communication between the various wireless devices in your network. In this section, we describe how to set up a typical AP.

Preparing to install a wireless AP

The procedure for installing and configuring most wireless APs is similar from one manufacturer to the next . . . but not exactly the same. You're most likely to be successful if you locate the documentation for the AP that you have chosen and follow its installation and configuration instructions carefully.

Because having a network makes it easy to share an Internet connection, the best time to set up the AP for that purpose is during initial setup (but we give you the details for setting up Internet sharing in Chapter 9). In terms of setting up a shared Internet connection, you'll already have a wired computer on your broadband (cable or digital subscriber line [DSL]) or dialup Internet connection. This is very helpful as a starting place for most AP installations because most of the information that you need to set up your AP is already available on your computer. If you don't have a wired computer on your Internet connection — that is, this is the first computer that you're connecting — first collect any information (special log-in information, such as username or password) that your Internet service provider (ISP) has given you regarding using its services.

  ✔ **Ensure that your computer has a standard wired Ethernet connection.** Most AP configurations require wired access for their initial setup. An Ethernet port is normally found on the back of your computer; this port looks like a typical telephone jack, only a little bit wider. If you don't have an Ethernet adapter, you should buy one and install it in your computer. Alternatively, if your computer does have a Universal Serial Bus (USB) port (preferably USB 2.0, also known as USB High Speed), you can purchase an AP that connects to the USB port.

  ✔ **Collect your ISP's network information.** You need to know the following. If you don't already know this stuff, ask the tech support folks at your ISP.

   • **Your Internet protocol (IP) address:** This is the equivalent of your network's phone number. Your IP address identifies your network on the Internet and enables communications.

- **Your gateway address:** This is the IP address of the networking device that connects the devices attached to your home network to the Internet.

- **Your subnet mask:** Your local area network (LAN) — your home network — uses this to define the location of the computers within the network and allows them to connect to Internet.

- **Your Domain Name System (DNS) server:** This is a special computer within your ISP's network that translates IP addresses into host names. *Host names* are the (relatively) plain English names for computers attached to the Internet. For example, the *wiley.com* part of `www.wiley.com` is the host name of the Web server computers of our publisher.

- **Whether your ISP is delivering all this to you via Dynamic Host Configuration Protocol (DHCP):** In almost all cases, the Internet service that you get at home uses DHCP, which means that a *server* (or computer) at your ISP's network center automatically provides all the information listed in the bullets above, without you needing to enter anything manually. It's a great thing!

✔ **Collect the physical address of the network card used in your computer** *only if you are already connected.* Many ISPs use the physical address as a security check to ensure that the computer connecting to its network is the one paying for the service. Many of the AP and Internet access devices available today permit you to change their physical address (Media Access Control [MAC] address) to match the physical address of your existing network card, eliminating the need for you to get your service provider to adjust your account — or in many cases, charge you more.

Installing the AP

If you're connecting your first computer with your ISP, the ISP should have supplied you with all the information that we list in the preceding section except for the physical address of the network card (which isn't needed if you aren't already connected).

Before you install your wireless gear, buy a 100-foot Ethernet cable. If you are installing your AP at a distance farther than that away from your router or Internet-sharing PC, you might get a longer cable. Trust us . . . this is one of those things that comes with having done this a lot. You need a wired backup to your system to test devices and debug problems. And to do that (unless you want to keep moving your gear around, which we don't recommend), you need a long cable. Or two. Anyone with a home network should have extra cables, just like you have electrical extension cords around the house. You can get good quality 100-foot cables online at RadioShack (www.radioshack.com) or Fry's (www.frys.com) for around $25.

1. **Gather the necessary information for installing the AP (see the preceding list).**

   If you're using Windows 95/98/Me, do the following:

   a. **Choose Start➪Run, type** winipcfg **in the Run dialog box that appears, and then click OK.**

   This brings up the Windows IP configuration tool.

   b. **Select the network adapter that you are connecting to your physical network and then click the More Info button.**

   c. **Copy all the networking information from the screen and save it for later use in configuring the AP in Step 4.**

   The information that you need to know includes the physical address, IP address, default gateway, subnet mask, DNS server(s), and whether DHCP is enabled.

Note that if your network adapter has more than one DNS server assigned, you will see a square button with three dots on it to the right of the DNS servers box. Clicking this button will cycle through the available DNS servers that you have access to. In most cases, you will have at least two.

   If you're using Windows NT/2000/XP, do the following:

   a. **Choose Start➪Programs➪Accessories➪Command Prompt.**

   This will bring up the command prompt window that's similar to a DOS screen.

   b. **Type** IPCONFIG /ALL **and then press Enter.**

   The information that you receive will scroll down the screen. Use the scroll bar to slide up to the top and write down the networking information that we listed earlier (physical address, IP address, default gateway, subnet mask, DNS server(s), and whether DHCP is enabled). You will use this information to configure the AP in Step 4.

2. **Run the setup software that accompanies the AP or device containing your AP like a wireless or Internet gateway.**

   The software will probably start when you insert its CD-ROM into the CD drive. In many cases, this software will detect your Internet settings, which makes it much easier to configure the AP for Internet sharing and to configure the first computer on the network. For example, Figure 6-1 shows the Microsoft Broadband Networking Setup utility that accompanies the Microsoft Wireless Base Station, which is a wireless gateway from Microsoft.

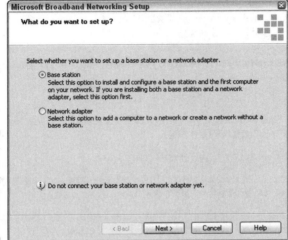

 Figure 6-1:
The
Microsoft
Broadband
Networking
Setup.

3. **When prompted by the setup software to connect the AP (see Figure 6-2), unplug the network cable that connects the broadband modem to your computer from the computer's Ethernet port and plug this cable into the Ethernet port that's marked *WAN* or *Modem* on your network's cable/DSL router or Internet gateway.**

   If you're using an Internet or wireless gateway, run a Cat 5e cable from one of its Ethernet ports to the computer on which you are running the setup software. (*Cat 5e cable* is a standard Ethernet cable or patch cord with what look like oversized phone jacks on each end. You can pick one up at any computer store or RadioShack.)

   If you're not, you need to connect a Cat 5e cable between the AP and one of the router's Ethernet ports and then connect another cable from another one of the router's Ethernet ports to the computer on which you are running the setup software.

4. **Complete the installation of the setup software and when prompted, enter the information that you collected in Step 1 (so have that information handy).**

5. **Record the following access point parameters.**

   The following list covers AP parameters that you will most often encounter and need to configure, but it is not comprehensive. (Read more about them in the following section, "Configuring AP parameters.") You will need this information if you plan to follow the steps on modifying AP configuration, which we cover in the later section, "Changing the AP Configuration." (What did you expect that section to be called?) Other settings that you probably don't need to change include the transmission rate (which normally adjusts automatically to give the best throughput), RTS/CTS protocol settings, the beacon interval, and the fragmentation threshold.

- Service set identifier (SSID)
- Channel
- WEP keys
- Password
- MAC address
- Dynamic or static wide area network (WAN) IP address
- Local IP address
- Subnet mask
- PPPoE (Point-to-Point Protocol over Ethernet)

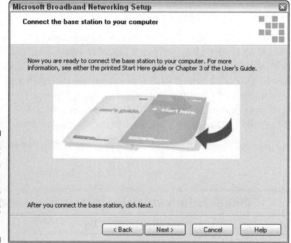

Figure 6-2:
It's time to connect the AP or Internet gateway.

6. **Complete the installation software and you're finished.**

After you complete the AP setup process, you should now have a working access point ready to communicate with another wireless device.

Configuring AP parameters

Here's a little more meat on each of the access point parameters that you captured in Step 5 of the preceding section.

✔ **Service set identifier (SSID):** The SSID (sometimes called the *network name*, *network ID,* or *service area)* can be any alphanumeric string, including upper- and lowercase letters, up to 30 characters in length. The AP manufacturer might set a default SSID at the factory, but you should change this setting. Assigning a unique SSID doesn't really add much security; nonetheless, establishing an identifier that is different than the factory-supplied SSID makes it a little more difficult for intruders to access your wireless network. And if you have a nearby neighbor with a wireless AP of the same type, you won't get the two networks confused. When you configure wireless stations, you need to use the same SSID/network name that is assigned to the AP.

✔ **Channel:** This is the radio channel over which the AP will communicate. If you plan to use more than one AP in your home, you should assign a different channel (over which the AP will communicate) for each AP to avoid signal interference. If your network uses the IEEE 802.11b or IEEE 802.11g protocols, 11 channels, which are set at 5 MHz intervals, are available in the United States. However, because the radio signals used by the IEEE 802.11b standard spread across a 22 MHz-wide spectrum, you can only use up to three channels (typically 1, 6, and 11) in a given wireless network.

If you're setting up an 802.11a AP, you have 11 channels from which to choose. But because these channels are 20 MHz wide and do not overlap, you really have 11 channels with which to work, compared with only 3 with IEEE 802.11b or 802.11g. If you operate only one AP, all that really matters is that all wireless devices on your network must be set to the same channel. If you operate several APs, give them as much frequency separation as possible to reduce the likelihood of mutual interference.

Table 6-1 contains the channel frequencies for the different wireless standards.

Table 6-1	Channel Frequencies for Wireless Standards
2.4 GHz (802.11b/g)	*5 GHz (802.11a)*
Channel 1–2.412 GHz	Channel 36–5.180 GHz
Channel 2–2.417 GHz	Channel 40–5.200 GHz
Channel 3–2.422 GHz	Channel 44–5.220 GHz
Channel 4–2.427 GHz	Channel 48–5.240 GHz
Channel 5–2.432 GHz	Channel 52–5.260 GHz
Channel 6–2.437 GHz	Channel 56–5.280 GHz
Channel 7–2.422 GHz	Channel 60–5.300 GHz
Channel 8–2.447 GHz	Channel 64–5.320 GHz
Channel 9–2.452 GHz	

2.4 GHz (802.11b/g)	5 GHz (802.11a)
Channel 10–2.457 GHz	
Channel 11–2.462 GHz	
Channel 12–2.467 GHz	
Channel 13–2.472 GHz	
Channel 14–2.477 GHz (Japan only)	

Notes
802.11b/g:
Channel 3 is default FCC, ETSI, Japan.
Channel 12 is for ETSI countries only.
For France, Channels 10–13 are applicable only.
802.11a:
These channels are valid only in US/Canada and Japan at this time.
Source: ORiNOCO

Some access points, such as some from ORiNOCO, offer an automatic channel selection feature, which is cool. For instance, the ORiNOCO AP-2000 Access Point selects its own frequency channel, based on interference situation, bandwidth usage, and adjacent channel use, using its Auto Channel Select feature. This is beneficial when first deploying your AP-2000 or adding an AP-2000 unit in an existing environment. For instance, for the 5 GHz radio card (used for 802.11a), the default channel is 52 (5.260 GHz). When a second AP-2000 unit is turned on in the vicinity of the currently active AP-2000 device, the Auto Channel Select feature changes the frequency channel of the second unit so there is no interference between the units. Multiple AP-2000 units can be turned on simultaneously to establish proper channel selection. That's pretty nice; you might wonder why it's necessary to pay more for more business-class access points — this is a good reason.

When you have multiple access points and set your 802.11a, b, or g access points all to the same channel, sometimes roaming won't work when users move about the house, and the transmission of a single access point blocks all others that are within range. As a result, performance degrades significantly. (You notice this when your *throughput,* or speed of file/data transfers, decreases noticeably.) Use different, widely separated channels for b and g; you only have to use different channels for a because they are non-overlapping.

✔ **WEP keys:** You should always use Wired Equivalent Privacy (WEP) encryption. Only a determined hacker with the proper equipment and software will be able to crack the key. (By the time that you're reading this, newer encryption protocols such as Wi-Fi Protected Access [WPA] might have been implemented that are nearly impossible to break.) If you don't use WEP or some other form of security, any nosy neighbor with a laptop, wireless PC card, and range-extender antenna might be able to see and access your wireless home network. Whenever you use encryption, all wireless stations in your house attached to the wireless home network must use the same key. Sometimes the AP manufacturer will assign a default WEP key. Always assign a new key to avoid a security breach.

Read Chapter 10 for great background info on WEP and WPA.

✔ **Password:** Configuration software might require that you enter a password to make changes to the AP setup. The manufacturer might provide a default password (see the user documentation). Use the default password when you first open the configuration pages, and then immediately change the password to avoid a security breach. (***Note:*** This is not the same as the WEP key, which is also called a *password* by some user interfaces [UIs].)

✔ **MAC address:** The *Media Access Control (MAC) address* is the physical address of the radio in the AP. You should find this number printed on a label attached to the device. You might need to know this value for troubleshooting, so write it down. The AP's Ethernet (RJ-45) connection to the wired network also has a MAC address that is different than the MAC address of the AP's radio.

✔ **Dynamic or static wide area network (WAN) IP address:** If your network is connected to the Internet, it must have an IP address assigned by your ISP. Most often, your ISP will dynamically assign this address. Your router or Internet gateway should be configured to accept an IP address dynamically assigned by a DHCP server. It is possible, but unlikely, that your ISP will require a *set* (static) IP address.

✔ **Local IP address:** In addition to a physical address (the MAC address), the AP will also have its own network (IP) address. You need to know this IP address to access the configuration pages using a Web browser. Refer to the product documentation to determine this IP address. In most cases, the IP address will be 192.168.*xxx.xxx* where *xxx* is between 1 and 254. It's also possible an AP could choose a default IP that's in use by your cable/DSL router (or a computer that got its IP from the cable/DSL router's DHCP server). Either way, if an IP conflict arises, you might have to keep the AP and cable/DSL routers on separate networks while configuring the AP.

✔ **Subnet mask:** In most cases, this value will be set at the factory to 255.255.255.0. If you're using an IP addressing scheme of the type described in the preceding paragraph, 255.255.255.0 is the correct number to use. This number, together with the IP address, establishes the subnet on which this AP will reside. Network devices with addresses on the same subnet can communicate directly without the aid of a router. You really don't need to understand how the numbering scheme works except to know that the AP and all the wireless devices that will access your wireless network must have the same subnet mask.

✔ **PPPoE:** Most DSL ISPs use of Point-to-Point Protocol over Ethernet (PPPoE). The values that you need to record are the user name (or user ID) and password.

Changing the AP Configuration

Each brand of AP has its own configuration software that you can use to modify the AP's settings. Some products provide several methods of configuration. The most common types of configuration tools for home/small office APs are

- ✔ **Software-based:** Some APs come with access point setup software that you run on a workstation to set up the AP over a wireless connection, a USB cable, or an Ethernet cable.

- ✔ **Web-based:** Many of the newer lines of APs intended for home and small office use have a series of HyperText Markup Language (HTML; Web) forms stored in firmware. You can access these forms by using a Web browser over a wireless connection or over a network cable in order to configure each AP.

To access your AP's management pages with a Web browser, you need to know the local IP address for the AP. If you didn't make note of the IP address when you initially set up the AP, refer to the AP's user guide to find this address. It will be a number similar to 192.168.2.1. If you're using an Internet gateway, you can also run `winipcfg` (on Windows 9*x*/Me machines) or `ipconfig` (Windows NT, 2000, XP), as we describe in Chapter 7. The Internet gateway's IP address is the same as the default gateway.

When you know the AP's IP address, run your Web browser software, type the IP address in the Address line, and then press Enter or click the Go button. You'll probably see a screen that requests a password. This is the password that you established during initial setup for the purpose of preventing unauthorized individuals from making changes to your wireless AP's configuration. After you enter this password, the AP utility will display an AP management screen. If you're not using a Web-based tool, you need to open up the application that you initially installed to make any changes.

Within the AP's management utility, you can modify all the AP's settings such as the SSID, the channel, and WEP encryption key. The details of how to make these changes vary from manufacturer to manufacturer. Typically, the AP management utility also enables you to perform other AP management operations, such as resetting the AP, upgrading its firmware, and configuring any built-in firewall settings.

AP manufacturers periodically post software on their Web site that you can use to update the AP's firmware that's stored in the circuitry inside the device. If you decide to install a firmware upgrade, follow the provided instructions very carefully. ***Note:*** Do *not* turn off the AP or your computer while the update is taking place.

The best practice is to modify AP settings only from a computer that's directly connected to the network or the AP by a network cable. If you must make changes over a wireless connection, think through the order that you will make changes, or you could orphan the client computer. For example, if you want to change the wireless network's WEP key, change the key on the AP first and make sure that you write it down. As soon as you save the change to the AP, the wireless connection will effectively be lost. No data will pass between the client and the AP, so you will no longer be able to access the AP over the wireless connection. To re-establish a useful connection, you must change the key on the client computer to the same key that you entered on the AP.

Chapter 7

Setting Up Your Windows PCs for Wireless Networking

· ·

In This Chapter

▶ Installing wireless network interface adapters

▶ Windows XP's Wireless Zero Configuration

▶ Going wireless with Pocket PC 2002

· ·

*I*n this chapter, we describe the installation and configuration of wireless devices on Windows computers. To that end, we explain how to set up and configure the wireless network interface adapter in each of your computers (and other wireless devices) so that they can communicate with the access point (AP) and with one another. Finally, we also include special coverage for installing and configuring wireless network adapters in computers running Windows XP (it's amazingly easy) and in handheld computers running Microsoft Pocket PC 2002.

Read through Chapter 6 for information about physically installing APs, and see Chapter 8 for a discussion of setting up a Mac-based wireless network. And if you find yourself lost in the acronyms, check out Chapter 2 for the background on this equipment.

Setting Up Wireless Network Interface Adapters

After you have the AP successfully installed and configured (see Chapter 6), you're ready to install and set up a wireless network interface adapter in each client device. Wireless network adapters all require the same information to be installed, although the installation on different platforms might differ to some degree. From most manufacturers, the initial setup procedure differs somewhat depending on the operating system that is running your computer.

In this section, we walk you through installing device drivers and client software before addressing the typical setup procedure for various wireless network interface adapters.

If you're using Windows XP, you can also set up your wireless network interface adapter by using Windows XP's built-in support for wireless networking. Refer to the "Windows XP's Wireless Zero Configuration" section, later in this chapter, for more information.

The installation procedure for most types of PC devices consists of installing the hardware (the device) in your computer and then letting Windows detect the device and prompt you to supply a driver disk or CD. With most wireless network adapters, however, it is important to install the software that is provided with the wireless networking hardware *before* installing the hardware. This ensures that the setup software can examine your computer's hardware, software, network, and Internet settings *before* you have installed any wireless hardware.

Installing device drivers and client software

Whenever you install an electronic device in your Windows PC, including a wireless network interface adapter, Windows needs to know certain information about how to communicate with the device. This information is a *device driver*. When you install a wireless network adapter, depending on which version of Windows you're using, you might be prompted to provide the necessary device driver. Device driver files typically accompany each wireless networking device on an accompanying CD-ROM. Most wireless device manufacturers also make the most up-to-date device driver files available for free download from their technical support Web sites.

When you install the wireless adapter into your computer, Windows uses the device driver file(s) to add the adapter into your computer's hardware configuration. The new network adapter's driver also must be configured properly in order for it to communicate with other computers over the Windows network.

Even if you receive a driver CD with your wireless network interface adapter, we still recommend checking the manufacturer's Web site for the most recent software. Wireless networking technology is still evolving, so keeping up with the changes is paramount. For example, to address the security flaws in WEP (which we talk about in Chapter 10), different security (or encryption) protocols are becoming available or will soon be available. For example, as we discuss in Chapter 10, a new system called WPA will soon be available. To take advantage of this, you need to download the newest driver software as well as the newest *firmware,* which is the special software that resides in the flash memory on your network adapter and which enables it to do its job.

The exact procedure for installing the drivers and software for the wireless network adapters varies from manufacturer to manufacturer, so read the documentation that accompanies the product that you are installing *before* you begin. Although the details might differ from the instructions that accompany your product, the general procedure is as follows:

Because antivirus programs often mistake installation activity for virus activity, shut down any antivirus programs that you might have running on your PC *before* you begin any installation of software or hardware. (And remember to turn it back on when you're done!)

1. **Insert the CD that accompanies the wireless network adapter into the CD-ROM drive.**

   If the CD's startup program doesn't automatically begin, choose Start➪ Run or use Windows Explorer to run the Setup.exe program on the CD.

2. **Install the software for configuring the network adapter by following the instructions on your screen.**

   Typically, you'll be following along with an installation wizard program.

   Do not insert the network adapter until prompted to do so by the installation software (see Figure 7-1). In some cases, you might be prompted to restart the computer before inserting the adapter. For some older versions of Windows, you will be prompted to insert your Windows CD in order for the setup program to copy needed networking files.

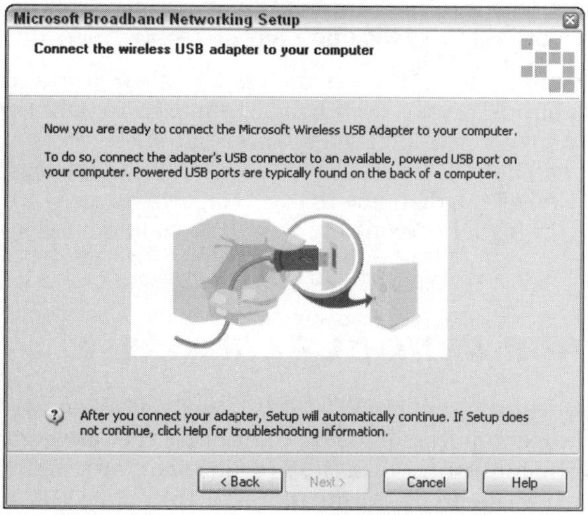

Figure 7-1:
Don't connect your wireless network adapter until prompted by the setup software.

Because you installed the wireless network adapter's drivers and configuration software prior to inserting the adapter, the operating system should be able to automatically locate the driver and enable the new adapter.

Note: If Windows can't find the driver, it might start the Found New Hardware (or Add/Remove Hardware, or even New Hardware — it depends on which OS you're using) Wizard. If this does happen, don't panic. You can direct Windows to search the CD-ROM for the drivers that it needs, and they should install without issues (although you might have to reboot again).

After you insert or install your wireless network adapter (and restart the computer, if prompted to do so), you will be prompted to configure the new adapter.

3. **At a minimum, you need to make sure that the following settings match those of your network's wireless AP:**

   • **SSID (network name or network ID):** Most wireless network adapter configuration programs will display a list of wireless networks that are in range of your adapter. In most instances, you will see only one SSID listed. If you see more than one, that means one (or more) of your neighbors also have a wireless network that is close enough for your wireless adapter to "see." Of course, that means that your neighbor's wireless adapter can see your network, too. This is one good reason to give your wireless network a unique SSID (network name), and it's also a compelling reason to use encryption.

   • **WEP key:** Enter the same key that you entered in the AP's configuration.

After you configure the wireless network adapter, the setup program might announce that it needs to reboot the computer. Newer versions of Windows, such as Windows XP, don't have to reboot.

One of the common applications installed with a wireless adapter is a bandwidth monitor. This is a very handy tool used to debug problems and inform you of connection issues. Almost all these tools are graphical in nature and can help you determine the strength of the signal to your AP device as well as the distance that you can travel away from the device before the signal becomes too weak to maintain a connection.

PC Cards and mini-PCI cards

Most wireless network adapters are PC Cards. Nearly all Windows laptops and some Mac laptop computers have PC Card ports that are compatible with these cards. The hottest new wireless (draft) standard, IEEE 802.11g, however, is available on some platforms (notably, the Apple Macintosh) only on mini-PCI cards capable of transmitting data at speeds that are faster than the PC Cards are capable of handling. IEEE 802.11g interfaces will come on mini-PCI cards or standard size PC Cards. The Apple AirPort Extreme (draft) IEEE 802.11g wireless adapter, for example, comes only in a mini-PCI version that will not install in most older Macs. Nevertheless, Linksys, NETGEAR, D-Link, and others offer an IEEE 802.11g PC Card wireless network interface adapter. In the future, most such devices will come pre-installed in computers.

The installation procedure for most types of PC Cards, peripherals (such as modems), and wired network cards consists of plugging the card into the PC Card slot and supplying a driver disk or CD when prompted to do so. With most PC Card wireless network adapters, however, installing the software drivers *before* inserting the PC Card for the first time is important. Doing so ensures that the correct driver is present on the computer when the operating system recognizes that you've inserted a PC Card. Installing the drivers first also ensures that you can configure the software when you install the device.

If you're installing a PC Card in a Windows-based computer with a PC Card slot, use the following general guidelines but don't forget to refer to the documentation that comes with the card for detailed instructions. (Refer to Chapter 8 if you are a Mac user.)

Even if you received a CD with the PC Card, checking the manufacturer's Web site for the most recent drivers and client station software is a good idea. Wireless networking technology is still evolving, so we recommend that you keep up with the changes. For example, to address the security flaws in WEP, a new version of the encryption protocol is available from some manufacturers.

1. **Insert the CD that accompanies the PC Card into the CD-ROM drive.**

   If the setup program doesn't automatically start, choose Start⇨Run (in Windows) or open Windows Explorer to run the Setup.exe program on the CD.

2. **Install the wireless client software.**

   During this installation, you might be asked to indicate the following:

   - Whether you want the PC Card set to infrastructure (AP) mode or to ad hoc (peer-to-peer) mode. Choose infrastructure mode to communicate through the AP. We talk about the difference between infrastructure and ad hoc modes in Chapter 2.

   - The SSID (network name).

   - Whether you will use a network password (which is the same as WEP encryption).

3. **After the wireless station software is installed, restart the computer.**

4. **While the computer restarts, insert the PC Card wireless network adapter into the available PC Card slot.**

   Windows 95/98/Me/2000 are Plug and Play-compliant, so they should recognize that you have inserted a new device in the PC Card slot and will automatically search the hard disk for the driver.

Windows XP comes with generic drivers for many wireless PC cards to make installation much simpler than ever before. Some newer PC Cards, which are made specifically for XP, have no software included, relying on XP to take care of it. Even so, we recommend that you follow the directions that come with your PC Card and check whether your card is compatible with XP. Later in this chapter, we discuss XP's *Net Zero* configuration tools, which provide software for many XP-compliant and noncompliant cards.

When Windows finds the driver, it will enable the driver for the card, and you're finished.

 Wireless network interface adapter manufacturers periodically post software on their Web sites that you can use to update the *firmware* (software that's stored in the circuitry and chips inside the card). In most cases, firmware updates address-specific hardware or software issues. If you aren't aware of a problem with the card or an important new feature that you need, you should probably leave well enough alone. However, if you like to stay on the cutting edge, we suggest that you regularly check the manufacturer's Web site for updates.

Compact Flash cards

Some Pocket PCs have optional attachments that make it possible to add PC Card devices. Most Pocket PC manufacturers provide either standard or optional support for add-on cards built to the Compact Flash (CF) form factor. We cover CF cards in more detail in Chapter 2.

Installing a wireless network interface adapter in a Pocket PC is about as easy as it gets (we show you how in a moment), but configuring the device so that you can both synchronize with your PC and use your Pocket PC to access the Internet can be a little tricky (and we show you that later in this chapter).

The installation procedure varies in precise detail from manufacturer to manufacturer, but you can follow these general steps:

1. **Install the software that came with the Compact Flash (CF) card and then insert the CF card into the CF slot in your Pocket PC when prompted to do so.**

2. **Connect the Pocket PC to the desktop or laptop PC that you plan to use to configure your Pocket PC.**

   This step usually involves placing the Pocket PC in the cradle that's attached by a cable to your desktop or laptop computer, just like you do when you're synchronizing your calendar.

3. **Insert the setup CD that came with the wireless network interface CF card into your computer's CD-ROM drive.**

   If the setup software doesn't run automatically, choose Start⊏>Run (in Windows) or open Windows Explorer to start it.

4. **Install the software by following the onscreen instructions.**

   If prompted to choose between infrastructure mode and ad hoc mode, choose infrastructure mode (which is the mode that causes your CF card to talk to the AP) rather than directly to other wireless devices (ad hoc mode).

5. **When prompted to enter the network name or SSID, enter the name that you used when you set up the AP.**

   Refer to the discussion of Pocket PC 2002 (later in this chapter) for more information about configuring wireless client software on your Pocket PC.

6. **On the Pocket PC, run the wireless network adapter's configuration program.**

   To run the configuration utility for the Linksys WCF11 wireless adapter, for example (shown in Figure 7-2), you choose Start⊏>Programs and then click the WCF11 Config icon. You might have to unplug the card and rein-sert for the configuration utility to be able to "see" the card the first time.

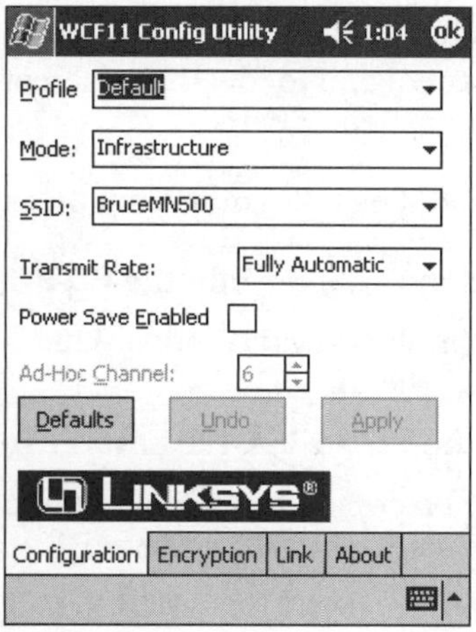

Figure 7-2:
The con-
figuration
utility for
the Linksys
WCF11
wireless
adapter.

7. **Using the wireless adapter's configuration utility on the Pocket PC, turn on the encryption feature and enter the same encryption key that you entered in the AP's configuration software.**

   At this point, you should have a valid link between the wireless network adapter in the Pocket PC and the AP. (The Linksys utility, for example, has a Link button that you can click to display a screen showing link quality and signal strength.) You aren't quite ready to use the wireless card to synchronize your Pocket PC with your PC, however. You must follow the steps in the later section, "Getting Set for Synchronizing and Internet Access," to do just that.

PCI and ISA cards

If you purchased a wireless networking adapter that fits inside your PC, you must make sure that you have the right type for your computer. Most desktop computers built in the last five years contain at least one PCI slot. Older desktop computers might have only Industry Standard Architecture (ISA) slots. Refer to your computer's documentation to determine which type of slot is inside your computer and then purchase a wireless network interface adapter to match.

Some manufacturers choose to mount a PC Card on a PCI or an ISA adapter. Some of the newest PCI adapters consist of a mini-PCI adapter mounted to a full-sized PCI adapter. In either of these configurations, a black rubber dipole-type antenna, or another type of range-extender antenna, is attached to the back of the PCI or ISA adapter.

Most PCI or ISA cards come with specific software and instructions for installing and configuring the card. We can't tell you exactly what steps you'll need to take with the card that you buy, but we can give you some generic steps. And don't forget to read the manual and follow the onscreen instructions on the CD that comes with your particular card.

Follow these general guidelines for installing a PCI or ISA adapter card:

1. **Insert the CD that accompanied the adapter into the CD-ROM drive.**

   If necessary, choose Start⇨Run (in Windows) or open Windows Explorer to run the Setup.exe program on the CD.

2. **Select the option for installing the PCI or ISA card driver software.**

   At this point, the driver will only be copied to the computer's hard drive. The driver will be added to the operating system in Step 4.

3. **If prompted to restart the computer, select No, I Will Restart My Computer Later and then click the Next (or Finish) button.**

   During the install process, many Windows-based computers will prompt you to restart the computer by displaying a pop-up box with a question similar to "New drivers have been installed, do you want to restart for the changes to take effect?" The normal reaction might be to do what it asks and click the OK button — but don't! The software installation needs to fully complete before the computer can be restarted. You will know it's completed because the installation wizard (not a Windows pop-up) will prompt you for your next step. After the software has completed its installation process, *it* will prompt you in its own software window to restart your computer, or it will inform you that you need to restart to complete the installation.

4. **After the computer restarts, install the PC Card wireless station (client) software in accordance with the instructions that came with it.**

   In some cases, Steps 2 and 4 are accomplished in a single software-installation step. In other cases, you will only install the wireless station software at this point.

   While the wireless station software is installing, you might need to indicate whether you want the PC Card to be set to infrastructure (AP) mode or to ad hoc (peer-to-peer) mode. Choose infrastructure mode to cause the wireless network adapter to use the AP to communicate with other network devices. You might also need to provide the SSID (network name) and to indicate whether you will use WEP encryption.

5. **After both the PCI card or ISA card driver and the wireless station software are installed, shut down the computer.**

6. **Unplug the computer and install the PCI card or ISA card in an available slot.**

7. **Plug in the computer and restart it.**

Although most internal Wi-Fi adapters use the PCI bus in your PC, a few use the ISA bus. (This is an older system that's gradually being phased out of newer computers.) Most of the time, PCI systems will automatically detect the new hardware that you've installed (the wireless network adapter) when you restart the computer. If you're using an ISA adapter, you might have to manually prompt the computer to recognize the new card by using the Add/Remove Hardware Wizard. To start the wizard, choose Start➪Settings➪Control Panel and then double-click the Add/Remove Hardware icon.

Windows will recognize that you have installed new hardware and will automatically search the hard drive for the driver. When Windows finds the driver, it will enable the driver for the adapter, and you're done.

USB adapters

If you purchased a USB adapter, these are easy to install in your USB port. All new PCs and laptops come with at least one (and usually two) USB port(s). Most USB adapters attach to the USB port via a USB cable. Some new devices are so lightweight and compact that you can plug them directly into the USB port. (Refer to Chapter 8 if you are a Mac user.)

The general guidelines for installing a USB wireless NIC are as follows:

1. **Insert the CD that accompanied the USB adapter into the CD-ROM drive.**

   If the CD's AutoRun feature doesn't cause the setup program to start, use the Run command from the Start button (in Windows) or open Windows Explorer to run the `Setup.exe` program on the CD.

2. **Install the wireless station (client) software.**

   During the installation of the wireless station software, you might be asked to indicate whether you want the USB wireless adapter to be set to infrastructure (access point) mode or to ad hoc (peer-to-peer) mode. Choose infrastructure mode to cause the wireless network adapter to use the AP to communicate with other network devices. You might also be asked for the SSID (network name) and to indicate whether you will use WEP encryption.

3. **After the wireless station software is installed, restart the computer.**

4. **After the computer restarts, attach the USB adapter to one of the computer's USB ports by running a USB cable from the network adapter to the USB port.**

   Windows should recognize that you have installed new hardware and will automatically search the hard disk for the driver. When Windows finds the driver, it will enable the driver for the adapter. That's it — you're all finished.

Modifying Wireless Network Adapters

Some occasions might warrant modifying one or more of the adapters' parameters. For example, you might need to change the adapter's WEP key or SSID to match changes that you have made to the AP. The wireless network adapter's manufacturer has provided utility software for this purpose. For example, Figure 7-3 shows the ORiNOCO (`www.proxim.com`) Client Manager program that you can use to select a different wireless network SSID or to change the WEP key. (For more about SSIDs and WEP keys, see the step lists in the first section of this chapter.)

Figure 7-3:
The
ORiNOCO
Client
Manager.

If you use Windows XP, however, you can use the operating system's utilities to change settings in your wireless network interface adapter. Windows XP is the first Windows OS that has support for wireless networking built in. We talk about this built-in support in the later section "Windows XP's Wireless Zero Configuration."

Synchronizing and Internet Access

To get your Pocket PC to synchronize with your PC through the wireless adapter — and to enable wireless access to the Internet — follow these general steps:

1. **On the Pocket PC, choose Start⇨Settings⇨Connections⇨Network Adapters. Then select the wireless network adapter from the list of installed adapters on the Network Adapters screen and click Properties.**

   A screen similar to what's shown in Figure 7-4 appears. Click the IP Address tab. Marking the default setting (the Use Server-Assigned IP Address radio button) is easiest. The DHCP server on your network that assigns the IP addresses for all the other devices on the network will also assign the IP address for your Pocket PC.

Settings   4€ 1:42 ok
Instant Wireless Network CF Card
● Use server-assigned IP address
○ Use specific IP address
IP address: .   .   .
Subnet mask: .   .   .
Default gateway: .   .   .
IP Address │ Name Servers

Figure 7-4: Assigning an IP address for your Pocket PC.

2. **Determine the IP address of the PC with which the Pocket PC will synchronize.**

   • If your PC runs Windows 95/98/SE/Me, choose Start⇨Run, type winipcfg, and then click OK to display the IP Configuration window. Select the PC's network adapter from the drop-down list. Copy down the IP address for the PC's network adapter and then close the IP Configuration window.

- If your PC runs Windows 2000/XP, choose Start⇨(All) Programs⇨Accessories⇨Command Prompt. In the command prompt window that appears, type ipconfig, and then press Enter. Copy the IP address for the PC's network adapter and then close the command prompt window.

3. **On the Pocket PC, go to the Name Servers tab of the wireless network adapter's Properties screen.**

   You accessed the Properties screen in Step 1; it should still be visible on the Pocket PC.

4. **In the WINS text box, enter the PC's IP address that you copied in Step 4.**

   Figure 7-5 shows the Name Servers tab with WINS address filled in.

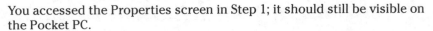

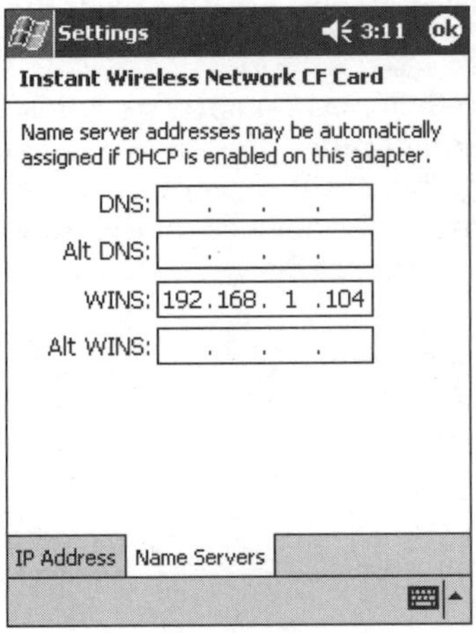

Figure 7-5: Supplying a WINS address.

You should now be able to wirelessly synchronize the Pocket PC with the PC. And if your wireless network is connected to the Internet, you should be able to wirelessly access the Internet on your Pocket PC. To check for the functionality of these two features, proceed to Steps 5 and 6.

5. **While the Pocket PC is not in its cradle, choose Start⇨ActiveSync and then click the Sync button (on the ActiveSync screen that appears).**

   You should see the ActiveSync pop-up window on the PC and a message on the Pocket PC telling you that the two computers are synchronizing.

6 **Launch Internet Explorer and browse the Internet to find out whether you have wireless access to the Internet.**

Wireless Zero Configuration with XP

Windows XP promises to make connecting to new wireless networks easier through a service that Microsoft has dubbed *Wireless Zero Configuration*. Although Microsoft's claim of zero configuration is a bit of an exaggeration, configuration is pretty easy. When installing or configuring a wireless adapter that's supported by Windows XP, you don't need to use software provided by the manufacturer. Instead, Windows XP itself recognizes the adapter and provides the necessary driver and configuration software.

Easy installation

As an alternative to the manufacturer's installation and configuration software, follow these steps to install and configure a supported wireless network adapter. (***Note:*** We recommend that you check the documentation that accompanies your wireless adapter to determine whether it is supported by Windows XP Zero Configuration before continuing with these steps.)

1. **If you plan to use a wireless network interface adapter that you have to install inside the case of the computer, turn off the computer and install the PCI or ISA adapter.**

2. **Log on to Windows XP as a user with administrator rights.**

   If you installed Windows XP, you probably have administrator rights. To check, choose Start⇨Settings⇨Control Panel⇨User Accounts to display the User Accounts screen that shows the accounts on your computer. If you're not listed as Computer Administrator, you need to find out who is the administrator and get that person to change your account.

3. **Insert the PC Card or attach the USB adapter.**

   Windows XP displays a message that your new hardware is installed and ready to use.

   Because your computer is within range of your network's wireless AP (they have to be close enough to talk to each other), Windows XP announces that one (or more) wireless network is available and suggests that you click the Network icon to see a list of available networks.

4. **Click the Network icon in the notification area of the task bar at the bottom-right of the screen.**

   Windows XP displays the Wireless Network Connection dialog box, as shown in Figure 7-6.

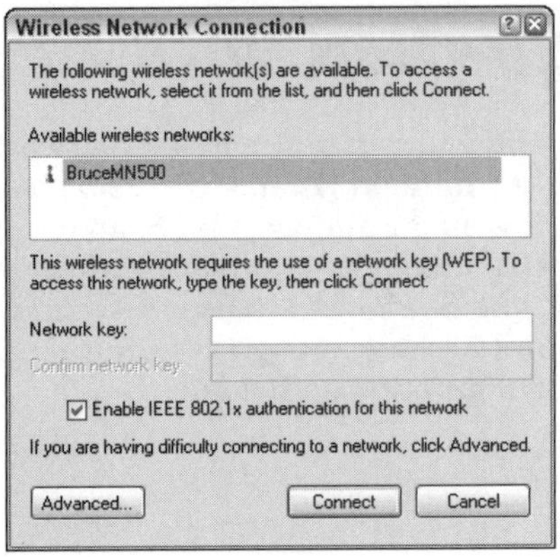

Figure 7-6:
The
Wireless
Network
Connection
dialog box.

5. **In the Network Key text box, type the WEP key that you used in the AP configuration, enter the key again in the Confirm Network Key text box, and then click the Connect button.**

   The dialog box disappears, and Windows XP displays a balloon message that announces a wireless network connection and indicates the connection's speed and signal strength (poor, good, or excellent). The Network icon in the status bar flashes green occasionally to indicate network traffic on the wireless connection.

In a matter of minutes, you have installed and configured a wireless network connection. If you have trouble connecting, you can access more configuration information by clicking the Advanced button in the Wireless Network Connection dialog box (refer to Figure 7-6) to display the Wireless Network Connection Properties dialog box (shown in Figure 7-7).

Automatic network connections

Easy installation and configuration is only half of the Windows XP wireless networking story. If you know that you will use your computer to connect to several different wireless networks — perhaps one at home and another at work — Windows XP enables you to configure the wireless adapter to automatically detect and connect to each network on the fly, without further configuration.

To configure one or more wireless networks for automatic connection, follow these steps:

1. **In the notification area of the status bar at the bottom of the screen, click the Network icon to display the Wireless Network Connection dialog box and then click the Properties button.**

2. **In the Wireless Network Connection Properties dialog box (see Figure 7-7) that appears, click the Wireless Networks tab.**

   Notice that your home wireless network is already listed. If your computer is in range of the second wireless network, its SSID will also be listed.

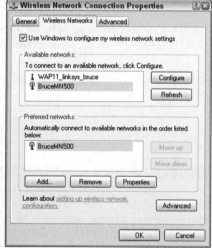

Figure 7-7:
The
Wireless
Network
Connection
Properties
dialog box.

3. **To add another network to the list, click the Add button on the Wireless Networks tab.**

4. **In the Wireless Network Properties dialog box that appears, type the network name (SSID) of the other wireless network to which you will be connecting your computer in the Network Name text box.**

   You'd want to enter the network name (SSID) for the wireless network at your office, for example.

5. **If you're connecting to a wireless network at your office, make sure that you have appropriate authorization and check with the network administrator for encryption keys and authorization procedures that he or she has implemented.**

   If the network administrator has implemented a system for automatically providing users with WEP keys, click OK.

   If the wireless network to which you plan to connect doesn't have an automatic key distribution system in place, do this:

   a. **Deselect the The Key Is Provided for Me Automatically check box.**

   b. **Enter the WEP key.**

   c. **Click OK to save this network SSID.**

6. **Move on to the next network (if any) that you want to configure.**

Notice the Key Index scroll box near the bottom of the dialog box. By default, the key index is set to 1. Your office network administrator will know whether you need to use the key index. This feature is used if the system administrator has implemented a *rotating key system,* which is a security system used in some office settings. You won't need to mess with this unless you're setting up your computer to use at work — it's not something that you'll be using in your home wireless network.

7. **After adding all the necessary wireless networks, click OK on the Wireless Networks tab of the Wireless Network Connection Properties dialog box.**

Windows XP now has the information that it needs to automatically connect the computer to each wireless network whenever the wireless station comes into range.

Tracking Your Network's Performance

After you have your network adapters and APs installed and up and running, you might think that you've reached the end of the game — wireless network Nirvana! And in some ways, you have, at least after you go through the steps in Chapter 9 and get your network and all its devices connected to the Internet. But part of the nature of wireless networks is the fact that they rely upon the transmission of radio waves throughout your home. And if you've ever tried to tune in a station on your radio or TV but had a hard time getting a signal (who hasn't had this problem — besides kids who've grown up on cable TV and Internet radio, we suppose), you probably realize that radio waves can run into interference or just plain peter out at longer distances.

Obviously, the transmitters used in Wi-Fi systems use very low power levels — at least compared with commercial radio and television transmitters — so the issues of interference and range that are inherent to any radio-based system are even more important for a wireless home network.

Luckily, the client software that comes with just about any wireless network adapter includes a tool that enables you to take a look at the performance of your network — usually in the form of a signal strength meter and perhaps a link test program. With most systems (and client software), you'll be able to view this performance monitoring equipment in two places:

✔ **In your system tray:** Most wireless network adapters will install a small signal strength meter in the Windows system tray (usually found on the bottom-right corner of your screen, although you might have moved it elsewhere on your screen). This signal strength meter will usually have a series of bars that light up in response to the strength of your wireless network's radio signal. It's different with each manufacturer, but most that we've seen light up the bars in green to indicate signal strength. The more bars that light up, the stronger your signal.

✔ **Within the client software itself:** The client software that you installed along with your network adapter will usually have some more elaborate signal strength system that graphically (or using a numerical readout) displays several measures of the quality of your radio signal. This is often called a *link test* function, although different manufacturers call it different things. (Look in your manual or in the online help system to find this in your network adapter's client software.) The link test usually measures several things:

- **Signal strength:** Also called *signal level* in some systems, this is a measure of the signal's strength in dBm. The higher this number is, the better, and the more likely that you'll be getting a full speed connection from your access point to your PC.

- **Noise level:** This is a measure of the interference that is affecting the wireless network in your home. Remember that electronics in your home (such as cordless phones and microwaves) can put out their own radio waves that interfere with the radio waves used by your home network. Noise level is also measured in dBm, but in this case, lower is better.

- **Signal to Noise Ratio (SNR):** This is really the key determinant to how good the performance of your wireless network is. This ratio is a comparison of the signal (the good radio waves) with the noise (the bad ones). SNR is measured in dB, and a higher number is better.

Many link test programs provide not only an instantaneous snapshot of your network performance but also give you a moving graph of your performance over time. This can be really helpful in two ways. First, if you have a laptop PC, you can move it around the house to see how your network performance looks in different parts of the house . . . or even just in different parts of the house. Second, it can let you watch the performance while you turn various devices on and off. For example, if you suspect that a 2.4 GHz cordless phone is killing your wireless LAN, turn on your link test and keep an eye on it while you make a phone call.

When you grow more comfortable with your wireless LAN — and start using it more and more — you can leverage these tools to really tweak your network. For example, you can have your spouse or a friend sit in the living room watching the link test results while you move the access point to different spots in the home office. Or you could use the link test with a laptop to find portions of the house that have really weak signals and then use these results to decide where to install a second access point.

Chapter 8

Setting Up a Wireless Mac Network

In This Chapter

▶ Installing and configuring the Apple AirPort Card under OS 9 and OS X

▶ Installing and configuring the Apple AirPort Base Station under OS 9 and OS X

▶ Adding a computer to an existing wireless network

*I*f you're an Apple Macintosh user and you've just decided to try wireless networking, this chapter is for you. This chapter covers installing and setting up the AirPort Card in an Apple computer as well as setting up an AirPort Base Station. Because both Mac OS 9.2 and Mac OS X (v. 10.2) are the most current versions of the Mac operating system at the time of this writing, the chapter covers setting up the AirPort Card and Base Station for each of these operating systems.

Note: Apple is beginning to phase out OS 9 support in its new computers. Over time, it's possible that fewer AirPort features will be available for computers running this OS.

Apple AirPort Hardware

On July 21, 1999, Steve Jobs, then the interim CEO of Apple, introduced wireless networking to mainstream computing in a speech at the Macworld trade show in New York. In this speech, Jobs launched Apple's new iBook laptop computer for consumers. One of the innovative features of the iBook was a wireless networking card developed by Apple and Lucent: the AirPort Card. This device, when used in conjunction with the AirPort Base Station, enabled consumers to wirelessly connect their iBook to a network from as far away as 150 feet. The audience that viewed Jobs' speech was fascinated by the technology. The iBook quickly became one of Apple's most popular computer models. Apple now offers the AirPort Card as an option that can be installed inside any of its computers.

Apple's AirPort products use the same Wireless Fidelity (Wi-Fi) IEEE 802.11b technology that has become the most popular wireless networking standard. Apple computers equipped with AirPort Cards can connect to any Wi-Fi–compatible 2.4 GHz wireless network — regardless of whether the network uses Apple equipment — including Windows wireless networks.

At the Macworld tradeshow in January 2003, Apple announced a new AirPort Extreme Card and Base Station that uses the draft IEEE 802.11g technology that can transfer data up to 54 Mbps and can handle up to 50 Mac and Windows users simultaneously. These new products are backward compatible with the older AirPort equipment; however, the new AirPort Extreme Card will install only in Apple computers that have a mini-PCI (Peripheral Component Interconnect) slot inside.

Pick an AirPort Card, any card

Apple computer models were the first on the market to feature a special wireless adapter — the AirPort Card — as an option. The AirPort Card, with a retail price of $99, is very similar to a PC Card (a Personal Computer Memory Card International Association [PCMCIA] Card) but is designed to be installed in a special AirPort slot inside an Apple computer. You should not try to use it in a PC Card slot found on most laptop computers.

The AirPort Extreme Card is a mini-PCI card. It is designed to fit inside an Apple computer, such as several of the newest PowerBook G4s, but will not fit in the original AirPort slot. Likewise, an AirPort Card will not fit in a mini-PCI slot. The AirPort Extreme card also has a retail price of $99. It will connect to the original AirPort Base Stations but will also connect to the new AirPort Extreme Base Station that can transmit data up to 54 Mbps, almost five times faster than the original AirPort.

Lucent designed and manufactures the AirPort Card for Apple and also manufactures a very similar card for other vendors (such as ORiNOCO, a Proxim brand) but with an antenna built into the card. These Lucent PC Cards are too long and fat to fit in the slot intended for AirPort Cards, but they can be used in PC Card-slot–equipped PowerBook laptop computers, as well as in current and older Apple desktop computers, through the use of a special adapter card that fits into a Macintosh PCI slot.

A few other vendors (such as Proxim) offer wireless networking cards that will work in Apple Macintosh computers' PCI slots or PC Card slots, but most Apple computer users buy the AirPort Card because it can be installed inside the computer and attached to the built-in antenna.

Apple AirPort-ready computers

The Apple computer models that are compatible with the AirPort Card are

- ✔ **iBook:** All iBook models.

- ✔ **PowerBook:** The PowerBook (FireWire) and some PowerBook G4. Several of the newest PowerBook G4 models are AirPort Extreme-ready rather than Airport-ready.

- ✔ **iMac:** The iMac (slot-loading except 350 MHz model), iMac (Summer 2000 except Indigo 350 MHz model), iMac (early 2001), iMac (Summer 2001), and iMac (flat panel). You also need an AirPort Card Adapter to install an AirPort Card into any AirPort-ready, G3-based, slot-loading iMac.

- ✔ **Power Mac G4:** All models except Power Mac G4 (PCI Graphics).

Apple computers that are equipped for installation of an AirPort Card have an antenna built into the body of the computer. When you install the AirPort Card, you attach the AirPort Card to the built-in antenna. (All radios need an antenna to be able to send and receive radio signals, and wireless networking cards are no exception.)

You can use any standard PC Card Wi-Fi card in an older PowerBook (or Power Mac with a PC Card adapter installed) if you can find drivers. The open source driver project is located at SourceForge (http://wireless driver.sourceforge.net/).

Installing an AirPort Card

Apple considers the AirPort Card a user-installable upgrade, which means that the procedure is very straightforward and easy to accomplish. The exact steps vary depending on which computer you have.

Your Apple dealer or local Apple retail store will probably install an AirPort for you rather cheaply ($20 or so) if you don't feel comfortable getting inside your Mac.

If you purchase the AirPort Card in a retail box, it often comes installed in an iMac AirPort Card adapter. This adapter is required to install the card in an iMac, but you must remove it if you're going to install the card in an iBook, a PowerBook, or a Power Mac G4.

1. **Shut down the computer.**

2. **Unplug the appropriate cabling:**

   • **For models except the iMac and Power Mac G4:** Unplug all cables, such as the power, keyboard, mouse, printer cables, modem, and so on.

   • **For the iMac and Power Mac G4:** Leave the power cord plugged in for now.

3. **To avoid discharging damaging static electricity through the AirPort Card, be sure to touch a metal part on the computer chassis before touching the AirPort Card to the computer.**

   Or even better, purchase an electrostatic discharge (ESD) strap from a local electronics or computer store. Place the strap on your wrist and clip the end of the cable to the computer's chassis.

   • **For the iBook:** Turn it over, use a coin to remove the battery cover, and remove the battery. Turn the computer back over so that the keyboard is facing up and then release the keyboard by sliding the two plastic tabs (between the Esc and F1 keys and between the F8 and F9 keys) away from the display. Lift the keyboard, turn it over, and lay it on the front portion of the computer.

   If you are not wearing an ESD strap: To discharge static electricity, touch any one of the metal surfaces inside the iBook with your hand — *not* with the AirPort Card.

   • **For the PowerBook:** Remove the battery from the expansion bay. If you've locked down the keyboard, open the locking screw (between the F4 and F5 keys) and then release the keyboard by sliding the two plastic tabs away from the display. Lift the keyboard, turn it over, and lay it on the front portion of the computer.

   If you are not wearing an ESD strap: To discharge static electricity, touch any one of the metal surfaces inside the PowerBook with your hand — *not* with the AirPort Card.

   • **For the iMac:** You can use a coin to open the access panel on the back of the computer and then touch the metal shield inside the recessed latch. Then unplug the power cord.

   • **In a Power Mac G4:** You can touch the metal PCI access covers on the back of the computer and then unplug the power cord.

4. **Locate the antenna cable and plug it into the end of AirPort Card.**

   • **In the iBook:** The antenna cable is tucked under a wire clip that's exposed when you remove the keyboard. Insert the round connector at the end of the cable into the hole at the end of the AirPort Card.

   • **In a PowerBook:** Remove the screws that hold down the internal heat shield and lift out the heat shield. Locate the antenna cable and plug it into the end of the AirPort Card.

- **In an iMac:** The antenna cable is attached to the left rail guide. Detach it and remove the cap from the end of the cable. Insert the cable's connector into the hole at the end of the AirPort Card.

- **In a PowerMac G4:** Release the latch on the side of the computer and lower the side. You'll find the antenna in the side of the PCI card guide. Plug the cable into the AirPort Card.

5. **Insert the card, with the cable attached, into the AirPort Card slot.**

- **For the iBook:** Flip up the wire clip and then slide the card, with the AirPort label facing down, under the clip and between the edge guides until it fits snuggly in the slot that's beneath the back edge of the trackpad. Then flip down the clip to hold the card and cable in place. Replace the keyboard, slip the plastic tabs (between the Esc and F1 keys and between the F8 and F9 keys) closed, and reinstall the battery.

- **In a PowerBook:** Insert the card, with antenna cable attached, into the AirPort Card slot at the upper-left corner of the compartment beneath the keyboard, just above the PowerBook's PC Card slot. The card's AirPort label should be facing downward, and any bar code or product ID numbers should be facing upward. Replace the heat shield and the keyboard.

- **In an iMac:** Turn the AirPort Card (still in the iMac AirPort Card Adapter) sideways and insert the AirPort Card into the slot while aligning the edges of the card with the card-edge guides. Close the access panel and reconnect the cables.

- **In a Power Mac:** Slide the card through the opening in the PCI card guide and into the AirPort Card socket on the main logic board. Close the case and reconnect the cables.

"Come in, AirPort Base Station, over . . ."

The Apple access point (AP) is the AirPort Base Station (ABS, to those in the know). In addition to serving as a wireless AP, it can act as a cable/digital subscriber line (DSL) router and Dynamic Host Configuration Protocol (DHCP) server, which automatically assigns a network address to every computer on a network. It even has a built-in dialup modem in case you connect to the Internet that way.

The ABS can be used to connect to American Online (AOL) — most access points don't even have dialup modems any more. And very few can connect to AOL. If you don't have broadband and use AOL, consider buying an ABS as your access point for a Mac network (or even a Windows network) to get this capability.

The exterior of the original version of the AirPort Base Station is a gray color (Graphite). The newest AirPort Base Station is white — the Snow AirPort. The Graphite AirPort Base Station has one Ethernet port that you can use to connect to a cable or a DSL modem so that you can share Internet connectivity among your networked computers. The Snow AirPort Base Station has two Ethernet ports: a local area network (LAN) and a wide area network (WAN). The WAN port connects to your broadband modem, and the LAN port enables you to connect a small, wired network to the Base Station and use the Base Station as a DHCP server and as a cable/DSL router for your wired network as well as your wireless network. (Skip back to Chapter 2 for more about DHCP servers and cable/DSL routers.)

The AirPort Base Station, both the Graphite and Snow versions, also has a 56 Kbps dialup modem that enables you to connect your wireless network to the Internet via a regular phone line, assuming that you have an account with a dialup Internet service provider (ISP). (But see the discussion of connecting to AOL in the "AirPort 2.0 software" section of this chapter.)

The AirPort Extreme Base Station is white, like the Snow version, but is based on the draft IEEE 802.11*g* technology rather than IEEE 802.11*b* technology. (Jump back to Chapter 2 for more about these two technology standards.) As a result, the AirPort Extreme Base Station is capable of transmitting data at 54 Mbps, nearly five times faster than the Graphite and Snow AirPort Base Stations. AirPort Card-equipped Macs can still connect to the AirPort Base Station Extreme but will not enjoy the higher speed. You need an AirPort Extreme card equipped Mac to take full advantage of this state-of-the-art Base Station. In addition, the AirPort Extreme Base Station includes a Universal Serial Bus (USB) port to which you can connect a printer. All computers accessing the wireless network can then print to this printer.

Another new feature of the AirPort Extreme Base Station is a bridging feature. You can now use two base stations together to extend the range of your wireless network without the need to run network cabling between the two base stations.

The AirPort Extreme Base Station offers all these new features and is less expensive than its predecessors. (Both earlier Base Station models had a retail price of $299.) There are two models of the AirPort Extreme Base Station. The basic model has all the features described earlier (sells for $199), and the deluxe model (retail price of $249) adds a v.90 (56 Kbps) modem and a port for attaching an external range-extending antenna.

Apple AirPort Software Updates

Apple has been a pioneer in wireless networking, but as more and more people use wireless networking and as the number of companies producing Wi-Fi equipment grows, Apple has continued to improve its wireless products. Amazingly, the majority of the improvements can be applied to the original AirPort Card and AirPort Base Station through software upgrades. In general, if you keep your Mac OS software current (as of this writing, Mac OS v. 10.2.3) and your AirPort firmware up to date, you will be able to take advantage of most of the new wireless networking features. (*Note:* You cannot upgrade an AirPort Card to an AirPort Extreme Card through a firmware update.)

Rather than waiting to release all new features at once, Apple continually puts out updates to its AirPort software. Read on to discover how each of the new versions of AirPort software can benefit your wireless network.

AirPort 2.0 software

When Apple released the Snow AirPort Base Station, it upgraded the AirPort software to version 2.0. Your computer must have Mac OS v. 9.0.4 or later to install this software. Compared with the original Graphite AirPort Base Station, AirPort 2.0 adds the following features:

✔ **America Online compatibility:** If you use AOL to connect to the Internet over a dialup phone connection, AOL's unique login protocol has been a stumbling block that has prevented you from connecting to the Internet through your AirPort's built-in modem — until now. Apple and AOL have collaborated and come up with a way to enable AOL customers to use AirPort. At the time of this writing, AirPort is the only wireless AP with a built-in modem that also works with AOL. (*Note:* AOL users can wirelessly connect to AOL using any Wi-Fi wireless network that's connected to the Internet via a cable or DSL modem.)

✔ **128-bit encryption:** The security features have been improved in several ways including support for 128-bit encryption. Earlier versions of the base station software supported only 64-bit encryption. *Note:* You cannot upgrade the Graphite Base Station to 128-bit encryption, but you can upgrade your AirPort Cards to 128-bit.

✔ **RADIUS authentication and Cisco LEAP client support:** Remote Authentication Dial-In User Service (RADIUS) and Lightweight Extensible Authentication Protocol (LEAP) are enhanced security options of interest to corporate and university IS departments . . . and are a nice bonus for a wireless home network.

✓ **Support for up to 50 users:** The Graphite AirPort Base Station can handle as many as ten wireless network client devices. The Snow AirPort Base Station can handle up to 50 users (up to about 30 simultaneously). For home use, however, you probably will never exceed ten users.

AirPort 2.0.4 software

But Apple didn't stop adding features with AirPort 2.0. The last version of AirPort 2.0 software that will install on Mac OS 9 (actually version 9.2.1 or higher) is AirPort 2.0.4. In addition to the features in AirPort 2.0, it adds the following:

✓ **Windows VPN support:** The AirPort Base Station is now compatible with Windows Virtual Private Networking (VPN) software that uses Point-to-Point Tunneling Protocol (PPTP) or Internet Protocol Security (IPSec). This is big for businesses and home offices of employees who want to connect to the main company network over the Internet.

✓ **Incoming remote connections:** The AirPort Base Station now supports incoming calls from other computers to the modem port to allow remote access to the network to which the AirPort Base Station is attached.

✓ **Multiple connections to port-mapped services:** This feature is for advanced users and small business owners who plan to host one or more servers on their network. If you plan to host a Web server, File Transfer Protocol (FTP) server, or other public server on your system, you can now map the public ports on the AirPort Base Station to specific private ports on one or more computers on your private network. This feature also comes in handy if you want to connect other devices, such as an Xbox game console, to the AirPort and to Xbox live gaming service.

Most home broadband ISPs don't permit you to operate a server on your home computer because you could potentially hog the bandwidth on their broadband network. For this reason, many broadband service providers meter the upload speeds on home accounts to a rate that would be too slow to host a Web site or other Internet site.

AirPort 2.0.5 software

If you want to take advantage of future upgrades to the AirPort software beyond version 2.0.4, you'll have to upgrade your computer's operating system to at least OS X version 10.1.5. AirPort 2.0.5 is not available for Mac OS 9 computers. You can use AirPort 2.0.5 software to configure or upgrade your AirPort hardware to add the following features:

✔ **Updated firmware:** Version 2.0.5 of the AirPort software includes the latest version of the *firmware* (the product's feature set stored as software on chips inside the card or base station) for both AirPort Cards and AirPort Base Station (v. 4.0.7). Apple recommends this firmware update to customers who have problems connecting to their ISP or to secure Web sites.

✔ **Improved PPPoE support:** Many DSL broadband ISPs use a special protocol — Point-to-Point Protocol over Ethernet (PPPoE) — to provide a very fast Internet connection over normal telephone lines. AirPort 2.0.5 offers improved PPPoE support compared with previous software versions.

AirPort 2.1.1 software

The most current AirPort software (at the time of this writing) is AirPort 2.1.1. If your Mac is running OS version 10.2 (Jaguar) or later, you can use AirPort 2.1.1 to configure or upgrade your AirPort hardware. As is true with AirPort 2.0.5, version 2.1.1of the AirPort software includes the latest version of the firmware for both AirPort Cards and AirPort Base Station. In addition, AirPort 2.1.1 adds the following features:

✔ **Verizon DSL:** This update corrects problems that sometimes occurred with e-mail when an AirPort network was connected to the Internet via Verizon DSL services.

✔ **Added security:** The Base Station administrator (you) can now turn off the capability to configure the AirPort Base Station over the second Ethernet port (the WAN port of the Snow Base Station; see the earlier section "Come in, AirPort Base Station, over . . ."). This eliminates the possibility that someone could reconfigure your Base Station over the Internet.

✔ **Password compatibility:** AirPort 2.1.1 software makes it easier to enter network passwords when you want to connect to a Microsoft Windows-based wireless network. The new software automatically distinguishes between alphanumeric (American Standard Code for Information Interchange; ASCII) and hexadecimal passwords. With earlier versions of the software, to connect to a Wired Equivalent Privacy protocol- (WEP) encrypted Windows-based network, you had to type quotation marks around alphanumeric values and type a dollar sign character ($) in front of hexadecimal numbers. Read the "Connecting to Non-Apple-Based Wireless Networks" section of this chapter for more on this issue.

OS 9 Wireless Networks

When Apple released the first AirPort wireless network concurrently with the release of the first iBook, the most current Apple operating system software was Mac OS 8.6. Apple has since updated the original Mac OS to version 9.2 (9.2.2 at the time of this writing). All Apple computers that are AirPort ready can be upgraded to Mac OS 9.2, although it might not be a free upgrade. This section of the chapter covers configuring your AirPort Card in Mac OS 9.2 but doesn't cover earlier versions of this operating system. If your computer runs Mac OS X (which isn't an update of the original Mac OS; it's a completely new operating system), see the "OS X Wireless Networks" section later in this chapter.

Although you still might be able to find an original (Graphite) AirPort Base Station to purchase, the most current and full-featured model is the dual-Ethernet port (Snow) AirPort Base Station with AirPort 2.0 (or higher) software. Nonetheless, AirPort 2.0 software will install and configure the Graphite or Snow AirPort Base Stations. The major differences between the two versions are the second Ethernet port and 128-bit encryption of the Snow Base Station. And don't forget that the new AirPort Extreme Base Station that can transmit data at 54 Mbps and comes with a built-in print server.

AirPort 2.1.1 is the most current version of the AirPort software at the writing of this book, but it won't install under OS 9.2. Consequently, the following discussion describes the steps and shows screen images that relate to AirPort 2.0.4, which is the last version that will install and set up an AirPort Base Station on OS 9.

If you have access to a computer that has OS X installed, consider using that computer to configure your AirPort Base Station. The AOL compatibility feature of AirPort 2.0.4 software and later versions of the AirPort software can be added and configured only from OS X.

Even though a CD containing AirPort software is distributed with both the Base Station and the AirPort Card, check out the Apple Web site `www.info.apple/support/downloads.html` to make sure that you have the latest version of the AirPort software before setting up your AirPort network.

To set up an AirPort Base Station using the AirPort 2.0.4 software, you must have the Base Station itself as well as the following:

- An AirPort-ready computer with an AirPort Card, or a PowerBook G3 with either a Lucent WaveLAN or an ORiNOCO PC Card
- Mac OS v. 9.2.1 or later

When you run the AirPort software installation, you first install (or upgrade) software on your computer and then upgrade the firmware that's built into the AirPort Base Station. Finally, you configure the Base Station. The sections that follow take you through the process step by step.

Installing AirPort software on Mac OS 9

To install AirPort software on your computer, follow these steps:

1. **Close all open applications.**

   The installation process will cause the computer to restart, and you certainly don't want to lose any of your work.

2. **If you're installing the software from a CD-ROM, insert the CD-ROM and double-click the** Install Mac OS 9 **file.**

   Alternatively, you can download the most current version of the software from the Apple Web site (www.info.apple/support/downloads.html) and then double-click the Apple SW Install file.

   The Welcome window appears, as shown in Figure 8-1.

Figure 8-1:
The AirPort
2.0.4 Install
AirPort
Welcome
screen.

3. **Click the Continue button to display the Select Destination window, choose the drive where you want the software to be installed from the Destination Disk list, and then click the Select button to display the Software License Agreement.**

4. **Read the license agreement; if you agree, click the Continue button and then click the Agree button to display the About AirPort window.**

5. **After reading and/or printing the contents of the About AirPort window, click the Continue button to display the Install/Remove Software window.**

6. **In the Install/Remove Software window, click the Start button to display a warning screen that the software installation will restart your computer, which requires it to first quit all applications that are running.**

You can click the Stop button to abort the installation program and return to any application that you accidentally left open so that you can save your work and close it down yourself. You'll just have to start the AirPort software installation again when you're ready.

7. **After you click the Continue button, the installer closes all running applications and then copies the AirPort software to your computer's drive.**

A message displays that the installation process is finished.

8. **Click the Restart button to restart your computer.**

Upgrading AirPort Base Station firmware on OS 9

This section explains how to upgrade the firmware of a new AirPort Base Station. Upgrading the firmware on your AirPort Base Station through a direct Ethernet cable connection is the easiest route. Use an Ethernet cable (either a straight-through cable or a cross-over cable; the Base Station automatically detects the type of cable that you're using) to connect your computer's Ethernet port to the Base Station's LAN port.

To make sure that your computer can recognize the AirPort Base Station in order to upgrade its firmware, execute the following steps:

1. **Open the Control Panels menu by clicking the Apple menu icon (**🍎**) in the upper-left corner of your screen and then selecting Control Panels.**

2. **Choose TCP/IP to display the TCP/IP control panel.**

3. **Choose Ethernet from the Connect Via pop-up menu and then choose Using DHCP Server from the Configure pop-up menu.**

These settings will cause your computer to request an Internet Protocol (IP) address from the AirPort Base Station that will enable your computer and the Base Station to communicate.

4. **Close the control panel; if prompted to save changes, click the Save button.**

5. **To check whether TCP/IP is properly configured, repeat Steps 1 and 2.**

   The IP address should now be listed as 10.0.1.2 with subnet mask 255.255.255.0 and router address 10.0.1.1. If you don't see these numbers, check that the AirPort Base Station is turned on and that the Ethernet cable is plugged in securely on both ends. Then go through these steps again.

To upgrade the firmware of a new AirPort Base Station that you're setting up for the first time, follow these steps:

1. **Double-click the desktop icon for the hard disk on which you installed the AirPort software.**

   The AirPort folder is located in the Apple Extras folder, which can be found in the Applications folder.

2. **When the hard disk's folder opens, open the Applications (Mac OS 9) folder, the Apple Extras folder, and the AirPort folder, in that order.**

   The open AirPort folder is shown in Figure 8-2.

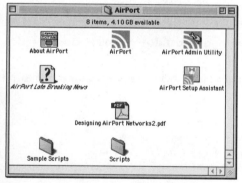

Figure 8-2:
The AirPort
2.0.4 AirPort
folder.

3. **Double-click the AirPort Admin Utility icon to display the Select Base Station window, as shown in Figure 8-3.**

   You should see Base Station in the Name list. This is the factory-supplied name for your AirPort Base Station. It should have the IP address 10.0.1.1.

4. **Click Base Station to highlight it and then click the Configure button.**

   A message pops up requesting a password.

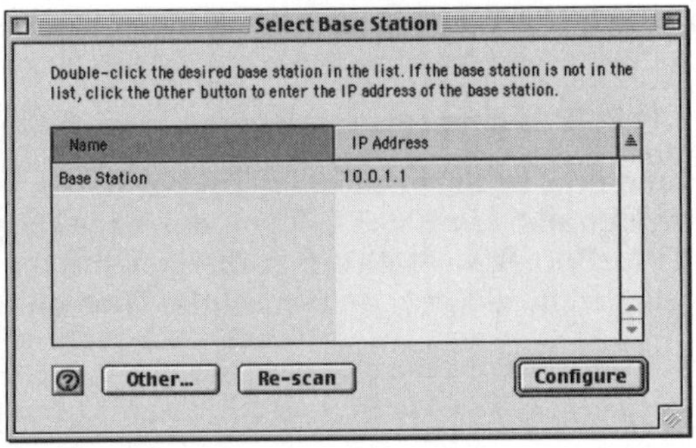

Figure 8-3:
The AirPort
2.0.4 Select
Base
Station
window.

5. **Enter** public **as the password and then click OK.**

   If the firmware installed in the Base Station is older than the firmware that was supplied with your updated software, you see a message prompting you that a newer version of the Base Station software is available.

   • In this message window, click the Upload button to install the newer software.

   • If a message pops up stating that uploading the software will cause the wireless network to be disconnected, click OK.

   The new firmware is copied to the Base Station, and a message box displays showing progress.

6. **When the Select Base Station window returns, close it (click the X in the upper-right corner).**

7. **Disconnect the Ethernet cable between your computer and the Base Station.**

Configuring the AirPort Base Station on OS 9

After you're sure that your AirPort Base Station has the most current firmware, the easiest way to set it up for use in your wireless home network is to use the AirPort Setup Assistant. The AirPort Setup Assistant reads the Internet settings from your computer and transfers them to the Base Station so that you can access the Internet over your wireless network. To use the AirPort Setup Assistant, follow these steps:

1. **Before running the AirPort Setup Assistant, set up your computer to connect to the Internet by dialup modem or by broadband (cable or DSL) modem.**

   Your ISP will provide instructions for getting connected.

   - **If you connect to the Internet by dialup modem:** Connect the telephone line to the phone line port on the Base Station.

   - **If you connect to the Internet by DSL or cable modem:** Use an Ethernet cable to connect the modem to the Base Station's WAN port.

2. **Double-click the desktop icon for the hard disk on which you installed the AirPort software.**

3. **When the hard disk's folder opens, open the Applications (Mac OS 9) folder, the Apple Extras folder, and the AirPort folder, in that order.**

4. **In the AirPort folder, double-click the AirPort Setup Assistant icon to display the AirPort Setup Assistant pane, shown in Figure 8-4.**

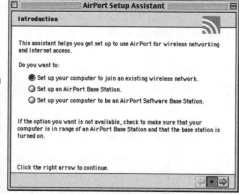

Figure 8-4:
The OS 9
AirPort
Setup
Assistant
window.

5. **Select the Set Up an AirPort Base Station radio button and then click the right arrow in the lower-right corner of the window to display the Internet Choice panel.**

   The Internet Choice panel asks whether your computer is set up to access the Internet.

6. **To copy the Internet settings — such as the logon ID and password to connect to a dialup ISP or to a DSL account — from your computer to the Base Station, click Yes.**

The Setup Assistant displays the PPPoE panel. Most DSL service providers use Point-to-Point Protocol over Ethernet (PPPoE).

- **If your service provider uses PPPoE:** Click the Yes button.

- **If your DSL provider doesn't use PPPoE, or if you connect to the Internet via a dialup connection or by cable modem:** Click the No button.

If your computer is in range of only your one wireless network, the Setup Assistant will automatically configure your AirPort Card to select that network. However, if you happen to be in range of more than one wireless network, you'll be asked to select your network from a list. Your network will have the name assigned at the factory, similar to *Apple Network xxxxxx* where *xxxxxx* is a hexadecimal number assigned by the software.

7. **Click the right arrow at the lower-right corner of the window to display the Internet Access panel.**

8. **In the Internet Access panel, select the Internet settings to use to configure your Base Station.**

   - In most cases, you should use the default setting that permits the Base Station to assign an IP address to each computer on the wireless network through its DHCP server's software. Just leave the setting as it is.

   - If your service has assigned a specific IP address to your system, click the Details button and enter the settings manually in the panel that pops up as directed by your ISP.

9. **Click the right arrow at the lower-right corner of the window to display Network Name and Password panel.**

10. **In the Network Name and Password panel, enter the name and password that you want to use for your wireless network.**

11. **Click the right arrow to display the Base Station Password panel.**

    The Base Station Password panel gives you the options to use the network password as your Base Station password or to assign a different password for changing the settings on your Base Station.

    - **If you're the only person who will be entering the password:** Using the same password both places is probably easiest.

    - **If you plan to share the network password with other users:** Assign a different password to the Base Station so that only you can change the Base Station's settings.

12. **Click the right arrow to display the Conclusion panel.**

    The Conclusion panel informs you that the Setup Assistant is ready to set up your Base Station.

13. **Click the Go Ahead button to proceed.**

    After the AirPort Setup Assistant downloads the new settings to the Base Station, it displays a message that it's waiting for the Base Station to restart. As soon as the Base Station restarts, it displays a panel announcing that it's finished and that it's ready to connect to the Internet.

14. **Click the Connect Now button.**

    The Setup Assistant closes itself, launches Internet Explorer, and connects to the browser's default home page. You're in!

Adding a computer to your AirPort network on OS 9

When you set up your AirPort Base Station by following the directions in the "Configuring the AirPort Base Station on OS 9" section of this chapter, you also set up the AirPort Card in the computer that you used to configure the Base Station. However, you still need to configure the AirPort Cards in the other Mac computers in your house. Follow these steps:

1. **Double-click the desktop icon for the hard disk on which you installed the AirPort software.**

2. **When the hard disk's folder opens, open the Applications (Mac OS 9) folder, the Apple Extras folder, and the AirPort folder, in that order.**

3. **In the AirPort folder, double-click the AirPort Setup Assistant icon to display the AirPort Setup Assistant window (refer to Figure 8-4).**

4. **Select the Set Up Your Computer to Join an Existing Wireless Network radio button and then click the right arrow in the lower-right corner of the window to display the Select an AirPort Network panel.**

    If your AirPort Base Station is the only wireless network within range, its network name will be displayed to the right of the AirPort Networks Available heading.

    If you live close enough to a neighbor who also has a wireless network, you might see the network name of your neighbor's network.

    a. **To replace your neighbor's network name with your own, click the double arrow to the right of the network name and then select your network name from the pop-up list that appears.**

    b. **Click the right arrow in the lower-right corner of the window to go to the next panel.**

5. **Type the network password for your wireless network in the Password text box and then click the right arrow in the lower-right corner of the window to go to the final panel.**

6. **Click the Go Ahead button.**

7. **When a message displays that the AirPort Setup Assistant is done, click the Connect Now button.**

   The assistant closes itself and launches Internet Explorer. If a Web page displays, the connection is a success, and you've added another computer to your wireless home network.

OS X Wireless Networks

AirPort 2.1.1 is the most current version of the AirPort software as of the writing of this book. Consequently, the following discussion describes the steps and shows screen images that relate to AirPort 2.1.1. If you use a later version to set up your AirPort network, the screens might look slightly different.

Even though a CD containing AirPort software is distributed with both the AirPort Base Station and the AirPort Card, check out the Apple Web site www.info.apple/support/downloads.html to make sure that you have the latest version of the AirPort software before setting up your AirPort network.

To set up an AirPort Base Station using the AirPort 2.1.1 software, you must have the Base Station itself as well as the following:

- ✔ An AirPort-ready computer with an AirPort Card
- ✔ Mac OS X version 10.2 or later

If you have a third-party wireless networking card in your PowerBook PC Card slot, use the software that came with the card to configure your network.

When you run the AirPort software installation, you first install (or upgrade) software on your computer and then upgrade the firmware that's built into the AirPort Base Station. Finally, you configure the Base Station. The sections that follow take you through the process step by step.

Installing the AirPort software on OS X

To install AirPort software on your computer under OS X, follow these steps:

1. **Close all applications.**

   The installation process will restart your computer, so save your work and close all applications before starting the installation procedure.

2. **If you're installing the software from a CD-ROM, insert the CD-ROM and double-click the** Install Mac OS X.pkg **package file.**

   Alternatively, you can download the most current version of the software from the Apple Web site (www.info.apple/support/downloads. html).

   If you download the software, the file will bear a .dmg extension denoting it as a disk image file.

3. **Double-click the file name.**

   The Disk Copy application runs, creates a Disk icon on the desktop, and then opens the disk in the Finder.

4. **Double-click the package file** AirPortSW.pkg **in the Finder window.**

5. **If an Authenticate pane pops up prompting you for a password, enter the password that you use to log on to your computer.**

   The Welcome to the AirPort Installer panel displays.

6. **Click the Continue button to display Important Information; read this information and then click the Continue button to display the Software License Agreement.**

7. **Read the license agreement; if you agree, click the Continue button and then click the Agree button to display the Select a Destination panel.**

8. **Chose the drive where you want the software to be installed from the Destination Disk list and then click the Continue button to display the Easy Install panel.**

9. **Click the Upgrade button and then click the Continue Installation button.**

   The Installation program installs the software and optimizes system performance, showing you a progress bar while it's doing so.

10. **When a message displays announcing that the software installation was successful, click the Restart button to close the installation software and to restart your computer.**

Upgrading AirPort Base Station firmware on OS X

In this section, we explain how to upgrade the firmware of a new AirPort Base Station. Upgrading the firmware on your AirPort Base Station through a direct Ethernet cable connection is easiest. Use an Ethernet cable (either a straight-through cable or a cross-over cable; the Base Station automatically detects the type of cable that you're using) to connect your computer's Ethernet port to the Base Station's LAN port. You can also do the upgrade over a wireless connection.

To upgrade the firmware of a new AirPort Base Station that you're setting up for the first time, follow these steps:

1. **Double-click the desktop icon for the hard disk on which you installed the AirPort software.**

2. **When the hard disk's folder opens, open the Applications folder and then open the Utilities folder.**

3. **Double-click the AirPort Admin Utility icon to display the Select Base Station window, shown in Figure 8-5.**

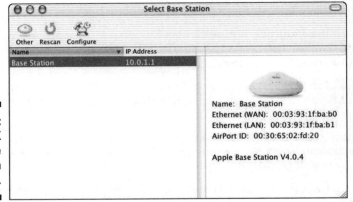

Figure 8-5:
The OS X
Select Base
Station
window.

You should see Base Station in the Name list. This is the factory-supplied name for your AirPort Base Station. It should have the IP address 10.0.1.1.

4. **Highlight the Base Station name and then click the Configure button.**

5. **After a message pops up requesting a password, enter** public **as the password and then click OK.**

   • If the firmware installed in the Base Station is older than the firmware that was supplied with your updated software, you see a message prompting you that a newer version of the Base Station software is available. Click the Upload button to install it.

   • If a message pops up stating that uploading the software will cause the wireless network to be disconnected, click OK. The new firmware is copied to the Base Station.

   Note: If the Base Station window displays when you click the Configure button — rather than a message that a newer version of the Base Station software is available — your Base Station already contains the most recent firmware. Close the Base Station window and then close the AirPort Admin Utility.

6. **After a message displays that the system is waiting for the Base Station to restart and that the Base Station has been successfully updated, click OK.**

7. **When the Select Base Station window returns, close it.**

8. **Disconnect the Ethernet cable between your computer and the Base Station.**

Configuring the AirPort Base Station on OS X

After you're sure that your AirPort Base Station has the most current firmware, the easiest way to set it up for use in your wireless home network is to use the AirPort Setup Assistant. The AirPort Setup Assistant reads the Internet settings from your computer and transfers them to the Base Station so that you can access the Internet over your wireless network. To use the AirPort Setup Assistant, follow these steps:

1. **Before running the AirPort Setup Assistant, set up your computer to connect to the Internet by dialup modem or by broadband (cable or DSL) modem.**

   Check with your ISP for instructions on getting connected.

   • **If you connect to the Internet by dialup modem:** Connect the telephone line to the phone line port on the Base Station.

   • **If you connect to the Internet by DSL or cable modem:** Use an Ethernet cable to connect the modem to the Base Station's WAN port.

2. **Double-click the desktop icon for the hard disk on which you installed the AirPort software.**

3. **When the hard disk's folder opens, open the Applications folder and then open the Utilities folder.**

4. **In the Utilities folder, double-click the AirPort Setup Assistant icon to display the AirPort Setup Assistant window, as shown in Figure 8-6.**

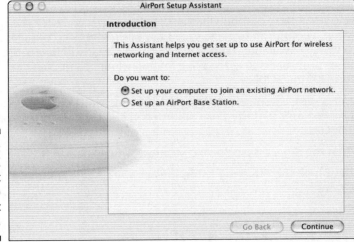

Figure 8-6:
The OS X
AirPort
Setup
Assistant
window.

5. **Select the Set Up an AirPort Base Station radio button and then click the Continue button in the lower-right corner of the window.**

   If your computer is in range of only your one wireless network, the Setup Assistant automatically configures your AirPort Card to select that network and proceeds to the America Online Access panel. However, if you happen to be in range of more than one wireless network, you see the Select an AirPort Network panel that asks you to select your network from a pop-up list. Your network will have the name assigned at the factory, similar to *Apple Network xxxxxx* where *xxxxxx* is a six-digit hexadecimal number. After selecting your network, click the Continue button to go to the next panel.

6. **In the America Online Access panel:**

   • **If you connect to the Internet via AOL:** Select the I Am Using American Online radio button and then click the Continue button.

   • **If you're not using AOL:** Select the I Am Using Another Internet Service Provider radio button and then click the Continue button to display the Internet Access panel.

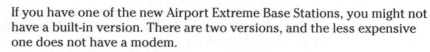

7. **In the Internet Access panel, choose one of the following options and then click the Continue button:**

   - **Telephone Modem:** Select this radio button if you connect to the Internet through a dialup modem. The AirPort Base Station is one of the few wireless access points that includes a 56 Kbps modem. By choosing this option, all the computers connected to your wireless network might be able to share a single dialup connection.

If you have one of the new Airport Extreme Base Stations, you might not have a built-in version. There are two versions, and the less expensive one does not have a modem.

   - **Local Area Network:** You should select this radio button if your computer is connected to a high-speed LAN.

   - **Cable Modem or DSL Using Static IP or DHCP:** Select this radio button if you connect to the Internet by cable modem or by DSL but only if your ISP doesn't use the PPP over Ethernet (PPPoE) protocol.

   - **Cable Modem or DSL Using PPPoE:** If your ISP uses the PPPoE protocol, select this radio button. It is important that you make a successful connection to the Internet with your computer connected directly to the cable or DSL modem before attempting to configure the Base Station. The AirPort Setup Assistant will then be able to copy the PPPoE settings from your computer to the Base Station so that the Base Station can log on to the Internet with your user ID and password. All the computers on your wireless network will then be able to share the Internet connection without needing to log on.

The next panel that you see at this step depends on the choice that you make in Step 7:

   - **Telephone Modem:** If you choose Telephone Modem, you see the Modem Access panel with text boxes available for various dialup parameters such as user name, password, and phone number. In most cases, the setup assistant copies this information from your computer.

   - **LAN, or Broadband Using Static IP or DHCP:** If you choose either a LAN or a broadband (cable modem or DSL) connection that doesn't use PPPoE, the Ethernet Access panel presents the option to use DHCP or to assign a static IP address. If your ISP has assigned you a static IP address — along with other values such as subnet mask, router address, domain name, and/or DHCP client name — you have to enter this data if it isn't automatically copied from your computer.

- **Broadband Using PPPoE:** If you select the Cable Modem or DSL Using PPPoE option, the PPPoE Access panel presents text boxes for entering an account name, password, and other account information sometimes required by PPPoE providers. Again, in most cases, this information is automatically copied from your computer.

After you enter the appropriate information, click the Continue button to display the Network Name and Password panel.

8. **In the Network Name and Password panel that appears, enter the name and password that you want to use for your wireless network and then click the Continue button to display the Base Station Password panel.**

The Base Station Password panel gives you the options to use the network password as your Base Station password or to assign a different password for changing the settings on your Base Station. If you're the only person who'll be configuring the computers on the network, using the same one both places is probably the easiest. However, if you plan to share the network password with other users, assign a different password to the Base Station so that only you can change the Base Station's settings.

9. **Click the Continue button to display the Conclusion panel.**

The Conclusion panel informs you that the Setup Assistant is ready to set up your Base Station.

10. **Click the Continue button.**

After the Setup Assistant downloads the new settings to the Base Station, it displays a message that it's waiting for the Base Station to reset. As soon as the Base Station resets, the Setup Assistant displays a panel announcing that it's finished and that it has been able to configure this computer to connect to the Internet.

11. **Click the Done button to close the AirPort Setup Assistant.**

Adding another computer to your AirPort network on OS X

When you set up your AirPort Base Station by following the directions in the preceding section ("Configuring the AirPort Base Station on OS X"), you also set up the AirPort Card in the computer that you used to configure the Base Station. However, you need to configure the AirPort Cards in the other Mac computers in your house to enable them to connect to the AirPort network. Follow these steps:

1. **Double-click the desktop icon for the hard disk on which you installed the AirPort software.**

2. **When the hard disk's folder opens, open the Applications folder and then open the Utilities folder.**

3. **In the Utilities folder, double-click the AirPort Setup Assistant icon to display the AirPort Setup Assistant window (refer to Figure 8-6).**

4. **Select the Set Up Your Computer to Join an Existing AirPort Network radio button and then click the Continue button to display the Select an AirPort Network panel.**

   If your AirPort Base Station is the only wireless network within range, the next panel will prompt you to enter the network password. However, if you happen to live close enough to neighbors who also have a wireless network, you might see the network name of that neighbor's network.

5. **Select your network name from the pop-up list and then click the Continue button to display the Enter Network Password panel.**

6. **Type the network password for your wireless network in the Password text box and then click the Continue button to display the Conclusion panel.**

7. **Click the Continue button.**

8. **When a message displays that the AirPort Setup Assistant is finished, click the Done button.**

   The assistant closes itself.

Adding a Non-Apple Computer to Your AirPort Network

One of the reasons why wireless home networking has become so popular is the interoperability between wireless networking equipment from different vendors. Apple wireless networking equipment is no exception. You can even use a Windows or Linux computer to connect to an Apple AirPort Base Station.

The procedure for entering the wireless network parameters in non-Apple wireless software for configuring a wireless network adapter varies by manufacturer. Follow these general steps to add your non-Apple computer (or even Apple computer with non-Apple wireless hardware and software) to your AirPort Network:

1. **Select the network name of the AirPort Base Station.**

   The wireless network adapter configuration software will usually present a list of available wireless networks in range of the adapter. Select the network name that you assigned to the AirPort Base Station from the list.

   For example, in Windows XP, right-click the Network icon in the notification area of the task bar and then select View Available Wireless Networks from the pop-up menu that appears. Then select the AirPort Base Stations network name from the list presented in the Wireless Network Connection dialog box.

2. **Enter the network password.**

   The password that you entered in the AirPort Base Station setup probably won't work. Here's how to find the password — the WEP key — that will work. Apple uses a different password naming convention than other wireless manufacturers. Fortunately, Apple has provided the AirPort Admin Utility that does the conversion for you:

   a. **Open the AirPort Admin Utility.**

   b. **Select your Base Station from the list and then click the Configure icon.**

   c. **When presented with a pop-up window, enter the password for configuring the base station and then click the OK button to display the main AirPort Admin Utility window.**

   d. **If you're using OS X, click the Password icon in the toolbar at the top of the window.**

      Note: If the toolbar isn't visible, click the View menu and choose Show Toolbar.

      The utility opens a drop-down window that displays the equivalent network password (WEP key) that you should enter in the configuration software for your non-Apple wireless network adapter.

   e. **If you're using OS 9, choose Equivalent Network Password from the Base Station menu.**

      A pop-up window appears with the equivalent network password (WEP key) that you should enter in the configuration software for your non-Apple wireless network adapter.

3. **Make sure that you set the adapter to obtain an IP address automatically.**

   How you do this depends on what kind of PC and which PC operating system you're using.

4. **Close the configuration software, and you should be connected to the AirPort network.**

   If you're not connected, go through the steps again, paying particular attention that you enter the equivalent network password correctly.

If you're really having a hard time, try turning WEP off on your AirPort Base Station (deselect the Use Encryption check box in the Airport Setup Program) and see whether you can connect without any encryption. If this works, double-check your Equivalent Network Password and look in the manual for your network adapter. You might need to enter a special code before the Equivalent Network Password — we discuss this in Chapter 10.

Connecting to Non-Apple-Based Wireless Networks

One scenario that you might encounter in a home network is the need to connect a Macintosh computer to a non-Apple-based network. Follow the procedures outlined in this chapter for adding a computer to a wireless network. If you have any trouble, it will almost certainly relate to the network password. Here are a few troubleshooting tips to resolve password issues:

✔ **Try turning off encryption on the wireless network.** If you can successfully connect your Mac to the network without the need of a password, you can be sure that the password was the problem. Don't leave the network unprotected, however. Read on.

✔ **Check the password configuration.** When you turn on the access point's encryption, determine whether the password is an alphanumeric value or a hexadecimal number. Some hardware vendors provide configuration software that has you enter a pass phrase, but the software then generates a hexadecimal number. You have to enter the hexadecimal number in the AirPort software, not the pass phrase.

✔ **Watch for case-sensitivity.** If the Windows-based access point configuration software enables you to enter an alphanumeric password, keep in mind that the password is case sensitive. The password should be either exactly 5 characters (letters and/or numbers) for 64-bit encryption or 13 characters for 128-bit encryption. You should then enter exactly the same characters in the Password text box in the AirPort configuration software.

✔ **Use current software.** Make sure that you're using the most current version of AirPort software. The most up-to-date software makes it easier to enter passwords connecting to a Windows-based wireless network. The new software automatically distinguishes between alphanumeric and hexadecimal passwords. With earlier versions of the software, to connect to a WEP-encrypted Windows-based network, you have to type quotation marks around alphanumeric values and type a $ in front of hexadecimal numbers.

These guidelines should help you get your Mac connected to a Windows wireless network, including the capability to share the Internet. Keep in mind, however, that other factors determine whether you can also share files, printers, and other resources over the wireless network. Mac OS X is generally more PC friendly than Mac OS 9, but OS 9-based utility software such as the DAVE software from Thursby Software Systems (www.thursby.com) is available that enables you to add your Mac to a Windows network to share files and printers.

Chapter 9

Setting Up Internet Sharing

● ●

In This Chapter

▶ Using an Internet gateway or router

▶ Obtaining an IP address automatically in Windows 9*x*/2000/XP and Mac OS 9/X

▶ Internet connection sharing in Windows 98/98 SE/2000/Me/XP and Mac OS X

● ●

*O*ne of the most popular uses of personal computers is to access the Internet. In this chapter, we describe how you can use a network, including a wireless network, to share a single Internet connection among all the computers on the network. We also describe how to obtain an Internet Protocol (IP) address automatically in Windows 9*x*/2000/XP and Mac OS 9/X. In addition, the chapter explains how to set up sharing of Internet connections without the need to buy a router in Windows 98/98 SE/2000/Me/XP and Mac OS X.

In Chapter 7, we describe how to set up and configure wireless network interface adapters using the installation software that accompanies the adapters. When you set up wireless adapters that way, the installation software (in most cases) properly configures the adapter to make it possible for computers on the network to communicate and to take advantage of the Internet-sharing capabilities of Internet gateways, Dynamic Host Configuration Protocol (DHCP) servers, and cable/digital subscriber line (DSL) routers. Occasionally, however, you might need to change network settings of a wireless network adapter.

Deciding How to Share Your Internet Connection

Whether you've installed a wireless network or are using some other type of network devices to create a home network, you no doubt want all your networked computers to have access to an Internet connection. Here are two ways to share an Internet connection over the network:

✔ **Connection sharing:** All network users access the Internet via one computer that's specifically set up for doing just that.

✔ **A router or an Internet gateway:** A router handles the traffic management to enable all network users access to the Internet. An Internet gateway is a broadband modem with a bundled-in router. A wireless Internet gateway adds an access point (AP) to the mix.

Connection sharing

Windows 98 and later versions of Windows enable Internet connection sharing, as does Mac OS X. When using this method to share an Internet connection, each computer in a wired or wireless network is set up to connect to the Internet through the computer that's connected to the modem that's connected to the Internet. The disadvantage with this system is that you can't turn off or remove the computer that's connected to the modem without also disconnecting all computers from the Internet. In addition, simultaneous usage (several people on the network using the Internet at once) can slow down the computer providing the connection.

Mac OS 9 and Mac OS X v. 10.2 (called Jaguar) or later include a program for the Apple AirPort system called AirPort Software Base Station. The Base Station enables you to share an Internet connection by creating a software-based wireless Base Station in one of the computers on your network. Other computers on the network with wireless network adapters can access the Internet through the soft Base Station. Again, the computer that's running this Base Station software has to be turned on for the other computers in the wireless network to gain access to the Internet, and this Base Station computer is affected by the same performance degradation as in the preceding scenario.

Routers and gateways

By connecting a router between the broadband modem and your home network, all computers on the network can access the Internet without going through another computer. The Internet connection no longer depends on any computer on the network.

The types of routers used in homes are often cable/DSL routers. These devices are also DHCP servers and also include Network Address Translation (NAT) services. The most popular type of device for sharing an Internet connection over a home network, often described as a *wireless gateway*, combines the features of a router, a DHCP server, a NAT server, and the capabilities of a wireless AP. In addition to wireless connectivity, most of these devices also have several Ethernet ports for connecting computers with network cable, giving you the flexibility of adding wired devices and expanding your network connections. Each computer connects to the wireless gateway; the wireless gateway device connects to the broadband (usually DSL or cable) modem; and the modem connects to the Internet.

The nature of the Internet and Transmission Control Protocol/Internet Protocol (TCP/IP) networking requires that every machine or device connecting has to have a unique IP address. For information to get to its proper destination, every piece of information has to contain the IP address that it came from and the IP address that it's going to for it to get from one point to another.

A NAT server allows for the conversion of one IP address to one or many other IP addresses. This means that a whole group of computers can look like just one computer to the rest of the Internet. This is becoming more the norm in both home and corporate networks these days because we have many more computers and devices using the Internet today than we have IP addresses to give them. Connecting to an Internet service provider (ISP) will typically deliver one IP address to the device performing the connection. This is true for dialup, cable, and satellite modems as well as DSL. That IP address is used by the computer or Internet gateway that the modem connects to.

If you have one computer, getting an IP address assigned to your computer is very simple because the modem device delivers the IP address to the computer, and the computer uses that address as its own and connects to the Internet. If you have more than one computer or device to connect, you have to share that one IP address that the modem receives among those machines. NAT creates an internal addressing scheme using one of the reserved IP address ranges that the Internet does not use. (192.168.$x.x$ is one of two Class B networks that are used internally to home or office networks using NAT.) Many companies and almost all cable/DSL routers use these address ranges on the networks behind them. In many cases, it's a given that the IP address of the cable/DSL router will be 192.168.1.1 or 192.168.2.1, depending on which address NAT is configured to use.

After the address translation is in place, a DHCP server then assigns the local IP addresses for all the devices connected inside your home network. The Internet gateway's NAT function enables all computers connected to the Internet through the Internet gateway device to share the same IP address on the Internet. Figure 9-1 depicts a wireless home network that uses an Internet gateway providing NAT and DHCP to share Internet access to three computers over wireless connections and to two more over wired connections.

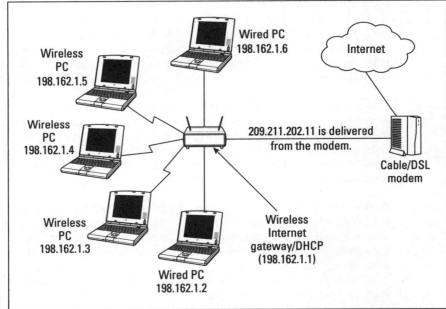

Figure 9-1:
A wireless
home
network
using a
wireless
Internet
gateway
device
shares an
Internet
connection
with wired
and
wireless
computers.

Sharing dialup Internet connections

You can use connection sharing and a home network to share a single dialup connection. This would be especially practical if you have a dedicated telephone line for Internet access. You can use a dialup modem to connect to the Internet on the dedicated line, leave the connection running, and then share this connection with all the computers on your home network so that they can access the Internet.

Similarly, if you purchase an Internet gateway that includes a dialup modem, you can use the gateway to share a dialup connection. You can connect the gateway to the Internet using the dialup modem and then use the gateway's router feature to share this connection with all the networked computers. Some Internet gateways (usually those designed for small businesses) combine both a broadband (DSL usually) modem and a dialup modem in one box. You can use the dialup modem as a backup system if your broadband connection ever goes down.

Apple's AirPort Base Station does include a dialup modem (standard on older AirPort Base Stations and optional on the AirPort Extreme Base Station) and also includes ISP logon features that can successfully connect to AOL, but you still need multiple AOL accounts for multiple users to access the Internet simultaneously through AOL.

Obtaining an IP Address Automatically

For the computers in your home network to communicate effectively with one another, whether connected to the network by wire or wirelessly, all computers must have IP (network) addresses on the same *subnet* — the network address equivalent of having house addresses in the same Zip code or having phone numbers in the same area code. For example, the local IP addresses 192.168.*0*.1 and 192.168.*0*.55 are on the same subnet, but the IP addresses 192.168.*0*.1 and 192.168.*1*.55 are not. Note that the number after the second dot (referred to by computer geeks as the *third octet*) must be the same for the address to be in the same subnet. In addition, all must have the same subnet mask, which is typically 255.255.255.0.

A *subnet* (or subnetwork) is simply a portion of a network (like your home wireless network) that has been portioned off and grouped together as a single unit. When you use a wireless Internet gateway, all your computers are placed into the same subnet. The single IP address assigned to your modem can provide Internet access to all the computers on the subnet. The actual numbers used to identify the subnet are the *subnet mask*. As we mention previously, you'll typically use 255.255.255.0 as your subnet mask. The important thing is to ensure that all the computers and devices connected to your wireless home network also have that same subnet mask assigned to them — otherwise, they won't connect to the Internet. Most of the time, you don't have to do anything here because your computer should have this subnet mask set up by default.

You can manually assign the IP address of each device connected to the network, but (luckily) you usually don't have to worry about using this feature. For some applications, such as gaming or videoconferencing — and for some non-computer devices on your network such as game consoles — you might have to enter a static IP address into your router's configuration. In the majority of cases, however — that is, for most normal PC Internet connections — the DHCP server built into cable/DSL routers and wireless Internet gateways takes care of IP address assignments for you.

One of the most common errors when setting up a home network comes from using a router providing DHCP and NAT and combining it with a wireless access point that also provides DHCP and NAT. If you're using two devices rather than a combined one, you need to be sure that you only enable the DHCP and NAT services on the router that's connected to the modem device. The AP should have an option when it's configured to be set up as a bridge device. This turns off its services and allows the device to be a wireless conduit to the network created by the DHCP and NAT services of the Internet gateway. Failing to do this can result in a segmented home network in which the wired devices cannot share with the wireless devices, or the wireless devices won't be able to share with anything but themselves and will be unable to access the Internet through your ISP.

Suppose that you install a network adapter (refer to Chapter 7), launch your Web browser, and try to reach the Internet. If you then have problems (assuming that everything else is connected and other computers on the network can successfully access the Internet), perhaps the IP address wasn't properly assigned to the adapter. Before you start panicking, try shutting down and restarting the computer. Often, restarting the computer will cause the network adapter to properly obtain an IP address from the network's DHCP server. If you still can't reach the Internet, follow the instructions in this section to configure the network adapter to automatically obtain an IP address. (Also check out Chapter 18, where we cover some basic troubleshooting techniques for home wireless networks.)

Configuring a device on the network (wired or wireless) to automatically obtain an IP address from a DHCP server is very easy. Throughout the rest of this section, we outline the steps necessary for automatically obtaining an IP address from a DHCP server for various operating systems: Windows 9*x*/2000/XP and Mac OS X. After you complete the applicable procedure, the DHCP server leases a local IP address to the device that you are configuring, enabling it to communicate with other IP devices on the network.

Sometimes you have to restart your computer to successfully achieve the desired result.

When a DHCP server *leases* an IP address, the server will not assign that IP address to another device until the lease runs out or the device that is leasing the address releases it. Each time when you restart your computer — or on a periodic basis if you leave your computer on all the time — the DHCP server will renew the lease, allowing the computer to keep the IP address that it has been given.

Domain Name System (DNS) servers

When the DHCP server assigns an IP address, it also specifies the IP addresses for Domain Name System (DNS) servers and for a default gateway. *Domain names* are text-based names that represent one or more registered IP addresses used on the Internet. When you type a Uniform Resource Locator (URL) in your Web browser, DNS servers translate the text-based domain names in the URL into the equivalent IP addresses. You don't have to know the IP addresses, just the domain names. The DNS server addresses will be supplied by your ISP's DHCP server and will be passed on by your home network's DHCP server to each workstation. The *default gateway* takes care of sending network traffic to devices that have IP addresses outside the local subnet. The wireless Internet gateway device or the cable/DSL router that you installed in your wireless network is the default gateway for each of the computers on your network.

Windows 9x

If your computer is running the Windows 9x (95, 98, 98 SE, or Me) operating system, the steps in this section are for you. To instruct the network adapter to obtain its IP address automatically from a DHCP server, follow these steps:

1. **Choose Start⇨Settings⇨Control Panel.**

2. **Double-click the Network icon in the Control Panel.**

   The Network dialog box appears.

3. **In the Configuration tab, highlight the TCP/IP item for the network adapter that you want to configure and then click the Properties button.**

   For example, Figure 9-2 shows the Network dialog box in Windows 9x with the TCP/IP item for Microsoft Broadband Networking Wireless USB Adapter selected.

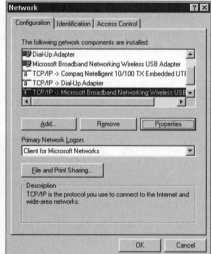

Figure 9-2:
The Network dialog box in Windows 9x.

The TCP/IP Properties dialog box appears, as shown in Figure 9-3.

4. **On the IP Address tab, select the Obtain an IP Address Automatically radio button and then click OK.**

   You're returned to the Network dialog box.

5. **Click OK again to return to the Control Panel.**

6. **Close the Control Panel.**

   Depending on your version of Windows, you might be prompted to insert the Windows CD in the CD drive.

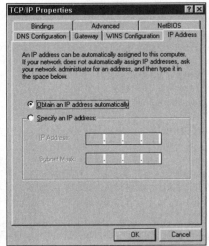

Figure 9-3:
The TCP/IP
Properties
dialog box in
Windows 9x.

7. **Insert the Windows CD and then click OK.**

Windows copies the needed files to your computer's hard drive and then has to restart the computer before the change takes affect. When the computer restarts, Windows will lease an IP address from your network's DHCP server.

Windows 2000

If the computer is running the Widows 2000 operating system, follow these steps to set the network adapter to obtain its IP address automatically from a DHCP server:

1. **Choose Start⇨Settings⇨Network and Dial-up Connections.**

   The Network and Dial-up Connections window appears, as shown in Figure 9-4.

2. **Highlight the Local Area Connection item for the network adapter that you want to configure.**

   In Figure 9-4, the wireless network interface adapter is listed as ORiNOCO PC Card.

3. **Choose File⇨Properties.**

   The Local Area Connection Properties dialog box appears.

4. **Highlight the Internet Protocol (TCP/IP) option and then click the Properties button.**

   The Internet Protocol (TCP/IP) Properties dialog box appears, as shown in Figure 9-5.

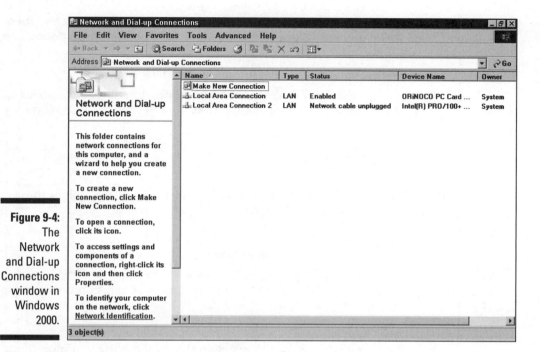

Figure 9-4:
The
Network
and Dial-up
Connections
window in
Windows
2000.

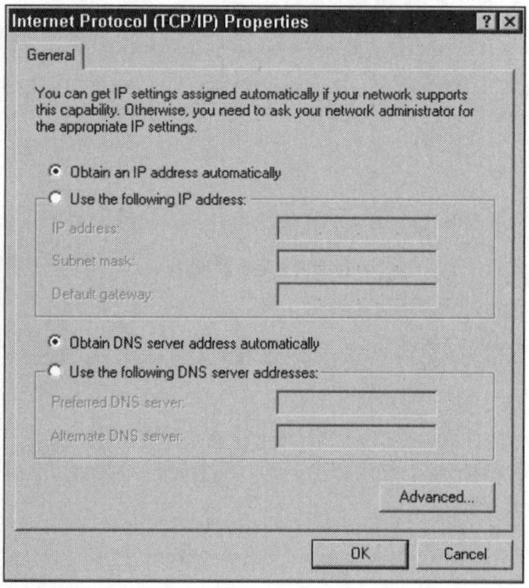

Figure 9-5:
The Internet
Protocol
(TCP/IP)
Properties
dialog box in
Windows
2000.

5. **On the General tab, select both the Obtain an IP Address Automatically and the Obtain DNS Server Address Automatically radio buttons.**

6. **Click OK to return to the Local Area Connections dialog box and then click OK again to return to the Network and Dial-up Connections window.**

7. **Close the Network and Dial-up Connections window.**

   Windows 2000 applies the change to the network settings and obtains an IP address for the network adapter from your network's DHCP server.

Windows XP

If your computer is running the Windows XP operating system, follow these steps to set the network adapter to obtain its IP address automatically from a DHCP server:

1. **Choose Start⇨Network Connections.**

   If Network Connections doesn't appear in the Start menu, choose Control Panel and then double-click the Network Connections icon in the Control Panel.

   The Network Connections window appears, as shown in Figure 9-6.

2. **In the LAN or High-Speed Internet section of the Network Connections window, highlight the Wireless Network Connection item for the network adapter that you want to configure.**

   For example, in Figure 9-6, the wireless network interface adapter device is listed as ORiNOCO PC Card (5 Volt) in the Network Connections window.

3. **Choose File⇨Properties.**

   The Wireless Network Connection Properties dialog box appears.

4. **On the General tab, highlight the Internet Protocol (TCP/IP) option, and then click the Properties button.**

   The Internet Protocol (TCP/IP) Properties dialog box appears, as shown in Figure 9-7.

5. **On the General tab, select both the Obtain an IP Address Automatically and the Obtain DNS Server Address Automatically radio buttons and then click OK.**

   You're returned to the Wireless Network Connection Properties dialog box.

6. **Click OK again to return to the Network Connections window and then close that window.**

   Windows XP applies the change to the network settings and obtains an IP address for the network adapter from your network's DHCP server.

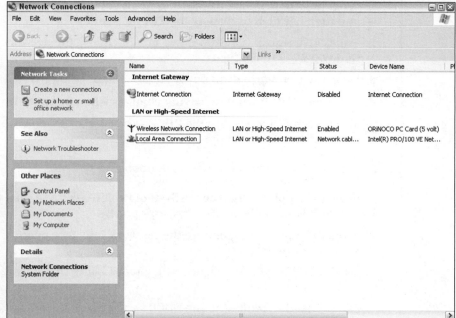

Figure 9-6:
The
Network
Connections
window in
Windows
XP.

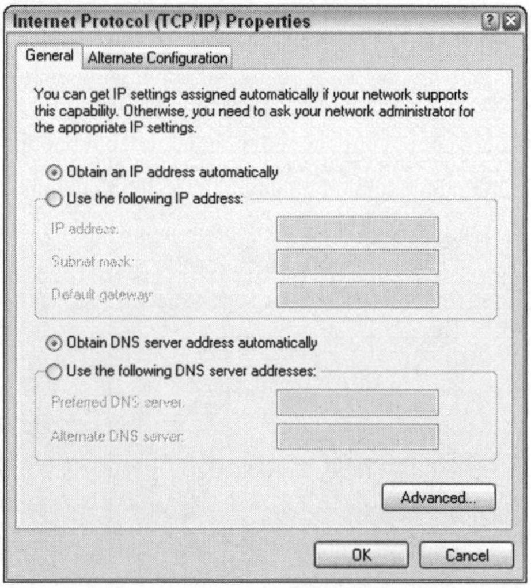

Figure 9-7:
The Internet
Protocol
(TCP/IP)
Properties
dialog box in
Windows
XP.

Mac OS

If the computer is running the Mac OS 9.*x* operating system, follow these
steps to set the network adapter to obtain its IP address automatically from a
DHCP server:

1. **From the Apple menu, display the Control Panels list, select TCP/IP, and then click OK to display the TCP/IP window.**

2. **From the Connect Via drop-down menu, choose the network device that you want to configure.**

3. **From the Configure drop-down menu, choose Using DHCP Server.**

4. **Close the TCP/IP window, saving changes when prompted.**

   Mac OS sends a request to the DHCP server for an IP address and assigns that address to the network device.

If the computer is running the Mac OS X operating system:

1. **From the Apple menu, choose System Preferences and then click the Network icon to display the Network pane.**

2. **From the Show menu, choose the network interface adapter that you want to configure.**

3. **On the TCP/IP tab (see Figure 9-8), choose Using DHCP from the Configure menu.**

   Mac OS sends a request to the DHCP server for an IP address and assigns that address to the network adapter.

Figure 9-8:
The TCP/IP tab of the Mac OS X Network pane.

Setting Up Internet Connection Sharing

Internet gateways and cable/DSL routers are certainly the easiest way to accomplish Internet connection sharing, but we know of a more economical method — software-based sharing using an attached PC. We should say, right up front, that we think that the *hardware* approach — that is, using a wireless Internet gateway or a cable/DSL router — is the best way to go. But if you really need to save a few bucks (and we mean only a few because you can get a router for $50 these days), try this approach. It works, but it's not as good as the hardware approach because it can affect the performance of both your network overall as well as the particular computer that you use for Internet connection sharing. Windows 98 Second Edition (SE) and later versions of Windows provide a software-based solution for sharing an Internet connection over a local area network (LAN). This option is available whether you're using a wired network, a wireless network, or a combination of the two.

Software-based Internet connection sharing is not efficient if you have more than four computers trying to share an Internet connection simultaneously. The cost of a broadband router is far less than the cost of a dedicated computer in most cases. And broadband routers usually contain other features that this software connection sharing doesn't offer, such as port forwarding (Port Address Translation; PAT) to forward incoming requests to specific machines based on port, as well as offering a demilitarized zone (DMZ). (A *DMZ,* in the network world, is a network zone that has no firewall protection — we discuss this more in Chapter 10.) On the other hand, if you have an extra computer lying around and have time on your hands to maintain it, software-based Internet connection sharing could be your best option. (We're still not convinced.)

When you set up a Windows software-based shared Internet connection, you select one computer to be the *Internet connection host* — the computer (running Windows 98 or later) that is always turned on and always connected to the Internet so that any other networked computer is able to access the Internet through it. This Internet connection host computer also must have two network adapters: one that connects to the Internet and another that communicates with the local area network. The connection to the Internet could be through a dialup modem, a broadband modem, or a connection to another larger network that connects to the Internet. After you complete the setup wizard, Windows turns the Internet connection server computer into both a DHCP server and your gateway to your broadband connection and the Internet.

You need to understand what Windows Internet Connection Sharing does *not* do: It does not convert the Internet connection host into a wireless access point. By contrast, software included with Mac OS 9 and Mac OS X v. 10.2 or later is capable of turning your AirPort-enabled Mac into an AP.

Using Windows Internet Connection Sharing software is equivalent to adding a cable/DSL router to your network. You could, for example, purchase a *standalone* AP — one that's not also a router and DHCP server — and attach it to your PC via an Ethernet port. All wireless PCs in your house can then connect to the AP, which in turn connects to your host PC. You then connect a dialup modem to your computer (or perhaps installed inside your computer) or connect the modem to a second Ethernet port. You can then share your Internet connection (through the dialup modem or through a broadband modem) with the computers that connect wirelessly to the AP. Figure 9-9 depicts a wireless home network that uses Windows Internet Connection Sharing to provide an Internet connection to all wireless PCs on the network.

Figure 9-9:
A wireless home network using Windows Internet Connection Sharing to provide an Internet connection to all wireless PCs on the network.

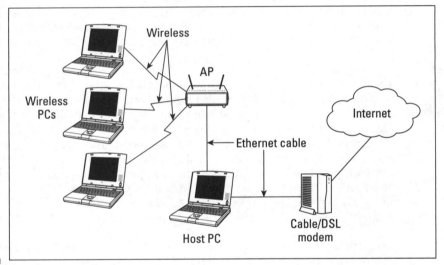

When using Windows Internet Connection Sharing, the host computer must always be on, with Windows running, so that the other computers in the home network can access the Internet. In addition, each of the other computers on the network must be set up to obtain an IP address automatically, which we describe in the earlier section "Obtaining an IP Address Automatically."

Windows 98 SE and Windows Me

To set up Windows Internet connection sharing in Windows 98 SE or Windows Me:

1. **Choose Start⇨Settings⇨Control Panel.**

2. **Double-click the Add/Remove Programs icon in the Control Panel.**

3. **When the Add/Remove Programs Properties dialog box appears, click the Windows Setup tab.**

   Windows Setup will take a few moments to search your hard drive to determine what Windows components are currently installed on your computer.

4. **When Windows Setup displays the list of Windows components, highlight the Internet Tools option but make sure that its check box remains marked (see Figure 9-10).**

Figure 9-10:
The Windows Setup tab of the Add/Remove Programs Properties dialog box in Windows 98 SE or Me.

5. **Click the Details button and then select the Internet Connection Sharing check box (if it's not already marked).**

6. **Click OK twice.**

7. **Insert the Windows CD when prompted and then click OK again.**

8. **When the Copying Files dialog box appears, make sure that the drive letter in the Copying Files From text box is the drive letter assigned to your CD-ROM drive and then click OK once more.**

   Windows Setup copies a few files to your computer's hard drive and then displays the Internet Connection Sharing Wizard.

9. **On the wizard's opening screen, click Next to display a list of network adapters (all the adapters ever installed on this computer).**

10. **Select the network adapter that you plan to use to connect to the Internet and then click Next.**

If you're using a cable or DSL modem, be sure to select the adapter that's connected to the cable/DSL modem. If you're using a dialup modem, select this modem from the list.

The next screen that appears looks almost the same as the previous screen but no longer lists the adapter that you selected in this step.

11. **Select the adapter that communicates with your network and then click Next.**

If you plan to use your PC as a router for your wireless network, you should select the Ethernet adapter to which your AP is connected.

12. **When the wizard prompts you to create a disk for the client computers, click Next, insert a floppy disk, and then click OK.**

The wizard copies two files to the floppy disk: `icsclset.exe` and `ReadMe.txt`.

If one of the client computers has been connecting to the Internet through a dialup connection, you might need to run the `icsclset.exe` program that the wizard copied onto the floppy disk. This program reconfigures your Web browser to connect to the Internet through the network adapter rather than through the dialup adapter. Run this program after finishing the wizard if you can't connect to the Internet from one of the computers on your network.

13. **Click Finish to complete the wizard.**

When the wizard completes its magic, the PC on which you ran the wizard is now both a DHCP server and a NAT server (refer to the discussion in Chapter 2) — equivalent to a broadband router. You might need to restart any PC or AP that is connected to the PC for the changes to take effect.

The host PC has to be turned on for the other computers sharing its connection to be able to access the Internet.

To remove Internet connection sharing, repeat Steps 1 through 6 — except that in Step 5, clear the Internet Connection Sharing check box.

Windows 2000

To set up Internet connection sharing in Windows 2000:

1. **Choose Start⇨Settings and then click the Network and Dial-up Connections menu item to display Network and Dial-up Connections window.**

2. **Highlight the Local Area Connection item for the network connection device that will be connected to the Internet.**

3. **Choose File⇨Properties to display the Local Area Connection Properties dialog box.**

4. **On the Sharing tab, select the Enable Internet Connection Sharing for This Connection check box, as shown in Figure 9-11, and then click OK.**

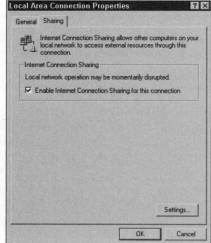

Figure 9-11:
Enable
Internet
connection
sharing in
Windows
2000.

A pop-up message informs you of the local IP address that will be assigned to the host computer (192.168.0.1) when it restarts. The message also instructs you to set each of the client computer's TCP/IP settings to obtain an IP address automatically (which we discuss earlier in this chapter).

5. **If you're that sure you want to enable Internet Sharing, click the Yes button.**

You're returned to the Network and Dial-up Connections window.

6. **Close the Network and Dial-up Connections window.**

After completing these steps, this Windows 2000 PC is now both a DHCP server and a NAT server, equivalent to a broadband router. You might need to restart any PC or AP that is connected to the PC for the IP addresses to be reassigned.

To remove Internet connection sharing, display the Sharing tab of the Local Area Connection Properties dialog box and then clear the Enable Internet Connection Sharing for This Connection check box.

Windows XP

To set up Internet connection sharing in Windows XP:

1. **Choose Start⇨Control Panel.**

2. **Double-click the Network Connections icon in the Control Panel to display the Network Connections window.**

3. **Highlight the Network Connection item for the network device that you want to use to connect to the Internet and then choose File⇨Properties.**

   The Local Area Connection Properties dialog box appears.

4. **On the Advanced tab, select the Allow Other Network Users to Connect through This Computer's Internet Connection check box, as shown in Figure 9-12.**

   By default, the Allow Other Network Users to Control or Disable the Shared Internet Connection check box is selected. Unless you want other users on the network to be able to enable and disable the shared connection, clear this check box. For dialup modems, you can also cause the modem to dial automatically when another computer on the network attempts to access the Internet.

   Using the same process as above on your dialup networking connection, select the Establish a Dial-up Connection Whenever a Computer on My Network Attempts to Access the Internet check box. Then click OK. See Figure 9-12.

   You're returned to the Network Connections window.

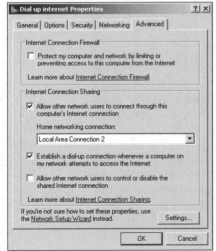

Figure 9-12: Enable Internet connection sharing in Windows XP.

5. **Close the Network Connections window.**

When you complete these steps, this Windows XP PC is now both a DHCP server and a NAT server, equivalent to a broadband router. You might need to restart any PC or AP that is connected to the PC for the IP addresses to be reassigned.

To remove Internet connection sharing, display the Advanced tab of the Local Area Connection Properties dialog box and clear Allow Other Network Users To Connect through This Computer's Internet Connection check box.

Mac OS X v. 10.2 (Jaguar)

To set up Internet connection sharing in Mac OS X v. 10.2 or later:

1. **From the Apple menu, click System Preferences to display the System Preferences pane.**

2. **Click the Sharing icon in the System Preferences panel to display the Sharing panel.**

   If you don't see the Sharing icon, click the Show All button on top of the System Preferences pane, and it will appear.

3. **Click the Internet tab, as shown in Figure 9-13.**

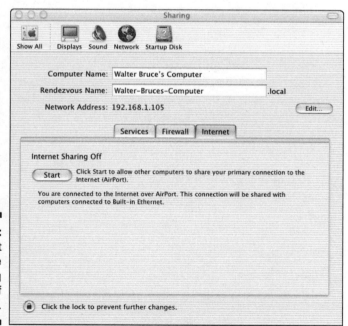

Figure 9-13: The Internet tab in the Sharing pane of Mac OS X.

Mac OS X senses which adapter is currently connected to the Internet and offers an option to share that connection with other computers on your local network.

4. Click the Start button to start sharing.

5. Close the Sharing panel and the System Preferences panel.

After you complete these steps, this Mac OS X computer is now both a DHCP server and a NAT server, equivalent to a broadband router. You might need to restart any computer or AP that is connected to the PC for the IP addresses to be reassigned.

To remove Internet connection sharing, display the Internet tab of the Sharing pane in System Preferences and click the Stop button.

The host PC has to be turned on for the other computers sharing its connection to be able to access the Internet.

Chapter 10

Securing Your Wireless Home Network

In This Chapter

▶ Worrying about wireless home network security

▶ Understanding Wired Equivalent Privacy (WEP)

▶ Getting security on your network

▶ Checking out future security enhancements

*I*f you read the news — well, at least if you read the same networking news sources that we do — you've probably seen and heard a thing or two (or a hundred) about wireless local area network (LAN) security. In fact, you really don't need to read specialized industry news to hear about this. Many major newspapers and media outlets — *The New York Times*, the *San Jose Mercury News*, and *USA Today*, among others — have run feature articles documenting the insecurity of wireless LANs. Most of these stories have focused on *wardrivers*, those folks who park in the lot in front of an office building, pull out their laptops, and easily get onto corporate networks.

In this chapter, we talk a bit about these security threats and how they might affect you and your wireless home network. We also (being the helpful types that we are) give you some good advice on how you can make your wireless home network more secure. And finally, we talk about some new solutions that are being developed by the wireless LAN industry to beef up wireless LAN security.

The advice that we give in this section applies equally to your wireless network, whether it uses 802.11b, a, or g. We're not going to be specific to any particular 802.11 technology in this chapter because the steps that you take to batten down the hatches on your network are virtually identical, regardless of which version of 802.11 you choose. (If you've missed our discussion on 802.11 basics, jump back to Chapter 2.)

No security at all!

The vast majority of wireless LAN gear (access points, network cards, and so on) is shipped to customers with all the security features turned off. That's right: zip, nada, zilch, no security at all. Just a wide-open access point, sitting there waiting for anybody who passes by (with a Wi-Fi–equipped computer, at least) to associate with the access point and get on your network.

Now this isn't a bad thing in and of itself; initially configuring your network with security features turned off and then enabling the security features after things are up and running is easier than doing it the other way 'round. Unfortunately, many people never take that extra step and activate their security settings. So a huge number of access points out there are completely open to the public (when they are within range, at least). Folks who've spent some time wardriving (which we describe in this chapter's introduction) say

that up to 60 percent of all access points that they encounter have no security methods in place at all.

Now, we should add that some people *purposely* leave their access point security off in order to provide free access to their neighborhoods. (We talk about this in Chapter 16.) But we find that many people don't intend to do this but have done so unknowingly. We're all for sharing, but keep in mind that it could get you in trouble with your broadband provider (who might cancel your line if you're sharing with neighbors). If you don't want other people on your network, take the few extra minutes that it takes to set up your network security. You can test your network — to make sure WEP is really enabled — by using a program like Network Stumbler (which we discuss at length in Chapter 16).

 No network security system is absolutely secure and foolproof. And, as we discuss in this chapter, Wi-Fi networks have some inherent flaws in their security systems, which means that even if you fully implement the security system in Wi-Fi (WEP), a determined individual could still get into your network.

We're not trying to scare you off here. In a typical residential setting, chances are good that your network won't be subjected to some sort of determined attacker like this. So follow our tips, and you should be just fine.

Assessing the Risks

The biggest advantage of wireless networks — the fact that you can connect to the network just about anywhere within range of the base station (up to 300 feet) — is also the biggest potential liability. Because the signal is carried over the air via radio waves, anyone else within range can pick up your network's signals, too. It's sort of like putting an extra RJ-45 jack for a wired LAN out on the sidewalk in front of your house: You're no longer in control of who can access it.

General Internet security

Before we get into the security of your wireless LAN, we need to talk for a moment about Internet security in general. Regardless of what type of LAN you have — wireless, wired, a LAN using powerlines or phonelines, or even no LAN — when you connect a computer to the Internet, some security risks are involved. Malicious *crackers* (the bad guys of the hacker community) can use all sorts of tools and techniques to get into your computer(s) and wreak havoc.

For example, someone with malicious intent could get into your computer and steal personal files (such as your bank statements that you've downloaded using Quicken) or mess with your computer's settings . . . or even erase your hard drive. Your computer can even be hijacked (without you knowing it) as a jumping off point for other people's nefarious deeds; as a source of an attack on another computer (the bad guys can launch these attacks remotely using your computer, making them that much harder to track down); or even as source for spam e-mailing.

What we're getting at here is the fact that you need to take a few steps to secure *any* computer attached to the Internet. If you have a broadband (digital subscriber line [DSL], satellite, or cable modem) connection, you *really* need to secure your computer(s). The high speed, always-on connections that these services offer make it easier for a cracker to get into your computer. We recommend that you take three steps to secure your computers from Internet-based security risks:

✔ **Use and maintain antivirus software.** Many attacks on computers don't come from someone sitting in a dark room, in front of a computer screen, actively cracking into your computer. They come from viruses (often scripts embedded in e-mails or other downloaded files) that take over parts of your computer's operating system and do things that you don't want your computer doing (like sending a copy of the virus to everyone in your e-mail address book and then deleting your hard drive). So pick out your favorite antivirus program and use it. Keep the *virus definition files* (the data files that tell your antivirus software what's a virus and what's not) up to date. And for heaven's sake, use your antivirus program!

✔ **Install a personal firewall on each computer.** *Personal firewalls* are programs that basically take a look at every Internet connection entering or leaving your computer and check it against a set of rules to see whether the connection should be allowed. After you've installed a personal firewall program, wait about a day and then look at the log. You'll be shocked and amazed at the sheer number of attempted connections to your computer that have been blocked. Most of these attempts are relatively innocuous, but not all are. If you've got broadband, your firewall might block hundreds of these attempts every day.

We like ZoneAlarm — www.zonelabs.com — for Windows computers, and we use the built-in firewall on our Mac OS X computers.

✔ **Turn on the firewall functionality in your router.** Whether you use a separate router or one integrated into your wireless access point, it will have at least some level of firewall functionality built in. Turn this function on when you set up your router/access point. (It'll be an obvious option in the configuration program and might well be on by default.) We like to have both the router firewall and the personal firewall software running on our PCs. It's the belt-and-suspenders approach, but it makes our networks more secure.

In Chapter 12, we talk about some situations (particularly when you're playing online games over your network) where you need to disable some of this firewall functionality. We suggest that you do this only when you must. Otherwise, turn on that firewall — and leave it on.

Some routers use a technology called *stateful packet inspection* firewalls, which examine each packet (or individual group) of data coming into the router to make sure that it was actually something requested by a computer on the network. If your router has this function, we recommend that you try using it because it's a more thorough way of performing firewall functions. Others simply use Network Address Translation (NAT, which we introduce in Chapter 2 and further discuss in Chapter 16) to perform firewall functions. This isn't quite as effective as stateful packet inspection, but it does work quite well.

There's a lot more to Internet security — like securing your file sharing (if you've enabled that) — that we just don't have the space to get into. Check out Chapter 11 for a quick overview on this subject. To get really detailed about these subjects, we recommend that you take a look at *Home Networking For Dummies*, by Kathy Ivens (Wiley Publishing, Inc.) for coverage of those issues in greater detail.

After you've set up your firewall, test it out. Check out this great site that has a ton of information about Internet security: `www.grc.com`. The guy behind this site, Steve Gibson, is a genius on the topic, and he's built a great tool called ShieldsUP!! that lets you run through a series of tests to see how well your firewall(s) is working. Go to `www.grc.com` and test yourself.

Airlink security

The area that we really want to focus on in this chapter is the aspect of network security that's unique to wireless networks: the airlink security. In other words, these are the security concerns that have to do with the radio frequencies being beamed around your wireless home network.

Traditionally, computer networks use wires that go from point to point in your home (or in an office). When you've got a wired network, you've got physical control over these wires. You install them, and you know where they go. The physical connections to a wired LAN are inside your house. You can lock the doors and windows and keep someone else from gaining access to the network. Of course, you've got to keep people from accessing the network over the Internet, as we mention in the previous section, but locally it would take an act of breaking and entering by a bad guy to get on your network. (Sort of like on *Alias* where they always seem to have to go deep into the enemy's facility to tap into anything.)

Wireless LANs turn this premise on its head because you've got absolutely no way of physically securing your network. Now you can do things like go outside with a laptop computer and have someone move the access point around to reduce the amount of signal leaving the house. But that's really not going to be 100 percent effective, and it can reduce your coverage within the house. Or you could join the tinfoil hat brigade ("The CIA is reading my mind!") and surround your entire house with a Faraday cage. (Remember those from physics class? Us neither, but they have something to do with attenuating electromagnetic fields.)

Some access points have controls that let you limit the amount of power used to send radio waves over the air. This isn't a perfect solution (and it can dramatically reduce your reception in distant parts of the house), but if you live in a small apartment and are worried about beaming your Wi-Fi signals to the apartment next door, you might try this.

Basically, what we're saying here is that the radio waves sent by your wireless LAN gear are going to leave your house, and there's not a darned thing that you can do about it. Nothing. What you can do, however, is make it difficult for other people to tune into those radio signals, thus (and more importantly) making it difficult for those who can tune into them to decode them and use them to get onto your network (without your authorization) or to scrutinize your e-mail, Web surfing habits, and so on.

You can take several steps to make your wireless network more secure and to provide some airlink security on your network. We talk about these in the following sections, and then we discuss some even better methods of securing wireless LANs that are coming down the pike.

Introducing Wired Equivalent Privacy (WEP)

The primary line of defense in a Wi-Fi network is *Wired Equivalent Privacy* (WEP). WEP is an encryption system, which means that it scrambles — using the encryption key (or WEP key, in this case) — all the data packets (or individual chunks of data) that are sent over the airwaves in your wireless network. Unless someone on the far end has the same key to decrypt the data, he (theoretically) won't be able to make heads nor tails of it. It'll be gibberish. So even though your data is beamed right through the side of the house into that snooper's PC, it will arrive in an unreadable form.

WEP also has a second security function: Not only does it encrypt your data being transmitted over the airlink, it also can be used to authenticate users connecting to the access point. In other words, not only do you need a WEP key to decode data transmitted over the airlink, but you also need a WEP key to get your computer connected to the access point in the first place. If an access point has WEP enabled and you don't have the key, you can try and try, but you'll never get connected to it.

Although the WEP key itself is a long series of numbers and letters, you often don't have to make up this key yourself. (It's harder than you think to just spew out some random numbers and letters.) Instead, you just have to enter a *pass phrase* (some regular English words that you can remember), and the software will use this pass phrase to generate the key for you.

How about a bit more about WEP?

WEP encrypts your data so that no one can read it unless they have the key. That's the theory behind WEP, anyway. WEP has been a part of Wi-Fi networks from the beginning. (The developers of Wi-Fi were initially focused on the business market, where data security has always been a big priority.) The name itself belies the intentions of the system's developers; they wanted to make wireless networks as secure as wired networks.

In order for WEP to work, you must activate WEP on all the Wi-Fi devices in your network via the client software or configuration program that came with the hardware. And every device on your network must use the same WEP key to gain access to the network. (We talk a bit more about how to turn on WEP in the "Clamping Down on Your Wireless Home Network's Security" section of this chapter.)

For the most part, WEP is WEP is WEP. In other words, it doesn't matter which vendor made your access point or which vendor made your laptop's PC card network adapter — the implementation of WEP is standardized across vendors. Keep this one difference in mind, however: WEP key length. Encryption keys are categorized by the number of bits (1s or 0s) used to create the key. Most Wi-Fi equipment these days uses 128-bit WEP keys, but some early gear (like the first generation of the Apple AirPort equipment) supported only a 64-bit WEP key.

A few access points and network adapters on the market even support longer keys, such as equipment from D-Link, which can support a 256-bit key. Keep in mind that the longest standard (and common) key is 128 bits. Most equipment enables you to decide how long to make your WEP key; you can often choose between 64 and 128 bits. Generally, for security purposes, you should pick the longest key available. If, however, you have some older gear that can't support longer WEP key lengths, you can use a shorter key. If you have one network adapter that can handle only 64-bit keys but you've got an access point that can handle 128-bit keys, you need to set up the access point to use the shorter, 64-bit key length.

You can almost always use a shorter-than-maximum key length (like using a 64-bit key in a 128-bit-capable system), but you can't go the other way. So if you set your access point up to use a 128-bit key, your older 64-bit network adapter won't be able to connect to it.

What's wrong with WEP?

WEP sounds like a pretty good deal, doesn't it? It keeps your data safe while it's floating through the ether by encrypting it, and it keeps others off your access point by not authenticating them. In fact, it's pretty good. Notice that we didn't say that WEP is *great* or *superb* or *awesome*. Just pretty good.

We're actually being somewhat generous. With the proper tools and enough network traffic to analyze, a dedicated network cracker can break WEP (or independently figure out the WEP key by using some mathematical techniques) in a relatively short time. In the business environment, where a ton of traffic is traveling over the wireless network and valuable business secrets are part of this traffic, this is a pretty big deal. The math to break WEP is pretty hard (you're not going to do it in your head), but plenty of freely available tools are on the Web that let a computer do it relatively quickly.

We're being generous with WEP because we strongly believe that in the home environment — particularly in the suburbs and other less-than-densely populated areas — the chances of you having someone who can pick up your signals AND be motivated to go through all the trouble of breaking your WEP code are pretty darn slim. No one's ever tried to do it to us, and we don't know any folks who have had this happen to them at home. So we don't sweat it all that much.

But we do think that WEP needs to be improved. We use wireless networks at work too, and we'd like additional security. The final section of this chapter, "Looking into the Crystal Ball," talks about some newer systems that are on the way which will complement or supplant WEP entirely and offer greater security.

We're writing *Wireless Home Networking For Dummies* here, not *Secure Office Wireless Networks For Dummies*. More sophisticated security systems are available now for business networks that can improve upon the security of a wireless LAN. Many of these systems rely upon using stronger encryption systems called Virtual Private Networks (VPNs), which encrypt all data leaving the PC (not just wireless data) with very strong encryption. You might even have a VPN system on that work laptop that you bring home with you every night. VPN is great, and as long as your router supports VPN tunneling, you should be able to connect to the office network from your home LAN using your VPN client. But VPN technology is not anywhere close to being cheap, simple, and user-friendly enough to be something that we'd ever recommend that you install in your house to secure your wireless LAN.

Clamping Down on Your Wireless Home Network's Security

Well, enough of the theory and background. Time to get down to business. In this section, we discuss some of the key steps that you should take to secure your wireless network from intruders. None of these steps are difficult, will drive you crazy, or make your network hard to use. All that's really required is the motivation to spend a few extra minutes (after you've got everything up and working) battening down the hatches and getting ready for sea. (Can you tell that Pat used to be in the Navy?)

The key steps in securing your wireless network, as we see them, are the following:

1. Change all the default values on your network.

2. Enable WEP.

3. Close your network to outsiders (if your access point supports this).

Hundreds of different access points and network adapters are available on the market. Each has its own unique configuration software. (At least each vendor does; and often, different models from the same vendor have different configuration systems.) You need to RTFM (Read the Fine Manual!). We're going to give you some generic advice on what to do here, but you really, really, really need to pick up the manual and read it before you do this to your network. Every vendor has slightly different terminology and different ways of doing things. If you mess up, you might temporarily lose wireless access to your access point. (You should still be able to plug a computer in with an Ethernet cable to gain access to the configuration system.) You might even have to reset your access point and start over from scratch. So follow the vendor's directions (as painful at that may be — there's a reason why people buy *For Dummies* books). We tell you the main steps that you need to take to secure your network; your manual will give you the exact line-by-line directions on how to implement these steps on your equipment.

WEP key length: Do the math

If you're being picky, you might notice that WEP keys aren't really as long as their names say that they are. The first 24 bits of the key are actually something called an *initialization vector*, and the remaining bits comprise the key itself. Therefore, 128-bit keys are really only 104 bits long, and 64-bit keys are really only 40 bits long. So when you enter a 128-bit key (and you do the math), you'll see that there are only 26 alphanumeric characters (or digits) for you to enter in the key (4 bits per digit × 26 = 104 bits). This isn't something that you really need to know because everyone adds the 24 initialization vector bits to the WEP key length number, but just in case you were curious. . . .

Most access points also have some wired connections available — Ethernet ports that you can use to connect your computer to the access point. You can almost always use this wired connection to run the access point configuration software. When you're setting up security, we recommend making a wired connection and doing all your access point configuration in this manner. That way, you can avoid accidentally blocking yourself from the access point when your settings begin to take effect.

Getting rid of the defaults

It's incredibly common to go to a Web site like Netstumbler.com, look at the results of someone's Wi-Fi reconnoitering trip around their neighborhood, and see dozens of access points with the same exact Service Set Identifier (SSID, or network name; see Chapter 2). And it's usually *Linksys* because Linksys is the most popular vendor out there. Many folks bring home an access point, plug it in, turn it on, and then do nothing. They leave everything as it was set up from the factory. They don't change any of the default settings.

Well, if you want people to be able to find your access point, there's nothing better (short of a sign on the front door; check out our discussion of *warchalking* — the practice of leaving marks on sidewalks to point out open APs — in Chapter 16) than leaving your default SSID broadcasting out there for the world to see. In some cities, you could probably drive all the way across town with a laptop set to Linksys as an SSID and stay connected the entire time. (We don't mean to just pick on Linksys here. You could probably do the same thing with an SSID set to default, D-Link's default, or any of the top vendor's default settings.)

When you begin your security crusade, the first thing that you should do is to change all the defaults on your access point. At a minimum, you should change the following:

- ✔ Your default SSID
- ✔ Your default administrative password

You want to change this password because if you don't, someone who gains access to your network can guess at your password and end up changing all the settings in your access point without you knowing. Heck, if they wanted to teach you a security lesson — the tough love approach, we guess — they could even block you out of the network until you reset the access point. These default passwords are well known and well publicized. Just look on the Web page of your vendor, and we bet that you'll find a copy of the user's guide for your access point available for download. Anyone who wants to know them does know them.

When you change the default SSID on your access point to one of your own making, you'll also need to change the SSID setting of any computers (or other devices) that you want to connect to your LAN. To do this, follow the steps that we discuss in this part's earlier chapters.

This tip really falls under the category of Internet security (rather than airlink security), but here goes: Make sure that you turn off the Allow/Enable Remote Management function (it might not be called this exactly but something like that). This function is designed to allow people to connect to your access point over the Internet (if they know your IP address) and do any or all the configuration stuff from a distant location. If you need this turned on (perhaps you have a home office, and your IT gal wants to be able to configure your access point remotely), you'll know it. Otherwise, it's just a security flaw waiting to happen, particularly if you haven't changed your default password. Luckily, most access points have this set to Off by default, but take the time to make sure that yours does.

Enabling WEP

After you eliminate the security threats caused by leaving all the defaults in place (see the preceding section), it's time to get some encryption going. Get your WEP on, as the kids say.

We've already warned you once, but we'll do it again, just for kicks: Every access point has its own system for setting up WEP, and you need to follow those directions. We can only give generic advice because we have no idea which access point you're using.

To enable WEP on your wireless network, we suggest that you perform the following generic steps:

1. **Open your access point's configuration screen.**

2. **Go to the Wireless, Security, or Encryption tab or section.**

   We're being purposely vague here; bear with us.

3. **Select the radio button or check box labeled Enable WEP or Enable Encryption or Configure WEP.**

   You should see a menu similar to the one shown in Figure 10-1. (This is for a Siemens SpeedStream access point/router.)

4. **Select the check box or the pull-down menu to the appropriate WEP key length for your network.**

   We recommend 128-bit keys if all the gear on your network can support it. (See the earlier section, "How about a bit more about WEP?," for the lowdown on WEP keys.)

5. **Create your own key if you prefer (we prefer to let the program create one for us):**

   a. **Type a pass phrase into the Passphrase text box.**

   b. **Click the Generate Keys button.**

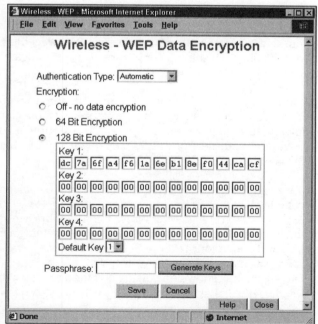

Figure 10-1: Setting up WEP on a Speed-Stream access point.

Remember the pass phrase. Write it down somewhere, and put it some place where you won't accidentally throw it away or forget where you put it. Danny likes to tape his pass phrase note to the box that his Wi-Fi gear came in so he'll always be able to track it down.

Whether you created your own key or let the program do it for you, a key should now have magically appeared in the key text box. ***Note:*** Some systems allow you to set more than one key (usually up to four keys), such as the system in Figure 10-1. In this case, use Key 1 and set this as your default key by using the pull-down menu.

Remember this key! Write it down. You'll need it again when you configure your computers to connect to this access point.

Some access point's configuration software won't necessarily show you the WEP key that you've generated — just the pass phrase that you've used to generate it. You'll need to dig around in the manual and menus to find a command to display the WEP key itself. (For example, Apple's AirPort software shows just the pass phrase; you need to find the *Network Equivalent Password* in the Airport Admin Utility to display the WEP key — in OS X, this is in the Base Station Menu.)

The built-in wireless LAN client software on Windows XP numbers its four keys from 0–3 instead of 1–4. So if you're using Key 1 on your access point, select Key 0 in Windows XP.

6. **Click OK to close the WEP configuration window.**

You're done turning on WEP. Congratulations.

Can we repeat ourselves again? Will you indulge us? The preceding steps are *very* generic. Yours might vary slightly (or in rare cases, significantly). Read your user's guide. It will tell you what to do.

Some access points will make you go through the extra step of requiring all users to use WEP to connect to the access point. Look for a check box or pull-down menu on your configuration screen with this option. If you don't do this, computers without your network's WEP key might still be able to connect to your access point.

After you configure WEP on the access point, you must go to each computer on your network, get into the network adapter's client software (as we describe in Chapters 7 and 8), turn on WEP, and enter either the pass phrase or the WEP key. Typically you'll find an Enable Security dialog box containing a check box to turn on security and one to four text boxes for entering the key. Simply select the check box to enable WEP, enter your key in the appropriate text box, and then click OK. Figure 10-2 shows this dialog box for a Proxim ORiNOCO PC Card network adapter; the dialog box that you see is likely to be similar.

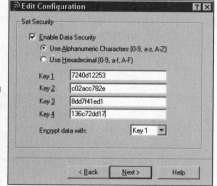

Figure 10-2:
Setting up
WEP on an
ORiNOCO
PC Card.

One area that is consistently confusing when setting up a WEP key — and often a real pain in the rear end — is the tendency of different vendors to use different formats for the keys. The most common way to format a key is to use *hexadecimal* (hex) characters. This format represents numbers and letters by using combinations of the numbers 0–9 and the letters A–F. (For example, the name of Pat's dog, Opie, would be represented in hexadecimal as *4f 70 69 65*.) A few other vendors use *ASCII*, which is simply the letters and numbers on your keyboard.

Although ASCII is an easier-to-understand system for entering WEP codes (it's really just plain text), most systems make you use hexadecimal: It's the standard. The easiest way to enter hex keys on your computers connecting to your access point is to use the pass phrase that we discuss previously. If your network adapter client software lets you do this, do it! If it doesn't, try entering the WEP key itself that you wrote down when you generated it (it's probably hexadecimal). If that doesn't work either, you might have to dig into the user's manual and see whether you need to add any special codes before or after the WEP key to make it work. Some software requires you to put the WEP key inside quotation marks; others might require you to put an *0h* or *0x* (that's a zero and an h or an x character) before the key or an *h* after it (both without quotation marks).

Closing your network

The last step that we recommend you take in the process of securing your wireless home network (if your access point allows it) is to create a *closed network* — a network that allows only specific, pre-designated computers and devices onto it. You can do two things to close down your network, which makes it harder for strangers to find your network and gain access to it:

✔ **Turn off SSID broadcast:** By default, most access points broadcast their SSID out onto the airwaves. This makes it easier for users to find the network and associate with it. If the SSID is being broadcast and you're in range, you should see the SSID on your computer's network adapter client software and be able to select it and connect to it. That is, assuming that you have the right WEP key, if WEP is configured on that access point. When you create a closed network, you turn off this broadcast so that only people who know the exact name of the access point can connect to it.

You can find access points even if they're not broadcasting their SSID (by observing other traffic on the network with a network *sniffer* program), so this is an imperfect security measure — and no substitute for enabling WEP. But it's another layer of security for your network. Also, if you're in an area where you will have a lot of people coming into your home and wanting to share your connection, you might not want to close off the network, thus balancing convenience for your friends against the small exposure of a more open network.

✔ **Set access control at the MAC layer:** Every network adapter in the world has a unique number assigned to it known as a Media Access Controller (MAC) address. You can find the MAC address of your network adapter either by looking at it (it's usually physically printed on the device) or using software on your computer:

- **Open a DOS window and use the** `winipcnfg` **command in Windows 95/98/Me or the** `ipconfig/all` **command on Windows NT/2000/XP.**

- **Look in the Network Control Panel/System Preference on a Mac.**

With some access points, you can type in the MAC addresses of all the devices that you want to connect to your access point and block connections from any other MAC addresses.

Again, if you support MAC layer filtering, you'll make it harder for friends to log on to when visiting. If you've got some buddies who like to come over and mooch off your broadband connection, you'll need to add their MAC addresses as well, or they won't be able to get on your network. Luckily, you need to enter their MAC address only one time to get them "on the list," so to speak, so you won't need to do it every time they show up — at least until you have to reset the access point (which shouldn't be that often).

Neither of these "closed" network approaches is absolutely secure. MAC addresses can be *spoofed* (imitated by a device with a different MAC address, for example), but both are good ways to add to your overall security strategy.

Looking Into the Crystal Ball

The limitations of WEP have become a bit of an embarrassment to the wireless industry. Although a whole big boatload of businesses has begun using wireless LANs, many are waiting on the sidelines until security issues are a bit better sorted out. And although we think that WEP is okay (but not great) for home use, it's certainly not good enough for a business that relies upon the security of its data.

Several efforts are underway to create newer, better, and more secure ways of protecting wireless LANs . . . efforts that will pay off for home users in the long run. In this section, we talk about some of the most important of these efforts and give you a quick overview of them.

This is our "Gaze into the crystal ball and chant voodoo incantations" section of the chapter. None of this stuff is available yet (although some of it *is* due in 2003 . . . sometime . . .).

Waiting for WPA

The Institute for Electrical and Electronics Engineers (IEEE — the group that developed the standards for 802.11 networks; see Chapter 2) is working on a long-term solution to WEP's weaknesses (which we discuss in the following section about 802.11i). In the meantime, the Wi-Fi Alliance (the group of vendors that ensure the compatibility of Wi-Fi gear) has put together its own interim solution for wireless LAN security called *Wi-Fi Protected Access* (WPA).

WPA is a new set of forward-compatible encryption and authentication enhancements for 802.11 networks. *Forward-compatible* means that WPA will work with newer systems that are currently being developed by the IEEE. Other reasons to get excited about WPA include the following features that it will offer:

✔ **More random encryption techniques:** WPA has basically been designed as an answer for all the current weaknesses of WEP, with significantly increased encryption techniques. One of WEP's fatal flaws is that its encryption is not sufficiently random, meaning that an observer can more easily find patterns and break the encryption. WPA's encryption techniques will basically be more random — and thus harder to break.

✔ **Automatic key changes:** WPA also has a huge security advantage in the fact that it automatically changes the key (although you, as a user, get to keep using the same password to access the system). So by the time a bad guy has figured out your key, your system would have already moved on to a new one.

✔ **More user-friendly:** WPA will also be easier for consumers to use because there's no hexadecimal stuff to deal with . . . just a plain text password. The idea is to make WPA much easier to deal with than WEP, which takes a bit of effort to get up and running (depending on how good your access point's configuration software is).

✔ **Backward compatibility:** The best thing about WPA is that it's being designed to be backward compatible, too. Thus, existing Wi-Fi certified equipment should be able to be upgraded to WPA by just installing a downloadable software update.

The Wi-Fi alliance expects to begin certifying WPA equipment sometime in early 2003. (We haven't seen any yet, but it's just a matter of time, as we write.)

The future: 802.11i

WPA is a great next step in wireless LAN security (see the preceding section), but it's not the end of the road. Well, face it . . . there is no end of the road. Computers get more powerful, and the bad guys in the black hats who want to break into the networks get smarter — so no system is going to be immune to security breakdowns forever. Don't think of security as something that you can just figure out and put behind you; security is a continuous trek of upgrades and refinements — and it always will be.

802.1x: The corporate solution

Another new standard that's being slowly rolled out into the Wi-Fi world is 802.1x. This isn't an encryption system but instead, an authentication system. An 802.1x system, when built into an access point, would allow users to connect to the access point but give them only extremely limited access (at least initially). In an 802.1x system, the user would be able to connect to only a single network port (or service). Specifically, the only traffic that the user could send over the network would be to an authentication server, which would exchange information (such as passwords and encrypted keys) with the user to establish that he was actually allowed on the network. After this authentication process has been satisfactorily completed, the user is given full (or partial, depending on what policies the authentication server has recorded for the user) access to the network.

802.1x is *not* something that we expect to see in any wireless home LAN anytime soon. It's really a business-class kind of thing, requiring lots of fancy servers and professional installation and configuration. Just thought we'd mention it because you'll no doubt hear about it when you search the Web for wireless LAN security information.

The next step on this road, after WPA, is 802.11i. This is an entirely new reconfiguration of wireless LAN security. Unlike WPA, it likely won't work on existing access points and network adapters, at least not all aspects of the system. But sometime down the road, probably in 2004, you should start seeing new generations of wireless LAN gear that incorporates 802.11i security systems.

Perhaps the biggest advance that you'll see when 802.11i hits the streets is the system's adoption of the Advanced Encryption Standard (AES). AES uses very sophisticated encryption techniques and super-long keys (much bigger than the 128-bit keys used by WEP) that take a really, really long time (even with really fast computers) to break. With today's technology, at least the technology available to regular people, AES is essentially unbreakable.

802.11i also includes other security measures (like support for 802.1x, which we discuss in a nearby sidebar) that help really tighten up wireless LAN security. So 802.11i should be worth the wait. In the meantime, use what you have (WEP), and you'll be fine.

Part IV
Using a Wireless Network

The 5th Wave   By Rich Tennant

EXPERIMENTING WITH THE
WIRELESS LASER BEAM NETWORK

"Okay—did you get that?"

In this part . . .

And here's where things get fun: After you get your wireless home network installed and running, you probably can't wait to use it, both in practical and fun ways. In this part, we cover the basics on what you can do with your network, such as sharing printers, files, folders, and even hard drives. But there are many other cool things that you can do over a wireless network, too, such as playing multi-user computer games, connecting your audio-visual equipment, and operating various types of "smart home" conveniences. We cover all these great topics here. This part also contains a chapter on using Bluetooth-enabled devices and another chapter that describes how to find and use wireless *hot spots* so that you can access the Internet in public locations.

Chapter 11

Putting Your Wireless Home Network To Work

In This Chapter

▶ Checking out Network Neighborhood

▶ Finding files on other computers

▶ Sharing printers and other peripherals

▶ Securing your network through sensible sharing

▶ Exploring Mac-friendly sharing

*R*emember that old Cracker Jack commercial of the guy sitting in the bed when the kid comes home from school? "What'd you learn in school today?" he asks. "Sharing," says the kid. And then out of either guilt or good manners, the old guy shares his sole box of caramel popcorn with the kid.

You shouldn't hog your caramel popcorn, and you shouldn't hog your network resources, either. We're going to help you share your Cracker Jacks now! (After all, that's kinda the purpose of the network, right?) You've got a wireless network installed. It's secure. It's connected. Now you can share all sorts of stuff with others in your family — not just your Internet connection, but printers, faxes, extra disk space, Telephony Application Programming Interface (TAPI) devices (telephone-to-computer interfaces and vice versa for everybody else), games, A/V controls . . . oodles and oodles of devices.

In this chapter, we give you a taste of how you can really put your wireless network to work. We talk about accessing shared network resources, setting up user profiles, accessing peripheral devices across the network (such as network printing), checking out your Network Neighborhood, and other such goodies.

Entire books have been written about sharing your network, such as *Home Networking For Dummies* (by Kathy Ivens), and other books, such as *Mac OS X All-In-One Desk Reference For Dummies* (by Mark L. Chambers, Erick Tejkowski, and Michael L. Williams) and *Windows XP For Dummies* (by Andy Rathbone; all from Wiley Publishing, Inc.), include some details about networking. These are all good books. In fact, some smart bookstore should bundle these together with *Wireless Home Networking For Dummies* because they're very complementary. In this chapter, we expose you to the network and what's inside it (and there's probably a free prize among those Cracker Jacks somewhere, too!), and that should get you started. But if you want to know more, we urge you to grab one of these more detailed books.

It's one thing to attach a device to the network — either directly or as an attachment — but it's another to share it with others. Sharing your computer and devices is a big step. Not only do you open yourself up to a lot of potential unwanted visitors (like bad folks sneaking in over your Internet connection), but you also make it easier for friendly folks (like your kids) to erase stuff and use things in unnatural ways. That's why you can (and should!) control access by using passwords or by allowing users to only read (open and copy) files on your devices (instead of changing them). In Windows 2000 and XP, security is paramount, and you must plan how, what, and with whom you share. Definitely take the extra time to configure your system for these extra security layers. We tell you in this chapter about some of these mechanisms (see the later section "Setting permissions"); the books that we mention previously go into these topics in more detail.

A Networking Review

Before we go too far into the concept of file sharing, we should review basic networking concepts a bit (that we touch upon in earlier chapters of this book): that is, what a network is and how it works.

Basic networking terminology

Simply defined, a *network* is something that links computers, printers, and other devices together. These days, the standard protocol used for most networking is Ethernet. A *protocol* is the language that devices use to communicate to each other on a network.

For one device to communicate with another under the Ethernet protocol, the transmitting device needs to accomplish a few things. First, it must announce itself on the network and declare what device it's trying to talk to. Then it must authenticate itself with that destination device — confirming that the sending device is who it says it is. This is done by sending a proper name, such as a domain or workgroup name, and also a password that the receiving device will accept.

For our purposes here, when we talk about networking, we're talking about sharing devices on a Windows-based network. Windows 95/98/Me start the network tour with *Network Neighborhood*. In Windows XP (both Professional and Home) and Windows 2000 Professional, this is called *My Network Places*. Although both show the same information and serve the same function, My Network Places has more layers. In Network Neighborhood, you see all the computers and other network devices that are currently on your network. Your computer knows this because it has been monitoring your Ethernet network and has seen each device announce itself and what it has to offer to the entire network when each one first powered up.

With the release of Windows XP Professional and Home, Microsoft introduced a new look and feel to the desktop. The differences in the new look were drastic enough that during the beta testing of XP, Microsoft decided to offer people a choice as to which look and feel they would like by implementing *themes*. When we reference the XP desktop in this chapter, we are referencing what's known as the *Windows Classic Theme* in XP. If, at any point, you're having trouble following any of our steps, do this:

1. **Right-click the desktop and then choose Properties from the pop-up menu that appears.**

2. **On the Themes tab of the Display Properties dialog box, choose Windows Classic from the Themes pull-down menu.**

   You can always change the theme back without doing any damage to any personal preferences that you set up for yourself.

Setting up a workgroup

To set up networking on any Windows-based computer, you need to decide on a few basic networking options. A lot of these will be decided for you, based on the equipment that you happen to be using on your network. As an example, if you have a server on your wireless network, you have many more options as to the type of network that you might create. With a server on your network, you gain the ability to centralize your security policies and to use domains to control devices. In Windows, a *domain* is a set of network resources (applications, printers, and so on) for a group of users. The user only has to log on to the domain to gain access to the resources, which might be located on one or a number of different servers in the network.

If you don't have a server (which most of us don't on our home networks), you'll end up using the most common type of network: a *workgroup*.

The distinction between a workgroup and a domain can best be summed up in one word: security. Domains make managing, maintaining, and modifying security much simpler. In many cases, the *domain controller* — the server that controls the domain — can set up security on each device on the network remotely, and security can be managed in groups so that you don't have to add every family member to every machine or device on the network. Of course, all this great management comes at a price. Servers tend to be expensive and require a much higher skill level to maintain. The initial setup of a domain can take a lot of planning and time to implement. We don't take you through setting up your own domain because you can find more detailed books already written on the subject. If you do happen to choose some type of domain for networking, keep in mind that the security of your domain is only as strong as the security on each individual piece of equipment attached to your network — and that includes *all* your wireless devices.

On the other hand, setting up a workgroup is relatively simple. All that's really required is to decide on the name of your workgroup. Many people use family names or something similar. Microsoft has a default of *Workgroup* MSHome for workgroups in Windows, for instance. Keep in mind that domain and workgroup names can only be 15 characters long and cannot contain any spaces or special characters.

To set up a workgroup in Windows 95/98/Me, you start by right-clicking the Network Neighborhood icon on your desktop or choosing Start⇨Settings⇨ Control Panel and then double-clicking the Network icon. On the Identification tab of the Network dialog box that opens, enter the following:

- A simple *computer name* of eight characters that describes the machine
- The *workgroup name* of no more than 15 characters
- A good *computer description* so others on the network will have an idea of what's on this computer (such as *Danny's Office Machine*)

To set up a workgroup in Windows 2000/XP, start by right-clicking the My Computer icon (in the upper-left of your desktop) or by choosing Start⇨ Settings⇨Control Panel and then double-clicking the System icon. On the Network Identification tab of the System Properties window that opens, you can click the Network ID button to have a wizard walk you through the process of setting up your networking options. A simpler method is to click the Properties button and just enter the computer name, description, and workgroup name (and a handy way to quickly check — and rename if necessary — workgroup names on the computers on your network.)

Will You Be My Neighbor?

"Hello! I'm here!" When a computer attached to a network is turned on, it broadcasts its name to every other device on the network and asks every device to broadcast as well. If that computer is sharing something, such as a folder or a printer, the other devices can see it. By asking the other devices to broadcast, it can then see all of them. This process is repeated (on average) every 15 minutes in most networks with Windows computers attached to them.

The "Hello, I'm here" process is a great way to add devices to a network. Unfortunately, it's not too great at detecting if a device falls off or is disconnected from that network. If a machine or shared device seems to be visible on your network but doesn't respond when you try to access it, the problem might not be on your computer. Devices that get disconnected from your network don't immediately appear to be disconnected on some of your other computers. They usually only get removed from the list of available networked computers if they fail to answer the every-15-minute "Hello" call from the other machines.

The Network Neighborhood (or My Network Places) icon is your ticket to the network and seeing what shared resources are available, like a printer. (The risk versus rewards of sharing these types of items just makes sense. The chances of a bad guy getting into your printer and printing out documents is really rather low — there's not much reward for doing that.)

You can see what's shared on your network by checking out your PC's Network Neighborhood (or My Network Places).

  ✔ **Windows 95/98/Me:** Double-click your Network Neighborhood icon (usually on your desktop), and you will see all the devices in your workgroup or domain. You will also see an item labeled Entire Network. Under this, you can see devices residing in other workgroups or domains that happen to be on the same physical network as the computer that you're working from.

  ✔ **Windows 2000 and XP:** Double-click the My Network Places icon (also usually found on your desktop) to see options such as Entire Network and Computers Near Me. Microsoft added a layer to the old Network Neighborhood icon and consolidated the devices in the same workgroup or domain to the Computers Near Me folder. The Entire Network folder still shows all the available devices on your physical network. The root of the My Network Places folder is now reserved for shortcuts to network resources that you tend to use on a regular basis.

Looking at Network Neighborhood (see Figure 11-1) shows you all the computers on the network, including the PC that you're using at that particular moment — if it happens to be set up for sharing. If a computer is networked but not turned on, you wouldn't see it — only turned-on computers show up in Network Neighborhood. When you double-click a computer listed in Network Neighborhood, a new window pops up showing you what is shared on that computer or device.

Networked computers

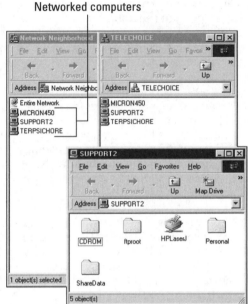

Figure 11-1:
See
networked
Windows
95/98/Me
computers
in Network
Neighbor-
hood.

If you're using Windows 2000 or XP, My Network Places (see Figure 11-2) serves a similar (but enhanced) purpose. My Network Places gives you access to your entire network resources and also enables you to add shortcuts to your favorite places. To check out everything that's on your home network, click the Entire Network icon. This will show you your workgroup.

Regardless of the operating system, you'll always see devices set up to share represented by small computer icons. If you double-click one of these icons, you can see any shared printers, folders, or other devices represented by appropriate icons. Sometimes you have to *drill down* (continue to double-click icons) a little bit to find all the shared items on your network.

In general, you'll see two types of devices on your network:

- **Standalone network devices:** These are computers, storage devices, gaming devices, and so on that have a network port and are on the network in their own right.

- **Attached devices:** These are peripherals, drives, or other devices that are on the network because they're attached to something else, like a PC.

Just double-click your workgroup to see all your home computers and other networked devices. Click any to see what you can share within them.

All this mouse clicking can be a pain. Save your wrist and create a shortcut to your shared resources by clicking the Add Network Place icon within My Network Places. Shortcuts are especially handy for people who have networked devices out on the Internet that they visit often, such as File Transfer Protocol (FTP) sites.

If you find a computer that you expect to be on the network but it's not, make sure that its workgroup name is the same as the other machines — this is a common mistake. (See the earlier section "Setting up a workgroup.")

We find using Windows Explorer to be the best way to visualize what's on your computer and your network. You can get to Windows Explorer in all Windows operating systems the same two ways. Either right-click the Start button and select Explore, or choose Start➪Programs➪Windows Explorer. Figure 11-3 shows Windows Explorer looking at available network resources.

Just because you see a device in the Network Neighborhood or My Network Places doesn't mean you can *share* with that device — where *share* means that you can view, use, copy, and otherwise work on files and resources on that device. The devices need to be set up for sharing for that to happen. (Think of it like your regular neighborhood, where you can see a lot of the houses, but you can't go in some of them because they're locked.) To set up sharing, see the next section.

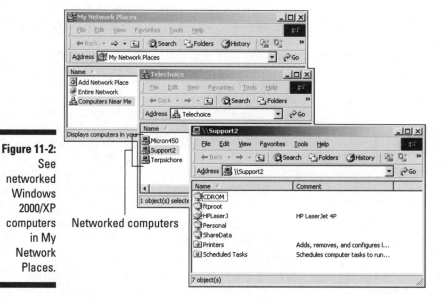

Figure 11-2:
See networked Windows 2000/XP computers in My Network Places.

Networked computers

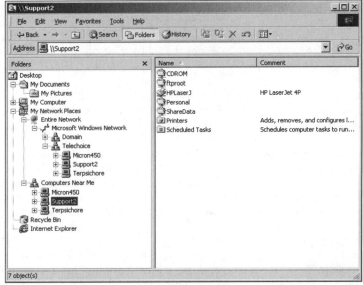

Figure 11-3:
Use
Windows
Explorer to
see network
resources.

Sharing — I Can Do That!

File sharing is a basic feature of any home network. Whether sharing MP3 files on a computer with other devices (including your stereo as we discuss in Chapter 13) or giving access to financial files for mom and dad to access on each other's computers, sharing files is a way to maintain one copy of something and not have a zillion versions all over the network.

You can share your whole computer, you might want to share only certain things (documents or folders), or you might want to share some stuff only in certain ways. Here's an idea of what you can share in your network:

✔ **The whole computer:** You can choose to make the whole computer or device accessible from the network. (We really don't advise sharing your whole computer because it exposes all your PC to anyone who accesses your network.)

✔ **Specific internal drives:** You can share a specific hard drive, such as one where all your MP3s are stored or your computer games.

✔ **Specific peripheral drives:** You can share PC-connected or network-enabled peripheral drives, like an extra Universal Serial Bus (USB)-attached hard drive, a Zip or Jaz backup drive, or an external CD/DVD read/write drive.

✔ **Files:** You can set up particular folders or just a specific file to share across your network. *Note:* File storage schemes on devices are *hierarchical:* If you share a folder, all files and folders within that folder will be shared. If you want to share only one file, select just that file or share a folder with only the one file in it.

Enabling file sharing on Windows 95/98/Me

Luckily for you, file sharing is easy. But to share files in Windows 95/98/Me, you first must enable sharing on your PC.

After you set up sharing, your computer will need to reboot, so we recommend that you close any and all other applications before following these steps.

To enable file sharing on your Windows 95/98/Me PC, do this:

1. **Choose Start⇨Settings⇨Control Panel and then double-click the Network icon.**

2. **On the Configuration tab of the Network dialog box, click the File and Print Sharing button.**

3. **In the File and Print Sharing dialog box that appears, select the I Want to Be Able to Give Others Access to My Files check box and then click OK twice.**

   If you want to share a printer from this machine, you could also select the I Want to Be Able to Give Other Access to My Printers check box.

4. **Click OK in the dialog box that asks to restart your computer.**

   Your computer reboots, and your files are now ready for sharing.

Sharing a document or folder on Windows 95/98/Me

You don't need to share your entire C: drive in order to share just one file. We recommend that you create a shared folder where you put all the files that you want to share. Because you're opening just this one shared folder to the network, the rest of your documents are protected.

You can never be too protected

The number of ways that someone can get on your network multiplies with each new technology that you add to your network. We note in Chapter 10 that wireless local area networks (LANs) seep out of your home and make it easy for others to log in and sniff around. If someone does manage to break into your network, the most obvious places to snoop around and do damage are the shared resources. Sharing your C: drive (which is usually your main hard drive), your Windows directory, or your My Documents directory makes it easier for people to get into your machine and do something you'd rather they not.

You see, sharing will broadcast to the rest of the network the fact that something is shared,

telling everyone who's got access, your computer's name on the network, and how to find it. Sharing can broadcast that availability across firewalls, proxies, and servers. Certain types of viruses and less-than-friendly hackers look for these specific areas (like your shared C: drive) in broadcast messages and follow them back to your machine.

If you're going to share these parts of your system on your network, run a personal firewall on your machines for an added layer of security, or it will likely be compromised at some point. Get virus software. Protect your machine, and limit your exposure to risk. (And by all means be sure to follow our advice in Chapter 10 for securing your wireless network.)

To share a document on your now sharing-enabled Windows PC (whether it's running 95/98/Me), follow these steps:

1. **Set up a space to share from.**

   In Windows, you do this at the folder level. If, like most of us, you use the My Documents folder to store and organize your files, either create or use an existing folder inside My Documents to share your files with others.

2. **Right-click the folder that contains the document that you want to share and then choose Sharing from the shortcut menu that appears.**

   If you want to share full disk drives, choose the entire drive here, not just a folder.

3. **On the Sharing tab of the Properties dialog box, click Shared As.**

4. **Identify the shared folder on the network by using the active folder name or entering a different name in the Share Name text box.**

   If you have a mixed network that has older Mac or Windows 95/98/Me/NT computers on it, keep your folder names to just eight characters with no spaces. Eight-character names are the standard form, compatible with those platforms, and if you want to effectively share without problems you will not have a choice — keep those names short.

To provide a longer description of the folder, enter a comment in the Comment box. (We recommend that you do this because some shared documents and devices sometime have non-intuitive names.)

5. **Windows 95/98/Me will allow everyone full access to any share you set up by default.**

   If you want to protect your shared folder, you have the option to set up an Access Type (see Figure 11-4), which allows read-only access or full control based on the password, or passwords, that you set on the folder.

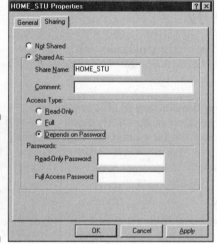

Figure 11-4: The dialog box where you config- ure your shared folder.

Enabling sharing on Windows 2000/XP

In Windows 2000/XP, sharing is enabled by default on each network connection on your machine. If you have a wired network card and a wireless card, you can have sharing enabled On on one card and Off on the other. This is very helpful if you only want to share files on one of the networks that you connect to. For example, if you want to share files when connected to your home wireless network but turn off sharing when you plug your laptop in at work, turn sharing On for your wireless card and Off for your wired Ethernet card. When you first install a new network card, or wireless network card for our purposes, the default is to have sharing turned On.

To enable sharing on a Windows 2000/XP machine, follow these steps, which are quite similar to those in the preceding section:

1. **Choose Start⇨Settings⇨Network and Dial-up Connections.**

2. **Right-click the icon of the network connection over which you wish to enable File and Printer Sharing and then choose Properties from the pop-up menu that appears.**

3. **On the General tab for network cards and on the Network tab for dialup connections, you select the check box for File and Printer Sharing for Microsoft Networks.**

This enables your PC to share files and also printers.

Use Windows Explorer to find and move shared files.

When you right-click any folder or file and then select Sharing from the pop-up menu that appears, you can control the sharing of that file.

Setting permissions

In Windows 95/98/Me, you set file-sharing permissions on a folder-by-folder basis; see the earlier section "Sharing a document or folder on Windows 95/98/Me."

In Windows 2000/XP, controlling the sharing of files is a bit more complex because of the enhanced security that comes with those operating systems. To share folders and drives, you must be logged on as a member of the Server Operators, Administrators, Power Users, or Users groups. Throughout the rest of this section, we describe these user types and then show you how to add users to your 2000/XP network.

User types

The *Server Operators* group is really only used on large networks that incorporate Microsoft's Active Directory technology; if you're trying to set up your office computer at home, you might run into this (but it's not very likely). The groups that you need to concern yourself with are the Administrators, Power Users, and Users groups:

- **Administrators** are system gods. Anyone set up as an administrator can do anything they like — no restrictions.

- **Power Users** can't do as much as administrators, but they can do a lot — as long as what they're doing doesn't change any of the files that make Windows operate. In other words, Power Users can add and remove software, users, hardware, and so on to a system as long as their actions don't affect any files keeping the system running the way that it's running.

- **Users** are just that: Users simply use what the system has to offer and aren't able to do anything else. The Users group provides the most secure environment in which to run programs, and it's by far the best way to give access to your resources *without* compromising the security of your computer and network.

How do you know what kind of access you have? Unfortunately, that's not an easy thing to find out unless you're an administrator. If you know that you're not an administrator, the only way to find out what you *can* do is by trying to do it. If you don't have the proper access to do something, you will get a warning message telling you exactly that — sometimes the message might tell you what access you need to have in order to do what you want.

Adding users

For others to get access to what you have shared, you need to give them permission. You do that by giving them a logon on your computer and assigning them to a group — essentially adding them to the network as a user. The group is then given certain rights within the folder that you have shared; every user in the group has access only to what the group has access to. For more details on this process, we strongly recommend that you use the Windows Help file to discover how to set up new users and groups on your system.

In Windows 2000/XP, creating users and adding them to groups is best done by using the administrator logon. If you're using an office computer and you're not the administrator or a member of the Power Users group, you won't be able to create users. Talk to your system administrator to get permission and help setting up your machine.

We're guessing that you are the administrator of your home-networked computer (it's your network, right?), and so you do have access to the administrator logon. Thus, you can set up new users by logging onto the machine as administrator. Like the hierarchical folder permissions, user permissions are hierarchal as well. If you're a Power User, you can only create users who have less access than yourself. By using the administrator logon, you can create any type of user account that you might need.

Unless you're very comfortable with the security settings of Windows 2000/XP, you should never give new user accounts more access than the Users group provides. (For a description of user types, see the preceding section.) Keep in mind that by creating these accounts, you're also creating a logon that can be used to turn on and access your computer directly. For the purposes of sharing files and peripherals, the standard Users group provides all the access that any individual on the network would normally need.

To add users to your network, follow these steps:

1. **Choose Start⇨Settings⇨Control Panel and double-click the Users and Passwords icon.**

   This brings up the Users and Passwords dialog box.

2. **Click the Add button to launch the New User Wizard and add users to your machine.**

3. **Follow the wizard's onscreen prompts to enter a name, logon name, description, password, and then which group the user will be part of.**

   New users should always start as part of the Users group (also referred to as the Restricted Access group), which is the lowest possible access level. Starting users at the lowest possible access level is the best way for you to share your files without compromising your network's security.

Accessing shared files

Whether drives, folders, or single files are set up for sharing on your wireless home network, you access the shared thing in pretty much the same way. On any networked PC, you simply log onto the network, head for Network Neighborhood (or My Network Places, as the case may be), and navigate to the file (or folder or drive) that you want to access. It's really as easy as that.

Just because you can *see* a drive, folder, or file in Network Neighborhood, however, doesn't necessarily mean that you have *access* to that drive, folder, or file. It all depends on set permissions.

Be Economical: Share Those Peripherals

Outside of the fact that there is only so much space on your desk or your kitchen countertop, you simply don't need a complete set of peripherals at each device on your network. For instance, digital cameras are becoming quite popular, and you can view pictures on your PC, on your TV, and even in wireless picture frames around the house. But you probably only need one color printer geared toward printing high-quality photos for someone to take home (after admiring your wireless picture frames!).

The same is true about a lot of peripherals: business card scanners, backup drives (such as Zip and Jaz drives), and even cameras. If you have one device and it's network enabled, anyone on the wireless network should be able to access that for the task at hand.

Setting up a print server

The most common shared peripheral is a printer. Setting up a printer for sharing is really easy, and using it is even easier.

You might have several printers in your house, and different devices might have different printers — but they all can be shared. You might have the color laser printer on your machine, a less expensive one (with less expensive consumables like printer cartridges, too) for the kid's computer, and a high-quality photo printer maybe near the TV set plugged into a USB port of a net-workable A/V device. Each of these can be used by a local device . . . if properly set up.

Here are the steps that you need to take to share a printer:

1. Enable printer sharing within the operating system of the computer to which the printer is attached.

2. Set up sharing for the installed printer.

   We say *installed* printer because we assume that you've already installed the printer locally on your computer or other device.

3. Remotely install the printer on every other computer on the network.

   We describe remote installation in the aptly named section "Remotely installing the printer on all network PCs."

4. Access the printer from any PC on the network!

Throughout the rest of this section, we go through these four general steps in much more detail.

Enabling printer sharing

Your first task is to enable the printer sharing within the Windows OS of the computer to which the printer is attached. This is the same process as shar-ing a folder (see the earlier section "Sharing a document or folder") and is available by default in Windows 2000/XP.

Windows 95/98/Me shares the printer drivers for that printer. It's the same as sharing a folder. Because most people will be using a workgroup type of net-work (see the earlier section "Setting up a workgroup"), having the printer drivers easily accessible makes adding those shared printers to your other computers a lot simpler.

In the shared folder that you create, copy the printer software that came with your printer. These days, most printers have their software on CD-ROM. The simplest way to make that accessible is to share the CD-ROM drive of the computer that the printer is attached to. Now you have full access to the printer's software without having to use up space on one of your hard drives.

Setting up sharing for the installed printer

After you enable printer sharing, it's time to . . . can you guess? . . . share your installed printer.

Windows 95/98/Me

To share a printer on Windows 95/98/Me, just follow these steps:

1. **Go to your Printers folder by choosing Start⇨Settings⇨Printers and then right-clicking the printer that you want to share.**

2. **From the pop-up menu that appears, choose the Sharing option.**

3. **Select the appropriate radio button to share the printer and then consider adding some descriptive words in the Comment field like *Photo Printer in Living Room*.**

   Keep in mind the eight-character limit for device names that we mention earlier.

   Just like in file sharing, you can set a password at the same place where you activate sharing in the Sharing dialog box. We can't see a reason to add a password for a printer, but you might want to because some printers (like photo printers) have high consumables costs (photo paper often costs more than a buck per sheet). This is likely one of the reasons why Windows 2000/XP carries its security policy to printers as well as files.

4. **Click OK.**

   Your printer is shared. Didn't we tell you that this was simple?

Windows 2000/XP

Windows 2000/XP are more sophisticated operating systems and subsequently have a *server type* of print sharing. In other words, they offer all the features of a big network with servers on your local machine. These features include the ability to assign users to manage the print queue remotely, embed printer software for easier installation, and manage when the printer will be available based on a schedule that you define.

To share a printer on Windows 2000/XP, follow these steps:

1. **Choose Start⇨Settings⇨Printers and Faxes (or simply choose Start⇨Printers and Faxes, depending on how your Start menu is configured).**

2. **Right-click the printer in the Printers folder and choose Properties from the pop-up menu that appears.**

3. **On the Sharing tab of the dialog box that appears, click the Additional Drivers button.**

4. **Select which operating systems you want to support to use this shared printer and also select the other types of drivers needed for your other computer systems and devices; then click OK.**

5. **When prompted, insert a floppy disk or CD-ROM and direct the subsequent dialog boxes to the right places on those devices to get the driver for each operating system that you chose.**

   Windows finds those drivers and downloads them to the Windows 2000/XP's hard drive. Then, when you go to install the printer on your other computers (see the next section), the Windows 2000/XP machine, which is sharing the printer, automatically transfers the proper printer drivers and finishes the installation for you. Darned sweet if you ask us!

Remotely installing the printer on all network PCs

The third step is done at every other PC in the house. Basically, you install the printer on each of these computers, but in a logical way — *logically* as opposed to *physically* installing and connecting the printer to each computer. You install the printer just like any other printer except that you're installing a *network* printer, and the printer installation wizard will search the network for the printers that you want to install.

The process that you'll use will vary depending on the operating system that you use and the type of printer that you're trying to install. In every case, read the printer documentation before you start because some printers require their software to be partially installed before you try to add the printer. We've seen this a lot with multifunction printers that support scanning, copying, and faxing.

With Windows, the easiest way to start the installation of a printer is to look inside Network Neighborhood (or My Network Places), find the computer sharing the printer, and double-click the shared printer. This starts the Add Printer Wizard, which takes you through the process of adding the printer. This wizard works like any good wizard — you'll make a few selections and click Next a lot. When asked for the printer drivers, use the Browse button to direct the wizard to look in the shared folder or CD-ROM drive where you put the printer software on the computer that the printer is attached to.

You have two options for installing a network printer:

✔ **From your Printers folder:** In Window 95/98/Me, choose Start➪Settings➪Printers to see the Printers folder where your installed printers are shown. Double-click the Add Printer icon.

In Windows 2000/XP, choose Start➪Settings➪Printers and Faxes (or simply Start➪Printers and Faxes, depending how your Start menu is configured).

✔ **From Network Neighborhood or My Network Places:** From within Network Neighborhood in Windows 95/98/Me (or My Network Places in Windows 2000/XP), double-click the computer that has the printer attached. An icon will appear showing the shared printer. Right-click it and then choose Install from the pop-up menu that appears.

Either route leads you to the Add Printer Wizard, which guides you through the process of adding the network printer.

Don't start the Add Printer Wizard unless you have the disks or CDs for your printer handy. The Add Printer Wizard will install the printer *drivers* (software files that contain the info required for Windows to talk to your printers and exchange data for printing). The wizard gets these from the CD that comes with your printer. If you don't have the CD, go to the Web site of your printer manufacturer and download the driver to your desktop and install from there. And don't forget to delete the downloaded file(s) from your desktop when done with installing them on the computer.

Note also that the wizard will allow you to browse your network to find the printer that you want to install. Simply click the plus sign next to the computer that has the printer attached, and you should see the printer below the computer. (If not, then recheck that printer sharing is enabled on that computer.)

At the end of the wizard screens, you have the option to print a test page. We recommend that you do this. You don't want to wait until your child has to have a color printout for her science experiment (naturally she waits until 10 minutes before the bus arrives to tell you!) to find out that the printer doesn't work.

Accessing your shared printer(s)

After you have the printers installed, how do you access them? Whenever your Print window comes up (by pressing Ctrl+P in most applications), you will see a field labeled Name for the name of the printer accompanied by a pull-down menu of printer options. Use your mouse to select any printer — local or networked — and the rest of the printing process remains the same as if you had a printer directly plugged into your PC.

You can even make a networked printer the default printer by right-clicking the printer and then choosing Set as Default Printer from the pop-up menu that appears.

Sharing other peripherals

Sharing any other peripheral is quite similar to sharing printers. You need to make sure that you're sharing the device on the computer that it's attached to. Then you need to install that device on another PC by using that device's installation procedures. Obviously, we can't be very specific about such an installation because of the widely varying processes that companies use to install devices. Most of the time — like with a printer — you need to install the drivers for the device that you're sharing on your other computers.

Note that some of the devices that you attach to your network have integral Web servers in them. This is getting more and more common. Danny's AudioReQuest (www.request.com) music server, for instance, is visible on his home network and is addressable by any of his PCs. Thus, he can download music to and from the AudioReQuest server and sync it to his other devices that he wants music on. Anyone else in the home can do the same — even remotely, over the Internet. We talk more about the AudioReQuest system in Chapter 13.

Danny has also set up a virtual CD server in his home to manage all the CDs that his kids have for their games. This server is shared on the home network. By using Virtual CD software from H+H Zentrum fuer Rechnerkommunikation GmbH (www.virtualcd-online.com/default_e.htm; $75 for a five-user license), Danny has loaded all his CDs onto a single machine so that the kids (he's got four kids) can access those CDs from any of their individual PCs (he's got four *spoiled* kids). Instead of looking to the local hard drive for the CD, any of the kids' PCs looks to the server to find the CD — hence the name *virtual CD*. Now those stacks of CDs (and moans over a scratched CD!) are gone.

Sharing between Macs and Windows-based PCs

We could tell you about all sorts of ways that you can get files from Macs to PCs — as well as kludgey ways to send them via FTP from computer to computer — but the simple fact of the matter is this: If you have a Mac and want to get it on a PC network, you buy a software program for the Macintosh called *DAVE*. If you have a non-Apple computer that you want on your Mac network, you go to Chapter 8 where we show you how to do that. If you have a Mac network on which you want to share files, printers, and other peripherals, check out the nearby sidebar, "Care for a Rendezvous?"

Care for a Rendezvous?

One cool feature that Apple has added to its newest version of Mac OS — Mac OS v. 10.2 (often called Jaguar) — is a networking system called Rendezvous. Rendezvous is based on an open Internet standard (IETF [Internet Engineering Task Force] Zeroconf) and is being adopted by a number of manufacturers outside of Apple.

Basically, Rendezvous (and Zeroconf) is a lot like Bluetooth (which we discuss in Chapter 15) in that it allows devices on a network to discover each other without any user intervention or special configuration. Rendezvous is being incorporated into many products, such as printers, storage devices (basically, networkable hard drives), and even household electronics like TiVos (hard drive-based television personal video recorders [PVRs]).

Here's one great feature about Rendezvous: On Macs that are equipped with Apple AirPort network adapter cards, it lets two (or more) Macs in range of each other (in other words, within Wi-Fi range) *automatically* connect to each other for file sharing, Instant Messaging, and such without going through any extra steps of setting up a peer-to-peer network.

Rendezvous is enabled automatically in Mac OS v. 10.2 computers if you turn enable Personal Fire Sharing (found in the System Preferences; look for the Sharing Icon) or use Apple's iChat Instant Messaging Program, Apple's Safari Web browsers, or any Rendezvous-capable printer connected to your Airport network.

If you have a Mac, you've probably heard about DAVE from someone. Using DAVE enables you to share CDs, printers, hard drives, folders, and so on. DAVE (www.thursby.com; $149 for a single-user license) uses the fast, industry standard Transmission Control Protocol/Internet Protocol (TCP/IP) protocol instead of AppleTalk and is designed specifically for the Apple Macintosh. It's installed on the Macintosh, and no additional hardware or software is required on the PC. There are versions for all current versions of Mac OS, including OS X.

When you install DAVE on your Mac and launch it for the first time, the DAVE setup assistant will launch. Follow the onscreen steps — you'll need to tell DAVE what type of Windows network you'll be connecting to. (You need to mark a check box to specify if your Windows network uses Windows NT or Windows 2000.) You'll also need to enter a name for your Mac as well as identify the name of the Windows network workgroup, as we discuss earlier in this chapter. DAVE will then automatically connect your Mac to the PC network, asking you whether you want to share files from your Mac with PCs in the network.

If you're using the latest version of Mac OS X — Jaguar, or OS X v. 10.2 — your Mac can basically work right out of the box with any Windows network for things like file sharing. That is, if you have Mac OS X v. 10.2 (or later), you don't need DAVE.

Thursby also sells the program MacSOHO that enables file and printer sharing between PCs and Macs. We don't suggest you get this because it won't work with Windows XP. Microsoft has decided to eliminate support for NetBEUI from its new release, Windows XP, and MacSOHO uses the NetBEUI protocol. Get DAVE instead.

Chapter 12

Gaming over a Wireless Home Network

. . . .

In This Chapter

▶ Unwiring your gaming PCs: Hardware and networking requirements

▶ Getting your gaming consoles online

▶ Forwarding those ports

▶ Setting up a demilitarized zone (DMZ)

. . . .

*I*n case you missed it, gaming is huge. We mean HUGE. The video gaming industry is, believe it or not, bigger than the entertainment industry generated by Hollywood. Billions of dollars per year are spent on PC game software and hardware and on gaming consoles such as PlayStation and Xbox. You probably know a bit about gaming — we bet you've at least played Minesweeper on your PC or Pong on an Atari when you were a kid. But what you might not know is that video gaming has moved online in a big way. And for that, you need a network.

All three of the big gaming console vendors — Sony (www.us.playstation.com), Microsoft (www.xbox.com), and Nintendo (www.gamecube.com) — have created inexpensive networking kits for their latest consoles that let you connect your console to a broadband Internet connection (such as a cable or digital subscriber line [DSL]) to play against people anywhere in the world. Online PC gaming has also become a huge phenomenon, with games such as EverQuest Online attracting millions of users.

A big challenge for anyone getting into online gaming is finding a way to get consoles and PCs in different parts of the house connected to your Internet connection. For example, if you have an Xbox, it's probably in your living room or home theater, and we're willing to bet that your cable or DSL modem is in the home office. Lots of folks string a Cat 5e Ethernet cable down the hall and hook it into their game machine — a great approach if you don't mind tripping over that cable at 2 a.m. when you let the dogs out. Enter your wireless home network, a much better approach to getting these gaming devices online.

In this chapter, we talk about some of the hardware requirements for getting a gaming PC or game console online. In the case of gaming consoles, you'll need to pick up some extra gear because none of the current online kits contain wireless gear. We also talk about some of the steps that you need to take in order to configure your router (or the router in your access point [AP], if they're the same box in your wireless local area network [LAN]) to get your online gaming up and running.

We're approaching this chapter with the assumption that your wireless gaming network will be connecting to the Internet using some sort of always-on, broadband connection such as DSL or a cable modem, using a home router (either the one built into your access point or a separate one). We have two reasons for this assumption: First, we think that online gaming works much, much better on a broadband connection; second, because with some console systems (particularly the Xbox), you are *required* to have a broadband connection to use online gaming.

One of the biggest things that broadband brings is speed to your gaming experience. A big part of online gaming is not so much how quickly you can kill your opponent or crossover your dribble but how quickly the central gaming host computer in the middle of it all knows that you performed a certain action (and recognizes it). How frustrating to fire a missile at a helicopter only to find out that the helicopter blew you up first because the system registered its firing before yours. The time that it takes for your gaming commands to cross the Internet — in gaming, at least — is often a matter of virtual life or death.

Get your online game on!

The biggest trend in PC gaming (besides the ever-improving quality of graphics enabled by the newest hardware) is the development of online gaming. Broadband Internet connectivity has become widespread — about a quarter of Americans use broadband at home, according to the Pew Internet Life Survey. This has allowed online PC gaming to grow beyond simplistic (and low-speed) Java games (which still can be fun — check out games.yahoo.com) and move toward high-speed, graphics–intensive, multi-player games like Quake III.

If you've not yet checked out online gaming, you might not realize what a big deal it is. In parts of the world where broadband is ubiquitous — like South Korea, where almost every home is wired with DSL or cable — broadband online games boast tens of millions of users. Here in the United States, this trend has not quite reached those proportions, but there are still millions of users playing various multi-player online games. Face it — it's just plain fun to reach out and blow up your buddy's tank from 1,000 miles away.

You can find out how fast your connection is by pinging the other machines or the central server. (*Pinging* is a process where you use an application on your computer — usually just called *ping*, accessible from the DOS or CMD window — to send a signal to another computer and see how long it takes to get there and back, like a sonar beam on a submarine pinging another sub.)

PC Gaming Hardware Requirements

We should preface this section of the book by saying that this book is not entitled *Gaming PCs For Dummies*. Thus, we're not going to spend any time talking about PC gaming hardware requirements in any kind of detail. Our gamer pals will probably be aghast at our brief coverage here, but we really just want to give you a taste of what you might want to think about if you decide to really outfit a PC for online gaming. In fact, if you're buying a PC for this purpose, check out the classes of computers called *gaming PCs* optimized just for this application. Throughout this chapter, we use the term *gaming PC* generically to mean any PC in your home that you're using for gaming — not just special-purpose gaming PCs.

Your best resource, we think, is to check out an online gaming Web site that has a team of experts who review and torture-test all the latest hardware for a living. We like CNET's www.gamespot.com and www.gamespy.com.

At the most basic level, you really just need any modern multimedia PC (or Macintosh for that matter) to get started with PC gaming. Just about any PC or Mac purchased since 2002 or so will have a fast processor and a decent graphics or video card. (You'll hear both terms used.) If you start getting into online gaming, start thinking about upgrading your PC with high-end gaming hardware or even consider building a dedicated gaming machine. Some of the key hardware components to keep in mind are the following:

- **Fast processor:** A lot of the hard work in gaming is done by the video card, but a fast Pentium 4 or AMD Athlon (or PowerPC G4, for Macs) central processing unit (CPU) is always a nice thing to have.

- **Powerful video card:** The latest cards from ATI and nVIDIA (www.nvidia.com) contain incredibly sophisticated computer chips that are dedicated to cranking out the video part of your games. If you get to the point where you know what frames per second (fps) is all about and you start worrying that yours are too low, it's time to start investigating faster video cards.

  We're big fans of the ATI (www.ati.com) All-In-Wonder 9700 PRO, but then, we're suckers for fast hardware that can crank out the polygons (the building blocks of your game video) at mind-boggling speeds.

✔ **Fancy gaming controllers:** Many games can be played by using a standard mouse and keyboard, but you might want to look into some cool specialized game controllers that connect through your PC's Universal Serial Bus (USB) ports. For example, you can get a joystick for flying games or a steering wheel for driving games. Check out Creative Technologies (www.creative.com) for some cool options.

✔ **Quality sound card:** Many games include a *Surround sound* soundtrack, just like DVDs provide in your home theater. If you've got the appropriate number of speakers and the right sound card, you'll hear the bad guys creeping up behind you before you see them on the screen. Très fun.

Networking Requirements for PC Gaming

Gaming PCs might (but don't have to) have some different innards than regular PCs, but their networking requirements don't differ in any appreciable way from the PC that you use for Web browsing, e-mail, or anything else. So you shouldn't be surprised to hear that connecting a gaming PC to your wireless network is no different than connecting any PC.

You'll need some sort of wireless network adapter connected to your gaming PC to get it up and running on your home network (just like you need a wireless network adapter connected to *any* PC running on your network, as we discuss in Chapter 5). These adapters can fit in the PC Card slot (of a laptop computer, for example) or connect to a USB or Ethernet port of a desktop computer. If you have a Mac that you're using for gaming, you'll probably use one of the Apple AirPort or AirPort Extreme cards (which we discuss in Chapter 8). There's nothing special that you need to do, hardware-wise, with a gaming PC.

When it comes to actually playing online games, you might need to do some tweaking to your home network's router — which might be a standalone device or might be part of your access point. In the upcoming sections "Dealing with Router Configurations" and "Setting Up a Demilitarized Zone (DMZ)," we discuss these steps in further detail.

Depending upon which games you're playing, you might not need to do any special configuring at all. Some games play just fine without any special router configurations — particularly if your PC isn't acting as the *server* (meaning that other people aren't connecting to your PC from remote locations on the Internet).

Getting Your Gaming Console on Your Wireless Home Network

Although PC gaming can be really cool, we find that many people prefer to use a dedicated game console device — such as a PlayStation 2 (PS2) or an Xbox — to do their gaming. And although hard-core gamers might lean toward PC platforms for their gaming (often spending thousands of dollars on ultra high-end gaming PCs with the latest video cards, fastest processor and memory, and the like), we think that for regular gamers, consoles offer some compelling advantages:

- ✔ **They're inexpensive.** Price points are always dropping, but as we write, you could buy a PS2 or Xbox for $199 or a Nintendo GameCube for even less ($149). Even if you dedicate an inexpensive PC for gaming, you'll probably spend closer to $1,000 — and even more if you buy the fancy video cards and other equipment that gives the PC the same gaming performance as a console.

- ✔ **They're simple to set up.** Although it's not all that hard to get games running on a PC, you are dealing with a more complicated operating system on a PC. You have to install games and get them up and running. On a game console, you simply shove a disc into the drawer and you're playing.

- ✔ **They're in the right room.** Most folks don't want a PC in their living room or home theater, although some really cool models are designed just for that purpose. A game console, on the other hand, is relatively small and inconspicuous and can fit neatly on a shelf next to your TV.

- ✔ **They work with your biggest screen.** Of course, you could connect a PC to a big-screen TV system (using a special video card), and it's getting easier. But consoles are designed to plug right in to your TV or home theater system, using the same cables that you use to hook up a VCR or DVD player. You can even use the Xbox or PS2 as a DVD player!

Today's game consoles can offer some awesome gaming experiences. Try playing the Xbox game Halo on a big-screen TV with a Surround sound system in place . . . it's amazing — you can even get a full HDTV (High Definition TV) picture on the Xbox, with certain games. And because these gaming consoles are really nothing more than specialized computers, they can offer the same kind of networking capabilities that a PC does — in other words, they can fit right into your wireless home network.

You can't just take your console out of the box and connect it to your wireless network, however. Here are three steps that you need to take; we talk about each in more detail in the following sections:

1. Get the networking kit appropriate to your console.

2. Get signed up with an online gaming service.

3. Get a wireless Ethernet bridge (see Figure 12-1) to make the connection.

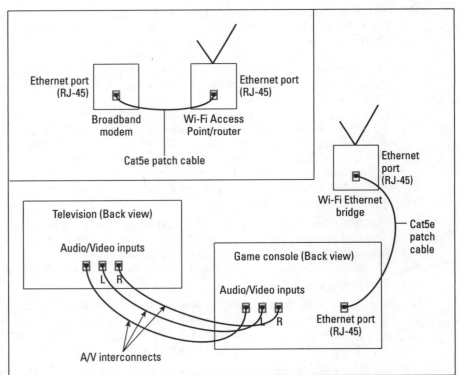

Figure 12-1:
Connecting
a game
console
wirelessly.

Ethernet port
(RJ-45)

Broadband
modem

Cat5e patch cable

Wi-Fi Access
Point/router

Ethernet port
(RJ-45)

Ethernet
port
(RJ-45)

Wi-Fi Ethernet
bridge

Cat5e
patch
cable

Television (Back view)

Audio/Video inputs

L   R

Game console (Back view)

Audio/Video inputs

L   R

Ethernet port
(RJ-45)

A/V interconnects

Console online gaming services and equipment

In this section, we conjoin our discussion of the first two requirements listed previously: the networking kit and the online gaming service. For the Xbox, these two items are one and the same. Conversely, for PlayStation and GameCube, they're separate steps, as we discuss shortly.

Can your games get online?

As you get into online gaming with your game console, keep this one common requirement in mind: You need to have games that are online capable. As we write this book, online gaming services have been available for only a few months, and the number of games that can be played online is relatively limited. Most of the games that you already own (if you have one of these consoles now) probably don't have online gaming capabilities. Fortunately, all the gaming software companies that we know are bringing out a ton of online-capable games, so this won't be a major limiting factor if you're just now getting into online gaming.

Online capable games cost about the same as regular games for these consoles — about $20–$50, and the price of the service depends upon the game and console you're using. Microsoft, for example, charges $50/year for its gaming service, which covers all the games available.

The cost of getting into online gaming will be higher than just the price of the kit or service. You also need to account for the cost of new, online-ready games. Plus, none of the gaming services that we discuss here includes the broadband Internet access that you need to make them work. You've got to have a broadband Internet service, and *then* you need to buy the equipment and get the online gaming service set up.

Living large with Xbox

In many ways, Microsoft's Xbox is the most online-ready of the gaming consoles that we discuss. Xbox is the only console to come with a built-in networking port (an RJ-45, or Ethernet, jack). And Microsoft's online gaming service, Xbox Live (www.xboxlive.com) is (in our opinion) the furthest along so far in terms of games available and number of participants. Remember that all these services are quite new.

To get online with Xbox Live, you need to buy a $50 kit (available at www.xbox.com/live), which is a combination of hardware and service. In other words, you get the components that you need to get online as well as a year of gaming service. As of this writing, 14 Xbox Live-enabled games are on the market.

Microsoft doesn't provide the broadband service for Xbox Live (none of the gaming companies do) — just the gaming service itself. Thus, you need to already have a cable or DSL modem set up in your home. What Microsoft *does* do — and this is a bit different from what Sony and Nintendo do with their online gaming — is host its own online service that you connect to when you sign on to Xbox Live. You need to sign up for only one service to play online games with your Xbox. Sony and Nintendo rely on game software vendors to set up their own online gaming services, so you might need to subscribe to one service for Game A and another for Game B.

Xbox Live includes a software disc to get things set up on your console as well as a headset that plugs into one of the Xbox's controller ports. This headset enables a really cool feature of Xbox Live — voice chat during game play. With this, you can add your own running commentary to the game while you blow past your opponent on the racecourse or blow up her tank.

Because the Xbox comes out of the box with a built-in Ethernet port, the Xbox Live kit doesn't contain any other networking hardware. You just need to connect your Xbox to the wireless network (using a wireless Ethernet bridge as we discuss in the upcoming section "Console wireless networking equipment"), insert the Xbox Live disc into your Xbox, and follow the on-screen instructions. You'll be prompted to enter a *Gamertag* — your online "handle" or screen name — as well as your actual name, address info, credit card number, and a subscription code (you'll usually find this inside the disc case that your Xbox Live disc came in). After you do all this, your account is registered, and you're ready to game.

Microsoft doesn't let you change your Gamertag after the fact, so pick one you like — you're stuck with it.

Playing online with PlayStation 2 (PS2)

Although the Xbox, with its Xbox Live service, is probably the most advanced online gaming console, it has one big disadvantage when compared with Sony's PS2 console — a lot less users. The PlayStation is the numero uno, most popular gaming console these days, with tens and tens of millions of users. This popularity led to a greater number of game software companies creating a greater number and variety of games for the PS2 console.

As we discuss in the earlier section "Can your games get online?," most existing games will not work online. As we write this, 15 PS2 games allow online gaming. So even though there are a lot more PS2 games than Xbox or GameCube games on the market, you won't find a lot more online-capable PS2 games.

Because the PS2 does not come from the factory with an Ethernet port, you need to spend 40 bucks for the Sony PlayStation 2 Network Adaptor to get into online gaming. The adaptor plugs into a port on the back of the PS2 and has an Ethernet port (like the port that's already on the back of an Xbox) for connecting to your wireless home network using a wireless Ethernet bridge. The network adaptor also has a dialup modem built in, so even if you don't have broadband, you can still get into online gaming (unlike Xbox Live, which is broadband only).

We think that you really need broadband to do online gaming right . . . otherwise, the play is just too choppy and lagging. If you don't have broadband, we also recommend that you don't bother connecting your PS2 to your wireless LAN. Just plug the network adapter in the nearest phone jack. If you don't have a phone jack near your PS2, consider getting one of RCA's wireless phone jacks (search for this term on www.rca.com to find more information). Although these aren't wireless LAN equipment, they are a cheap way (about $50) to put a phone jack where one isn't.

You can find more information about PS2 online gaming at Sony's site (www. us.playstation.com/onlinegaming). As we mention in the previous section, the big difference between PS2 and Xbox Live online gaming relates to who provides the online gaming service itself. With the Xbox, you sign up for your account with Microsoft, and you can then play any Xbox Live game using that account. With the PS2, you need to sign up for accounts with the individual game developers — so if you want to be the Duke Blue Devils in Sega's NCAA 2K3 Hoops game, you need to sign up for Sega's online game hosting service. Luckily, the game manufacturers are not currently charging for this service, but you might end up having to remember account names and passwords for multiple services when your game collection grows.

GameCube

Without a doubt, the Nintendo GameCube is the cutest of the three major game console systems. Although it's positively tiny compared with the PS2 — and especially when compared with the huge Xbox — it's still loaded with powerful computer chips that give you some big gaming fun. And like the other two consoles, the GameCube can be a part of your wireless LAN, with just a few additions.

Like the PS2, the GameCube doesn't have a built-in Ethernet port with which you can connect the console directly to a wireless Ethernet bridge. So (like the PS2), you need to buy an adapter — a Broadband Network Adapter, to be precise, which costs about $39 — that plugs into the back of the GameCube and contains an Ethernet port that you can use for hooking the console into your wireless home network. You can find more details about this network adapter — as well as lots of info about the GameCube itself — at Nintendo's Web site (www.gamecube.com).

As of this writing, you can play only one GameCube game online — Phantasy Star Online — that requires an $8.95 per month subscription and works with most online services (but not, unfortunately, with the biggest one — AOL). We expect more GameCube online games to become available, but so far, that's it.

Like the PS2, the GameCube also has a dialup modem adapter for online gaming. As we discuss in the "Playing online with PlayStation 2 (PS2)" section of this chapter, we think that the best way to deal with dialup modem gaming is to just plug this adapter into a nearby phone jack and not to try to connect the console to your wireless LAN.

Console wireless networking equipment

In case we haven't made it abundantly clear in our discussion so far, we reiterate: *None* of the consoles that we've discussed comes with any kind of built-in wireless LAN capabilities, and *none* of the networking kits or adapters that you need to buy from the console maker includes wireless LAN equipment. What all these consoles do have, when outfitted for online gaming, is an Ethernet port. This will undoubtedly change, but for now that's it.

And really, that's all you need, thanks to the availability of relatively inexpensive wireless Ethernet bridges. The deeper you get into the networking world, the more likely you are to run into the concept of a *bridge,* which is simply a device that connects two segments of a network together. Unlike hubs or switches or routers or most other network equipment (we talk about a lot of this stuff back in Chapters 2 and 5), a bridge doesn't do anything with the data flowing through it. It basically just passes the data straight through without manipulating it, rerouting it, or even caring what it is. A wireless Ethernet bridge's sole purpose in life, then, is to send data back and forth between two points. (Not too tough to see where the name came from, huh?)

While we're discussing these wireless Ethernet bridges in terms of game consoles networks in this chapter, they're actually quite handy devices that can be used for a lot of different applications in your wireless LAN. Basically, any device that has an Ethernet port — such as a TiVo or ReplayTV personal video recorder (PVR), an MP3 server (such as the AudioReQuest), even an Internet refrigerator (such as Samsung's Internet Refrigerator) — can hook into your wireless home network using a wireless Ethernet bridge.

Wireless Ethernet bridges are a relatively new phenomenon in the wireless LAN world — which is really saying something considering the fact that wireless LANs have been a mainstream technology for only a couple of years. As we write, only a couple of wireless Ethernet bridges are on the market. We don't expect this situation to last — our contacts at just about every wireless networking equipment company that we know tell us that they, too, are working on their own products in this category.

As we write, you can find two widely available models, which we discuss in detail momentarily:

- **D-Link's D-Link*Air* DWL-810**
- **Linksys WET11**

Both of these wireless Ethernet bridges use the common 11 Mbps 802.11b system. That means that they won't work on the faster 802.11a networking system. They should work on the new 802.11g system but only at the lower 802.11b 11 Mbps speed (which should be fast enough for your gaming needs!). Also, keep in mind that although 802.11b gear *is supposed to* work on 802.11g networks, a lot of "g" gear is pretty new on the market and has not yet undergone extensive interoperability testing.

The great thing about wireless Ethernet bridges — besides the fact that they solve the very real problem of getting non-computer devices onto the wireless network — is that they are the essence of Plug and Play. You might have to spend three or four minutes setting up the bridge itself (getting it connected to your wireless network), but you don't need to do anything special to your game console besides plug the bridge in. All the game consoles that we discuss in this chapter (at least when equipped with the appropriate network adapters and software) will "see" your wireless Ethernet bridge as just a regular Ethernet cable. You don't need any drivers or other special software on the console. The console doesn't know (nor does it care in its not-so-little console brain) that there's a wireless link in the middle of the connection. It just works!

Not many wireless Ethernet bridges are on the market yet, and none are yet available in the faster 802.11a or 802.11g flavors of wireless LANs. We fully expect that to change and to change fast. So if you're using one of these newer technologies in your LAN, don't despair. Keep an eye on the vendor Web sites or on one of the other wireless LAN news sites that we discuss in Chapter 20. You'll probably see a solution for your network before too long.

D-LinkAir DWL-810

D-Link (www.dlink.com) has developed this product with gaming consoles in mind. And in fact, D-Link even has its own online Gamer's Haven site with lots of great gaming information on it (games.dlink.com). The $129 list price DWL-810 (see Figure 12-2) doesn't need any special drivers or configuration but does include a Web-browser based configuration program that enables you to do things like enter your Wired Equivalent Privacy (WEP) keys. (Check out Chapter 10 for more information on this.)

Figure 12-2:
The D-Link
DWL-810
Ethernet
bridge.

Because this bridge can also be used to connect to wired Ethernet hubs and switches, you need to use a special kind of Ethernet cable — a crossover cable — to connect the DWL-810 to your console. (A *crossover cable* is basically an Ethernet cable that's used to interconnect two computers by crossing over [reversing] their respective pin assignments.) Luckily, D-Link includes one in the box — just remember to use that cross-over cable and not a regular Ethernet cable when you hook things up. If you use this bridge with one of D-Link's access points, you can actually take advantage of their proprietary system that speeds up the network to throughputs up to 22 Mbps.

Linksys WET11

The Linksys WET11 ($129; www.linksys.com), like the DWL-810, allows an easy connection between any Ethernet device and your Wi-Fi network. The only substantial difference between the WET11 and the DWL-810 is the addition of an uplink switch on the WET11. Instead of using a cross-over cable to connect to a game console (or any other individual device), you simply slide a switch on the back of the WET11 to a particular position. On the WET11 devices that we've seen, the switch position for connecting to game consoles is labeled *X* — the position labeled *II* is used for connecting to a hub or switch. Because of this switch, you use a standard straight-through Ethernet cable with the WET11 instead of a cross-over Ethernet cable.

Dealing with Router Configurations

So far in this chapter, we talk a bit about the services and hardware that you need to get into online gaming using your wireless network. What we haven't covered yet — getting online and playing a game — will be either the easiest or the hardest part of the equation. The difficulty of this task depends upon two things:

- **The platform that you're using:** If you're trying to get online with a PC (whether it's Windows-based or a Mac) . . . well, basically there's nothing special to worry about. You just need to get it connected to the Internet as we describe in Chapter 9. For certain games, you might have to do a few fancy things with your router, which we'll discuss later in this chapter. If you're using a gaming console, you might have to adjust a few things in your router to get your online connection working, but when using a game console with many routers, you can just plug in your wireless equipment and go, too.

- **What you're trying to do:** For many games, after you establish an Internet connection, you're ready to start playing. Some games, however, will require you to make some adjustments to your router's configuration. If you're planning on hosting the games on your PC (meaning that your online friends will be remotely connecting to your PC), you're definitely going to have to do a bit of configuration.

Don't sweat it, though. It's usually not all that hard to get gaming set up, and it's getting easier every day. We say that it's getting easier because the companies that make wireless LAN equipment and home routers realize that gaming is a growth industry for them. And they know that they can sell more equipment if they can help people get devices like game consoles online.

You need to accomplish two things to get your online gaming — well, we can't think of a better term — online:

1. **Get an Internet Protocol (IP) address.**

   Your access point needs to recognize your gaming PC's or console's network adapter and your console's wireless Ethernet bridge, if you've got one in your network configuration. If you've got WEP configured (see Chapter 10), your game machine will need to provide the proper password. And your router (whether it's in the access point or it's separate) will need to provide an IP address to your gaming machine.

2. **Get through your router's firewall.**

   The previous step is really pretty easy. The step that's going to take some time is configuring the firewall feature of your router to allow gaming programs to function properly.

Getting an IP address

For the most part, if you've set up your router to provide IP addresses within your network using DHCP (as we discuss in Chapters 5 and 7), your gaming PC or gaming console will automatically connect to the router when the device is turned on and will send a Dynamic Host Configuration Protocol (DHCP) request to the router asking for an IP address. If you've configured your gaming PC like we discuss in Chapters 7 and 8, your computer should get its IP address and be online automatically. Or, as we like to say about this kind of neat stuff, auto*magically*. You might need to go into a program to select an access point and enter your WEP password, but otherwise, it should just work without any intervention.

If you've got a game console with a wireless Ethernet bridge, the process should be almost as smooth. The first time that you use the bridge, you might need to use a Web-browser interface on one of your PCs to set up WEP passwords; otherwise, your router should automatically assign an IP address to your console. Sometimes, however, a router might not be completely compatible with a gaming console. Keep in mind that online console gaming was introduced in November of 2002, and many home router models have been around much longer than that.

Before you get all wrapped around the axle trying to get your game console connected to your router, check out the Web site of your particular console maker *and* your router manufacturer. We have no doubt that you'll find a lot of information about how to make this connection using those resources. In many cases, if you're having troubles getting your router to assign an IP address to your console, you'll need to download a firmware upgrade for your router. *Firmware* is the software that lives inside your router and that tells your router how to behave. Most router vendors have released updated firmware to help their older router models work with gaming consoles.

Some older router models simply aren't going to work with gaming consoles. If online gaming is an important part of your plans, check the Web sites that we mention earlier above *before* you choose a router.

In most cases, if your console doesn't get assigned an IP address automatically, you'll need to go into your router's setup program — most use a Web browser on a networked PC to adjust the configuration — and manually assign a fixed IP address to the console. Unlike DHCP-assigned IP addresses (which can change every time a computer logs onto the network), this fixed IP address will always be assigned to your console.

Every router has a slightly different system for doing this, but typically you'll simply select an IP address that isn't in the range of DHCP addresses that your router automatically assigns to devices connected to your network.

You will need to assign an IP address that isn't in the range of your router's IP address pool but that is within the *same subnet*. In other words, if your router assigns IP addresses in the 192.168.0.*xxx* range, you'll need to use an IP address beginning with 192.168.0 for your game console. For example, if your router uses the range of 192.168.0.0 to 192.168.0.32 for computers connected to the network, you'll want to choose an IP address like 192.168.0.34 for your console. Every router's configuration program is different, but you'll typically see a box that reads something like `DHCP Server Start IP Address` (with an IP address next to it) and another box that reads something like `DHCP Server Finish IP Address` with another box containing an IP address. (Some routers might just list the start address, followed by a *count* — meaning that the finish address is the last number in the start address plus the count number.)

The key thing to remember here is that you've only got to come up with the last number in the IP address — the number after the third period in the IP address. The first three (which are usually 192.168.0) won't change. All you need to do to assign this IP address is to pick a number between 0 and 254 that *is not* in the range that your router uses for DHCP.

Dealing with port forwarding

After you have your gaming PC or game console assigned an IP address and you're connected to the Internet, you might very well be ready to start playing games. Our advice: Give it a try and see what happens. Depending upon the games that you play, any additional steps might not be needed.

The steps that we're about to discuss shouldn't be required for a game console. And although we haven't checked out every single game out there, we haven't run into any incidences where you need to get involved with the port forwarding that we're about to discuss with a game console. After you get your console assigned an IP address and connected to the Internet, you should be ready to start playing. If you have an older router that doesn't work well with console games, you might consider putting your console on the router's DMZ as we discuss in the upcoming section "Setting Up a Demilitarized Zone (DMZ)."

If, however, your games don't work, you might need to get involved in configuring the firewall and Network Address Translation (NAT). As we discuss in Chapters 5 and 9, home network routers use a system called NAT to connect multiple devices to a single Internet connection. What NAT does, basically, is translate between public Internet IP addresses and internal IP addresses on your home's network. When a computer or other device is connected to your home network (wirelessly or even a wired network), the router assigns it an internal IP address. Similarly, when your router connects to the Internet, it's assigned its own public IP address: that is, its own identifying location on the Internet. Traffic flowing to and from your house uses this public IP address to find its way. After the traffic (which can be gaming data, an e-mail, a Web page . . . whatever) gets to the router, the NAT function of the router figures out to which PC (or other device) in the house to send that data.

One important feature of NAT is that it provides a firewall functionality for your network. NAT knows which computer to send data to on your network because that computer has typically sent a request over the Internet for that bit of data. For example, when a computer requests a Web page, your NAT router knows which computer made the request so that when the Web page is downloaded, it gets sent to the right PC. If no device on the network has made a request — meaning that an unrequested bit of data shows up at your public IP address — NAT doesn't know where to send it. This provides a security firewall function for your network because it keeps this unrequested data (which could be some sort of security risk) off your network.

NAT is a cool thing because it lets multiple computers share a single public IP address and Internet connection and because it helps keep the bad guys off your network. NAT can, however, cause problems with some applications that might require this unrequested data to work properly. For example, if you have a Web server on your network, you would rightly expect that people would try to download and view Web pages without your PC sending them any kind of initial request. After all, your Web server isn't clairvoyant. (At least ours isn't!)

Gaming can also be an application that relies upon unrequested connections to work properly. For example, you might want to host a game with your friends on your PC, which means that their PCs will try to get through your router and connect directly with your PC. Even if you're not hosting the game, some games will send chunks of unrequested data to your computer as part of the game play. Other applications that might do this include things such as audio and video conferencing programs (such as Windows Messenger) and remote control programs (such as pcAnywhere).

In order to get these games (or other programs) to work properly over your wireless home network and through your router, you need to get into your router's configuration program and punch some holes in your firewall by setting up NAT port forwarding.

Of the many routers out there, they don't all call this *port forwarding*. Read your manual. (Really, we mean it. Read the darn thing. We know it's boring, but it can be your friend.) Look for terms like *special applications support* or *virtual servers*.

Port forwarding effectively opens a hole in your firewall that will not only allow legitimate game or other application data through but might also let the bad guys in as well. Only set up port forwarding when you have to and keep an eye on the logs. (Your router should keep a log of who it lets in — check the manual to see how to find and read this log.) We also recommend that you consider using personal firewall software on your networked PCs (we like ZoneAlarm, www.zonelabs.com) and that you keep your antivirus software up to date.

Some routers let you set up something called *application triggered* port forwarding, which basically allows your router to look for certain signals coming from an application on your computer (the triggers), and then enable port forwarding. This is a more secure option, if it's available to you, because when the program that requires port forwarding (your game, in this case) is not running, your ports are closed. They only open when the game (or other application) requires them to be opened.

When you set up port forwarding on your router, you are selecting specific ports (ports are actually a subsegment of an IP address — a computer with a specific IP address will use different numbered ports to connect different applications to the network) and sending any and all incoming requests using those ports to a specific computer or device on your network. When you get involved in setting up port forwarding, you'll notice two kinds of ports: TCP (Transmission Control Protocol) and UDP (User Datagram Protocol). These names relate to the two primary ways by which data is carried on the Internet, and you might have to set up port forwarding for both TCP and UDP ports, depending upon the application.

Every router or access point will have its own unique system for configuring port forwarding. Generally speaking, you'll find the port forwarding section of the configuration program, and simply type the port numbers you want to open up into a text box on the screen. For example, Figure 12-3 shows port forwarding being configured on a Siemens SpeedStream router/access point.

As we mention earlier, ports are assigned specific numbers. And to get some gaming applications to work properly, you'll need to open (assign) port forwarding for a pretty big range of port numbers. The best way to find out which ports need to be opened is to read the manual or search the Web page of the game software vendor. You can also find a relatively comprehensive list online at practicallynetworked.com/sharing/app_port_list.htm.

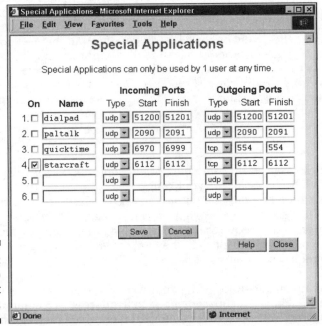

Figure 12-3:
Setting up port forwarding.

If your router is UPnP-enabled (Universal Plug and Play, a system developed by Microsoft and others, that — among other things — automatically configures port forwarding for you) and the PC game that you're using uses Microsoft's DirectX gaming, the router and the game should be able to talk to each other and automatically set up the appropriate port forwarding. Just make sure that you enable UPnP in your router's configuration system — this will usually be a check box in the router's configuration program.

Setting Up a Demilitarized Zone (DMZ)

If you need to do some special port forwarding and router tweaking to get your games working, you might find that you're spending entirely too much time getting it all up and running. Or you might find that you open up what *should* be the right ports — according to the game developer — and that things still just don't seem to be working correctly. It happens — not all routers are equally good at implementing port forwarding.

Here's another approach that you can take — setting up a *demilitarized zone* (DMZ). This term has been appropriated from the military (think the North/South Korean border) by way of the business networking world, where DMZs are used for devices such as Web servers within corporate networks. In a home network, a DMZ is a virtual portion of your network that's completely outside of your firewall. In other words, a computer or device connected to your DMZ will accept any and all incoming connections — your NAT router will forward all incoming connections (on any port) to the computer connected to the DMZ. You don't need to configure special ports for specific games because everything will be forwarded to the computer or device which you have placed "on the DMZ."

Most home routers that we know of will set up a DMZ for only one of your networked devices, so this approach might not work for you if you've got two gaming PCs connected to the Internet. However, for most people, a DMZ will do the trick.

Although setting up a DMZ is perhaps easier to do than configuring port forwarding, it comes with bigger security risks. If you set up port forwarding, you lessen the security of the computer that the ports are being forwarded to . . . but if you put that computer on the DMZ, you've basically removed all the firewall features of your router from that computer. Be judicious when using a DMZ. If you've got a computer dedicated only to gaming, a game console, or a kid's computer that doesn't have any important personal files configured to be on your DMZ, you'll probably be okay. If you're gaming on your work computer — the one with all the classified work documents and your downloaded credit card statements — you might want to think twice about setting up a DMZ.

Depending on the individual router configuration program that comes with your preferred brand of router, setting up a DMZ is really typically quite simple. Figure 12-4 shows a DMZ being set up on a Siemens SpeedStream router/access point. It's a dead-simple process. In most cases, you need only to mark a check box in the router configuration program to turn on the DMZ and then use a pull-down menu to select the computer that you want on the DMZ.

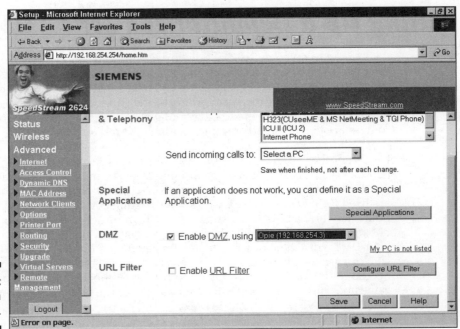

Figure 12-4:
Setting up a
DMZ.

Chapter 13

Networking Your Entertainment Center

In This Chapter

▶ Buying audio/video (A/V) gear with wireless inboard

▶ Plugging into wireless with wireless A/V adapters

▶ Understanding your home theater PC options

*W*ithout doubt, the most significant news in wireless home networking — outside of the general price drops that are driving growth in the industry — is the movement of the 802.11-based networking outside of the realm of computers and into the realm of entertainment.

The linkage of the two environments really yields the best of both possible worlds. You can use your hard drive on your PC to store audio and video tracks for playback on your TV and through your stereo. You can stream movies from the Internet and play them on your TV. You can take pictures with your digital camera, load them on your PC, and view them on your TV. You get the picture (oops, pun).

You will simply not believe how much the ability to link the home entertainment center with the PC is going to affect your computing and entertainment experience. It could affect which PC you buy. For example, Microsoft has teamed up with leading hardware manufacturers such as Hewlett-Packard (HP) and Gateway to offer Windows XP Media Center Edition PCs, designed to power your home entertainment system (it's really too irresistible). It could affect how you rent movies — why go all the way to Blockbuster when you can just download a movie over the Internet from Movielink (www.movie link.com) with a single click? It could even affect how you watch your favorite shows because with PC-based personal video recorders (PVRs), you can record the shows that you want to watch . . . but always miss because you could never figure out how to record on the VCR. Whew. That's *some* change.

In this chapter, we expose you to some of the ways wireless home networking is enabling this revolution toward a linked TV/PC world. You're going to find that a lot of what we talk about throughout the book will serve as the perfect foundation for linking PCs and audio/video systems.

You might be thinking, "Whoa, wait a minute, I thought wireless was just for data. Are you telling me that I need to move my PC to my living room and put it next to my TV?" Well, rest assured; we're not suggesting that, although you might find yourself putting a PC near your TV sometime soon. You could indeed put your PC next to your TV, link it with a video cable, and run your interconnection to the living room. But if that's your only PC and your wife wants to watch the latest basketball game, you might find it hard to do your work!

The revolution that we're talking about — and are just getting started with in this chapter and the ones that follow — is the whole home wireless revolution, where that powerful data network that you install for your PCs to talk to one another and the Internet can also talk to lots of other things in your home. You'll hear us talk a lot about your *whole home audio network* or a *whole home video network*. That's our code for "you can hear (view) it throughout the house." You built that wireless network (in Part III), and now other devices will come and use it. And coming they are, indeed. By the boxful. So be prepared to hear about all these great devices — things that you use every day, such as your stereo, refrigerator, and car — that want to hop onboard your home wireless highway.

Wirelessly Enabling Your Home Entertainment System

If you're like most of us, your home entertainment system probably consists of a TV, a stereo receiver, some components (like a record player, tape deck, or CD/DVD player), and a few speakers. For most parties, this is enough to make for a memorable evening!

And, if you're like most of us, you have a jumble of wires linking all this audio/visual (A/V) gear together. The mere thought of adding more wiring to the system — especially, say, to link your receiver to your computer to play some MP3s — is going to be a bit much.

We've got some good news for you. Regardless of whether you have a $250 television set or a $25,000 home theater, you can wirelessly enable almost any type of A/V gear that you've got. Before we get into the specific options on the market today, we need to discuss at a high level the wireless bandwidth requirements for the two major applications for your entertainment system: audio and video. Talking in general terms about this is okay because the differences among the bandwidth options are fairly great (so applications fall into clear camps), and we believe that most access points (APs) are moving toward 802.11a/g dual-mode designs, which is more than enough to handle your video and audio needs.

Here are the two predominant ways that audio and video files are handled with your entertainment/PC combo:

✔ **Streaming:** The file is played on your PC and sent via a continuous signal to your stereo for live playback.

✔ **File transfer:** The file is sent from your PC to your stereo system componentry, where it's stored for later playback.

These two applications are very different. The big issue here is where the file is played from. If it's played on the PC, for instance, it's streamed to the stereo for speaker amplification. If it's played on a source stereo system component, you just need to transfer the file. The wireless requirements are quite different.

With file transfer, a lot of transmissions take place in the background. For instance, many audio programs allow for automatic synchronization between file repositories, which can be scheduled during off hours to minimize the impact on your network traffic when you're using your home network. And in these cases, you're not as concerned with how long it takes as you would be if you were watching or listening to it live while it plays.

However, a streaming application is very sensitive to network delays and lost data packets. You tend to notice a bad picture pretty quickly. Also, with a file transfer, any lost data can be retransmitted when its loss was detected. But with streaming video and audio, you need to get the packets right the first time because most of the transmission protocols don't even allow for retransmission even if you wanted to. You just get clipped and delayed sound, which sounds bad.

A good-quality 802.11b signal is fine in most instances for audio or video file transfers and is also fine for audio streaming. Whether it's okay for *video* streaming depends a lot on how the video was encoded and how big the file is. The larger the file size for the same amount of running time, the larger the bandwidth that's required to transmit it for steady video performance. As a result, people tend to talk about 802.11g and 802.11a protocols for video simply because a lot of available bandwidth exists for any problems that might occur when sending the data over the airwaves.

In general, here are four generic ways that you can wirelessly enable your A/V system, each somewhat dependent upon where the source content resides.

Getting to the (access) point

Your wireless signal degrades the farther that you get from your access point, regardless of which protocol you're using. Thus, you might have a great signal near your AP, a pretty good signal 30–50 feet away, and an increasingly poorer signal as you get farther and farther away. The quality of signal isn't measured just in speed but also in the strength of the signal so that the data packets — whether carrying voice, data, video, audio, or whatever — are received and understood the first time by the recipient. (Check out Chapters 4 and 5 for more info about choosing an AP and where to place it in your home for best performance.)

There's no good absolute definition of what constitutes a good-quality signal; but for our purposes here, it means that the signal is consistent (not varying up and down), and it has at least enough throughput to be able to match the bandwidth of the source signal. So if you're streaming a 196 Kbps MP3 file, you want to make sure that you at least have that much throughput available on a consistent basis for that streaming file. In most instances, when streaming content from the Internet, your wireless network speeds will exceed that of your Internet connection, so your wireless connection probably won't be the bottleneck.

If the source content resides in the entertainment center:

- **Buy wirelessly functional equipment.** Some gear comes with wireless inboard. For example, Motorola makes the *simplefi* (www.motorola.com/simplefi), which is a wireless, digital audio receiver that enables you to stream audio from your PC or the Internet (through your broadband connection) directly to your home stereo. You just need to provide such equipment with the right Service Set Identifier (SSID) and Wired Equivalent Privacy (WEP) settings, and it's on your home wireless network. (Chapters 6, 7, and 8 cover SSID; Chapter 10 has the scoop on WEP.)

  This typically gives the equipment access to the Internet and users remote access to the device itself over these Internet connections. (In the next section, we introduce you to some of the ways that present entertainment gear is getting wirelessly enabled.)

- **Buy a wireless adapter or bridge.** Some A/V equipment is *network enabled* (meaning that it has some basic network interface capability such as an Ethernet or a Universal Serial Bus [USB] port) but lacks wireless functionality. In these instances, you can buy a wireless adapter to interface with that port to get the device on the home network. These typically have RCA jacks on one end of the wireless connection and Ethernet connections on the other. A wireless bridge is a perfect way to get it online. Gaming equipment, which we cover in detail in Chapter 12, commonly has an Ethernet port but no wireless capability; wireless bridges are perfect to allow multiplayer gaming over the Internet. Shortly, we talk about the range of wireless adapters and bridges available for the home user.

The simplefi and HomeRF

The current version of the simplefi uses a system called *HomeRF,* which was a competitor to 802.11. HomeRF is now defunct, and Motorola will be soon converting the simplefi to 802.11.

If you're shopping for a simplefi, make sure that you get one of these newer versions, which should be on the market by mid-2003.

If the source content resides in the personal computing center:

✔ **Buy a wireless media player.** Some A/V gear is complemented by a media player whose main goal is to coordinate the flow of audio, video, and other data between the PC/Internet environment and the entertainment system. A good example of this is the $249 PRISMIQ MediaPlayer (www.prismiq.com), which sits atop any television, stereo, or entertainment center and links to any computer via a wireless home network (or other Ethernet connection). It eliminates the requirement to be physically present at the PC in order to experience digital movies, MP3 audio, and digital pictures stored on the PC. The PRISMIQ MediaPlayer also connects to the Internet through the home network for relaxed, TV-based Web surfing, instant messaging, personalized TV-displayed news, and easy access to emerging next-generation broadband services. We introduce you to some of the leading media players on the market in a few moments.

✔ **Buy a home theater PC.** A high-powered PC designed to interact with the entertainment center is a perfect complement to your home. Instead of spending money on a new DVD player, why not use that CD/DVD player in your PC? In place of a bunch of home-created CDs, why not just leave them on a high-capacity hard drive on your PC and let the songs play through your stereo whenever you want? We talk about the home theater PC shortly.

Wireless Home Entertainment Gear

The ideal would be if all your stereo equipment came with 802.11 chips inboard so that they could just hop onto your wireless *backbone* (a technogeek way of talking about your wireless signal footprint in your home) and get to work. Although we think that's not all that unlikely as technology moves forward, it's not the case today.

Instead, what you find today is that a lot of home entertainment accessories are going wireless, like your MP3 players and portable speakers. One of the most major pieces of your home entertainment system going wireless is your

TV's set top box. Typically, to distribute video around the house, you had to wire a home with coaxial cable. The cable companies know that they don't make much (if any) money on that part of the equation, so they would just as soon run a cable into the home gateway set top box and then use wireless signals from there. Want to watch TV by the pool? No problem — your wireless TV signal can help you out. We expect that satellite, cable, and telephone company video set top boxes will all sport wireless options fairly soon. Instead of being hard-wired to your cable box, you can just pick up your TV (outfitted with a compatible wireless adapter) and carry it to the pool. And with your wireless remote control controlling the set top box back inside the house, you'll think you were in heaven. (Just keep the TV out of the hot tub, or you might really be in heaven.)

In Chapter 14, we introduce you to the next wave of remote controls — 802.11b-based remotes that control signals in other rooms. Right now, these signals actually go to infrared (IR) devices that mimic an IR remote control in that room. In the near term, you'll see onboard wireless interfaces in the set top boxes themselves, which will again allow remote control and access to files.

But alas, for now, only a few pieces of audio and video gear have standards-based wireless interfaces. You're starting to see video projectors sport 802.11b interfaces; for example, NEC Solutions (America), Inc. is shipping the first MT Series generation of portable projectors to offer the NEC ImageXpress networking technology option. With NEC ImageXpress, the MT60 Series of projectors can communicate continuously and in real time from a PC to the projector through a wireless system via 802.11b. The wireless option makes it easy to connect to the video projector from anywhere nearby, without the hassles of cables to trip over. Although this particular projector can double for home or office use, a lot of home theater projectors are moving towards wireless connectivity, too.

SONICblue (which at the time of this writing was unfortunately going through bankruptcy proceedings and was divesting the subsidiary that makes this product) has a wireless-enabled Go-Video D2730 DVD player (www.sonic blue.com; $299) and is the first player of its kind to be able to stream video files through a wireless network to a consumer electronics component. It supports Ethernet 10/100 through an RJ-45 wired interface as well as 802.11 through a Personal Computer Memory Card International Association (PCMCIA) Card/bus card slot where you can plug in 802.11b, 802.11a, 802.11g, and a Home Phoneline Networking Alliance (HPNA) card. The D2730 can play MP3 and WMA audio files, JPEG image files, and MPEG1 and MPEG2 video files.

Yamaha has an 802.11b-enabled audio server called the MusicCAST (see Figure 13-1). This system consists of a couple of pieces. The server is the centerpiece of the system and uses a large computer hard drive and a built-in CD drive to *rip* (convert to MP3) all your CDs and store the music. The server then uses 802.11b to send streaming music files to separate receivers throughout your home. The receivers contain built-in audio amplifiers, so you can plug a set of standard stereo speakers into them. Or if you have an existing stereo system in the room where the receiver is located, you can plug the receiver directly into that unit and use the speakers that you've already got. The MusicCAST system isn't cheap — the price of a server and a single receiver is about $2,800, and additional receivers (for other rooms in the house) go for about $800.

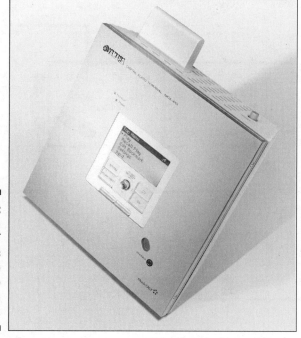

Figure 13-1:
The Yamaha
MusicCAST
enables
whole-home
audio
through
wireless.

Expanding Your Home Entertainment Center with Wireless Adapters

Nothing is worse than having a great piece of entertainment gear that you want to get onto your home network, but the nearest outlet is yards away, and you don't have a cable long enough to plug it in. So you can forgive Danny when he had his brand new, networking-capable ReQuest, Inc.

AudioReQuest system (www.request.com) with no Ethernet connection near it to plug it into. The *AudioReQuest* — a digital music server; see Figure 13-2 to see how the server sends music throughout the house — is a great example of the type of network-enabled audio gear coming down the pike. Capable of storing as many CDs as you have (you can add additional storage by their swappable hard drives or getting higher capacity units), this is the ultimate in CD listening pleasure.

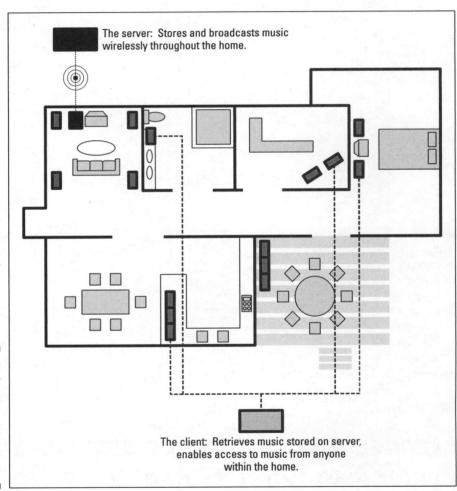

The server: Stores and broadcasts music wirelessly throughout the home.

The client: Retrieves music stored on server, enables access to music from anyone within the home.

Figure 13-2:
Wirelessly serving up digital music around the house with Audio-ReQuest.

And with a device like the AudioReQuest TV Navigator Interface, you can use your TV screen as the interface to your music collection. A bright, TV screen-based user interface enables you to select and play your music, create playlists from albums and artists stored in the system, and enjoy pulsating music-driven graphics on the TV set's display. That's a lot better than a two-line liquid crystal display (LCD) screen. And it's easy to use — loading (ripping) a new CD into the system is as easy as opening the CD tray and closing it. The AudioReQuest determines whether the CD is already loaded in your system and then looks up the name of the album and artist in its internal database of 650,000 albums; if the system can't find the CD, it checks a master database on the Internet.

The AudioReQuest has an onboard internal Web server that allows access to this music from wherever you want, be it in the house or over the Internet. You can also add other units to the system and network them. Danny has one unit in his house in Maine and another in his house in Connecticut, and they stay synchronized. What's more, multiple units enable you to have a backup of your collection in case your hard drive crashes.

Higher-end ReQuest units also support WAV and FLAK (*lossless compression* — meaning you'll get higher fidelity audio quality) protocols for those who want audio fidelity. (These protocols take up more space on the hard drive but preserve the nuances of the music.)

It's truly the future of music in the entertainment center. An entry-level Audio-ReQuest Nitro system costs about $2,500 and scales up from there depending on storage capacity and extra features. This is the box that you put in your home if you're serious about music!

The AudioReQuest also has onboard networking installed, just like your PC, with an Ethernet outlet for interconnecting with your home network. The only problem? No wireless connectivity, as we mention above. But because the AudioReQuest has an Ethernet outlet, it's easy to use a wireless bridge (which we discuss in Chapter 12) to bring it onboard to your wireless home network. Danny's using a D-Link (www.d-link.com) DWL-810 Wireless Ethernet Bridge (802.11b) to link it into his wireless network.

(As soon as he finishes this book, Danny's going to extend his AudioReQuest to syncing with his car stereos, too — over wireless computer network connections.)

Entertainment devices such as the Microsoft Xbox (www.xbox.com) and ReplayTV (www.replaytv.com) can also connect to a network with the D-Link Wireless Ethernet Bridge via their built-in Ethernet ports. The Ethernet bridge works because Danny has an Ethernet port on his audio server. But what about situations where there is no networking outlet option at all (no USB, no Ethernet, no onboard wireless)?

Not a problem. A new slew of wireless networking gear sports RCA jacks — the same jacks used to connect your sources into your receiver. These make it easy to connect non-audio gear into the home entertainment network. These wireless audio transmitters will transmit audio from your PC to your stereo without the use of cables.

Right now, most of this gear is using proprietary signaling — not Bluetooth or 802.11 — to transmit their signals. As a result, the signals are mostly point-to-point, linking a PC, say, with your entertainment center. As we write, 802.11b products are coming on the market that enable any compatible device in range to pick up the signals, making your entertainment center more accessible by lots of devices, from your PC to your audio server in your car. Get an 802.11-based product if you have the choice.

For instance, the RCA Model RD 900W Lyra Wireless (www.rca.com; $99) device sends crystal-clear digital audio from your PC to your stereo, as depicted in Figure 13-3. Just plug it into your PC's USB jack on the one end and the entertainment center's RCA jacks on the other, and you're ready to go. Unfortunately, as of this printing, the Lyra uses 900 MHz technology, not standardized 802.11 chips, to accomplish this. Jensen's Matrix Internet Audio Transmitter (www.jensen.com) Model JW901 works the same way: a 900 MHz connection between the PC and stereo. X10's Entertainment Anywhere (www.x10.com) uses a proprietary 2.4 MHz signal.

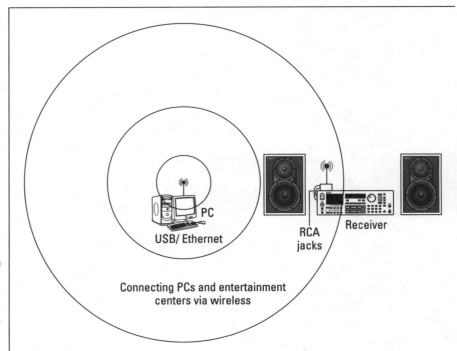

Figure 13-3:
Linking a PC
with any
piece of
stereo gear.

Connecting PCs and entertainment
centers via wireless

The Linksys (www.linksys.com; $120) Wireless Digital Media Adapter is an 802.11b-based transmitter. It resides in home entertainment centers next to the television and stereo. The device resembles the Linksys access point, with two 802.11b antennas. Instead of connecting to an Ethernet port like a normal AP, the device is equipped with audio/video connectors. To process JPEG, MP3, and WMA digital content from a networked PC, the adapter uses Intel's XScale architecture PXA250 application processor. By using Universal Plug and Play (UPnP) technology, the adapter can be easily set up to work with other UPnP devices on the network such as a Linksys wireless router or its car networking technology (under development in early 2003). The bottom line on these adapters: Look for wireless adapters that enable you to take ordinary devices and get them on your home wireless backbone.

The Home Media Player

A new intermediary that has thrust itself onto the scene is the *media player*, which is a device whose goal is to simplify the PC-to-entertainment system interface. Simply, these boxes give you an easy way to get at information on your PC, for playing or viewing on your TV and stereo system, by giving you an onscreen display, a remote control, and even a wireless keyboard.

Specifically, this device sits between your TV and your PC. And instead of using your computer display to see what's going on, the media player displays its own user interface on the TV set — a lot like the AudioReQuest that we mention earlier in this chapter. Thus, they can make it a lot simpler to merely play a song (a lot better than having to boot up a computer, open a program, and scroll around!). It interfaces with your PC via a wireless (or wired) connection.

The PRISMIQ system that we mention earlier in this chapter is a great example of this. By using an Internet-capable home computer and linking stored media and the Internet connection itself, the PRISMIQ system can perform a variety of functions:

- Play DVD-quality video
- Play Surround sound and CD-quality audio
- Stream a library of MP3 files
- Act as a video-on-demand set top box
- Display digital photos on the television
- Provide Web access on the television
- Show live, personalized news feeds to the television
- Connect users over the Internet to friends and family

The PRISMIQ MediaPlayer (see Figure 13-4) is a compact system, less than half the size of most DVD players. It can be used conveniently on any television in the house, yet it has all the capabilities of a high-end audio-visual component, such as Surround sound audio support and MPEG-1 and MPEG-2 video playback. The associated and bundled MediaManager software, which lets one or more computers in the home deliver content to the MediaPlayer, runs on Windows 98 SE, Me, 2000, and XP. Like the SONICblue DVD D2730, the PRISMIQ MediaPlayer supports Ethernet 10/100 natively and has embedded driver support for a variety of PCMCIA card/bus cards for 802.11b, 802.11a, 802.11g, and Home Phoneline Networking Alliance (HPNA) interfaces. It allows just about any sort of wireless connectivity through its PC Card slot

Figure 13-4:
The
PRISMIQ
MediaPlayer.

Other players are getting into the act, too. HP's Digital Media Receiver (www.hp.com/go/digitalmediareceiver; $299) 5000 Series extends digital music and photos on your PC to your TV and stereo systems. By using a standard remote control, the receiver enables you to browse through your favorite music and photos and choose what you want to view or listen to without having to go to your PC and use your mouse and keyboard. The HP Digital Media Receiver provides access to digital content from a PC on a user's wired Ethernet or wireless 802.11b home network.

The photos section will appeal to those with a digital camera. Digital photography enthusiasts can access JPEG, GIF, BMP, and PNG images and share their favorite moments with others in picture shows displayed on their TV in the living space of their choice instead of on a PC monitor. The receiver also allows users to print the currently displayed picture on any PC-connected printer with the simple push of a button on the remote control. In addition, the product allows users to combine music and photos on the TV and stereo for a multimedia experience.

What's neat is that multiple HP Digital Media Receivers can be connected to the home wireless network so that music and photos can be enjoyed throughout the home, simultaneously accessing digital files — including, if so desired, the exact same song or picture (say, during a party). In fact, the multiple devices can be controlled from each other to create a full-house listening experience.

The Home Theater PC

When you talk about your home entertainment center, you often talk about *sources:* that is, those devices such as tape decks, AM/FM receivers, phono players, CD units, DVD players, and other consumer electronics devices that provide the inputs of the content that you listen to and watch through your entertainment system.

So when you think about adding your networked PC(s) to your entertainment mix, the PC becomes just another high-quality source device attached to your A/V system — albeit wirelessly. To connect your PC to your entertainment system, you must have some special audio/video cards and corresponding software to enable your PC to "speak stereo." When configured like this, you've effectively got what is known as a *home theater PC* (or *HTPC*, as all the cool kids refer to them). In fact, if you do it right, you can create an HTPC that funnels audio and video into your system at a higher-quality level than many moderately priced, standalone source components. HTPC can be that good.

You can either buy an HTPC ready-to-go right off the shelf, or you can build one yourself. Building an HTPC, obviously, isn't something that we recommend unless you have a fair amount of knowledge about PCs. If that's the case, have at it. Another obvious point: It's a lot easier to buy a ready-to-go version of the HTPC off the shelf. You can find out more about HTPCs in *Home Theater For Dummies* (Pat and Danny wrote that, too), by Wiley Publishing, Inc. What we include here is the short and sweet version of HTPC.

What you expect from your home theater PC is going to be quite different from what, say, David Bowie expects from his HTPC. Regardless of your needs, however, a home theater PC should be able to store music and video files, play CDs and DVDs, let you play video games on the big screen, and tune in to online music and video content. Thus, it needs ample hard drive space and the appropriate software. (See the following section, "Internet Content for Your Media Players and HTPCs.") Also, your HTPC will act as a PVR (see the nearby "Checking out PC PVRs" sidebar for the lowdown on PC-based PVRs). In addition, an HTPC can

- ✔ **Store audio (music) files:** Now you can easily play your MP3s anywhere on your wireless network.

- ✔ **Store video clips:** Keeping your digital home video tapes handy is quite the crowd pleaser — you can have your own *America's Funniest Home Videos* show.

- ✔ **Play CDs and DVDs:** The ability to play DVDs is essential in a home theater environment.

- **Act as a PVR (personal video recorder):** This optional (but almost essential, we think) function uses the HTPC's hard drive to record television shows like a ReplayTV (www.replaytv.com) or TiVo (www.tivo.com).

- **Let you play video games on the big screen:** With the right hardware, PCs are sometimes even better than gaming consoles (which we cover in Chapter 12).

- **Tune in to online music and video content:** Grab the good stuff off the Internet (yes, and pay for it) and then enjoy it on the big screen with good audio equipment.

- **Provide a high-quality, progressive video signal to your TV video display:** This is behind-the-curtain stuff. Simply, an HTPC uses special hardware (it's pretty cheap, only about $200–$400) to display your PC's video content on a TV. Sure, PCs do have a built-in video system, but most are designed to display only on a PC monitor, not a TV. And high-definition TV, which is why you want high-definition content, is *progressive* (meaning all of the video "lines" are displayed at one time, rather than half in one frame and the other half in the next like most standard TVs today — providing a much smoother, more film-like, picture), and you need a special card or PC set up like an HTPC to facilitate it. (This investment also gives you better performance on your PC's monitor, which is never bad.)

- **Decode and send HDTV content to your high-definition TV display:** HTPCs can provide a cheap way to decode over-the-air HDTV signals and send them to your home entertainment center's display. You just need the right hardware (an HDTV-capable video card and a TV tuner card). If you have HDTV, this is a really cool optional feature of HTPC.

My name is Media, and I'll be your server

HTPCs and Windows XP Media Center Edition PCs are what their names say they are — *PCs.* Look to the horizon for a new generation of computer-like devices that serve up media. *Media servers* (creative name, no?) are really just a souped-up version of a standalone PVR (think TiVo) or a standalone MP3 server (like AudioReQuest, www.request.com). They don't run a PC operating system or do typical PC stuff. They just serve up media, and wireless is a key way, likely using 802.11a/g technology. You'll be able to hook media servers into your PC network *and* into your home theater, using them to store music, video, digital photographs, and more.

A good example of this is the Martian Net Drive Wireless (www.martian.com), a $399 802.11b-enabled accessible 40GB hard drive that allows you to store thousands of your favorite songs, digital pictures, or documents. Any network device can access them. The 802.11b is onboard. It even supports your WEP encryption. There are two steps to setting it up: 1. Unpack stylish brown shipping carton. 2. Plug in power cable. That's it. Cool.

Checking out PC PVRs

Using the HTPC's hard drive to record television shows like how a ReplayTV or TiVo does is an optional (but almost essential, we think) function. And using an HTPC as a PVR is a standard feature in a Windows XP Media Center PC — and something that we think you should consider adding to your home-built HTPC. Even if this were the only thing that you wanted to do with your HTPC, it would be worth it. You can simply install a PC PVR kit and skip a lot of the other stuff (such as the DVD player, decoder, and software).

Tip: Because the biggest limitation to any PVR system is the amount of space on your hard drive for storing video, consider a hard drive upgrade regardless of your other HTPC intentions.

PC PVR kits on the market include SnapStream Personal Video Station (www.snapstream. com), Pinnacle PCTV Deluxe (www.pinnacle sys.com), and ATI All-In-Wonder 9700 PRO (www.ati.com).

Internet Content for Your Media Players and HTPCs

If you're really into this HTPC thing, think about whether setting up an HTPC is really worth the trouble just to playback DVDs (although the quality would be way high). Probably not, huh? So, you might ask yourself, what else is in it for me? What really makes an HTPC useful is its ability to provide a portal to all sorts of great Internet-based content — that is, music and video content. A *portal* is simply a one-stop shop for movies, songs, animation clips, video voice mail, and so on. Think of it as a kind of a Yahoo! for your audio and video needs. (In fact, Yahoo!, a portal itself, is trying to position itself to be just that! You can play great music videos from its Web site at launch.yahoo.com.)

You're not getting much Internet content if your HTPC isn't connected to the Internet. And don't forget that a connection to your high-speed Internet access (digital subscriber line [DSL] or cable modem) is part of the overall equation. (Yup, a regular ol' vanilla dialup connection will work, but — we can't stress this enough — not nearly as well. Pony up the cash and come on into this century.)

Again, if you're really interested in your home entertainment system and home theater systems, you should check out *Home Theater For Dummies* for lots more info.

You'll find a load of good content on the Internet, just waiting for you to come around and get it. Note that these sites charge you for the services and content they provide, but the content is well worth the price. Take it from us. Some of the most popular online content providers include the following:

✔ **Listen.com** (www.listen.com): Listen.com's Rhapsody online music service is a great source of quality music for your home theater (via an HTPC). From its library of over 20,000 albums (and for a paltry $9.95 per month), you get unlimited, on-demand access. And check out its radio service ($5 per month) that offers differently themed radio stations. The Rhapsody player (the service uses its own proprietary player) is based on Windows Media Player, so it should work with just about any HTPC remote control.

✔ **MUSICMATCH MX** (www.musicmatch.com): Like Listen.com, MUSIC-MATCH MX comes in two versions: gold ($2.95 per month) that gives you radio access, and platinum ($4.95 per month) that gives you on-demand access to the catalogs of over 8,000 artists. MX is fully integrated into MUSICMATCH jukebox, so you've only got one interface to deal with.

✔ **Movielink** (www.movielink.com): Check out Movielink, which is a cool site from which you can download and play current Hollywood movies (meaning about when they make it to DVD). A six-day "rental" is about $3 per movie — the catch is that you gotta finish watching it within 24 hours after you start playing it.

Other wireless ways (Where there's a will . . .)

We are very obviously biased toward the 802.11x technologies because we believe in a home wireless network backbone. We think that with all the focus on standards, costs will decrease, new features will evolve, and the overall capability will continue to get better. Collectively, it simply gives you more options for the home.

That doesn't mean that standards are the only way to go. There are plenty of proprietary 900 MHz, 2.4 GHz, and 5 GHz approaches — as well as other frequency bands — that are popular because they're just cheap to manufacture and cheap to implement. For instance, the SoundLink (www.usr.com/products/device/p-device-product.asp?sku=USR6003) Wireless Audio Delivery System (Model USR6003, list price $105) uses FM frequency bands to link your PC and stereo over channels 88.1 or 88.3. This is basically an FM transmitter for your PC. (In *Home Theater For Dummies*, we tell you about how to use this type of transmitter to make your own drive-in!)

For another approach, check out Terk's (www.terk.com, $99.95) Leapfrog Series Wave Master 20 (Model LF-20S) that uses the same 2.4 GHz frequency spectrum as does 802.11b and 802.11g to carry audio and video around the house. So 802.11 is not the only way, but we prefer it. Just remember: The more signals that you put in the 2.4 GHz and 5 GHz ranges to compete with your 802.11 signals, the more problems you'll have.

Chapter 14

Other Cool Things You Can Network

In This Chapter

▶ Cruisin' with wireless onboard

▶ Looking good on Candid Camera, 802.11-style

▶ Controlling your home from afar

▶ Talking to your robo-dog (and having him talk back)

The wireless age is upon us, with all sorts of new devices and capabilities that you can add onto your network that save you time, enhance your lifestyle, and are simply fun. After you have your wireless local area network (LAN) in place (which we show you how to do in Parts II and III), you can do a nearly unlimited number of things. Sort of reminds us of the Dr. Seuss book, *Oh, the Places You'll Go!*.

In this chapter, we introduce you to some of the neater things that are available today for your wireless home network. And in Chapter 19, we talk about those things that are coming soon to a network near you! Together, with the gaming and A/V discussion in Chapters 12 and 13, you'll see why we say that wireless home networking isn't just for computers anymore.

In this chapter, we give you an overview of a lot of new products, but we can't really give you a lot of specific information about how to set up these products. In general, you have to provide your Service Set Identifier (SSID) and Wired Equivalent Privacy (WEP) codes, and that should be 95 percent of what you need to do to set up your device for your wireless network. In this chapter and in Chapter 19, we feel that it's important to expose you to the developments that are happening now so that you can look around and explore different options while you wirelessly enable your home. To say that your whole house is going to have wireless devices in every room within the next three years is *not* an understatement — it's truly coming on fast (so hold on tight!).

The wireless-enablement of consumer goods is spreading faster than a wild-fire. As we write, products are coming out daily. A lot of the products that we mention in this chapter represent some of the early forms of addressing the wireless enablement of some area of your home. If you're interested in seeing what else has popped up since we wrote the book, try searching Yahoo! (www.yahoo.com), as well as our book update site at www.dummies.com/extras, for the products that we mention in the book. The press likes to compare different items in articles, and you're likely to find other new products along with those referenced in this book.

Making a Connection to Your Car

For many people, their car is something more than a mechanism to get them from Point A to Point B. Some folks spend a considerable amount of time each day commuting — we know people who spend 1.5 hours in the car *each way* in a commute. For others, like those with RVs, their vehicle represents almost an entire vacation home.

If you think about the things you do in your car — listen to some music, talk on the phone, let your kids watch a movie — they're not all that different from things that you do around the house. Because your home's wireless connection can reach outside your walls and into your driveway or garage, your car can go online with your home network and access data ranging from your address book on your PC to your latest MP3s in your stereo. You can download these to your car, thus simplifying your life and making the car truly a second home. (No more calls home, "Honey, can you look on my computer for the number for . . .?")

Your car's path to wireless enlightenment

Although you might think that wireless is a new topic for your car, in fact, your car has been wirelessly enabled for years. Your car stereo gets wireless AM/FM signals from afar, and with the advent of satellite radio, now even farther than ever before. (See the nearby sidebar, "Satellite radio.") Wireless phone options — cellular and Bluetooth-based technologies — are quickly filtering into the car. (We discuss Bluetooth and cars more in Chapter 15.) And then there's the new wave of electronic toll systems that also predominantly use short range wireless technology to extract from your bank account that quarter (or dollar) every time that you cross a toll bridge. So wireless is all over your car . . . but just not centralized on any sort of wireless backbone, like we talk about for your home.

Satellite radio

Your wireless home is not always just about 802.11 technologies . . . other forms of wireless will enhance your home, and satellite radio is one of them, particularly for your car. If you're like us, you live somewhere where there isn't a whole lot of programming that you really want to listen to. Check out satellite radio, which offers a huge number of stations (over 100 each) beamed to your house or car from a handful of geostationary satellites hovering above the equator. We find a ton more diverse and just plain interesting stuff coming across these space-based airwaves than we find on our local radio today. Satellite radio services, from start-ups such as XM Radio or SIRIUS, require you to — gasp — *pay* for your radio (about $10 to $12 a month).

Check out the Web sites of the two providers (XM Radio, www.xmradio.com; and SIRIUS, www.sirius.com) to find the programming that you prefer. Then get your hands on a satellite radio tuner. (You can find a bunch of different models listed on each company's Web page.) The majority of these satellite tuners are designed for in-car use (because people tend to listen to the radio most while they're driving), but XM Radio offers some really cool tuners (from Sony and Delco) that can do double duty: You can put these tuners in your car, and when you get home, pull them out and plug them into your A/V receiver. As of this writing, SIRIUS doesn't yet offer a receiver for in-home use, but we expect that it will shortly.

Remember. These satellites are down by the equator, so no matter where you live in the United States, put your antenna in a south-facing window to pick up a good signal in your home.

Your car is also becoming more outfitted for computing and entertainment devices and functionality as manufacturers add as standard and optional features things such as DVD and VHS tape playback systems, Global Positioning Systems (GPSes), and even computers to operate your car.

All this spells "opportunity" for wireless. Bluetooth and 802.11 technologies are infiltrating the car, creating the same wireless backbone as in your home — a universal wireless network that any device or function can access to talk to other parts of the car, like your stereo, and to points outside the car. In fact, your wireless *home* network is going to play an important part in helping consolidate and integrate your *car's* wireless network within the car and with your home as these two areas converge towards each other.

The response has been a flurry of activity by the auto manufacturers and others to network-enable cars with wireless phone, data, video, audio, and control mechanisms that resemble (in a lot of ways) the same efforts that are going on inside your house by the other consumer goods manufacturers. In fact, you're starting to see whole product lines that include home and car wireless network products.

Linksys, for instance, has teamed with Zandiant Technologies (www.zandiant.com) to extend its digital home media products to wireless MP3 players in the car and other products that enable vehicles to connect with home, office, and hot spot networks. Very cool. A version capable of doing video is expected by the end of 2003, probably based on 802.11g. Other familiar home wireless product companies, like Kenwood, have similar efforts.

Synching your car stereo with home

The major area where 802.11 has initially started to take hold is in third-party add-ons to the car — a typical precursor to manufacturers directly bundling these add-ons into the car (in-car VCRs started the same way). One example is in the A/V arena. We show in Chapter 13 how simple it is to synchronize your audio and video server across the house and over the Internet — why not with your car, too? (See Figure 14-1.)

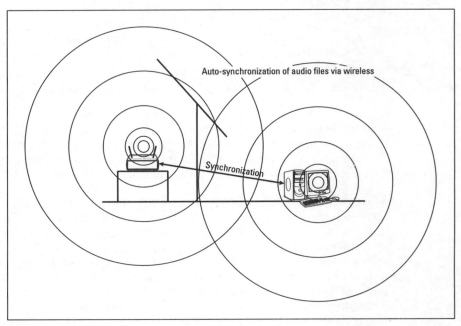

Figure 14-1:
Linking your car with your home wireless network is a matter of having your car's access point or wireless client log onto and sync with the home wireless network.

Auto-synchronization of audio files via wireless

Synchronization

Rockford Fosgate (www.omnifimedia.com), for instance, has an 802.11b-based car product Omnifi ($599 plus the $99 wireless option) that enables you to wirelessly transfer tunes from your home PC to the car, where they can be played on your in-dash stereo. The in-dash device can store up to 20GB of files; the home component is a standalone receiver capable of streaming media dispatched from the PC. (See Figure 14-2.)

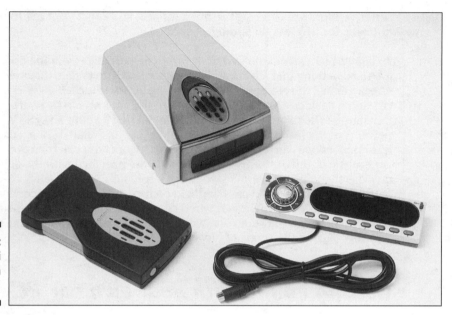

Figure 14-2:
The Omnifi
system in
your car!

Omnifi eliminates the legwork (the need to burn CDs) to listen to digital music in the car. It gives consumers the ability to download and transfer music and programs from the Internet to the PC hard drive to the consumer's car and home stereo/theater systems — using wireless technologies. The Omnifi comes with an Internet services package ($49.95 annually) that includes thousands of radio stations, news and information, and a host of additional content from providers, such as Live365, Yahoo!, Virgin Radio, AOL Shoutcast, Pinnacor, Gracenote, Tower.com, and Muze. Way cool.

Omnifi is a family of connected devices based on its SimpleWare software suite. You can manage your media files in one simple media player application, SimpleCenter, and then wirelessly deliver the content to your stereo or car-installed Omnifi devices. What's more, you can schedule delivery of information. The Omnifi scheduler gives users the ability to set information and music preferences in the SimpleCenter application and schedule the delivery of media automatically and wirelessly to devices in the car and at the stereo. This feature works with both local files and Internet-based files that a user can access through SimpleCenter's Internet services offerings. For example, a commuter might choose to schedule an information update of local weather and traffic, stock quotes, breaking news, and his daily horoscope to be automatically transferred to the Omnifi device in the car at 6:30 a.m. every day in time for his daily commute.

Other vendors are entering the marketplace, so expect your car to become a hot zone for wireless technologies soon.

Installing a wireless audio system in your car can range from the do-it-yourself job to something that a local audio installer needs to tackle. Generally, you have to install the electronics in your trunk or other tucked-away spots in your car. Some devices allow you to transmit to the car's stereo by short-range FM transmitter. (Rockford sells one for its Omnifi that's about $30.) So you run power (per the installation instructions) to your installed device, and the wireless connections can log onto your home network. You can then download all your music to the device by using the software provided with the device. That music is then played by tuning your car stereo into the frequency of the transmitter, like 99.1 FM. An in-car handheld control device is either connected to your main unit via a wireless or wired connection. More complex installations require you to run the audio and video cables to your stereo system, which is typically beyond the scope of the average homeowner.

Getting online with your own car PC

The previous products are great for syncing your audio at home with your car's audio system via wireless 802.11 networks. What about video? For auto video servers, the market is still beginning to develop, but it's more focused on putting a full PC in your car and storing and playing videos through that. Some very cool, wireless-capable auto PCs are currently on the market.

With a PC in your car (I don't recall seeing any of those plastic traffic signs in any car windows saying "PC on Board" — do you?), you can mimic your home wireless network in your car, almost in its entirety. You can sync up with your PC for audio and video to play over your car's radio and video display system. You can play computer games over those same systems. You can access your address books and calendars, just like at your desk. You can even use wireless keyboards.

G-NET Canada (`www.gnetcanada.com`) has a range of auto-enabling PCs that add all sorts of functionality to your car. Aurora Auto PC, for instance, is a $1,500 add-on that gives you just about all you'd want from your car. It includes an MP3 audio player, a DVD player, GPS navigation support, vehicle diagnostics, and a digital dash software interface, as well as a full Windows XP-based PC that can run any application you want. The Aurora Auto PC sports a PC Card slot so that you can add the wireless card of your choice — setup is the same procedure for setting up any Windows XP 802.11 client. The trimmed-down Memphis Auto PC model, which has all the same wireless access capabilities but no onboard DVD device, enables you to store and play audio and video files downloaded from your host home PC.

You can get additional accessories to boost your enjoyment of your car PC. A wireless keyboard makes it simple to interface with the PC for text-oriented tasks (as is common with kid's games) and for surfing the Internet. You can wirelessly connect to the Internet while driving by using a cellular PC Card like the Sierra Wireless AirCard 750.

So, you can now pull up to a hot spot and log on. (Check out Chapter 16 for more about hot spots.) Or, auto-sync when you enter your garage. It's just a matter of time until you can play games car-to-car while driving down the road with another wirelessly enabled car.

Installing your car PC is both easy and hard. It's easy in the sense that you screw the unit to your car and run power to the unit. It's hard in the sense that other than the wireless connections, any connections to your car stereo or video system might entail running wires, just like with the audio wireless car servers that we describe previously. But after you have all this in place, using a different application is just a matter of installing new software on your car PC. It's just like your home PC — after you install your printer, your monitors, and all the other parts of your system, the hard work is done. Just install new software to do new things.

We think that every car should have one of these wireless PCs! At least any car that has passengers in it — you don't want to be surfing the Web while you're driving.

Picking wireless gear for your car

The integration of external wireless connectivity options to cars is definitely in its infancy. However, some things to look for when shopping for auto-based audio/video gear include the following:

✔ **PC Card (PCMCIA) slots:** You get the ultimate in flexibility with PC Card slots because you can put any card that you want into the system. You need these for connecting to the home when parked in the yard and accessing the Internet when traveling. Ideally, you'd have two PC Card slots because it's probably going to be a while before a lot of dual-mode Wi-Fi/cellular cards are on the market.

✔ **FM modulator:** Some systems have an optional FM modulator that enables you to merely tune into an unused FM band in your area and broadcast your music from the server to your stereo system. Because some audio and video systems require you to have specific receivers (that is, your actual audio component where you will listen to the music) for your car to make full use of the new functionality, it can get expensive to install a system. FM modulators make it easy to put in a system without changing out your stereo; you do lose some of the onscreen reporting that comes with a hard-wired installation, but you still get access to the music (which is the important part).

✔ **Upgradeable storage hard-disk space:** Look for systems that allow you to add storage space when you need to. Storage is getting cheaper and coming in smaller form factors all the time. You'll probably want to keep adding storage space as your audio and video collection increases.

✔ **Lots of interfaces:** After your system is installed, you're going to want to plug a lot of things into it. Make sure that you have a good supply of Universal Serial Bus (USB), FireWire, Ethernet, PC Card, serial, and RCA ports. You might have already installed a VHS tape deck or DVD player in your car; if you did, you might be able to easily install an audio/video server right beside it and use available In jacks on the video player to feed your existing screen and audio system.

All in all, expect a wireless LAN in your car soon — it just makes sense.

Look Ma, I'm on TV — Video Monitoring over Wireless LANs

The heightened awareness for security has given rise to a more consumer-friendly grade of video monitoring gear for your wireless network, too — this is stuff that used to be the exclusive domain of security installers. You can get network-aware 802.11b-supporting video cameras that contain their own integrated Web servers, which eliminate the need to connect a camera directly to your computer. After installation, you can use its assigned Internet Protocol (IP) address on your network to gain access to the camera, view live streaming video, and make necessary changes to camera settings.

Panasonic sells its KX-HCM250 wireless network camera (www.panasonic.com; $750), complete with SSID filtering and 64/128-bit WEP encryption to help protect your wireless network from illegal intrusion. (See Figure 14-3 to see the product. We talk more about SSIDs and WEP in Chapters 6 and 10 if you need to know more.) The KX-HCM250 allows up to 30 simultaneous viewers to see up to 15 frames per second (fps) of live-motion video with resolution of up to 640 x 480. Through a Web-based interface, you can perform remote pan and tilt functions and click to eight preset angles.

D-Link is another vendor that has embraced the video aspects of wireless based video surveillance. Its D-LinkAir DCS-1000W (www.d-link.com; $329) — shown along with the Panasonic KX-HCM250 in Figure 14-3 — gives you VGA-quality streaming video with built-in automatic gain and white balance controls. It comes with IPView, which is a Microsoft Windows-compatible monitoring application. IPView allows you to control all your DCS-1000W cameras on your LAN from one location. IPView also lets you view as many as 16 cameras on one screen, supports manual and scheduled recording to an AVI movie file on your hard drive, and supports motion detection that triggers automatic recording.

Go to www.dlink.com/LiveDemo/ for a live demo of the D-Link*Air* DCS-1000W camera.

Installing a wireless network camera is incredibly simple. These are network devices and usually sport both an RJ-45 10Base-T wired network interface along with an 802.11b air interface. Installing the camera usually involves first connecting the camera to your network via the wired connection and then using the provided software to access your camera's settings. Depending on how complicated the camera is (whether it supports the ability to pan, to e-mail pictures on a regular basis, to allow external access, and so on), you might be asked to set any number of other settings.

Figure 14-3: The D-Link*Air* DCS-1000W and Panasonic KX-HCM250 wireless network cameras.

Photo courtesy of Panasonic

You might be asked to set a fixed (static) IP address for the camera on your home wireless network. In Chapter 6, we talk about how (in most cases) your wireless clients obtain an IP address (when on your network) through the Dynamic Host Configuration Protocol (DCHP). DHCP just gives you an address based on the next one that happens to be available on your network; it can change from time to time. However, to access the camera from outside your home, say from your office, you want that IP address to be the same all the time so that you don't have to guess what address it obtained from your DHCP host. When setting up your camera, it will probably ask you to give it a fixed address on your network. To do this, simply choose a number outside the range that's governed by your host's DHCP client range. If you let your router assign DHCP from within the range of numbers from 192.168.254.0 to 192.168.254.50, you can pick any number above 50 and below 254, such as 192.168.254.100. You need to make sure that you don't pick a number being assigned by the router's DHCP, or you might find that your number gets taken by another assignment.

The wireless communications doesn't have to be 802.11b, although we would argue that it makes sense to use standards-based gear when you can. Danny likes his X10 FloodCam (www.x10.com; $130) that videotapes all activity around the house, night or day, and sends the images to a VCR or PC. That system uses 2.4 GHz to send the signals, but it's not standardized wireless LAN traffic. Over time, we believe that many of these systems will move to 802.11 or Bluetooth when those chip and licensing costs continue to come down.

Controlling Your Home over Your Wireless LAN

Another area of wireless activity is home control. If you got excited about going from the six remote controls on your TV set to one universal remote control, you ain't seen nothin' yet. (And if you still have those six remote controls up there, we've got some options for you, too.)

The problem with controlling anything remotely is having an agreed-upon protocol between the transmitting functionality and the receiving functionality. In the infrared (IR) space, strong agreement and standardization exists for remote controls among all the different manufacturers, so the concept of a universal remote control is possible for IR. (IR remotes are the standard for the majority of home audio and video equipment.) But in the *radio frequency* (RF) space, there has not been the same rallying around a particular format, thus making it difficult to consolidate control devices except for within the same manufacturer's line. And then you have the issues of controlling non-entertainment devices, such as heating and air conditioning, security systems, and so on. Those have different requirements just from a user interface perspective.

TIP

Total Harmony with your wireless entertainment

A great idea demonstrating the power of consolidated remote controls is found in the Harmony Remote controls. With their Smart State Technology capabilities, they can interface with your A/V gear through macros. Select Watch TV, and the remote sequentially goes through all the motions to turn on the TV, turn on the receiver, select the TV mode, turn on the satellite receiver, and anything else that has to be activated to watch the television. What's more, these remotes have onscreen program guides to help you select what you want before you even turn on the TV. That's cool. You should check it out.

The advent of 802.11b and Bluetooth — as well as touchscreen LCDs and programmable handheld devices — offers the opportunity to change this because, at the least, manufacturers can agree upon the physical Transport layer of the signal and a common operating system and platform. Now we're starting to see the first moves toward collapsing control over various home functions towards a few form factors and standards. We talk about these in the next few sections.

Using your PDA as a remote control

One area that has seen some action is the personal digital assistant (PDA) marketplace. PDAs have a sophisticated operating system (OS), usually the Pocket PC or Palm OS. They have IR, 802.11, and sometimes Bluetooth wireless capabilities. And they have a programmable onscreen interface, making it easy to show different buttons for different devices. These features make PDAs ideal for wireless remote control of any entertainment, computing, or other networked device. You can cue up an MP3 on your computer and play it on your stereo system in your living room. You can find out what's playing on DirecTV tonight by wirelessly accessing TV schedules on the Internet and then turn your DirecTV receiver to the right channel to watch. With the ability to play in both the PC and entertainment (as well as home control) worlds, the PDA can do lots of things, as demonstrated by the following products:

- Philips offers **ProntoLITE** (www.pronto.philips.com; $19.95), which is a device that turns a Palm-based PDA into a universal remote control. ProntoLITE for Palm is compatible with versions 3.5x and 4.x. *Note:* As of this writing, it is not compatible with Palm OS version 5.0.

- Universal Electronic's **Nevo** (www.mynevo.com) has a more onboard remote control operating system solution, initially built into HP's iPAQ Pocket PCs.

✔ The popular Intrigue Technologies' Harmony Smart State Technology, which powers the **Harmony Remote** (www.harmonyremote.com) control, is being ported to PDAs. See the nearby sidebar ("Total *Harmony* with your wireless entertainment") for more about this cool product.

For people who want the flexibility of a big color screen, PDA-based programs allow you to take advantage of the dropping costs of PDAs to get a world-class, universal remote. Many PDA manufacturers are looking at making this a standard feature on their systems. Check out your PDA's home page on the manufacturer's site for any information on remote control software.

Whole home 802.11-based IR coverage

Other devices, namely Web tablets and standalone touchscreens, are sporting IR interfaces and can become remotes for your whole home, too. (*Whole home* means that you can use it anywhere that your wireless net reaches for a broad range of devices anywhere in your home; check out Chapter 1 for more details about whole home.)

One of the really cool wireless-enabled options is *iPronto* (www.pronto.philips.com; $1,699), which is a Web tablet-like device that enables you to do all sorts of chores. Phillips describes this wireless, mobile device as a "dashboard for the digital home" that combines home entertainment, security, and other systems control as well as 802.11b wireless LAN and broadband Internet access. That's a lot to pack in one device.

With iPronto (model TSi6400), you can control your A/V system components, check out program guides, and surf the Web — all while connected wirelessly to your home 802.11b network. Users can easily control devices via the high-resolution, touchscreen LCD, combined with a customizable user interface and exterior hard buttons. The system features a built-in microphone and stereo speakers, allowing users to listen to MP3s from the Internet and to future-proof themselves for applications such as voice recognition and telephony. Way cool.

One really neat capability of iPronto is its ability to link with your home's 802.11b network to communicate with IR-enabled, network-extender devices in other rooms. Suppose that you're in your master bedroom and you're listening to a Turtle Beach AudioTron (www.turtlebeach.com; $299) AT100 Digital Music Player through your remote wireless speakers, and you want to change stations. Just grab your iPronto and tap-tap-tap, you can change the song that's playing. Because the AT100 isn't wireless (although the higher-end AT200 model is), you'd have to go all the way downstairs to point the remote at the AT100 to change stations. That's the whole home advantage!

In an iPronto model, you could have a network extender in the room that has IR-emitter capability. The iPronto can communicate via 802.11b to the network extender, giving it the proper codes to send to the AudioTron via IR, and voilà! (or wal*la*! as a former employee once wrote in a presentation), you can change stations without leaving your bed. You could have whole home infrared-capability linked via 802.11. That's really neat.

The latest technology to hit the streets is the SST Component Framework. From Intrigue Technologies (makers of the popular Harmony Remote that we mention earlier in this chapter), this technology basically enables you to use its software and database on any devices that you want, such as personal computers, Web pads, Pocket PCs, Palm Pilots, or even cellular phones. This allows you to choose the particular components that are best for your house.

It works like this: You create an account on the Harmony Remote Web site and specify the devices in your house, along with the activities (such as *Watch a DVD*) that use those devices. Using the Harmony SST database, the Web site then creates a file that contains your house's personality. This personality file can then be sent to your control device either through a USB or wireless connection.

See me, feel me, hear me, touch me

Other neat touchpanels are ideal for whole home wireless control. You're probably familiar with touchscreens, if you've ever used a kiosk in a mall to find a store or at a hotel to find a restaurant. Touchpanels are smaller (typically 6–10" screens) and are wall mounted or simply lie on a table; you touch the screen to accomplish certain things.

Touchpanels have become a real centerpiece for expensive home control installations, where touchpanels allow you to turn on and off the air conditioning, set the alarm, turn off the lights, select music, change channels on the TV . . . and the list goes on. These are merely user interfaces into often PC-driven functionality that can control almost anything in your house, even the coffee maker.

Crestron (www.crestron.com) rules the upper end of touchpanel options with a whole product line for home control that includes wireless-enabled touchpanels. Crestron's color touchpad systems are to die for (or at least to second-mortgage for). We'd say, "The only thing these touchpanels cannot do is let the dog out on cold nights," but as soon as we said it, someone would retort, "Well, actually, they can."

Although some of Crestron's current products use 434 MHz wireless RF to communicate with each other, Crestron also has many 802.11 wireless solutions, including PDA control of Crestron via 802.11 using any PocketPC 2002-powered device, as well as full support for Microsoft Tablet PC OS. You can design your own graphical layouts for the devices using Crestron's touchpanel design software, VTPRO-e, so you can use a PDA/Web tablet for control, just like you would a wall-mounted Crestron touchpanel. In addition, Crestron is working very closely with Viewsonic to allow use of Viewsonic 802.11b-enabled Web tablets to control the home's systems.

Crestron is definitely high end — the average Crestron installation tops $50,000. But if you're installing a home theater, a wireless computing network, a slew of A/V, and home automation on top of that, you're probably going to talk to Crestron at one point or another.

An up-and-coming, lower-cost alternative to Crestron is CorAccess (www.coraccess.com), which offers a line of products that are 802.11b (and soon 802.11g) enabled. Dubbed the CorAccess Companion, these products are a pretty sleek and convenient way to interface with various home automation products, such as the HAI Omni and OnQ HMS home control software systems that allow you to manage the systems in your home (see Figure 14-4).

CorAccess also has added some nifty applications to boost this from just being a touchpanel for controls. Its PhotoMate software turns the Companion into a digital picture frame. When not in control mode, it displays a single picture or slideshow; images of the kids, your last vacation, or even updates of news and weather downloaded from the Internet. You can manage your Companion and its photo presentations from CorPhoto (www.corphoto.com), which is the CorAccess digital photo exchange site.

The Companion also comes equipped with a full Camera Monitoring application where you can view as many cameras as you'd like, one or four at a time. With just a touch, you can go to full screen, stop on particular cameras, or change the delay time between camera views. Or you can add camera views available through the Internet to see local traffic, weather, or any other IP-based camera (such as the Panasonic or D-Link cameras that we discuss earlier in the chapter).

The optional AudioMate application from CorAccess can be used to play music from your home network or streaming content from the Internet and can even become your home intercom system. An AudioMate intercom isn't limited to just inside the home, however. The CorAccess Voice over IP- (VoIP) based communication system allows Companion to talk to a multitude of other devices . . . from the Companion in the entryway to a laptop downtown or a PC halfway around the world.

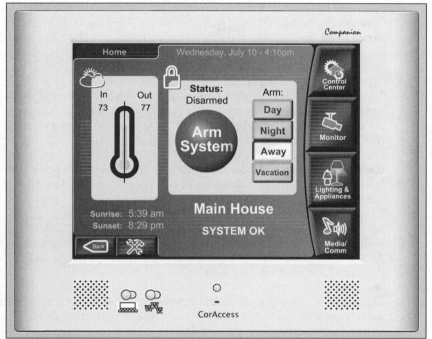

Figure 14-4:
The
CorAccess
Companion
10.

When linked to the HAI Omni system (www.homeauto.com), you add in an automation and security controller. Omni coordinates lighting, heating and air, security, scenes, and messaging based on activity and schedules. Omni comes with several standard modes, such as Day, Night, Away, and Vacation, and can accept customized scenes such as Good Night, Good Morning, or Entertainment that set temperatures, lights, and security to the desired levels — all with just one touch. Security and temperature sensors can be used to adjust lights, appliances, and thermostats; monitor activity; and track events.

So much control, so little time. The CorAccess products come in a wall mount or tablet version. Pricing ranges from $1,999 to $2,499. An HAI system adds about $1,500 to $3,500 to the mix.

If you're really interested in home automation and linking the various aspects of your home together, try _Smart Homes For Dummies,_ by Wiley Publishing, Inc. It's the best book on the topic. (Can you tell that Pat and Danny wrote it?)

Sit, Ubu, Sit . . . Speak!

Your wireless network can help with your pet tricks, too! Although we're not sure that this is what the pet trainer meant when she said that she'd teach your dog to speak, but speak he can if he's Sony's AIBO robotic dog (www.aibo.com; $1,500 and up). Don't be misled and think of this as a cute expensive toy — this is one incredible robot. If you don't know much about the AIBO, check out its Web site to find out about this robotic puppy. It's neat how Sony has wirelessly enabled its robo-dog with 802.11b.

All you need to do is buy an AIBO wireless LAN 802.11b card and a programming Memory Stick (assuming that you've already got an AIBO), and your pooch roves about constantly linked to your home wireless network. With AIBO Messenger software, AIBO can read your e-mail and home pages. AIBO will tell you when your receive e-mail in your inbox. AIBO will read your e-mail messages to you. ("Hey, Master, you got an e-mail from your girlfriend. She dumped you.") AIBO can read up to five pre-registered Web sites for you. And AIBO will remind you of important events.

With AIBO Navigator software, your computer becomes AIBO's remote-control unit. From the cockpit view on your PC, you can experience the world from AIBO's eyes in real-time. (You know, there are just some things that a dog sees that we really would rather not see!)

Through the control graphical user interface (GUI) on your PC, you can move your AIBO anywhere that you want. Use a joystick or your keyboard and mouse to move AIBO about. By using the sound transmission feature, you can make AIBO speak instead of you from a remote location. ("Hey, baby, how's about you and me going out for a cup of coffee?")

We're not sure that you're ready to start telling people that your dog has an SSID ("AIBONET"), but this is one good example today of robots using your home wireless highway. Above all, make sure that you turn on WEP and follow the security suggestions that we give you in Chapter 10. (Could you imagine taking control of your neighbor's un-secured AIBO — now THAT could be fun!) You can find out more about setting up an AIBO on your wireless LAN at www.us.aibo.com/lan/ers_210_lan_21.php.

Chapter 15

Using a Bluetooth Network

In This Chapter

▶ Delving into Bluetooth

▶ Enabling cell phone networking with Bluetooth

▶ Getting Bluetooth on your PDA or PC

▶ Discovering other Bluetooth devices

Most of the time, when people talk about wireless networks, they're talking about wireless local area networks (LANs). LANs, as the name implies, are *local*, meaning that they don't cover a wide area (like a town or a city block). Wide area networks (WANs), like the Internet, do that bigger job. For the most part, you can think of a LAN as something that's designed to cover your entire house (and maybe surrounding areas like the back patio).

Another kind of wireless network is being developed and promoted by wireless equipment manufacturers called the *personal area network* (PAN), which is designed to cover just a few yards of space and not a whole house (or office, or factory floor, or whatever). PANs are typically designed to connect personal devices (cell phones, laptop computers, and handheld computers/personal digital assistants [PDAs]) and also as a technology for connecting peripheral devices to these personal electronics. For example, you could use a wireless PAN technology to connect a mouse and a keyboard to your computer without any cables under the desk for your beagle to trip over.

The difference between LANs and PANs isn't all that clear cut. Some devices might be able to establish network connections by using either LAN or PAN technologies. The bottom-line distinction between LANs and PANs is this: If something connects to a computer by a network cable today, its wireless connection will usually be a LAN; if it connects by a local cable (like Universal Serial Bus [USB]), its wireless connection will usually be a PAN.

In this chapter, we discuss the most prominent wireless PAN technology: Bluetooth, which we introduce in Chapter 3. *Bluetooth* is a technology that's been in development for years and years. We first wrote about it in our first edition of *Smart Homes For Dummies* (Wiley Publishing, Inc.) in 1999. For a while, it seemed that Bluetooth might end up in the historical dustbin of wireless networking — a great idea that never panned out — but as we write, it appears that the technology has caught up with its promise. We expect to see a ton of new Bluetooth devices hitting the market over the next few years.

Bluetooth is still a relatively new technology. Although a lot of Bluetooth products (mainly cell phones and cell phone accessories) are now available, other Bluetooth products (such as keyboards) aren't widely available in the United States (where we're based). Bluetooth seems to be taking off first in Europe (and to a slightly lesser degree, in Asia) and moving over to the United States a bit more slowly. This isn't really surprising because a lot of mobile technologies (particularly cell phone-related technologies) have been developing faster in those places than they have in the U.S. We mention this because some of the Bluetooth categories that we discuss in this chapter are really in the coming-soon category when it comes to U.S. availability. We're confident that many of these devices will be available in the U.S. by the time that you read this (or soon thereafter), but as we write in early 2003, they're not quite here yet. A great resource for finding cool Bluetooth gear before it becomes generally available in the U.S. is the BlueUnplugged online store based in England (www.blueunplugged.com).

Discovering Bluetooth Basics

Let's get the biggest question out of the way first: What the heck is up with that name? Well, it's got nothing to do with what happens when you chew on your pen a bit too hard during a stressful meeting. Nor do blueberry pie, blueberry toaster pastries, or any other blue food. Actually, Bluetooth (www.bluetooth.com is the Web site for the industry group) is named after Harald Blåtand (Bluetooth), King of Denmark from 940 to 981, who was responsible for uniting Denmark and Norway. The idea here is that Bluetooth can unite things that were previously un-unitable. (We're a little rusty on our medieval Scandinavian history, so if we're wrong about that, blame our high school history teachers — if you're a Dane or Norwegian, feel free to e-mail us back with the story here!)

The big cell phone (and other telecommunications equipment) manufacturer Ericsson was the first company to promote the technology (back in the 1990s, as we mention earlier), and other cell phone companies joined in with Ericsson to come up with an industry de facto standard for the technology. The *Institute of Electrical and Electronics Engineers* (IEEE) — the folks who created the 802.11 standards that we've been talking about throughout *Wireless Home Networking For Dummies* — have since become involved with the technology under the auspices of a committee named *802.15*. The initial IEEE standard for PANs, 802.15.1, was adapted from the Bluetooth specification and is fully compatible with Bluetooth 1.1, which is the third and current version of Bluetooth.

If you're looking for a few facts and figures about Bluetooth, you've come to the right chapter. Here are some of the most important things to remember about Bluetooth:

- ✔ **Bluetooth operates in the 2.4 GHz frequency spectrum.** It uses the same general chunk of the airwaves as do 802.11b and 802.11g. (This means that interference between the two technologies is indeed a possibility.)

- ✔ **The Bluetooth specification allows a maximum data connection speed of 723 Kbps.** Compare this with the 11 Mbps of 802.11b. Bluetooth is much slower than wireless LAN technologies.

- ✔ **Bluetooth uses much lower power levels than do wireless LAN technologies (802.11x).** Thus, Bluetooth devices should have a much smaller impact, power-wise, than an 802.11 device. This is a huge deal for some of the small electronic devices that are being Bluetooth-enabled because it means that Bluetooth will eat up a whole lot less battery life than will 802.11 systems.

  Because Bluetooth uses a lower power level than does 802.11, it can't beam its radio waves as far as 802.11 does. Thus, the range of Bluetooth is considerably less than that of a wireless LAN. Theoretically, you can get up to 100 meters, but most Bluetooth systems use less than the maximum allowable power ratings, and you'll typically see ranges of 30 feet or less with most Bluetooth gear — meaning that you'll be able to reach across the room (or into the next room) but not all the way across the house.

- ✔ **Bluetooth uses a peer-to-peer networking model.** This means that you don't have to connect devices back through a central network hub like an access point (AP) — devices can connect directly to each other using Bluetooth's wireless link. The Bluetooth networking process is highly automated; Bluetooth devices actively seek out other Bluetooth devices to see whether they can connect and share information.

- ✔ **Bluetooth doesn't require line of sight between any of the connected devices.**

- ✔ **Bluetooth can also connect multiple devices together in a point-to-multipoint fashion.** One *master* device (often a laptop computer or a PDA) can connect with up to seven slave devices simultaneously in this manner. (*Slave* devices are usually things such as keyboards, printers, and so on.)

The really big deal that you should take away from this list is the fact that Bluetooth is designed to be a low-power (and low-priced!) technology for portable and mobile devices. Bluetooth (do they call it *Bleutooth* in France?) is not designed to replace a wireless LAN. It's designed to be cheaply built into devices to allow quick and easy connections.

Some of the PAN applications that Bluetooth has been designed to perform include the following:

- **Cable replacement:** Peripheral devices that use cables today — keyboards, mice, cell phone headsets, and the like — can now (or will soon, in the very near future) cut that cord and use Bluetooth links instead.

- **Synchronization:** Many people have important information (such as address books, phone number lists, and calendars) on multiple devices (such as a PC, PDA, and cell phone), and keeping this information *synchronized* (up-to-date and identical on each device) can be a real pain in the butt. Bluetooth (when combined with synchronization software) allows these devices to wirelessly and automatically talk with each other and keep up to date.

- **Simple file sharing:** If you've ever been at a meeting with a group of technology geeks (we go to these meetings all the time, but then, we're geeks ourselves), you might have noticed these folks pulling out their Palm PDAs and doing all sorts of contortions with them. What they're doing is exchanging files (usually electronic business cards) via the built-in infrared (IR) system found on Palms. This is an awkward system because you need to have the Palms literally inches apart with the IR sensors lined up. Bluetooth, because it uses radio waves, has a much greater range, which doesn't require that direct IR alignment . . . and is much faster to boot.

Look for even more cool applications in the future. For example, Bluetooth could be used to connect an electronic wallet (located on your PDA or cell phone — the line between these devices is becoming blurred, so perhaps your PDA/cell phone-combo device) to an electronic kiosk. For example, a soda machine could be Bluetooth enabled, and if you wanted a soda, you wouldn't need to spend ten minutes trying to feed that last, raggedy dollar bill in your wallet into the machine. You'd just press a button on your PDA/cell phone, and it would send a buck from your electronic wallet to the machine and dispense your soda. (Pat will have a root beer, thank you very much.)

Another common future application might be customized information for a particular area. Ever go to one of those huge conferences held in places like Las Vegas? The booth numbers tend to go from 0 to 20,000, and the convention floor is about the size of 50 football fields — in other words, it's a real pain in the rear to find your way around. With Bluetooth, you can simply walk by an info kiosk and have a floor map and exhibitor display downloaded to your PDA. We're hoping that this is in place next time that we go to the Consumer Electronics Show; we hate being late for appointments because we're spending an hour searching for a booth.

Bluetooth Mobile Phones

The first place where Bluetooth technology is really taking off is in the cell phone world. This probably shouldn't be a surprise because Ericsson (a huge, cell phone maker) was the initial proponent of the technology, and other big (huge, actually) cell phone companies such as Nokia are also huge proponents of the technology.

In early 2003, just about every new phone being announced (except for the really cheap-o ones) includes Bluetooth technology. Sony Ericsson (that's Ericsson's brand), Nokia, Motorola, Samsung, and Siemens, among others, have all begun selling Bluetooth-enabled phones. The adoption of the technology has been really spectacular. In 2002, it was a rarity, and in 2003, it's just about standard.

You can do a lot of things with Bluetooth in a cell phone, but the four most common applications are the following:

- **Replacing cables:** Many people use headsets with their cell phones. It's a lot easier to hear with an earpiece in your ear than it is to hold one of today's miniscule cell phones up to your ear . . . and a lot more convenient, too. The wire running up your torso, around your arm, and along the side of your head into your ear is a real pain, though. (Some people go to great lengths to keep from being tangled up in this wire — check out the jackets at www.scottevest.com.) A better solution is to connect your headset wirelessly — using Bluetooth, of course.

- **Synchronizing phone books:** Lots of us keep a phone book on our PC or PDA — and most of us who do have been utterly frustrated by the difficulty that we face when we try to get these phone books onto our cell phones. If you can do it at all (and you often can't), you end up buying some special cable and software and then you still have to manually correct some of the entries. But with Bluetooth on your cell phone and PC or PDA, the process can be automatic. (In the meanwhile, we've been using FutureDial, Inc.'s SnapSync [www.futuredial.com; $29] phone synchronization software to load numbers into our phones. It's the first software that we've found that does the trick easily and without error. Buy it until you get a Bluetooth phone!)

- **Going hands-free in the car:** Face it, driving with a cell phone in your hands isn't a very safe thing to do. Using a headset is better, but the best choice (except not using your phone while driving) is to use a completely hands-free system in your car, which uses a microphone and speakers (the speakers from your car audio system). This used to take a costly installation process and meant having someone rip into the wiring and interior of your car. And if you bought a new phone, you probably needed to have the old hands-free gear ripped out and a new one installed. No more — Bluetooth cars are here, and they let you use any Bluetooth-enabled cell phone to go hands-free. Just set the phone in the glove box or dashboard cubbyhole and don't touch it again. Keep your hands and eyes on the road!

✔ **Getting your laptop on the Internet while on the road:** We think that the best way to connect your laptop to the Internet, when you're out of the house, is to find an 802.11 hot spot (we talk about these in Chapter 16), but sometimes you're just not near a hot spot. Well, worry no more, because if you've got a cell phone and laptop with Bluetooth, you can use your cell phone as a wireless modem to connect to the Internet. With most cell phone services, you can establish a low-speed, dialup Internet connection for some basic stuff (like getting e-mail or reading text-heavy Web pages). If your cell phone system (and plan) includes a high-speed option (one of the so-called 2.5 or 3G systems), you can get online at speeds rivaling (although not yet equaling) broadband connections like digital subscriber line (DSL). All without wires!

The list of Bluetooth-enabled cell phones and accessories is already too long for us to list here. The Bluetooth Web site (listed earlier) maintains an up-to-date listing of all Bluetooth cell phones and cell phone accessories available. We expect that list to go from merely large (today) to huge in the very near future.

We also expect the list of applications for Bluetooth on cell phones to grow. For example, many new cell phones are camera phones with a built-in digital camera. The cell phone companies promote this concept because they can charge customers for multimedia messaging services (MMSes) and allow people to send pictures to other cell phone customers. But we can also foresee an application where you could use Bluetooth to send the picture that you just snapped to your buddy's cell phone when he's within range (for free!) or to download your pictures to your PC when you get home.

We're beginning to see Bluetooth headsets (like those currently available for cell phones) becoming available for home cordless phones as well. JABRA's FreeSpeak wireless headset and multi-adapter for non-Bluetooth phones (www.jabra.com; $179) plugs into any phone with a 2.5mm jack.

Bluetooth PDAs

In addition to cell phones, the other category of device that's really seeing a lot of action in the Bluetooth arena is the PDA category. In case you're not familiar with the concept, the term *PDA* (personal digital assistant) encompasses a wide range of handheld computing devices — and therefore, PDAs are also often referred to as *handhelds*.

The most common types of PDAs are the following:

- ✔ **PDAs that use the Palm operating system (OS):** These are the granddaddies of the PDA space. Palm's original model, the Palm Pilot, basically created the entire multibillion dollar PDA market back in the '90s. Today, Palm has been split into two separate groups: Palm, Inc. (www.palm.com), that makes a line of PDAs; and PalmSource, Inc. (www.palmsource.com), that develops the Palm OS. One of the reasons why the company has been split in two is the fact that a host of other companies (such as Sony, with its CLIÉ line [(www.sony.com/clie]) also manufacture and sell Palm OS-based PDAs. Speaking very generally (there are a few notable exceptions), Palm OS PDAs are the cheapest and easiest but also the least powerful (in terms of raw computing power) of the PDAs available today.

- ✔ **Handhelds that use Microsoft's Pocket PC operating system:** Pocket PC handhelds are typically (though not always) a bit more expensive and faster than Palm OS PDAs. The major manufacturers of Pocket PC systems include Hewlett-Packard (HP; www.hp.com), Toshiba (www.toshiba.com), and Dell (www.dell.com). In many ways, down to the user interface, Pocket PCs tend to mirror Windows-based desktop and laptop computers in a smaller, shrunken-down form. Pocket PC handhelds used to be considerably more expensive than Palm handhelds, but because of a price war among the vendors, the price differential has greatly decreased.

- ✔ **PDA/cell phone combinations:** As we mention earlier in the "Discovering Bluetooth Basics" section of this chapter, the line between PDAs and cell phones becomes a bit more blurry with each passing day. Companies such as Handspring (www.handspring.com) sell Palm OS-based devices that are cell phones and PDAs in one, and other companies such as Siemens (www.siemens.com) sell Pocket PC-based combos. Some cell phone/PDA combo devices use entirely different operating systems (such as Symbian, or even the open-source Linux operating system used on many business server computers).

Despite the variation in and among the PDA world, there's also a commonality — PDAs work a lot better as "connected" devices that can talk to computers and other PDAs. And because PDAs and cell phones are increasingly *converging*, or taking on the same functionality, any of the applications that we discuss in the preceding section ("Bluetooth Mobile Phones") might come into play with a PDA.

In particular, the synchronization application that we discuss in that section is especially important for PDAs because they tend to be mobile, on-the-road-again (thanks to Willie Nelson) extensions of a user's main PC. Most PDAs today require either a *docking cradle* (a device that you physically sit the PDA into, which is connected via a cable to the PC), or at least a USB or another cable to synchronize contacts, calendars, and the like with the PC. With Bluetooth, you just need to have your PDA in the same room as the PC, with no physical connection. You can even set up your PDA to automatically synchronize when it's within range of the PC.

Accordingly, we've begun to see Bluetooth functionality built into an increasing number of PDAs. For example, Palm's newest model, the Tungsten T, includes a built-in Bluetooth system, as does HP's Pocket PC OS iPAQ model and Toshiba's e740 series of Pocket PC handhelds.

You can also buy some cool Bluetooth accessories for handhelds. One big issue with handhelds is the process of entering data onto them. Most either have a tiny keyboard (a thumb keyboard really, which is too small for using all your fingers and touch typing) or use a handwriting system, where you use a stylus and write in not-quite-plain English on the screen. Both of these systems can work really well if you spend the time required to master them, but neither is optimal, especially if you want to do some serious data entry — like writing a book! In that case, you really need a keyboard. You can buy one today (with a wire) but we've heard around the grapevine that portable keyboards, which use Bluetooth and are compatible with any Bluetooth PDA, will be released in 2003. A dream come true for us — we can't wait.

If you already own a PDA and it doesn't have Bluetooth built in, what to do? Do you really have to go and replace that six-month-old PDA with a new model? Maybe not. Several manufacturers have begun selling add-on cards for existing PDAs that enable Bluetooth communications. For example, Palm sells the Palm Bluetooth Card ($129), which goes into the standard Secure Digital (SD) card slot found on many Palm OS PDAs. Speaking more generally, most PDAs have a slot like this — SD, Compact Flash, or Memory Stick — that is most often used to expand the amount of memory in the PDA but which can be used for other purposes. Just like the 802.11 cards in these formats that we discuss in Chapter 5, you can now (or will soon be able to) find Bluetooth cards in these formats.

Getting a Bluetooth card installed and set up on your PDA is really super easy. The first thing that you might (or might not) have to do is to install some Bluetooth software on your handheld. If this step is required, you'll simply put the software CD in your PC and follow the onscreen instructions, which will guide you through the process of setting up the software. After the software is on your PC, it should be automatically uploaded to your PDA the next time that you sync it (using your cable or cradle). After the software is on your PDA, just slide the Bluetooth card into the PDA. The PDA will recognize it and might (or might not — this process is so automated you might not notice anything happening) guide you through a quick set up wizard-type program. That's it — you're Bluetooth-ed!

After you get Bluetooth hardware and software on your PDA, you're ready to go. By its nature, Bluetooth is constantly on the lookout for other Bluetooth devices. When it finds something else (like your Bluetooth-equipped PC or a

Bluetooth printer) that can "talk" Bluetooth, the two devices communicate with each other and let each other know what their capabilities are. If there's a match (like you've got a document to print, and there's a printer nearby with Bluetooth), a dialog box pops up on your screen through which you can do your thing. It's usually really easy. In some cases (like syncing mobile phone address books with your PC), you'll need to finesse some software on one side or the other. We find that this is a good time to consult the owner's manual and/or the Web sites of the software and hardware companies involved.

Other Bluetooth Devices

Cell phone and PDAs aren't the only devices that can use Bluetooth, of course. In fact, the value of Bluetooth would be considerably lessened if they were. It's the *network effect* — the value (to the user) of a networked device that increases exponentially as the number of networked devices increases. To use a common analogy, think about fax machines (if you can remember them . . . we hardly ever use ours any more). The first guy with a fax machine found it pretty useless, at least until the second person got hers. As more and more folks got faxes, the fax machine became more useful to each one of them because they simply had a lot more people to send faxes to (or receive them from).

Bluetooth is the same way. Just connecting your PDA to your cell phone is kind of cool, in a geek-chic kinda way, but it's not going to set the world on its ear. But when you start considering wireless headsets, printers, PCs, keyboards, and even Global Positioning System (GPS) receivers — if you're a surveyor, check out Trimble's (`www.trimble.com`) GPS receivers with BlueCap technology — and the value of Bluetooth becomes much clearer.

In this section of the chapter, we discuss some of these other Bluetooth devices.

Printers

We talk about connecting printers to your wireless LAN in Chapter 11, but what if you want to access your printer from all those portable devices that don't have wireless LAN connections built into them? Or, if you haven't got your printer connected to the wireless LAN, what do you do when you want to quickly print a document that's on your laptop? Well, why not use Bluetooth?

You can get Bluetooth onto your printer in two ways:

✔ **Buy a printer with built-in Bluetooth.** These are relatively rare as we write but are becoming more widely available. An example of this comes from HP (www.hp.com), with its DeskJet 995c printer ($399 list price). In addition to connecting to laptops, PDAs (like the HP iPAQ) and other mobile devices using Bluetooth, this Mac- and Windows-compatible printer can connect to your PCs with a standard USB cable or by using an IR connection (using a standard computer system called *IrDA,* which stands for the *Infrared Data Association*). So you'll be able to connect just about any PC or portable device directly to this printer, with wires or wirelessly.

✔ **Buy a Bluetooth adapter for your existing printer.** Many printer manufacturers haven't got around to building printers with built-in Bluetooth yet, but they do recognize the potential in the market. So they've launched Bluetooth adapters that can plug into their existing lines of computers. Epson (www.epson.com), for example, offers a Bluetooth printer adapter for about $129 that plugs into the parallel port (this is the other standard connection that you'll find on printers — along with USB) of most Epson Stylus printers.

What we really expect to see happen in the printer world while the prices for the chips that allow Bluetooth and 802.11 wireless LAN technologies continue to plummet — you read our minds! — is printers that have both 802.11 *and* Bluetooth built into them.

Digital cameras

If you own a digital camera, you've probably spent a fair amount of time reaching behind your PC to connect the USB cable required to download the pictures from the camera to your PC. It's a real pain. And if you head over to your parents' house and want to download the pictures for them, you'd better have remembered that cable, or you'll have to wait until you get home. And then you've got to e-mail all those pictures to them, which can take forever, even on a broadband connection. (And if your parents only have a dialup modem, it'll take them even longer to download that huge e-mail.)

A better solution is to zap the pictures to their PC while you're there (or to your own computer at home, without any behind-the-desk acrobatics) using Bluetooth. Sony's got a solution for you (at least if you live in Japan — Sony hasn't released this model outside its home market yet): the Sony DSC-FX77. (And by the way, can we just ask — what's with Sony's product names? All these numbers drive us crazy.) The DSC-FX77 is a 4-megapixel camera (so you can take some really high-resolution shots that you can blow up into nearly poster-sized prints), and if it's anything like the other (non-Bluetooth) Sony digital cameras that we've used, it's gotta take some great pictures. You can find this camera on Sony's main Web page in Japan (www.sony.co.jp). Because this product is only currently available in Japan — and because we can't read Japanese, either — we can't offer you any setup tips. Because the camera is Bluetooth based, however, setup is probably like with all other Bluetooth-enabled devices . . . you might need to install a driver, and it works within range of other Bluetooth devices.

If you've got a baby (or you're a budding Scorsese) and are into digital camcorders, Sony has several models that have Bluetooth connectivity built in. This is great for sending still pictures over to your computer, but it might not work all that great for sending long videos. We'd love to see 802.11 get put into camcorders because the sheer size of video files means a long download with a slower wireless link. These cameras can be found on Sony's North American Web page (in English, even!) at www.sony.com.

Keyboards and meeses (that's plural for mouse!)

Wireless keyboards and mice have been around for a while (Danny's been swearing by his Logitech wireless mouse for years and years), but they've been a bit clunky. In order to get them working, you had to buy a pair of radio transceivers to plug into your computer, and then you had to worry about interference between your mouse and other devices in your home. With Bluetooth, things get a lot easier. If your PC (or PDA for that matter) has Bluetooth built in, you don't need to buy any special adapters or transceivers — just put the batteries in your keyboard and mouse and start working. (You probably won't even need to install any special software or drivers on your PC to make this work.) Check out the Bluetooth keyboard from the Korean company Bluelogic (www.bluelogic.co.kr) — it's a very cool device that should be available by the time you read this (it was announced but not yet being shipped as we wrote).

If your PC is not already Bluetooth equipped, you might consider buying Microsoft's Wireless Optical Desktop (www.microsoft.com/hardware/keyboard/wodbt_info.asp; about $160). This system includes both a full-function wireless keyboard (one of those cool Microsoft models with a ton of extra buttons for special functions such as audio volume, MP3 fast forward/rewind, and special keys for Microsoft Office programs), a wireless optical mouse (no mouse ball to clean — as an aside, if you haven't used an optical mouse yet, you really need to try one!), and a Bluetooth adapter that plugs into one of your PC's USB ports. This adapter turns your PC into a

Bluetooth PC. In other words, it can be used with any Bluetooth device, not just with the keyboard and mouse that come in the box with it. So this kit is a great way to unwire your mouse and keyboard *and* get a Bluetooth PC, all in one fell swoop.

The Wireless Optical Desktop is really easy to set up. You just need to plug the receiver into a USB port on the back of your computer and install the keyboard and mouse driver software. (This isn't really even a Bluetooth requirement, but rather, it allows you to use all the special buttons on the keyboard and extra mouse buttons on the mouse.) You do, however, have to have an up-to-date version of Windows XP (which you can update by using XP's built-in software update program) or a Macintosh with the latest version of OS X.

Bluetooth adapters

If your PC doesn't have built-in Bluetooth (and most don't, although a growing number of laptop computers, such as Apple's 17" G4 PowerBook — Pat really wants one of these — and some Toshiba and Sony VAIO laptops do ship with built-in Bluetooth), you'll need some sort of adapter, just like you'll need an 802.11 adapter to connect your PC to your wireless LAN. The most common way to get Bluetooth onto your PC is by using a USB adapter (or *dongle*). These compact devices (about the size of your pinkie — unless you're in the NBA, in which case, we'll say *half* a pinkie) plug directly into a USB port and are self-contained Bluetooth adapters. In other words, they need no external power supply or antenna. Figure 15-1 shows the D-Link USB Bluetooth adapter.

Figure 15-1:
D-Link's USB Bluetooth adapter is tiny — about the size of a small pack of gum.

Because Bluetooth is a relatively low-speed connection (remember the maximum speed is only 732 Kbps), USB connections — which are too slow for high-speed wireless LAN adapters like 802.11a and g adapters — are always going to be fast enough for Bluetooth. So you don't need to worry about having an available Ethernet, PC Card, or other high-speed connection available on your PC.

(Un)plugging into Bluetooth access points

Although most people use Bluetooth to connect to devices in a *peer-to-peer* fashion — connecting two devices directly together using a Bluetooth airlink connection — there might be situations where you want to be able to connect Bluetooth devices to your wireless home network itself (or to the Internet through your wireless home network). Enter the Bluetooth access point. Like the wireless access points that we discuss throughout the book, Bluetooth access points provide a means of connecting multiple Bluetooth devices to a wired network connection.

Bluetooth APs, like Belkin's Bluetooth Access Point ($169), have a high-powered Bluetooth radio system (meaning they can reach as far as 100 meters, although your range will be limited by the range of the devices that you're connecting to the AP, which is typically much shorter) and connect to your wireless home network with a wired Ethernet connection. Belkin's AP also includes a USB print server, so you can connect any standard USB printer to the AP and share it with both Bluetooth devices and any device connected to your wireless home network (including 802.11 devices — as long as your wireless home network is connected to the same Ethernet network).

Moving forward, we expect to see access points with both 802.11 *and* Bluetooth functionality built in — multipurpose access points that can connect to any wireless device in your home.

Because many people have more USB devices than USB ports on their computers, they often use USB *hubs,* which connect to one of the USB ports on the back of the computer and connect multiple USB devices through the hub to that port. When you're using USB devices (such as Bluetooth adapters) that require power from the USB port, it's best to plug them directly into the PC itself and not into a hub. If you need to use a hub, make sure that it's a *powered* hub (with its own cord running to a wall outlet or power strip). Insufficient power from an unpowered hub is perhaps the most common cause of USB problems.

If you've got a lot of USB devices, using a USB hub is really simple. We've never seen one that even required any special software to be loaded. Just plug the hub (use a standard USB cable — there should be one in the box with the hub) into one of the USB ports on the back of your PC. If it's a powered hub (which we recommend), plug the power cord into your power strip and into the back of the hub (there'll be a designated power outlet there), and you're ready to go! Easy as can be. Now you can plug any USB device that you've got (keyboard, mouse, digital camera, printer, you name it) into the hub and away you go.

Street prices for these USB Bluetooth adapters generally run under a hundred dollars, and you can find them at most computer stores (both online and the real brick-and-mortar store down the street). Vendors include companies such as D-Link (www.dlink.com), Belkin (www.belkin.com), and Sony (www.sony.com).

Chapter 16

Going Wireless Away from Home

In This Chapter

▶ Discovering public hot spots

▶ Tools of the hot spot trade

▶ Getting espresso and Internet at the same place

▶ Connecting wirelessly on the road

▶ Checking out what's coming soon

*T*hroughout *Wireless Home Networking For Dummies*, we focus — no big surprise here — on wireless networks located within your home. But wireless networks aren't just for the house. For example, many businesses have adopted wireless networking technologies in order to provide network connections for workers roaming throughout offices, conference rooms, and factory floors. And just about every big university has begun to build (or has already completed, in hundreds of cases) a campus-wide wireless network (CAN) that enables students, faculty, and staff to connect to the campus network (and the Internet) from just about every nook and cranny on campus.

These networks are great and very useful if you happen to work or teach or study at a business or school that's got a wireless network. But you don't need to be in one of these locations to take advantage of your wireless networking equipment. You can find literally thousands of *hot spots* (places where you can log onto Wi-Fi networks) across the United States (and the world, for that matter) where you can connect your laptop or handheld computer to the Internet via wireless local area network (LAN) technologies.

In this chapter, we give you some general background on public hot spots, and we discuss the various types of free and for-pay networks out there. We also talk about tools that you can use to find a hot spot when you're out of the house. Finally, we talk in some detail about some of the bigger for-pay hot spot providers out there and how you can get on their networks. The key thing to remember about hot spots — the really cool part — is that they use 802.11 wireless networking equipment. In other words, they use the same kind of equipment that you use in your wireless home network, so you can take basically any wireless device in your home (as long as it's portable enough to lug around) and use it to connect to a wireless hot spot.

Discovering Public Hot Spots

A wide variety of people and organizations have begun to provide hot spot services, ranging from individuals who have opened up their home wireless networks to neighbors and strangers to multinational telecommunications service providers who have built nation- or worldwide hot spot networks containing many hundreds of access points. There's an in-between here, too. Perhaps the prototypical hot spot operator is the hip (or wannabe hip) urban cafe with a digital subscriber line (DSL) and an access point (AP) in the corner. In Figure 16-1, you can see a sample configuration of APs in an airport concourse, which is a popular location for hot spots because of travelers' downtime when waiting for flights or delays.

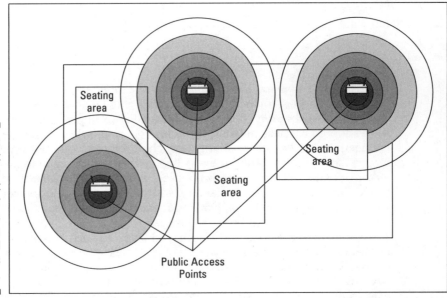

Figure 16-1: An airport concourse is a perfect location for a hot spot, using several access points.

Virtually all hot spot operators use the 802.11b standard for their hot spot access points — we don't know of a single one anywhere in the world that uses the newer standards. This is good because the majority of wireless networking equipment in use today uses this standard. *Note:* If your laptop or handheld computer has an 802.11a-only network adapter in it, you won't be able to connect these hot spot operator's networks. If you use 802.11g equipment, you should be able to connect because 802.11g equipment is backward compatible with 802.11b. Head to Chapter 2 for a refresher on the 802.11 Wi-Fi standards.

Of the myriad reasons why someone (or some company) might open up a hot spot location, the most common that we've seen include the following:

✔ **In a spirit of community-mindedness:** Many hot spot operators strongly believe in the concept of a connected Internet community, and they want to do their part by providing a hop-on point for friends, neighbors, and even passers-by to get online.

✔ **As a municipal amenity:** Not only individuals want to create a connected community. Many towns, cities, boroughs, and villages have begun exploring the possibility of building municipality-wide Wi-Fi networks. There's a cost associated with this, of course, but they see this cost as being less than the benefit that the community will receive. For example, many towns are looking at an openly accessible "downtown Wi-Fi network" as a way of attracting business (and businesspeople) into downtown areas that have suffered because of businesses moving to the suburbs.

✔ **A way to attract customers:** Many cafes and other public gathering spots have installed free-to-use hot spots as a means of getting customers to come in the door and to stay longer. These businesses don't charge for the hot spot usage, but they figure that you'll buy more double espressos if you can sit in a comfy chair and surf the Web while you're drinking your coffee.

✔ **As a business in and of itself:** Most of the larger hot spot providers have made public wireless LAN access their core business. They see (and we agree with them) that hot spot access is a great tool for traveling businesspeople, mobile workers (such as sales folks and field techs), and the like. They've built their businesses based around the assumption that these people (or their companies) will pay for Wi-Fi access mainly because of the benefits that a broadband connection offers them compared with the dialup modem connections that they've been traditionally forced to use while on the road.

Another group of hot spot operators exists that we like to call the *unwilling* (or *unwitting!*) hot spot operators. These are often regular Joes who have built wireless home networks but haven't activated any of the security measures that we discuss in Chapter 10. Their access points have been left wide open, and their neighbors (or people sitting on the park bench across the street) are taking advantage of this open access point to do some free Web surfing. Businesses, too, fall into this category: You'd really be shocked how many businesses have access points that are unsecured — and in many cases, that their IT staff doesn't even know about. It's all too common for a department to install its own access point (a *rogue access point*) without telling the IT staff that they've done so.

We tend to divide hot spot operators into two categories: free networks *(freenets)* that let anyone associate with the hot spot and get access without paying; and *for-pay* hot spots that require users to set up an account and pay per use or a monthly (or yearly) fee for access. In the following sections, we talk a bit about these two types of operators.

Freenets and open access points

Most open access points are just that: individual access points that have been purposely (or mistakenly) left open for others to use. Because this is essentially an ad hoc network created by individuals — without any particular organization behind them — these open hot spots can be hard to find. (**Note:** This is different than an ad hoc network that doesn't use an access point, as we describe in Chapter 7.) In some areas, the owners of these hot spots are part of an organized group, which makes these hot spots easier to find. But in other locations, you'll need to do some Web research and/or use some special programs on your laptop or handheld computer to find an open access point.

The more organized groups of open access points (often called *freenets*) can be found in many larger cities. See a listing of the Web sites of some of the most prominent of these freenets in Chapter 20. A few of the bigger and better-organized ones include

  ✔ **NYCwireless** (`www.nycwireless.net`): A freenet serving Manhattan, Brooklyn, and other areas of the metro New York City region

  ✔ **Bay Area Wireless Users Group** (`www.bawug.org`): A freenet in the San Francisco Bay area

  ✔ **AustinWireless** (`www.austinwireless.net`): Serving the Austin, Texas region

Many freenets are affiliated with larger, nation- or even worldwide efforts. Two of the most prominent are FreeNetworks.org (`www.freenetworks.org`) and the Wireless Node Database Project (`www.nodedb.com`). These organizations run Web sites and provide a means of communications for owners of hot spots and potential users to get together.

These aren't the only sources of information on open hot spots. The folks at 802.11 Planet (one of our favorite sources of industry news) run the Web site 802.11Hotspots.com (`www.80211hotspots.com`) that lets you search through its huge worldwide database of hot spots. You can search by city, state, or country. 802.11Hotspots.com includes both free and for-pay hot spots, so it's a pretty comprehensive list.

You're going to have a lot more luck finding freenets and free public access points in urban areas. The nature of 802.11 technologies is such that most off-the-shelf access points are only going to reach a few hundred feet with any kind of throughput. So when you get out of the city and into the suburbs and rural areas, the chances are that an access point in someone's house isn't going to reach any place that you're going to be . . . unless that house is right next door to a park or other public space. There's just a density issue to overcome. In a city, where there might be numerous access points on a single block, you're just going to have much better luck getting online.

Although these lists are pretty good, none of them are truly comprehensive because many individuals out there who have open hot spots haven't submitted them. If you're looking for a hot spot and haven't found it through one of these (or one of the many, many others online) Web sites, you might try using one of the hot spot-finding programs that we discuss in the upcoming section "Tools for Finding Hot Spots."

Some of the hot spots that you find using these tools, or some of the online Web pages that collect the reports of people using these tools, are indeed open, albeit unintentionally. As we discuss in Chapter 10, a whole wireless LAN subculture is out there — the *wardrivers* — who recreationally find open access points that should be closed. (Check out www.wifimaps.com for some results of their handiwork.) We're *not* going to get involved in a discussion of the morality or ethics of using these access points to get yourself online. We would say, however, that some people think that locating and using an open access point is a bad thing, akin to stealing. So if you're going to hop on someone's access point and you don't know for sure that you're meant to do that, you're on your own.

For-pay services

Freenets are cool. And, although we think that freenets are an awesome concept, if you've got an essential business document to e-mail or a PowerPoint presentation that you've absolutely got to download from the company server before you get to your meeting, you might not want to rely solely on the generosity of strangers. You might even be willing to pay to get a good, reliable, secure connection to the Internet for these business (or important personal) purposes.

And trust us: Someone out there is thinking about how he can help you with that need. In fact, a bunch of companies are focusing on exactly that business. It's the nature of capitalism, right? You've got a need that you're willing to part with some hard-earned cash to have requited. And some company is going to come along, fulfill that need, and separate you from your money.

The concluding sections of the chapter talk about a few of these companies, but for now, we just talk in generalities. Commercial hot spot providers are mainly focused on the business market, providing access to mobile workers and road-warrior types. And many of these providers also offer relatively inexpensive plans (by using either prepaid calling cards or pay-by-the-use models) that you might use for non-business (your personal) connectivity. (At least if you're like us, and you can't go a day without checking your mail or reading DBR — www.dukebasketballreport.com — even when on vacation.)

Unless you're living in a city or town right near a hot spot provider, you're probably not going to be able to pick up a hot spot as your primary ISP, although in some places (often smaller towns), ISPs are using Wi-Fi as the primary pipe to their customers' homes. You can expect to find for-pay hot spot access in a lot of areas outside the home. The most common include the following:

- Hotel lobbies and rooms
- Coffee shops and Internet cafes
- Airport gates and lounges
- Office building lobbies
- Train stations
- Meeting facilities

Basically, anywhere that folks armed with a laptop or a handheld computer might find themselves, there's a potential for a hot spot operator to build a business.

Opening up to your neighbors

We're not talking about group therapy or wild hot tub parties. Wireless networks can carry through walls, across yards, and potentially around the neighborhood. Although wireless LANs were designed from the start for in-building use, the technology can be used in outdoors settings. For example, most college campuses are now wired with dozens or hundreds of wireless access points so that students, staff, and professors can access the Internet from just about anywhere on campus. At UC San Diego, for example, freshmen are outfitted with wireless personal digital assistants (PDAs) to schedule classes, send e-mails, and instant messages, and even find their friends at the student center (by using a locator program written by a student). Many folks are adapting this concept when it comes to access in their neighborhood, setting up community wireless LANs.

Some creators of these community LANs have taken the openness of the Internet to heart and have opened up their access points to any and all takers. There's even an Internet subculture with Web sites and chalk markings on sidewalks

identifying these open access points. In other areas, where broadband access is scarce, neighbors pool money to buy a T1 or other business-class, high-speed Internet line to share it wirelessly.

We think that both of these concepts make a lot of sense, but we do have one warning: Many Internet service providers (ISPs) don't like the idea of you sharing your Internet connection without them getting a piece of the action. Beware that you might have to pay for a more expensive commercial ISP line. Before you share your Internet connection, check your ISP's Terms of Service (TOS) or look at the listing of wireless-friendly ISPs on the Electronic Frontier Foundation's Web page (www.eff. org). The same is true of DSL and cable modem providers. Your usage agreement with them basically says that you won't do this, and they're starting to charge high-use fees to lines that have *extranormal* traffic (that is, those lines that seem like there are a bunch of people on the broadband line sharing the connection).

Pretty soon, you'll even be able to plug into a Wi-Fi network on an airplane. Boeing and Cisco have been teaming up to get wireless Internet access on passenger planes. In fact, they've already got one plane — a Lufthansa 747 that makes regular trips between Frankfurt, Germany and Washington, DC — already outfitted with the system. The system connects to a satellite ISP and gives passengers a high-speed connection (up to 1 Mbps) in any seat on the plane (even back in 52b, that awful middle seat by the lavatory!). Here's a cool aside about this system: On the inaugural flight, a reporter wrote and submitted his story entirely online while flying on the plane.

The single biggest issue that's been holding back the hot spot industry so far (keeping it as a huge future trend instead of a use-it-anywhere-today reality) has been the issue of roaming. As of this writing, no one hot spot operator has anything close to ubiquitous coverage. Instead, dozens of different hot spot operators, of different sizes, operate in competition with each other. As a user, perhaps a sales person who's traveling across town to several different clients in one day, you might find yourself running into hot spots from three or four different hot spot providers — and needing accounts from three or four separate providers to get online with each.

This is a lot different, of course, from the cell phone industry, in which you can pretty much take your phone anywhere and make calls. The cell phone providers have some elaborate roaming arrangements in place that allow them to bill each other (and in the end, bill you, the user) for these calls. Hot spot service providers haven't quite reached this point. However, here are a couple of trends that will help bring about some true hot spot roaming:

- ✔ **Companies, such as Boingo Wireless, are entering the market.** Boingo (founded by Sky Dayton, who also founded the huge ISP EarthLink), doesn't operate any of its own hot spots but instead has partnered with a huge range of other hot spot operators from little mom-and-pop hot spot operators to big operations such as Wayport. Boingo provides all the billing and account management for end users. Thus, a Boingo customer can go to any Boingo partner's hot spot, log on, and get online. (We talk about both Boingo and Wayport in more detail later in the chapter.)

- ✔ **Cell phone companies are getting into the hot spot business.** Led by T-Mobile, cell phone companies are beginning to buy into the hot spot concept, setting up widespread networks of hot spots in their cellular phone territories. Although these networks aren't yet ubiquitous — the coverage isn't anywhere close to that of the cellular phone networks yet — it is getting better by the day.

Besides improving coverage and solving the roaming problem, commercial hot spot providers are also beginning to look at solutions that provide a higher grade of access — offering business class hot spot services, in other words. For example, they are exploring special hot spot access points and related gear that can offer different tiers of speeds (you could pay more to get a faster connection) or that can offer secure connections to corporate networks (so that you can safely log onto the office network to get work files).

In the next sections of this chapter, we talk about some of the most prominent commercial hot spot providers operating in the United States. We're not going to spend any time talking about the smaller local hot spot providers out there, although many of them are hooking up with companies like Boingo. We're not down on these smaller providers, but we're aiming for the maximum bang for our writing buck. So if you've got a local favorite that meets your needs, go for it!

Using T-Mobile Hot Spots

The biggest hot spot provider in the United States today — at least in terms of companies that run their own hot spots — is T-Mobile (www.t-mobile.com). T-Mobile has hot spots up and running in over 2,000 locations, primarily at Starbucks coffee shops in over 20 states. T-Mobile got into the hot spot business when it purchased the assets of a startup company named Mobilestar, which made the initial deal with Starbucks to provide wireless access in these coffee shops.

T-Mobile has branched out beyond Starbucks and currently is also offering access in American Airlines Admirals Clubs in a few dozen airports as well as a handful of other locations. T-Mobile charges $29.99 a month for unlimited local access (meaning at any T-Mobile location in your town) and $39.99 monthly for national unlimited access. A monthly download limit is imposed; if you download more than 500MB of data a month, you'll have to pay a small charge (a quarter) for each additional MB. And if you don't have the national plan, you'll pay 15 cents per minute of online time when you're using the service remotely.

T-Mobile also offers some corporate accounts (for those forward-thinking companies that encourage their employees to drink quadruple Americanos during working hours. . . Danny, are you listening?), prepaid account options, and pay-as-you-go plans.

To try T-Mobile hot spots out for free, register on T-Mobile's site at www.t-mobile.com/hotspot.

T-Mobile, like most hot spot companies, uses your Web browser to log you in and activate your service. You need to set the Service Set Identifier (SSID) in your wireless network adapter's client software to tmobile to get on the network. (Check out Part III of the book for information on how to do this on your laptop or handheld.)

Using Wayport Hot Spots

Another big commercial hot spot provider is Wayport (www.wayport.com). Wayport has made business travelers its number one focus: The company has hot spots in over 475 hotels and in 10 major airports nationwide. Besides just offering Wi-Fi access, Wayport offers wired Internet access in many hotels and airports. (You'll see Wayport Laptop Lane kiosks in many airports when you scurry from your security strip search to the gate.)

Wayport, like T-Mobile, offers a range of service plans, ranging from one-time, pay-as-you-go plans using your credit card to prepaid calling card plans. You can sign up as an annual customer for $29.95 a month (if you sign up for a year's worth of service; otherwise, it's $49.95 for a month-to-month plan) to get unlimited access to any of Wayport's Wi-Fi locations nationwide. Wayport also offers corporate plans, so consider bribing your IT manager if you travel a lot.

Like T-Mobile, Wayport uses your Web browser to authenticate you and collect your billing information. You need to set your SSID to Wayport_Access to get logged onto the access port.

Using Boingo Hot Spots

Boingo (www.boingo.com) made a big splash in 2002 when the company launched because it was the first company to bring a solution to the hot spot roaming issue. Boingo doesn't own its own network of hot spots; instead, it has partnered with a lot of other hot spot providers (including Wayport, which we discuss in the preceding section). Boingo provides you, the user, with some cool software, giving you access to all the hot spots of its partners with a single account, a single bill, and not too much hassle on your part.

As of this writing, Boingo has over 1,000 hot spots up and running on its network. Like the other providers, Boingo offers monthly plans ($24.95 for a plan that allows ten connections a month; $49.95 for unlimited access) as well as pay-as-you-go plans and corporate accounts. (Keep buttering up the IT manager at work!)

The big difference between Boingo and the other services is that Boingo uses its own software to control and manage the connection process. You download the Boingo software (available for most Windows computers and also for Pocket PC handhelds) and use the software to sign on to a Boingo hot spot. This approach has its limitations: For example, not all Wi-Fi cards work with the Boingo software — see a list of compatible cards on its Web site. However, this approach allows Boingo to offer a more consistent user experience when you roam around using its service. Boingo is also taking advantage of this software to offer a *Virtual Private Network* (VPN; a secured network connection that can't be intruded upon by others) service for business customers.

If you use a Mac laptop computer, don't bother with Boingo. The Boingo software is only available for the Microsoft platforms that we mention earlier in this section, and you can't get on the Boingo network without the software.

We talk a bit more about Boingo's software in the upcoming section "Tools for Finding Hot Spots" because you can use Boingo's software to sniff out open access points around you, regardless of whether they're Boingo's.

Tools for Finding Hot Spots

When you're on the road looking for a freenet, a community hotspot, or a commercial provider, here are a couple of ways that you can get your laptop or handheld computer to find available networks:

- ✔ **Do your homework:** If you know exactly where you're going to be, you can do some online sleuthing, find the available networks, and write down the SSIDs and/or Wired Equivalent Privacy (WEP) passwords (if required) before you get there. We talk about these in more detail in Chapter 10. Most hot spots don't use WEP (it's too hard for their customers to figure out), but you'll find the SSID (and the WEP password, if applicable), on the Web site of the hot spot provider that you're planning on using. Just look in the support or how-to-connect section.

- ✔ **Look for a sign:** Those providers that push open hot spots have adopted a standard logo that should be displayed prominently in a place where you can log on.

- ✔ **Rely on your network adapter's client software:** Many network adapter software systems will give you a nice pull-down list of available access points. In most cases, this won't really tell you any details about the access points, but you can do the trial-and-error thing to see whether you can get online.

- ✔ **Use a network sniffer program:** These programs work with your network adapter to ferret out the access points near you and provide a bit of information about them. In the next two sections, we describe sniffers from two companies: Netstumbler.com and Boingo. (*Note:* In most cases, *network sniffer programs* are used to record and decode network packets — something the highly paid network analysts at your company might use. In this case, we're referring to programs that are designed solely for wireless LANs and which sniff out radio waves and identify available networks.)

We find sniffer programs to be quite handy because they're a great way to take a quick survey of our surroundings when we're on the road. For example, Pat (one of the authors of this book) was recently staying at a hotel that belonged to a chain partnered with Wayport, but Wayport hadn't officially started offering service yet . . . and the hotel staff was clueless. No problem! A quick session using the Network Stumbler software (see the next section), and lo and behold! The Wayport access point in the lobby was up and running, and with a quick flip of the wallet (to pull out his prepaid card), Pat was up and running on high-speed wireless Internet. Take that, dialup!

Network sniffer programs are also a good way to help you evaluate the security of your own network. In fact, that's the main reason why the developers of Network Stumbler created the program. After you implement some of the security steps that we discuss in Chapter 10, you can fire up your favorite sniffer program and see whether you've been successful.

Netstumbler.com

The granddaddy of wireless network sniffer programs is Network Stumbler (www.netstumbler.com), which is a Windows program (works with Windows 95/98/Me/2000/XP) that connects to the PC Card network adapter in your laptop and lets you survey the airwaves for available Wi-Fi access points. Network Stumbler will list all available access points, giving you relatively detailed information about things such as the SSID and Media Access Control (MAC) address of the AP, whether WEP is enabled, the relative power of the signal, and more. You can even combine Network Stumbler with a Global Positioning System (GPS) card in your laptop to figure out exactly where you and the access point are located.

Network Stumbler users can upload their surveys to the Netstumbler.com Web page and contribute to a database of available access points that the Netstumbler.com folks maintain. You can see a map at www.netstumbler. com/nation.php to get an idea of places where people have already used the program. You can submit search queries on this Web page if you want to see other people's survey results.

Network Stumbler won't work with every Wi-Fi card. You can find a list of compatible cards on the Netstumbler.com Web site.

Figure 16-2 shows Network Stumbler in action in Pat's house, tracking down his two access points. (Looks like none of his neighbors are wireless yet!)

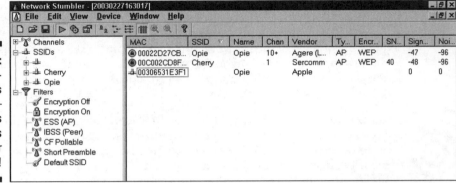

Figure 16-2: Netstumbling Pat's house — access points named after the dogs!

If you use a Pocket PC handheld computer, the folks at Netstumbler.com have a program for you: *Mini Stumbler*, available at the same Web site (`www.net stumbler.com`). There's also a similar program available for Mac OS X computers, called *MacStumbler* (`www.macstumbler.com`).

In fact, a growing number of these network sniffer programs are available, and most of them free to download. You can find a list at the Personal Telco Project at `www.personaltelco.net/index.cgi/WirelessSniffer`.

Boingo

Boingo's client software (available at `www.boingo.com`) can also be used as a network sniffer program (as long as you're using a compatible operating system and network adapter). The primary purpose of this software, of course, is to manage your connections to Boingo's network, but Boingo has also designed the software (and encourages the use of it) as a means of finding and connecting to freenets and other public open networks.

You can even use the Boingo software as a manager for all your Wi-Fi network connections. If you've got a wireless network at home, one or more in the office, plus some public networks that you want to connect to, try out Boingo's software. It's really pretty cool.

Part V
The Part of Tens

The 5th Wave   By Rich Tennant

"You the guy having trouble staying connected to the network?"

In this part . . .

This is the part you've been waiting for, right? We've
included four top-ten lists here that we hope you'll find
interesting as well as helpful — ten frequently asked questions about wireless home networking; ten ways to
improve the performance of your wireless home network;
ten way-cool devices that you'll (eventually) connect to
your wireless home network; and the top ten sources for
more information about wireless networking.

Chapter 17

Ten FAQs about Wireless Home Networks

In This Chapter

▶ Picking the right standard

▶ Dealing with dead Internet connections

▶ Getting games going

▶ Keeping things secure

▶ Finding out about firmware

*B*uilding a wireless network is getting a lot easier, but it still can be tough to figure things out. One of the toughest things about a wireless network is that when it breaks, it's not like you can go see where it's not plugged in, like you often can with a wired network. With the advent of new security and other logical layer configurations, it's easy for things to get out of sync . . . and yes, it can take a while to debug things.

As a starting point for issues, we asked vendors what questions pop up over and over. The following lists those most frequently asked questions that reflect some of the things that vendors felt users could benefit from knowing more about (we spend the rest of the chapter providing the answers):

1. What standard is right for me?

2. I can connect to the Internet by using an Ethernet cable but not by using my wireless local area network (LAN). What am I doing wrong?

3. How do I get my video games to work on my wireless LAN?

4. My videoconferencing application doesn't work. What do I do?

5. How do I secure my network from hackers?

6. How do I check to make sure that I'm secure?

7. What is firmware, and why might I need to upgrade it?

8. Isn't Network Address Translation (NAT) the same as a firewall?

9. How can I find out my Internet Protocol (IP) address?

10. If everything stops working, what can I do?

If you don't see the particular question that you're asking in the preceding list, we recommend that you at least skim through this chapter anyway. You never know; you might find your answer lurking where you least expect it, or you might come across a tidbit of information that will later come in handy. And throughout this chapter, we also steer you to where in the book we further discuss various topics — which might in turn lead you to your answer (or to other tidbits of information that will later come in handy). What we're saying is that reading this chapter can only help you. And also check out Chapter 18, where we give you some troubleshooting tips.

If you're new to *Wireless Home Networking For Dummies,* this chapter is a great place to start because you get a good overview to the things that a lot of people ask (when they haven't read the manual or this book!), and you can get to some meat (hope you're not vegetarian!) of the issues surrounding wireless. So don't feel bad if you feel like you're reading the book backward. (Just don't read it upside down.)

We firmly believe in the power of the Web and of using vendor Web sites for all they're worth. Support is a critical part of this process. When you're deciding on a particular piece of equipment for your home network, take a look at the support area on the vendor site for that device. Look at the frequently asked questions (FAQs) for the device. This is where you might find some of those hidden gotchas that you wish you knew *before* buying the gear.

Q. What standard is right for me?

This is probably the most-asked question, and you probably won't like our answer. No, it's not, "It depends," (we hate that answer, too); it's, "Buy an 802.11a/g device as your core access point (AP) so that you can figure this out down the road." If you have some 802.11b gear in your house, no problem — 802.11g will support it, albeit at the lower 802.11b speeds. As the g hardware comes down in price, you might find that you move your older b equipment to that vacation home or use it elsewhere.

Also, some of the cable industry companies are moving to implement 802.11a in their set top boxes, as are some specialty A/V companies. So you'll want some 802.11a around the house.

If we thought that you could get an a/g/Bluetooth device, we would say to grab that, too, but that's likely to be well down the pike. (Head over to Chapter 15 for the skinny on Bluetooth.)

Think of it this way: In the early days of radio, there were a lot of similar debates over whether to buy an AM or FM radio. In fact, both have perfectly valid uses and coexist nicely in AM/FM radios today. For the near term, 802.11a and 802.11b/g will both have their proponents, and both will likely be needed in your household at some point regardless of which standard you prefer. We think that by the end of 2003, a/g devices will be the standard offering by the equipment manufacturers.

If you're determined to pick one specific version, say 802.11b (after all, both the 802.11a and g technologies are still relatively early in their lifecycle), we respect that and feel that 802.11b will work great for almost all applications with the exception of the high-bandwidth requirements of high-quality streaming video. If you anticipate accessing video over your wireless network, such as for streaming MovieLink movies-on-demand through your PC over wireless to your home entertainment center, you'll probably want to boost this to an a or g connection. If you have a couple of microwaves and lots of 2.4 GHz cordless phones around, 802.11a might be better for your environment. Likewise, if your house is spread out and/or you've got 5 GHz phones, 802.11g could be your answer.

For longevity and investment protection, we advocate 802.11 a/g dual-mode APs.

Q. I can connect to the Internet by using an Ethernet cable but not by using my wireless LAN. What am I doing wrong?

In actuality, you are almost there. The fact that everything works for one configuration and not for another actually rules out many potentialities. As long as your AP and router are the same device (which is most common), you know that the AP can talk to your Internet gateway (whether it's your cable modem, digital subscriber line [DSL] model, dialup routers, and so on). You know that because when you're connected via Ethernet, there is no problem. So the problem is relegated to being between your AP and your client on your PC.

Most of the time, this is a configuration issue dealing with your Service Set Identifier (SSID) and Wired Equivalent Privacy (WEP) configurations. Your SSID denotes your service area ID for your LAN, and your WEP controls your encryption keys for your data packets. Without both, you can't decode the signals traveling through the air.

Bring up your wireless configuration program, as we discuss in Chapter 6 and recheck that your SSID is set correctly and that your WEP is likewise correct. Try typing the word **any** into the SSID to see whether it finds the AP at that point.

If neither of those is the problem, borrow a friend's laptop with a compatible wireless connection to see whether his card can find and sign onto your LAN when empowered with the right SSID and WEP codes. If it can, you know that it might be your client card. It could have gone bad.

Most cards (or any electronics, generally speaking) have technical problems within the first 30 days if they're going to go bad.

If your friend's PC cannot log on, the problem might be with your AP. At this point, we have to say, "Check out the vendor's Web site for more specific problem-solving ideas and call its tech support for further help."

Q. How do 1 get my video games to work on my wireless LAN?

This question has an easy answer and a not-so-easy answer. The easy answer is that you can get your Xbox, PlayStation 2, or GameCube onto your wireless LAN by linking the Ethernet port on your gaming device (if necessary, purchasing a network adapter kit to add an Ethernet port on your system) with a wireless bridge — which gets your gaming gear onto your wireless network in a very easy fashion. You just need to be sure to set your bridge to the same SSID and WEP as your LAN.

That's the easy part, and you should now be able to access the Internet from your box.

The tough part is allowing the Internet to access you and your gaming system. This is required for certain games, two-way voice, and aspects of multiplayer gaming. For this, you might need to open up certain ports in your router to enable those packets bound for your gaming system to get there. This is *port forwarding* (or something like that; vendors love to call things differently amongst themselves). Port forwarding basically says to the router that it should block all packets from accessing your system except those with certain characteristics that you identify (these types of data packets can be let through to your gaming server). We talk a lot about this in Chapter 11, so be sure to read up on that before tinkering with your router configuration.

If this is too complex to pull off with your present router, you might consider just setting up a demilitarized zone (DMZ) for your gaming application, where this sits fairly open to the network. This is not a preferred setup, however, for security reasons, and we recommend that you try to get port forwarding to work. We discuss setting up a DMZ in Chapter 12.

Q. My videoconferencing application doesn't work. What do 1 do?

In some ways, videoconferencing is its own animal in its own world. Videoconferencing has its own set of standards that it follows, typically has specialized hardware and software, and until very recently, has required special telephone lines to work.

The success of the Internet and its related protocols has opened this up to a more mass market with IP standards-based Web cameras and other software-based systems becoming popular.

Still, if you've installed a router with the appropriate protection from the Internet bad guys, videoconferencing can be problematic for all the same reasons as gaming that we mention earlier. You need to have packets coming into your application just as much as you are sending packets out to someone.

Now wait a minute. You might be thinking, "Data packets come into my machine all the time (like when I download Web pages), so what are you saying?" Well, those packets are requested, and the router in your AP (or your separate router, if that's how your network is set up) knows that they're coming and lets them through. Videoconferencing packets are often unrequested, which makes the whole getting-through-the-router thing a bit tougher.

As such, the answer is the same as with gaming. You need to open ports in your router (port forwarding) or to set up your video application in a DMZ. Again, Chapter 12 can be a world of help here.

Q. How do I secure my network from hackers?

Nothing is totally secure from anything. "Where there's a will, there's a way," tends to govern most discussions about someone hacking into your LAN. So we tend to fall back on, "Unless you have some major, super-secret hidden trove of something on your LAN that a lot of people would simply kill to have access to, the chances of a hacker spending a lot of time to get on your LAN is minimal." This means that as long as you do the basic security enhancements that we recommend in Chapter 10, you should be covered.

These basic enhancements cover

- **Securing your Internet connection:** At a minimum, you should turn on whatever firewall protection that your router offers. If you can, choose a router that's got Stateful Packet Inspection (SPI). You should also use antivirus software and seriously consider using personal firewall software on your PCs. It's defense in depth — after the bad guys get by your router firewall's Maginot line, you've got extra guns to protect your PCs. (For a little historical perspective on defense strategies, read up on Maginot and his fortification.)

- **Securing your airwaves:** Because wireless LAN signals can travel right through your walls and out the door, you should strongly consider turning on WEP (and taking other measures that we discuss in Chapter 10) to keep the next-door neighbors from snooping on your network.

Q. How do I check to make sure that I'm secure?

It's often easy to determine whether you've opened up your ports because your multiplayer gaming (or videoconferencing or whatever application requiring port forwarding) now works — where it didn't before.

However, the opposite is not always so easy to determine: that is, when you have open ports that should be closed. This often happens when you open ports for an application that you're no longer using (but forgot to close the ports again).

Plus, you might not have set things correctly in the first place.

We recommend the program ShieldsUP!! (`www.grc.com`). This program will systematically test your router, effectively trying to break into your system by using all commonly known techniques. The program will then issue you a report that tells you how secure your router is — and if it's not, what to do to fix it. We highly recommend this.

Q. What is firmware, and why might I need to upgrade it?

Any consumer electronics device is governed by software that's seated in onboard chip memory storage. When you turn on the device, it checks this memory for what to do and loads the software in that area. This turns the device on.

This *firmware*, as it's referred to, can be updated through a process that's specific to each manufacturer. Often you'll see options in your software configuration program for checking for firmware upgrades.

Some folks advocate never, ever touching your firmware if you don't need to. Indeed, reprogramming your firmware can upset a lot of the logical innards of your device that you struggled so hard to get right in the first place. In fact, you might see this advice on a vendor site (like this is from the D-Link site): "Do not upgrade firmware unless you are having specific problems ("If it ain't broke, don't fix it"). Upgrading firmware will reset the settings to default which means you will lose all your settings. You <u>cannot</u> use the backup settings feature and apply it to the newer firmware. Do **NOT** upgrade firmware with a wireless connection. You will damage the router." Although not all vendor firmware upgrades will reset your settings to default, many do. Be careful!

Okay, we don't necessarily disagree with any of that except to say, "Never say never." The standards in the wireless arena are changing, particularly in the 802.11a and 802.11g areas. One of the key ways that you can keep current with these standards is by upgrading your firmware. You will find over time that your wireless network will fall out of sync with these standards, and you'll have to upgrade at some point. When you do so, follow all the manufacturer's warnings.

In Chapter 10, we discuss a forthcoming security enhancement for 802.11 LANs called Wi-Fi Protected Access (WPA). Many existing APs and network adapters will be able to use WPA but only after they've had their firmware upgraded.

Q. Isn't NAT the same as a firewall?

If you finding networking confusing, you're not alone. (If it were so easy, we'd have no market for our books!) One area of a lot of confusion is Network Address Translation (NAT). And no, NAT is not the same as a firewall. It's important to understand the difference, too, to make sure that you set up your network correctly. Firewalls provide a greater level of security than a NAT router, and as a result, are generally more expensive than simple routers.

Often you'll hear the term *firewall* used to describe a router's ability to protect LAN IP addresses from Internet snoopers. But a true firewall actually goes deeper than this, using SPI. This allows the firewalls to look at each IP address and domain requesting access to the network; the administrator can specify certain IP addresses or domain names that are allowed to be let in while blocking any other attempt to access the LAN. (Sometimes you'll hear this called *filtering*.)

Firewalls can also add another layer of protection through a Virtual Private Network (VPN). This enables remote access to the private network through the use of secure logins and authentication. Finally, firewalls can help protect your family from unsavory content by enabling you to block content from certain sites.

So firewalls go well beyond NAT, and we highly recommend that you have a firewall in your home network. Check out Chapter 10 for more information on firewalls.

Q. How can I find out my IP address?

Well, first off, you have two IP addresses: your public IP address and your private IP address. There are instances where you need to know one or the other (or both) of these.

Your *private* IP address is your IP address on your LAN so that your router knows where to send traffic in and among LAN devices. If you have a LAN printer, that device will have its own IP address, as will any network device on your LAN.

The address that these devices have, however, is rarely the public IP address (the address is the "Internet phone number" of your network) mostly because public IP addresses are becoming scarce. Your Internet gateway has a public IP address for your home. If you want to access a specific device that's on your home network but from a public location, you typically have to enable port forwarding and address that port on your public IP address, something like 68.129.5.29:80, where 80 is the port.

You can usually find out your wide area network (WAN; public IP address) and LAN (private IP address) from within your router configuration software. You might see a Status screen; this is a common place where it shows your present IP addresses and other key information about your present Internet connection.

If you have Windows 2000 or XP, you can find your computer's private IP address by choosing Start➪Run. When the Run dialog box pops up, type **cmd** and then click OK. In the window that opens, type **ipconfig** at the command prompt and then press Enter. You'll see your IP address and a few other network parameters.

This IP address is your *internal* or *private* IP address, not the public address that people on the Internet use to connect to your network. So if you try to give this to someone (perhaps so that they can connect to your computer to do some videoconferencing or to connect to a game server that you're hosting), it won't work. You need the public IP address that you'll find in the configuration program for your access point/router.

Q. If everything stops working, what can I do?

The long time that it can take to get help from tech support these days actually does lead a lot of people to read the manual, check out the Web site, and work hard to debug their present situation. But what happens if you've tried everything, and it's still a dead connection — and tech support agrees with you?

In these instances, the last resort is to do a reset of the system back to the factory defaults and literally start over. If you do this, be sure to upgrade your firmware while you're at it because it will reset your variables, anyway. And who knows, the more recent firmware update might resolve some issues that could be causing the problems.

Resetting your device is considered a pretty drastic action and taken only after you've tried everything else. Make sure that you at least get a tech support person on the phone to confirm that you *have* tried everything else and that a reset makes sense.

Chapter 18

Ten Ways to Troubleshoot Wireless LAN Performance

In This Chapter

▶ Moving your access point(s)

▶ Flipping channels

▶ Boosting your signals

▶ Checking your cordless phones

Although troubleshooting any piece of network equipment can be frustrating, when you deal with wireless equipment, it's a little more so because there's so much that you just can't check. After all, radio waves are invisible. That's the rub with improving the throughput (performance) of your wireless home network, but we're here to help. And don't get hung up on the term *throughput* — it's just the actual rate of the data flowing when you take into account retransmissions attributable to errors.

The trick to successful troubleshooting anything is to be logical and systematic. First, think about the most likely issues and work from there (no matter how improbable). The second thing to do is to be systematic. Networks are complicated things, which mandates sequential troubleshooting thinking on your part. Patience is a virtue when it comes to network debugging.

But perhaps hardest of all is making sense of performance issues, which is the subject of this chapter. First of all, you can't get a lot of great performance reporting from consumer-level access points (the much more expensive ones sold to businesses are better at that). And even so, debugging performance based on performance data in arrears is tough. Fixing performance issues is a trial-and-error, real-time process. At least most wireless client devices have some sort of signal strength meter, which is one of the best sources of information that you can get to help you understand what's happening. (This is a key point, and these signal strength meters are used by the pros, says Tim Shaughnessy at NETGEAR: "I would highlight it as a tool." We agree.)

It's a good idea to work with a friend or family member. Your friend can be in a poor reception "hole" with a notebook computer with the wireless utility showing the signal strength. You can try moving or configuring the AP to see what works. Just be patient — it can take a few seconds for the signal meter to react to changes.

Because not all performance issues can be tracked down . . . or at least not easily . . . in this chapter, we introduce you to the most common ways to improve the performance or your wireless home network. These are tried-and-true tips, having been there ourselves. We're pretty good at debugging this stuff by now. We just can't seem to figure out when it's not plugged in! (Well, Pat can't . . . read the next section to see what we mean.)

Check the Obvious

Sometimes, what's causing you trouble is something simple — and which you can fix simply.

For instance, one of us (and we won't say who . . . *Pat*) was surprised that his access point (AP) just stopped working one day. The culprit was his beagle, Opie, who had pulled the plug out of the wall. As obvious as this sounds, it took the unnamed person *(Pat)* an hour to figure it out. Now if someone told you, "Hey, the AP just stopped working," you'd probably say, "Is it plugged in?" *The moral:* Think of the obvious and check that first.

Following are a couple more simple problems to think of first. . . .

Problem: The power goes out and then comes back on. Different equipment takes different periods of time to reset and go through to restart, causing loss of connectivity and logical configurations in your network.

Solution: Sometimes you need to just turn everything off and then turn them back on in order — from the wide area network (WAN) connection (your broadband modem, for instance) back to your machine — allowing each device to start up with everything upstream properly in place and turned on.

Problem: Your AP is working fine, with great throughput and a strong signal footprint, until one day when it all just drops off substantially. No hardware problem. No new interferers installed at home. No new obstructions. No changes of software. Nothing. *End cause:* The next door neighbor got an access point and was using his on the same channel.

Solution: This is hard to debug in the first place. How the heck do you find out who is charging invisible interference — by going door to door? "Uh, pardon me, I'm going door to door to try to debug interferers on my access point. Are you suddenly emitting any extraneous radio waves? No, I'm not wearing an aluminum foil hat, why?" Often with debugging performance issues, you need to try a lot of the one-step solutions, such as changing channels, to see whether that has an effect. If you can find the solution, you will have a lot of insight as to what the problem was. (If changing channels solved the problem, someone nearby was probably using the same channel, and you can then start tracking down whom!)

The wireless utility for the adapter might have a tab listing the APs in range called a *Site Survey* or *Station List.* It might show your neighbor's AP and the channel that it's on.

And before you chase a performance issue, make sure that there *is* one. The advertised rates for throughput for the various wireless standards are pretty misleading. What starts out at 54 Mbps for 802.11a is really more like a maximum of 36 Mbps in practice (less as distance grows). For 802.11b, it's more like 6 Mbps at best, rather than the 11 Mbps that you hear bandied about. You *will* occasionally see the high levels (like when you're within a few yards of the access point), but that's rare. The moral: If you think that you should be getting 54 Mbps but you're only getting 38 Mbps, consider yourself lucky.

Move the Access Point

Fact: A wireless signal degrades with distance. You might find that the place where you originally placed your AP doesn't really fit with your subsequent real-world use of your wireless local area network (LAN). A move might be in order.

After your access point is up and working, you'll probably forget about it — people often do. Access points can often be moved around and even shuffled aside by subsequent gear. Because the access connection is still up (that is to say, working), sometimes people don't notice that the access point's performance degrades when you hide it more or move it around.

Make sure that your AP is where you want it to be. Check that other gear isn't blocking your AP, that your AP isn't flush against a wall (which can cause interference), that the vertical orientation of the AP isn't too close to the ground (more interference), and that your AP isn't in line of sight of radio wave interference (like from microwaves and cordless phones).

Even a few inches can make a difference. The best location is in the center of your desired coverage area (remember to think in three dimensions!) and on top of a desk or bookcase.

For more about setting up access points, check out Chapter 6.

Move the Antenna(s)

Remember the days before everyone had cable or satellite TV? There was a reason people would fiddle with the rabbit ears on a TV set — they were trying to get the antennas into the ideal position to receive signals. Whether the antenna is on the client or on the access point, the same concept applies: Moving the antenna can yield results. Because different antennas have different signal coverage areas, reorienting it in a different declination (or angle relative to the horizon) will change the coverage pattern. And a strong signal translates to better throughput and performance.

Look at it this way: The antenna creates a certain footprint of its signal. If you're networking a multi-story home and you're not getting a great signal upstairs, try shifting your antenna to a 45° angle to increase a more vertical signal — that is, send more signal to the upstairs and downstairs, and less horizontally.

Change Channels

Each AP broadcasts its signals over portions of the wireless frequencies called *channels*. The 802.11b standard (the most common system as we write) defines 11 channels in the United States that overlap considerably, leaving only 3 channels that don't overlap with each other. The IEEE 802.11a standard specifies 12 (although most of today's products only support 8) non-overlapping channels. The 802.11g standard calls for the same 11 channels in the United States as 802.11b, again with overlapping channels.

This affects your ability to have multiple access points in the same area, whether your own or your neighbors'. Because channels can overlap, you can have the resulting interference. For 802.11b access points that are within range of each other, set them to different channels, five apart from each other (such as 1, 6, and 11), to avoid inter-access point interference.

We discuss the channel assignments for wireless LANs like 802.11b further in Chapter 6.

Check for Dual-Band Interference

Despite the industry's mad rush to wirelessly enable every networkable device that it makes, a whole lot hasn't been worked through yet, particularly interoperability. We're not talking about whether one vendor's 802.11b PC Card will work with another vendor's 802.11b AP — the Wi-Fi interoperability tests usually make sure that's not a problem (unless one of your products isn't Wi-Fi certified). Instead, we're talking about having Bluetooth (see Chapter 15 for more on this technology) working in the same area as 802.11b, or having 802.11a modems and 802.11b modems operating in the same area. In some instances, like the former example, Bluetooth and 802.11b operate in the same frequency range, and therefore do have some potential for interference. Because 802.11a and 802.11b operate in separate frequency bands, they're less likely to be exposed to interference.

There are also issues with how the different standards are implemented in different products. Some APs that support 802.11b and g, for instance, really support one or the other — not both simultaneously. If you have all g in your house, great. If you have all b, great. If you have some g and the AP detects that b is in the house, it will downshift to b rates. You might be all set, but then your neighbor upstairs buys a b modem (because you've said, "Sure, no problem, you can share my Internet connection."). Not only is he freeloading, but he's probably forcing your whole AP to shift down to the lower speeds.

To be fair, many of these very early implementation issues are rapidly going away while vendors refine their solutions. Check out how any multi-mode AP that you buy handles multiple forms of wireless connecting to the AP and asking for service. Some of the newer APs compartmentalize their signal so that they can handle two at once, which is very nice and almost necessary.

Check for New Obstacles

Wireless technologies are very susceptible to physical obstacles . . . some more than others. In Chapter 4, we show a Relative Attenuation of RF Obstacles table that tells you the relative attenuation of your wireless signals (radio frequency; RF) as they move through your house. One person in our neighborhood noticed a gradual degradation of his wireless signal outside his house, where he regularly sits and surfs the Net (by his pool). The culprit turned out to be a growing pile of newspapers for recycling. Wireless signals don't like such masses of paper.

Move around your house and think about it from the eyes of Superman, using his X-ray vision to see your access point. If you have a bad signal, think about what's in the way. If the obstacles are permanent, think about using a HomePlug wireless access point (which we discuss in Chapter 3) to go around the obstacle by putting an access point on either side of the obstacle.

 Another way to get around problems with obstacles is to switch technologies. In some instances, 802.11g could provide better throughput and reach than 802.11a when it comes to obstacles. 802.11g operates at a lower frequency, which does better moving through and around things. If you're in a dense environment with a lot of clutter and you're using 802.11a, switching to g might provide some relief.

Install Another Antenna

In Chapter 5, we point out that a detachable antenna is a great idea because you might want to add an antenna to achieve a different level of coverage in your home. Different antennas yield different signal footprints. If your AP is located at one end of the house, it's a waste to put an omnidirectional antenna on that AP because more than half of the signal might prove to be unusable. A directional antenna would better serve your home.

Antennas are inexpensive relative to their benefit and can also more easily help you accommodate signal optimization because you can leave the AP in the same place and just move the antenna around until the signal is the best. Within a home, there's not a huge distance limitation on how far the antenna can be away from the AP.

 For a more technical explanation of how antennas work, check out the technical white paper section on the Linksys site (`www.linksys.com/products/images/antennawhtpaper.pdf`), which at the time of this writing, had a good overview of antennas.

Add a Signal Booster

If you have a big house (or a lot of interference), you can add a *signal booster*, which essentially turns up the volume on your wireless home network transmitter. A stronger signal means that the receiving point gets a higher quality transmission. This increases throughput by reducing retransmissions of data that occurs when the signal strength is weak.

A signal booster can also improve the range of your access point (although this is much harder to quantify). Today's 802.11b and g products typically have a range of 100–150 feet indoors mainly because 802.11b/g products operate at a lower frequency. Although 802.11a products reach a shorter distance — up to 75 feet indoors — these products are getting better, and their distance is improving. A booster might add another 25–50 feet to this, but it won't take you to the Starbucks and back.

The signal range of the APs on the market today is steadily increasing because manufacturers are creating more efficient transceiver chipsets. We recommend reading the most recent reviews of products because products truly are improving month over month.

Linksys, for instance, sells its WSB24 Wireless Signal Booster (www.linksys.com; $90) that piggybacks onto a Linksys wireless access point (or wireless access point router) to increase the throughput, effective range, and coverage area of a resulting 802.11b network. (See Figure 18-1.)

This is really easy to install. Simply unscrew the antenna from the AP, connect the two linking wires (an SMA-to-TNC connector, if you're curious), reattach the antennas onto the booster, and then plug the electric cords in.

Signal boosters are *mated* devices, meaning that they're engineered for specific products. Vendors have to walk a fine line when boosting signals in light of federal limits on the aggregate signal that can be used in the unlicensed frequencies. For example, the Linksys Wireless Signal Booster is certified by the Federal Communication Commission (FCC) for use with the WAP11 Wireless Access Point and BEFW11S4 Wireless Access Point Router only. Linksys says that using the WSB24 with any other product from either Linksys or another vendor voids the user's authority to operate the device.

The main reason why companies like Linksys sell their signal boosters for use with only their own products is because of certification issues. The FCC has to approve any radio transmission equipment sold on the market. A lot of testing must be done for a piece of gear to get certified, and the certification testing must be done for the complete system — and the vendors will usually only do this expensive testing with their own gear.

That having been said, as some reviews have pointed out, you *can* use the WSB24 with any wireless LAN product that operates in the 2.4 GHz band — notably, 802.11b and 802.11g products. You cannot use it with 802.11a or any dual-band 2.4/5 GHz products; its design cannot deal with the higher frequency.

Figure 18-1:
The Linksys
WSB24
mated to a
Linksys
wireless
access
point.

Photo courtesy of Linksys

Add an AP

Adding another AP (or two) can greatly increase your signal coverage, as shown in Figure 18-2. The great thing about wireless is that it's fairly portable — you can literally plug it in anywhere. The main issues are getting power to it and getting an Ethernet connection (which carries the data) to it.

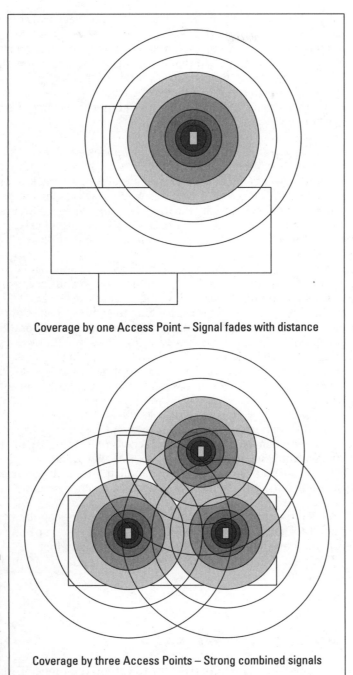

Coverage by one Access Point – Signal fades with distance

Coverage by three Access Points – Strong combined signals

Figure 18-2:
Three APs
provide
a much
stronger
signal than
a single AP.

The first item is usually not a problem because many electrical codes require that in a residence, a power outlet should be placed every eight feet. However, if you're mounting an AP high up on a wall, you might not want an electrical power jack running to the spot. In that case, you might consider getting an AP that supports a power over Ethernet (Power Over Ethernet; POE) option, which delivers power to run the unit over the same wiring as carries the data signal, meaning that only one Cat 5e (standard Ethernet cabling) wire has to be run to where you want your AP to be.

Leviton also has a neat product called the PowerJack (www.leviton.com/sections/prodinfo/newprod/powerjack/powerjack.htm; $25) that allows you to hide the power cable behind a four-conductor RJ-11 jack, avoiding that AC adapter cable strung across the wall as well. However, Leviton doesn't yet have a version for an eight-conductor RJ-45 jack, but we expect one soon. Check the Leviton site to see whether one is available — and get one of these if you have problems with an AC adapter cable with your cordless phone as well because they're great.

The second issue (getting the Ethernet connection to your access point) used to be a matter of running all sorts of wiring around the house, but depending on the actual throughput that you're looking to provide, you might be able to set up another access point by using the HomePlug, Home Phone Networking Alliance (HPNA), or even wireless repeater functionality that we mention in Chapter 3 and elsewhere in this chapter. We're not going to repeat those options here, but know that you have those options when moving away from your office or other place where a lot of your network connections are concentrated.

After you get the connectivity and power to the place you want it, what do you need to consider when installing a *second* access point? Choose the right channel: If you have auto channel selection in your AP, you don't need to worry about this because your AP's smarts will handle it for you. If you're setting this manually, don't choose the same channel that your other AP is set to.

Be sure to heed the previous advice about multiple access points on the same or nearby channels. Make sure that you have proper spacing of your channels if you have 802.11b or 802.11g access points (which have overlapping bands). Read "Change Channels" earlier in this chapter for more information on channels.

Add a Repeater or Bridge

Wireless repeaters are an alternative way to extend the range of an existing wireless network instead of adding more access points. We talk earlier in the book about the role of bridges and repeaters in a wireless network. The topic of bridges can be pretty complex, and we don't want to rehash here — go back and read Chapter 2 for all that juicy detail.

Not many standalone repeaters are on the consumer market. However, what's important for our discussion is that repeater capability is finding its way into the AP firmware from many AP vendors. A wireless AP *repeater* basically does double duty — it's an AP as well as a wireless connection back to the main AP that's connected to the Internet connection.

At its most basic level, a repeater simply regenerates a wireless network signal in order to extend the range of the existing wireless LAN. You set the two devices to the same channel with the same Service Set Identifier (SSID), thus effectively broadening the collective footprint of the signal.

If you're having throughput performance issues because of interference or reach, putting an access point into repeating mode might help you extend the reach of your network. One review of the D-Link (`www.d-link.com`) DWL-900AP+ saw a 50 percent improvement in reach.

However, it's not clear that adding a repeater helps actual throughput in all situations, unfortunately. Some testing labs have cited issues with through-put at the main AP because of interference from the new repeating AP (which is broadcasting on the same channel). Others note that the repeater must receive and retransmit each frame (or burst of data) on the same RF channel, which effectively doubles the number of frames that are sent. This effectively cuts throughput in half. Some vendors have dealt with this issue through software and claim that it's not an issue.

It's hard to make a blanket statement at this juncture about the basic effec-tiveness of doing an AP in repeater mode, particularly versus the option of running a high-quality Ethernet cable to a second AP set on a different chan-nel. If you can do the latter, that's preferable.

 When using the bridging/repeating functions of AP/bridges, we recommend that you use the same product at both ends of the bridge to minimize any issues between vendors. Most companies support this functionality between their products only.

Check Your Cordless Phone Frequencies

As we define in Part I of the book, the wireless frequencies at 2.4 GHz and 5.2 GHz are unlicensed, which means that you, as the buyer of an AP and opera-tor of a wireless broadcasting capability, don't need to get permission from the FCC to use these frequencies as long as you stay within certain power and usage limitations as set by federal guidelines. It also means you don't have to pay any money to use the airwaves — because no license is required, it doesn't cost anything.

A lot of consumer manufacturers have taken advantage of these free radio spectra and created various products for these unlicensed frequencies, such as cordless phones, wireless A/V connection systems, RF remote controls, wireless cameras, and so on.

A home that has grown up on RadioShack and X10.com gadgets can likely have a fair amount of radio clutter on these frequencies in the home. This clutter can cut into your performance. These sources of RF energy occasionally block users and access points from accessing their shared air medium.

As home wireless LAN usage grows, there are more reports of interference with home *X10 networks,* which use various wireless transmitters and signaling over electrical lines to communicate among their connected devices. If you have a home X10 network for your home automation and it starts acting weird (like the lights go on and off, and you think your house is haunted), consider your LAN as a potential problem source. A strong wireless LAN in your house can be fatal to an X10 network.

At some point, you've got to get better control over these interferers, and there aren't a lot of options. First, you can change channels, like we mention earlier in this chapter. Cordless phones, for instance, use channels just like your local area network; you can change them so that they don't cross paths (wirelessly speaking) with your data heading towards the Internet.

Second, you can change phones. If you have an 802.11b or g network operating at home on the 2.4 GHz band, consider one of the newer 5 GHz cordless phones for your house. (Or vice versa: If you have an 802.11a, 5 GHz network, get a 2.4 GHz phone). *Note:* An old-fashioned 900 MHz phone won't interfere with either.

You might find that your scratchy cordless phone improves substantially in quality and that your LAN performance improves, too. Look for other devices that can move to other frequencies or move to your 802.11 network itself. As we discuss in Chapter 19, all sorts of devices are coming down the road that will work *over* your 802.11 network and not compete with it. Ultimately, you need to keep the airwaves relatively clear to optimize all your performance issues.

At the end of the day, interference from sources outside your house is probably your own fault. If your neighbor asks you how your wireless connection works, lie and tell him or her that it works horribly. You don't want your neighbor getting one and sending any stray radio waves toward your network. And do the same about cable modems. You don't want your neighbor's traffic slowing you up because it's a shared connection at the neighborhood level. Interference is a sign of popularity — it means that a lot of other people have caught on. So keep it your little secret.

Chapter 19

More Than Ten Devices You'll Connect to Your Wireless Network in the Future

. . . .

In This Chapter

▶ Singing in the shower (and hot tub) with wireless tunes

▶ Looking under the hood (without lifting the hood)

▶ Losing weight with wireless exercise gear

▶ Wearing wirelessly connected apparel

▶ Tracking Junior and Fido

▶ . . . and more!

. . . .

We tell you throughout this book to think bigger-picture than just networking your home computers. In Chapter 11, we talk about adding various peripheral devices (such as a printer) to your home network. In Chapters 12 and 13, we talk extensively about all the gaming gear and audio/visual equipment that you'd want to hook into your wireless home network. In Chapter 14, you hear about lots of things you can connect today, ranging from cameras to cars.

Clearly, the boom is on among the consumer goods manufacturers to network-enable everything with chips. You get the convenience (and cool-factor) of monitoring the health of your gadgets, and vendors want to sell you add-on services to take advantage of that chip. This transformation is happening to everything — clocks, sewing machines, automobiles, toaster ovens . . . even shoes. If a device can be added to your wireless home network, value-added services can be sold to those who want to track their kids, listen to home-stored music in the car, and know when Fido is in the neighbor's garbage cans again.

In this chapter, we expose you to some things that you could bring very soon onto your wireless home network. These aren't pie-in-the-sky discussions because many of these products already exist. Expect in the upcoming years that they will infiltrate your home. Like the Borg say on *Star Trek,* "Prepare to be assimilated."

Your Bath

Yup, wireless toys are everywhere now, having traversed their way into the innermost sanctuary of your home: the bathroom. Not too many homes are wired for computer and video in the bathroom, and wireless may be the only way to get signals — like a phone — to some of these places. We've seen wireless-enabled toilets (don't ask) and all sorts of wireless controls for lighting in the bathroom to create just the right atmosphere for that bath. It's the wireless enablement of the bathtub itself that gets us excited. Luxury bathing combined with a home entertainment bathing center into one outfitted bathroom set is probably the ultimate for a wireless enthusiast.

Jacuzzi (www.jacuzzi.com) is the leader in this foray. Jacuzzi sells the only wireless waterproof remote control that we've seen, but it's what comes with the remote control that gets us. Jacuzzi's J-Allure shower comes standard with a built-in stereo/CD system, complete with four speakers. A digital control panel offers easy access to the whirlpool operation, underwater lighting, and temperature read-out. Talk about wired. The unit is also available with an optional television/VCR monitor. Cable ready, this feature allows you to enjoy the morning news or your favorite movie. The multi-channel, 9-inch unit is waterproof and includes a remote control. You can adapt the monitor for DVD or WebTV. All these features for a mere $12,500 retail price. The problem is that most homes aren't wired for audio or video in their bathroom. That's where your home wireless network comes into play. You can use the same wireless A/V extension devices used to link your PC and your stereo system to reach into the bathroom and bring your J-Allure online.

Jacuzzi's Vizion goes even further — it offers a whirlpool bath that boasts a state-of-the-art entertainment center for a mere $18,000 (not including installation). And for total indulgence, try a home theater in a tub. The La Scala model showcases a 42-inch, high-definition plasma monitor as well as a Surround sound system so powerful that it can make even the most subtle nuances spring to life. Price: black or white — $29,000; platinum — $31,000. But you'll need your wireless home network to get the signals there!

Your Car

Your car will also join the wireless revolution and in some neat ways. In Chapter 15, we discuss how cars are sporting Bluetooth interfaces to enable devices to interact with the car's entertainment and communications systems.

And in Chapter 14, we discuss the range of aftermarket devices that you can buy now that will provide 802.11-based connectivity between your home's wireless LAN and your car, whenever it's in range. (We guess that makes your garage a really big docking station!)

Because most cars already have a massive computing and entertainment infrastructure, reaching out and linking that to both the Internet and your wireless home network is simply a no-brainer.

A wireless connection in the car enables you to talk to your car via your wireless network. Now, before you accuse us of having gone loony for talking to our car, think about whether your lights are still on? Wouldn't it be great to check on it from your 40th-floor apartment instead of heading all the way down to the parking garage? Just grab your 802.11b-enabled PDA, surf to your car's own Web server, and check whether you left the lights on (again). Or perhaps you're filling out a new insurance form and forgot to check the mileage on your car. Click over to the dashboard page and see what it says.

You can also, on request, check out its exact location based on Global Positioning System (GPS) readings. (*GPS* is a location-finding system that effectively can tell you where something is, based on its ability to triangulate signals from three or more satellites that orbit the Earth. GPS can usually spot its target within 10–100 meters of the actual location.) You can, again at your request, even allow your dealer to check your car's service status via the Internet. You can also, say, switch on the lights or the auxiliary heating, call up numbers in the car telephone or addresses in the navigation system, unlock and lock the car — all from the wireless comfort of your couch (using some of those neat touchpanel remote controls that we talk about in Chapter 14). Just grab your wireless Web tablet, surf, and select. Pretty cool. The opportunities of being able to wirelessly connect to your automobile are truly endless.

Look for the following near-term applications for wirelessly linking your car to your home:

✔ **Vehicle monitoring systems:** These devices — usually mounted under a seat, under the hood, or in the trunk — monitor the speed, acceleration, deceleration, and various other driving and engine performance variables so that you can determine whether your kids are racing down the street after they nicely drive out of your driveway. When you drive into your driveway, the information is automatically uploaded to your PC over your wireless home network.

Devices like the Davis Instruments Corp. DriveRight (www.davisnet.com, $139) will likely be using 802.11b. Some of the pricier business products on the market, such as Road Safety International's SafeForce, already link to a base station computer using technologies such as 900 MHz spread-spectrum, RF data transceiver. Going 802.11b simply makes sense.

✔ **E-commerce:** You hear a great new song on your radio. Maybe you didn't catch the artist or song title. You push the Buy button on your audio system, which initiates a secure online transaction, and a legal copy of the song is purchased and downloaded to the car at the next wireless hot spot that your car senses. From now on, you can listen to the song over and over again, just like you would with a CD. When you get home, you can upload it to your home's audio system.

✔ **Remote control:** Use remote controls for your car to automatically open minivan doors or turn on the lights before you get in. And a remote car starter is a treat for anyone who lives in very hot or cold weather (get that heater going before you leave your home). Fancier remote controls, like the AutoCommand Deluxe Remote Starter with Keyless Entry & Alarm from DesignTech International (www.designtech-intl.com, $200) have a built-in car finder capability as well as a remote headlight control. AutoCommand can be programmed to automatically start your vehicle at the same time the next day, at low temperature, or at low battery voltage.

Okay, so these are not necessarily new and don't require a wireless home network. Where it can start to involve that wireless home network backbone is to start linking these remote control systems to your home's other systems so that this becomes part of your whole home experience. Imagine using that wireless connection to link to your home automation system, such as those we discuss in Chapter 14. So when you utter "Start the car," the system will communicate with the car and get it into the right temperature setting — based on the present temperature outside (it gets its readings from its Oregon Systems wireless weather station (www.oregonscientific.com).

Your Exercise Gear

Parts of exercise regimens are becoming network aware, and wireless plays a part, too. One of the more interesting applications of the Internet to the world of exercise comes from Icon Fitness (iFIT; www.ifit.com), which links your exercise equipment, the Internet, live personal coaches, and a library of audio and video slide tours to make each day of exercising a brand-new adventure. (Try the 30-day trial, or pony up $9.95 per month for a year-long contract.) Your iFIT-enabled exercise equipment can be controlled (either automatically by a preset program or live by a trainer) remotely via an Internet connection. The idea is to provide an environment where you can enjoy working out, be challenged, track your results, and learn about nutritional planning.

iFit.com can also remotely control more than 100 models of treadmills, elliptical trainers, stationary bikes, and incline trainers — from Icon's NordicTrack, Pro-Form, Reebok, HealthRider, and Image divisions (www.iconfitness.com). Each of these has an Ethernet connection into which you can put a wireless adapter to link your gear to the Internet.

If you don't like the audio and video programs, you can always get a live trainer, courtesy of Internet videoconferencing. For 45 minutes and $30, you see and hear the trainer — and the trainer sees and hears you. This is a great use of the wireless-enabled Web cameras that we talk about in Chapter 13.

Your Home Appliances

Most of the attempts to converge the Internet and home appliances have been prototypes and concept products — a few products are actually on the market, but we'd be less than honest if we said that the quantities being sold were anything but mass market yet.

LGE (www.lge.com) was the first in the world to introduce the Internet refrigerator — a Home Network product with Internet access capability — in June 2000 (see Figure 19-1). It soon introduced other Internet-based information appliance products in the washing machine, air conditioner, and microwave areas. The Internet refrigerator has a 15-inch detachable touchscreen that serves as a TV monitor, computer screen, stereo, and digital camera all in one. You can call your refrigerator from your cell phone, PDA, or any Internet-enabled device.

LGE also has an Internet air conditioner that allows you to download programs into the device so that you can have pre-programmed cooling times, just like with your heating system setbacks. Talk to your Digital Home Theater to preprogram something stored on your audio server to be playing when you get home. It's all interrelated, sharing a network in common. Wireless plays a part by enabling these devices to talk to one another in the home.

Samsung's (www.samsungelectronics.com) Digital Network Refrigerator is equipped with Internet access, a videophone, and a TV. In addition to storing food, consumers can send and receive e-mail, surf the Net, and watch a favorite DVD by using the refrigerator's touchscreen control panel, which also serves as a detachable wireless enabled handheld computer. Pretty neat.

All of this is still pricey; you'll spend $6,000 or more on an Internet refrigerator. But the future is one where most appliances have a network interface (and predominantly a wireless one) on board, and pricing will come down fast.

Figure 19-1:
LGE's
Internet
Refrigerator
is wirelessly
enabled.

And with the developments in radio frequency identification (RFID) and other technologies, you might indeed get to the point where your kitchen monitors all of its appliances (and what's in them — "We need more milk.").

Your Musical Instruments

A wireless home backbone will enable fast access to online music scores, like from www.score-on-line.com. Musical instruments are also growing more complex and wireless.

With ConcertMaster from Baldwin Piano (www.baldwinpiano.com), your home wireless LAN can plug into your ConcertMaster-equipped Baldwin, Chickering, or Wurlitzer piano and play almost any musical piece that you can imagine. You can plan an entire evening of music, from any combination of sources, to play in any order — all via a wireless RF remote control.

The internal ConcertMaster Library comes preloaded with 20 hours of performances in five musical categories, or you can create up to 99 custom library categories to store your music. With up to 99 songs in each category, you can conceivably have nearly 50,000 songs onboard and ready to play. Use your wireless access to your home's Internet connection to download the latest operating system software from Baldwin's servers, too. The system can accept any wireless MIDI interface. Encore!

You can record on this system, too. A one-touch Quick-Record button lets you instantly save piano performances, such as your child's piano recital. You can also use songs that you record and store on floppy disk with your PC to use within editing, sequencing, and score notation programs.

Your Pets

GPS-based tracking services can be used for pets, too! Just about everyone can identity with having lost their pet at some point. The GPS device's form factor can be collar-based or a subdermal implant. This can serve as your pet's electronic ID tag; it also can serve as the basis for real-time feedback to the pet or its owner, perhaps providing automatic notification if your dog goes out of the yard, for instance.

Check out www.homeagainid.com to find out about an Applied Digital-driven service for tracking your pet today. What makes this interesting is making the wireless connection more active than passive, adding 802.11 and GPS technologies so that there can be an ever-present signal to track your pet within the service area. Several companies are testing such capabilities so that soon, your LAN may indeed be part of a neighborhood wireless network infrastructure that provides a NAN — *neighborhood area network* — one of whose benefits is such continual tracking capability.

Your Phones

True, many phones in homes today are wireless. (And, of course, cell phones are, too.) But remember that your wireless home network uses the same 2.4 GHz and 5.8 GHz wireless frequencies that your cordless phones do. And when you factor in that your neighbor's phones and a bunch of other devices in home are also on these frequencies, the throughput and usability of your wireless home networking system can get watered down pretty fast.

Enter your *whole home* 802.11 network. It makes sense to migrate your cordless phones, for instance, to your home wireless network so that your wireless phones won't compete and interfere with your home wireless network; instead, you can get 802.11-based phones that ride over the same network in a very seamless way. (Chapter 2 has all the details about the 802.11 protocol.)

To do this, you will need to get an 802.11-enabled phone, which would work exactly like a cordless phone. In fact, you scarcely could tell the difference between the two. There are only a few such phones available today, and they are fairly pricey, but soon, you'll probably see a lot more home telephone products that support 802.11. You might also see 802.11 technology bundled inside your cell phone as well, although the early moves with cellular have focused on Bluetooth enablement, which we talk about in Chapter 15.

You can find 802.11b-based business phones today from Symbol Technologies (www.symbol.com) or SpectraLink (www.spectralink.com), but these are more business class products and require business telephone gear and VoIP (Voice over IP) gateways to work. We estimate that it will be a few years before these get to the price points that you'd pick one up at RadioShack or CompUSA. Expect to see your cell phone sporting an 802.11b/VoIP capability sometime in the next few years, too.

You can still use your wireless network and broadband connection to make low-cost phone calls. With a Cisco (www.cisco.com) ATA-186, which is a two-port analog telephone adapter that turns traditional analog phones into IP phones, you can place calls to any of a number of VoIP telephone companies (like www.vonage.com) that will carry your calls to their destination for low rates (less than the traditional long distance carrier rates for sure). Unlimited calling services like Vonage (www.vonage.com) take your normal ordinary phones and connect them to a special device, like the Cisco ATA-186, that allows you to place phone calls over IP networks, like your home wireless LAN and the Internet.

Just plug your cordless phone into the Cisco adapter and call away. You can also make calls over your laptop with software from companies like Net2Phone (www.net2phone.com); Net2Phone also has a strong line-up of hardware for VoIP calling.

Although the ATA-186 is not wireless itself yet, we expect it (or a similar model) to be so shortly. In the meantime, if you need to, you can get your ATA-186 onto your wireless network with a wireless bridge, such as the D-Link DWL-810+ (www.d-link.com), which we use with gaming devices in Chapter 12.

Your Robots

Current technology dictates that robots are reliant on special algorithms and hidden technologies to help them navigate. For instance, the $199 Roomba robotic vacuum cleaner from iRobot (www.irobot.com) relies on internal programming and virtual walls to contain its coverage area. The $499

Friendly Machines Robomow (www.friendlymachines.com) robotic lawn-mower relies on hidden wiring under the ground.

As your home becomes more wireless, devices can start to triangulate their position based on home-based homing beacons, of sorts, that help them sense their position at any time. The presence of a wireless home network will drive new innovation into these devices. Most manufacturers are busy designing 802.11 into the next versions of their products.

The following list highlights some other product ideas that manufacturers are working on now. We can't yet offer price points or tell you when these products will hit the market, but expect them to come soon.

- **Robotic garbage taker-outers:** Robotic firms are designing units that will take the trash out for you, on schedule, no matter what the weather. Simple as that.

- **Robotic mail collectors:** A robotic mail collector will go get the mail for you. Neither snow, nor rain, nor gloom of night, nor winds of change, nor a nation challenged will stay them from the swift completion of their appointed rounds. New wirelessly outfitted mailboxes will tell you (and the robots) when the mail has arrived.

- **Robotic snow blowers:** Manufacturers are working to perfect robotic snow blowers that continually clear your driveway and sidewalks while snow falls.

- **Robotic golf ball retrievers:** These bots retrieve golf balls. Initially being designed for driving range use, they are being modified for the home market.

- **Robotic guard dogs:** Companies such as iRobot (www.irobot.com) sell CoWorkers, which are robots that can roam areas and send back audio and video feeds.

- **Robotic gutter cleaners:** A range of spider-like robots are available that can maneuver on inclines, like a roof, and feature robotic sensors and arms that can clean areas.

- **Robotic cooks:** Put the ingredients in, select a mode, and wait for your dinner to be cooked — better than a TV dinner for sure.

- **Robotic pooper-scoopers:** The units that we've discovered roam your yard in search of something to clean up and then deposit the findings in a place that you determine.

You're more likely to see humanoid robots at special events demonstrating stuff than in your kitchen cooking dinner. Products such as Honda's ASIMO (Advanced Step in Innovative Mobility, world.honda.com/ASIMO/) are remarkable for the basic things they can do, like shake hands and bow, but the taskmasters that we mention above are really going to help you with day-to-day chores.

Your Wearing Apparel

Wireless is also making its way into your clothing. Researchers are already experimenting with so-called *wearables* — the merging of 802.11 and Bluetooth directly into clothing so that it can have networking capabilities. Want to synch your PDA? No problem — just stick it in your pocket. MIT Labs has been showing off some clothing that looks more like a Borg from *Star Trek* than anything practical, but there are all sorts of companies working on waterproof and washerproof devices for wirelessly connecting to your home wireless network.

Wireless technology will also infiltrate your clothing through radio frequency identification tags, or RFIDs, which are very small, lightweight, electronic read/write storage devices (microchips) that are half the size of a grain of sand. They listen for a radio query and when pinged, respond back by transmitting their ID code. Most RFID tags have no batteries because they use the power from the initial radio signal to transmit their response; thus, they never wear out. Data is accessible in real time through handheld and/or fixed-position readers, using RF signals to transfer data to and from tags. RFID applications are infinite, but when embedded in clothing, RFIDs will offer applications such as tracking people (like kids at school) or sorting clothing from the dryer (no more problems matching socks or identifying clothes for each child's pile).

A technology of great impact in our lifetime is GPS, which is increasingly being built into cars, cell phones, devices, and clothing. GPS equipment and chips are so cheap that you're going to find them everywhere. They are used in amusement parks to help keep track of your kids. Some shoe manufacturers are talking about embedding chips in shoes.

Most GPS-driven applications have software that enables you to interpret the GPS results. So you can grab a Web tablet at home while on your couch, wirelessly surf to the tracking Web site, and determine where Fido (or Fred) is located. Want to see whether your wife's car is heading home from work yet? Grab your PDA as you walk down the street, log onto a nearby hot spot, and check it out. A lot of applications are also being ported to cell phones, so you also can use those wireless devices to find out what's going on.

GPS-based devices — primarily in a watch form — are available that can track people. The Wherify Watch, shown in Figure 19-2, is a great device that allows you to track children and the elderly (such as Alzheimer's patients) who might wander off. The caretaker can then go to a Web site, view a map showing the wearer's location, and easily find the wanderer.

Figure 19-2:
The Wherify
Watch.

You can actually replay the signals received from the device over a period of time — sort of like a *Family Circus* cartoon showing the path of the little kid bopping around town. Watches are pricey, running about $300–$400 apiece plus monthly monitoring fees of $10–$50.

Check out companies like Wherify (www.wherify.com) and Applied Digital Solutions (www.digitalangel.net) for their products. Applied Digital has developed VeriChip (www.adsx.com/prodservpart/verichip.html) that can be implanted under the skin for people in high-risk (think kidnapping) areas overseas. This chip is an implantable, 12 mm x 2.1 mm radio frequency device, about the size of the point of a ballpoint pen. It contains a unique verification number.

Although watches are a great form factor for lots of wireless connectivity opportunities, they have been hampered by either wired interface requirements (like a USB connection) or an infrared (IR) connection (which requires line-of-sight to a specific on-ramp). Expect these same devices to very quickly take on Bluetooth and 802.11 interfaces so that constant updating — like with the Microsoft Smart Personal Objects Technology (SPOT) model (www.microsoft.com/SPOT/) — can occur. Watches are also popular for

- **Taking pictures:** The Casio (www.casio.com) WQV10D-2 Color Wrist Camera watch with color liquid crystal display (LCD) lets you snap up to 100 images in JPEG format. A 2X digital zoom enables you to get closer to your subjects, and IR transfer enables you to share your pictures with other Casio wrist cameras and your PC. An RF option is surely on the way.

- **Looking up phone numbers:** The Casio BZX201SCR PC Unite Watch is equipped with infrared capabilities, plus enhanced PC synchronization functions. In addition to being able to exchange personal information manager data with a computer, the PC Unite also can link with Microsoft Outlook and even exchange data with a portable terminal such as a PDA.

Creating wireless connectivity via jewelry bears its own set of issues because of the size and weight requirements of the host jewelry for any wireless system. The smaller the jewelry, the less power that the wireless transmitter can have to do its job. The less power, the shorter the range, and so the more limited the bandwidth and application of the device.

Chapter 20

Top Ten Sources for More Information

In This Chapter

▶ Shopping on CNET

▶ Blogging for 802.11

▶ Practically (wireless) networking

▶ Surfing the vendor sites

*W*e've tried hard in this book to capture all that's happening with wireless networks in the home. However, we can't cover everything in one book, and so, in fairness to other publications, we're leaving some things for them to talk about on their Web sites and in their print publications. (Nice of us, isn't it?)

We want to keep you informed of the latest changes to what's in this book. So we encourage you to check out the *Wireless Home Networking For Dummies* update site at www.dummies.com/extras — where you can find updates and new information.

Here's a listing of those publications that we read regularly (and therefore recommend unabashedly) and which you should get your hands on as part of your home wireless networking project. Many of these sources provide up-to-date performance information, which can be critical when making a decision about which equipment to buy and what standards to pursue.

The Web sites mentioned also have a ton of information online, but you might have to try different search keywords to find what you're looking for. Some publications like to use the term *Wi-Fi*, for instance, while others use *802.11*. If you don't get hits on certain terms when you're searching around, try other ones that you know. It's rare to come up empty on a search about wireless networking these days. All sites listed here are free.

CNET.com

CNET.com (www.cnet.com) is a simple-to-use, free Web site where you can do apples-to-apples comparisons of wireless equipment. You can count on finding pictures of what you're buying, editor ratings of the equipment, user ratings of the gear, reviews of most devices, and a listing of the places on the Web where you can buy it all — along with the actual pricing. What's great about CNET is that it covers the wireless networking aspect of Wi-Fi as well as the consumer goods portion of Wi-Fi (such as home theater, A/V gear, phones, and so on). You can count on being able to find all sorts of products and ideas in one place. It's your one-stop resource for evaluating your future home wireless purchases.

What we especially like is the ability to do a side-by-side comparison so that we can see who's got which features. You can go to the Wi-Fi portion of the site and see available gear from major manufacturers. By clicking the boxes next to each name, you can select that gear for comparison shopping. You can also filter the results by price, features, support, and so on at the bottom of the page. Then just click Compare to receive a results page.

Overall, this is a solid site that we often visit before buying anything.

802.11 Planet

802.11 Planet (www.80211planet.com) is a great resource for keeping up with industry news as well as getting reviews of access points, client devices, security tools, and software. Look for the tutorial section where you can find articles such as *Understanding Internal 802.11 Card Form Factors* and *Extending WLAN Range with Repeaters*.

One of the great parts of 802.11 Planet is its forum where you can ask questions to the collective readership and get answers. (You can ask a question, and the system will e-mail you with any responses — very nice.) The forum has sections on General, Security, Troubleshooting, Interoperability and Standards, Hardware, and Applications. The discussions are tolerant of beginners but can get quite sophisticated in their responses. All in all, this is a great site for info.

Broadband Wireless Exchange Magazine

The Broadband Wireless Exchange Magazine (www.bbwexchange.com) is a rapidly growing Web site dedicated to all things wireless, including coverage of lots of emerging products and services coming down the road. The site is a parent site for many sites-within-a-site. It started out covering fixed wireless topics for telephone companies and has grown to include all sorts of consumer, business, and industry content on wireless. If you're interested in just 802.11 products and services, the www.80211-news.com page is a good one for that, as are the firm's other sites on all aspects of wireless technologies. On any particular subsite, you'll find lots of information about industry news, new product announcements, buyer's guides, directories, article listings, and so forth.

This site is adding content and new capabilities daily, so it's hard to summarize in one paragraph. Suffice it to say that by the time you read this, it will probably have tripled in size. Definitely check it out.

80211b.weblogger.com

This site (80211b.weblogger.com) is a great site for finding out what's going on in the wireless world. You might have heard about *Weblogs:* They're link-running, rambling commentaries that people keep online about topics that are near and dear to their hearts. This is also called *blogging*.

Unless you want to track the wireless industry, though, you probably wouldn't want to check this daily, but it's a great resource for when you want to see what the latest news is about a particular vendor or technology. This is the site that we follow every day for interesting news and product or service developments.

Another big strength of this site is its coverage of the OS X/Apple world of wireless. If you have an Apple computer, do check out this site's AirPort Weblog on how to get the most out of your AirPort Extreme. If you've got a Mac, spend some time checking out their AirPort Forum threads and keep your eye on this page for the latest AirPort news! You can find a host of content to support your Apple efforts — lots besides just news.

Check out these other Weblogs about wireless topics: Bluetooth (bluetooth.weblogs.com) and Reiter's Wireless Data (reiter.weblogger.com) Weblogs in particular.

PC Magazine

The venerable *PC Magazine* (www.pcmag.com) is the go-to publication for PC users. This magazine regularly and religiously tracks all aspects of wireless, from the individual product reviews to sweeping buyer's guides across different wireless segments to updates on key operating system and supporting software changes. If you have a PC, you should be subscribing to this magazine.

We really like the First Look sections of the publication, which offer you the immediate insight on new product announcements, giving you hands-on, quick reviews of the latest developments on the market. This is great for those products that you've heard were coming but were waiting to actually be ready. *PC Magazine* is usually one of the first to review these products.

A one-year subscription (22 issues) runs only $34.97, and a two-year subscription (44 issues) is $59.97. You can subscribe to either electronic or print issues, which is nice if you want to catch up on your reading on the go but don't want to carry a bag of publications.

Electronic House Magazine

Electronic House (www.electronichouse.com) is one of our favorite publications because you can read a lot of very easy-to-understand articles about all aspects of an electronic home, including articles on wireless networking and all the consumer appliances and other non-PC devices that are going wireless. It's written for the consumer who enjoys technology.

Electronic House magazine includes articles on wireless home networking, wireless home control, and subsystems such as residential lighting, security, home theaters, energy management, and telecommunications. It also regularly looks at new and emerging technologies using wireless capabilities, such as wireless refrigerators and wireless touchpanels, to control your home.

Electronic House is a monthly publication with a 13th issue called the *Planning Guide* that's available at newsstands. The magazine costs $29.95 a year. Back issues are $5.95 each or six issues for $30 (plus shipping), so you can catch up on what you've missed (we always love doing that). You definitely want to subscribe to this one!

Home Automation Magazine

Home Automation magazine (www.homeautomationmag.com) — also from the publishers of *Electronic House* magazine — is a magazine for the do-it-yourselfer. It's geared more to the specific product reviews and discusses new technologies for the home and how to put them in. Articles show you how to carry out a range of wireless projects, including how you can add wireless access to an existing home network, set up a wireless video network, configure structured wiring, and much more.

The magazine comes out seven times a year and costs $29.95 a year. Back issues are $5.95 each or six issues for $30 (plus shipping).

The `www.homeautomationmag.com` Web site includes Web-only articles, so check it out as well. You also find links to the `www.ehstore.com` shopping site for books and videos.

Practically Networked

Practically Networked (`www.practicallynetworked.com`) is a free site run by the folks at Internet.com. It has basic tutorials on networking topics, background on key technologies, and a troubleshooting guide. The site can contain some dated information in places, but it does have monitored discussion groups where you can get some good feedback, and the reviews section gives you a listing of products with a fairly comprehensive buyer's guide-style listing of features.

ExtremeTech.com

Ziff Davis Media has a great site at `www.extremetech.com` that has special sections focused on networking and wireless issues. There is heavy traffic at the discussion groups, and people seem willing to provide quick and knowledgeable answers. (You'll find some seriously educated geeks on these groups.) Check out the links to wireless articles and reviews by ExtremeTech staff.

The site can be difficult to navigate because the layout is a little confusing. We recommend that you visit the *ExtremeTech Feature Story Index* that has "Links to all our great feature content in one place," as the editors put it. It's labeled ExtremeTech Index.

And if you're having a problem that you just can't seem to crack, check out the discussion groups on this site.

Network World

Network World (`www.nwfusion.com`) is the leading publication for networking professionals, and although this is a site geared primarily for businesses, it does have a lot of content about wireless because so much of the technology first appeared in commercial venues. The site has detailed buyer's guides that show features and functionality of wireless LANs products — almost all of which is applicable for your home. Importantly, you can also search the site for more content on Wi-Fi and 802.11 as well as Bluetooth. The publication has a large reporting staff and stays on top of everything networking-related.

Other Cool Sites

We can't list all the sites here that we regularly visit, but a lot of good information is out there. Here are some other sites worth looking at:

Topical sites/search engines

- ✔ **ZDNet:** www.zdnet.com
- ✔ **TechWeb:** www.techweb.com
- ✔ **searchNetworking.com** (look for the link to the Wireless LAN Info Center): www.searchnetworking.com

Industry organizations

The creation and maintenance of standards has really driven wireless to very low price points and great interoperability. Here are some of the organizations pushing for change in wireless; each site has info about wireless and networks:

- ✔ **IEEE 802 home page:** www.ieee802.org
- ✔ **Wi-Fi Alliance** (formerly WECA): www.wi-fi.net
- ✔ **Wireless LAN Association:** www.wlana.org
- ✔ **Freenetworks.org:** www.freenetworks.org

Roaming services and organizations

As we mention in Chapter 16, a range of potential services are available that you can use to log on when on the road. Most of these have sections of their sites devoted to helping you find out where you can log on near you. Here are some of the more mentioned services and initiatives:

- ✔ **Boingo Wireless:** www.boingo.com
- ✔ **Cometa:** www.cometanetworks.com
- ✔ **GRIC:** www.gric.net
- ✔ **iPass:** www.ipass.com

Local wireless groups

Many local groups are dedicated to offering free access around town for broadband Internet service. Here are some of the larger groups:

- ✔ **Austin Wireless** (Austin, TX): www.austinwireless.net
- ✔ **Bay Area Wireless Users Group (BAWUG)** (Bay Area, CA): www.bawug.org

- ✔ **Houston Wireless** (Houston, TX): www.houstonwireless.org
- ✔ **Marin Unwired** (Marin County, CA): www.digiville.com/
  wifi-marin/index.htm
- ✔ **NoCatNet** (Sonoma County, CA): nocat.net
- ✔ **NYCWireless** (New York, NY): nycwireless.net
- ✔ **Personal Telco** (Portland, OR): www.personaltelco.net
- ✔ **SeattleWireless** (Seattle, WA): www.seattlewireless.net

Manufacturers

Some of these firms are more oriented toward business products, but many of them have great educational FAQs and information that's helpful for people trying to read everything that they can (which we support!):

- ✔ **3Com:** www.3com.com
- ✔ *Actiontec:* www.actiontec.com
- ✔ **Alvarion:** www.alvarion.com
- ✔ **Apple:** www.apple.com/airport/
- ✔ **Asanté:** www.asante.com
- ✔ **Buffalo Technology:** www.buffalotech.com
- ✔ **Cisco:** www.cisco.com
- ✔ **D-Link:** www.d-link.com
- ✔ **Hewlett-Packard:** www.hp.com
- ✔ **Intel:** www.intel.com
- ✔ **Intermec:** home.intermec.com
- ✔ **Linksys:** www.linksys.com
- ✔ **Macsense:** www.macsense.com
- ✔ **Microsoft:** www.microsoft.com
- ✔ **NETGEAR:** www.netgear.com
- ✔ **Proxim (ORiNOCO):** www.proxim.com
- ✔ **Raylink:** www.raylink.com
- ✔ **Siemens/Efficient Networks:** www.speedstream.com
- ✔ **smartBridges:** www.smartbridges.com
- ✔ **SMC Networks:** www.smc.com
- ✔ **Symbol Technologies:** www.symbol.com
- ✔ **Xircom:** www.xircom.com

Index

• *Numerics* •

2Wire Web site, 59
3Com Web site, 343
802.11 Planet Web site, 294, 338
802.11 standards. *See* IEEE 802.11
    standards
802.11Hotspots Web site, 294
80211b Weblogger Web site, 339

• *A* •

ABS (AirPort Base Station)
  adding computer on Mac OS 9, 151–152
  adding computer on Mac OS X, 158–159
  adding non-Apple computer to, 159–161
  configuring on Mac OS 9, 148–151
  configuring on Mac OS X, 155–158
  definition of, 135–136
  features of, 139–143
  firmware upgrades on Mac OS 9, 146–148
  firmware upgrades on Mac OS X, 154–155
  Internet connection sharing using, 164
  setting up on Mac OS 9, 144–152
  setting up on Mac OS X, 152–159
access point (AP). *See also* ABS; wireless
    Internet gateway
  acting as a bridge, 29, 38, 167
  ad hoc mode for, 38
  antenna for, detachable, 94–95
  auto channel select, 94
  Bluetooth, 289
  cable/DSL router combined with, 70
  certification of, 88
  configuration, 97–99, 111–116, 191–192
  cost of, 84–85, 100
  definition of, 16
  DHCP address assignment by, 69–70, 91
  encryption key for, 37
  Ethernet port on, 94
  features of, 21–22, 69–70, 94–95
  firewall combined with, 70
  firmware upgrades for, 98–100
  form factor for, 90
  hardware platform support for, 89
  HomePlug built in to, 70
  as hot spot, unintentionally, 293
  HPNA built in to, 58, 70
  infrastructure mode for, 37–38
  installing, preparation for, 105–111
  Internet connection sharing with, 176
  location of, 71–76, 133, 315–316
  MAC address, changing, 108
  modem including, 70
  multiple, improving performance,
    320–322
  multiple, interfering with each other, 73
  NAT included in, 82
  network name for, 36
  operating system compatibility for, 89–90
  outdoor use of, 90
  password for, changing, 192
  PoE support, 94
  power output of, 39, 41
  print server combined with, 70, 93
  radio channel for, 37, 45–46, 112–113, 316
  range of, 16, 18, 76, 97
  repeater mode for, 323
  requirements for, list of, 87–88
  rogue, 293
  software platform support for, 89
  standards for, 68–69, 88–89, 306–307
  switches in, 69, 93
  technical support for, 101
  telnetting to, 99
  uplink port for, 95
  wall-mountable, 71, 90
  warranties for, 100–101
Actiontec Web site, 343
ad hoc mode, 38
Administrators group, 214
Advanced Step in Innovative Mobility.
    See ASIMO
AES (Advanced Encryption Standard), 199
AIBO robotic dog (Sony), 275–276
airlink security, 186–187. *See also* security

AirPort Base Station. *See* ABS
AirPort Card, 135–139, 161–162
AirPort Extreme Base Station, 136, 140
AirPort Extreme Card, 136, 140
AirPort software, 141–146, 152, 153
All-In-Wonder 9700 Pro (ATI), 227, 259
Alvarion Web site, 343
America Online. *See* AOL
antenna
  description of, 38–40
  gain of, 41
  moving to improve performance, 316
  multiple, improving performance, 94–95,
    318
  signal pattern of, 76
  Web site about, 318
antivirus software, 185
AOL (America Online), ABS connecting to,
  139, 141, 156, 166
AP. *See* access point
apparel. *See* clothing
Apple AirPort hardware. *See* ABS; AirPort
  Card
Apple AirPort Web site, 343
Apple Macintosh. *See* Macintosh
  computers
Apple Web site, 22, 144, 152
appliances, 329–330, 332–333
application triggered port forwarding, 241
Applied Digital Solutions Web site, 335
Asanté Web site, 343
ASCII format, for WEP keys, 195
ASIMO (Advanced Step in Innovative
  Mobility), 333
ATI All-In-Wonder 9700 Pro, 227, 259
attached network devices, 208
attenuation, signal, 40
AudioReQuest music server, 221, 251–253
AudioReQuest Web site, 252
AudioTron (Turtle Beach Systems), 27, 272
audio/video equipment
  adapter for, 248, 251–255
  in bathroom, 326
  bridge for, 248, 253
  in cars, 264–268
  digital music server, 221, 251–253
  HDTV, 258
  home theater PC, 249, 257–259
  IEEE 802.11 standards for, 247

  IR devices, controlling from wireless
    network, 272–273
  media player for, 249, 255–256
  network enabled, 248
  PDA as remote control for, 271–272
  streaming files for, 247
  transferring files for, 247
  transmitters on alternative frequencies
    for, 260
  video cameras, 13, 27, 48, 268–270, 287
  video projectors, 250
  wireless adapters for, 251–255
  wireless functionality built in to, 248,
    249–251
  wirelessly enabling, 79, 246–249
Austin Wireless freenet, 294
authentication, 52
AutoCommand Deluxe Remote Starter
  (DesignTech International), 328
automatic network connections, 130–132
automobiles. *See* cars

• *B* •

backbone, wireless, 8
Baldwin Piano Web site, 330
base station. *See* access point
bathroom, wireless devices in, 326
BAWUG (Bay Area Wireless Users Group)
  freenet, 294
Belkin Bluetooth Access Point, 289
BlueM (TDK Systems Europe), 54
Bluetooth technology
  access point for, 289
  adapters to enable PC for, 288–289
  applications for, 280
  communication used by, 50–53
  compared with/Wi-Fi, 49–50
  definition of, 48–49, 277–280
  history of, 278
  IEEE 802.15.1 standard for, 48, 278
  IrDA replaced by, 50
  security standards for, 52–53
  using in wireless network, 53–56
  Web sites for, 48, 53, 278, 339
Bluetooth Weblogs Web site, 339
Bluetooth-enabled devices
  in cars, 54, 282
  cell phones, 53–54, 281–282, 283

communication between, 50–53
connecting to wireless network, 289
digital camcorders, 48, 287
digital cameras, 56, 286–287
handheld computers, 54–55, 282–285
interfering with wireless network, 317
keyboards, 287–288
list of, 48–49, 53–54, 280
mice, 48, 287–288
printers, 56, 285–286
BlueUnplugged Web site, 278
Boingo
 hot spots, 297, 299–300
 network sniffer program, 302
 Web site, 299, 342
books
 about home automation, 275
 about home networking, 186, 203–204
 about home theater, 257
bridge
 access point acting as, 29, 38, 167
 adding to improve performance, 322–323
 AirPort Extreme Base Station acting as,
  140
 for audio/video equipment, 248, 253
 definition of, 29
 for gaming, 234–236, 308
 HomePlug as, 60
broadband connection. *See also* Internet
  connection
 discussion Web site about, 81
 for games, 226
 pinging to test speed of connection, 227
 restrictions on sharing by providers, 296
 sharing, 10–12, 80–81, 164–166
broadband router. *See* cable/DSL router
Broadband Wireless Exchange Magazine
  Web site, 338–339
Buffalo Technology Web site, 343
BZX201SCR PC Unite Watch (Casio), 336

• C •

cable box, wirelessly enabled, 250
cable connection. *See* broadband
  connection

cable modem. *See also* modems
 access point combined with, 70
 definition of, 11
 router for, 29
cable/DSL router
 ABS acting as, 139
 definition of, 29, 81, 92
 included in access point, 70
 included in wireless Internet gateway, 93
camcorders. *See* video cameras
cameras
 in cell phones, 282
 digital, 56, 286–287
 video, Bluetooth-enabled, 48, 287
 video, wireless network, 13, 27, 268–270
 in watches, 336
CAN (campus-wide area network), 291
cars
 Bluetooth used in, 54, 282
 choosing wireless equipment for, 267–268
 GPS for, 327
 MP3 players for, 264
 MP3 servers for, 9
 PCs for, 266–267
 shopping in, 328
 vehicle monitoring systems for, 327
 wireless audio systems for, 264–266
 wireless technologies used by, 262–264,
  326–328
Casio watches, 336
Cat 5e cable. *See* Ethernet cable
Cayman Systems 3500 Series Smart
  Gateways, 28, 30
CDs, virtual, 221
cell phones, 53–54, 281–282, 283
Centrino chip (Intel), 19
CF (Compact Flash) card, 24, 34–35, 55,
  122–124. *See also* network interface
  adapters
Chambers, Mark L. (*Mac OS X All-In-One
  Desk Reference For Dummies*), 203
channel. *See* radio channel
chips. *See also* firmware
 Centrino chip (Intel), 19
 embedded in clothing, 334
 implanted in people (VeriChip), 335
 implanted in pets, 331

Cisco products, 141, 332, 343
client computer. *See* computers
clothing, wireless technologies in, 334–336
CNET Web site, 100, 338
Cometa Web site, 342
computer network. *See* network
computers. *See also* devices; handheld computers; Macintosh computers; PCs
  connecting to Internet through, 164, 175–182
  definition of, 26
  home theater PC, 249, 257–259
  types of, 27–28
ConcertMaster (Baldwin Piano), 330–331
connection sharing, for Internet, 164, 175–182
CorAccess touchpanels, 274–275
cordless phones
  Bluetooth headsets for, 282
  interference caused by, 72, 74, 323–324
cost
  ABS, 140
  access point, 100
  AirPort Card, 136
  audio server, 251
  Bluetooth access points, 289
  Bluetooth adapters, 289
  IEEE 802.11 standards, 18
  media player, 256
  music server, 253
  online-capable games, 231
  touchpanels, 274, 275
  USB Bluetooth adapters, 289
  wired network, 14–15
  wireless Ethernet bridges, 235, 236
  wireless network, 15
crackers, 185
Crestron touchpanels, 273–274
crossover cable, 236

● ♪ ●

data and voice connection, Bluetooth, 51
data speed
  Bluetooth specification, 279
  HomePlug, 60

HPNA, 58
  IEEE 802.11 standards, 18, 42–44, 45, 315
  wired network, 14
  wireless network, 15–16
data-only connection, Bluetooth, 51
DAVE software, 162, 221–223
Davis Instruments Corp. DriveRight vehicle monitoring system, 327
dBm (decibels), 41
DCF-660W (D-Link), 35
demilitarized zone. *See* DMZ
DesignTech International Web site, 328
device drivers, for network interface adapters, 118–120
devices. *See also* audio/video equipment; Bluetooth-enabled devices; computers; gaming console
  multi-standard, 18
  peripherals, sharing, 9–10, 76–78, 216–221
  storage, sharing, 27, 210–216
  types of, 208
  viewing networked devices, 206–210
DHCP (Dynamic Host Configuration Protocol) server
  ABS acting as, 139
  definition of, 22, 27, 91, 165
  IP address automatically obtained from, 168–174, 238
  provided by both router and access point, 167
  provided by router for gaming, 238–239
  used by ISP, 108
dialup connection. *See also* Internet connection
  definition of, 80
  sharing, 81, 166
  WAN router for, 29
dialup modem. *See also* modems
  definition of, 11, 80
  included in ABS, 139–140, 166
  included in gaming console, 232, 233
digital camcorder. *See* video cameras
digital camera. *See* cameras, digital
Digital Media Receiver (HP), 256
digital music server. *See* music server
digital photographs. *See also* cameras, digital
  CorAccess touchpanel features for, 274
  displaying on TV, 256

digital subscriber line (DSL) connection. *See* broadband connection

digital subscriber line (DSL) modem. *See* DSL modem

dipole antenna, 39

directional antenna, 40

directories, sharing. *See* file sharing

disks. *See* storage devices

diversity antenna system, 39

D-Link
 D-Link DCF-660W CF card, 35
 Web sites, 22, 35, 59, 235, 289, 343

D-LinkAir
 DCS-1000W camera, 268–269
 DWL-810 bridge, 235–236, 253

DMZ (demilitarized zone), 92, 175, 243–244

DNS (Domain Name System) server, 108, 168

domain, Windows, 205–206

dongles, 34. *See also* form factor

DriveRight vehicle monitoring system (Davis Instruments Corp.), 327

DSL (digital subscriber line) connection. *See* broadband connection

DSL (digital subscriber line) modem, 11, 29, 70. *See also* modems

dual-mode devices. *See* multi-standard devices

dual-mode support. *See* multi-mode support

Dynamic Host Configuration Protocol server. *See* DHCP server

• E •

E-commerce, in cars, 328

802.11 Planet Web site, 294, 338

802.11Hotspots Web site, 294

80211b Weblogger Web site, 339

EIRP (effective isotropic radiated power), 41

electrical outlets, networking through. *See* powerline network

Electronic Frontier Foundation Web site, 296

Electronic House Magazine Web site, 340

E-mail server, 27

encryption. *See also* security (wireless network); WEP encryption protocol; WPA encryption protocol
 AirPort support for, 141
 Bluetooth standards for, 52
 HomePlug using, 60

Entertainment Anywhere (X10), 254

entertainment systems. *See* audio/video equipment

Epson Web site, 286

equipment for wireless network, 20–24. *See also* access point; devices; network interface adapters

Ericsson, Bluetooth and, 48, 278

ESSID (Extended Service Set Identifier), 36

Ethernet adapter, 58, 60

Ethernet bridge
 for AudioReQuest, 253
 for gaming, 230, 234–236
 HomePlug as, 60

Ethernet cable
 cost of, 67
 receiving AC power through (PoE), 94
 used for installing access point, 108, 110

Ethernet connection. *See also* wired network; wireless network
 definition of, 13
 included in access point, 94
 required for access point setup, 107, 320–321

Ethernet protocol, 12, 22, 204

Ethernet, wireless. *See* IEEE 802.11 standards

exercise equipment, 328–329

Extended Service Set Identifier. *See* ESSID

ExtremeTech Web site, 341

• F •

FCC (Federal Communication Commission)
 antenna regulations, 95
 AP power output regulations, 41

FCC (Federal Communication Commission)
 certification of radio equipment by, 319
 EIRP regulations, 41
 radio spectrum regulations, 44–45
 unlicensed frequencies set by, 72

fidelity. *See* wireless fidelity
file server, 27
file sharing, 8–9, 210–216, 221–223, 280
File Transfer Protocol server. *See* FTP server
filtering, 311
firewall
 compared with/NAT, 311
 definition of, 30
 included in access point, 70, 96
 personal, on each computer, 185
 port forwarding and, 240–242
 on router, 86, 186
firmware. *See also* software
 reasons to upgrade or not upgrade, 310
 upgrades for ABS, 143
 upgrades for ABS on Mac OS 9, 146–148
 upgrades for ABS on Mac OS X, 154–155
 upgrades for access points, 98, 99–100, 115
 upgrades for network interface adapters, 118, 122
fitness equipment, 328–329
FLAK lossless compression, 253
FM modulator, 267
folders, sharing. *See* file sharing
form factor. *See also* CF card; PC Card; PCI adapter; USB adapter
 for access point and network interface adapters, 90
 for GPS devices for pets, 331
 for HPNA products, 58
freenets, 294–295
FreeNetworks freenet, 294
FreeSpeak wireless headset (JABRA), 282
Friendly Machines Robomow robotic lawnmower, 333
Fry's Web site, 109
FTP (File Transfer Protocol) server, 142

● *G* ●

gain, antenna, 39, 41, 73
GameCube (Nintendo), 27, 225, 233
Gamer's Haven Web site, 235
Gamertag, 232

games
 configuring to work wirelessly, 308
 DMZ for, 92, 243–244
 Gamertag for, 232
 hardware requirements for, 227–228
 multi-user, playing, 12, 308
 network requirements for, 228
 online, 225–226, 230–233
 playing with home theater PC, 258
 router configurations for, 237–242
 Web sites for, 226, 227
gaming console
 benefits of, 229
 compatibility with router, 238
 connecting to wireless network, 78, 229–236
 definition of, 27
 online gaming with, 230–233
 port forwarding not required for, 239
 vendors of, 225
 wireless networking equipment for, 234–236
gaming controllers, 228
gaming PCs, 227
gateway address, for Internet connection, 108
gateways. *See* wireless gateway; wireless Internet gateway
Gibson, Steve (ShieldsUP!! software), 186
GPS (Global Positioning System), 285, 327, 331, 334
graphics card. *See* video card
Graphite ABS, 140
GRIC Web site, 342

● *H* ●

hacking, 95
HAI Omni system, 275
handheld computers. *See also* PDA
 Bluetooth add-on cards for, 284
 Bluetooth supported by, 54–55, 282–285
 Bluetooth-enabled, 48
 Bluetooth-enabled keyboard for, 284
 cell phones included in, 283
 CF card for, 34–35, 122–124
 docking cradle for, 283

enabling wireless Internet access, 127–128

remote control, using as, 271–272

sniffer program for, 302

synchronizing with PC, 127–128, 283–285

synchronizing with watches, 336

wireless uses of, 21

hard disks. *See* storage devices

hardware for wireless network. *See* equipment for wireless network

Harmony Remote (Intrigue Technologies), 272

HCI (Host Controller Interface), 54

HDTV (High Definition TV), 258

Hewlett Packard. *See* HP

hexadecimal format, for WEP keys, 195

H+H Zentrum fuer Rechnerkommunikation GmbH, Virtual CD software, 221

high-speed connection. *See* broadband connection

home

appliances, Internet-capable, 329–330

controlling IR devices from wireless network, 272–273

current technologies for, 270–271

PDAs as remote controls, 271–272

robots for, 275–276, 332–333

security for, 268–270, 274, 275

touchpanels, 273–275

Home Automation Magazine Web site, 340–341

home entertainment center. *See* audio/video equipment

home media player. *See* media player

Home Networking For Dummies (Ivens), 186, 203

Home Phoneline Networking Association. *See* HPNA

Home Theater For Dummies (Hurley, Briere), 257

home theater PC, 249, 257–260

HomePlug, 59–61

HomePNA. *See* HPNA

HomeRF standard, 57, 249

Honda ASIMO. *See* ASIMO

hopping scheme, 53

Host Controller Interface. *See* HCI

host, Internet connection, 175

hot spots

Boingo Wireless, 297, 299–300

definition of, 13, 291

finding, 300–302

for-pay, 295–298

freenets, 294–295

locations for, 296

public, 292–298

purposes of, 293

restrictions by ISPs and broadband providers, 296

roaming and, 297

T-Mobile, 297, 298

unintentional, 293

wardrivers finding, 295

Wayport, 299

Houston Wireless Web site, 343

HP (Hewlett-Packard)

Digital Media Receiver, 256

iPAQ Pocket PC H5450, 54

Pocket PC h5400, 35

Web site, 54, 256, 286, 343

HPNA (Home Phoneline Networking Association), 57–59

HTPC. *See* home theater PC

hub. *See also* network hub; switch

compared with/switch, 93

definition of, 22

USB, 289

• *I* •

iBook computer, 135, 137

Icon Fitness, 328–329

icons used in this book, 3–4

IEEE 802.11 standards

alternatives to, 260

channel frequencies for, 112–113

choosing, 68–69, 88–89, 306–307

descriptions of, 17–19, 41–44

future standards, 198–199

Web site for, 342

IEEE 802.11a standard

channel frequencies for, 112

description of, 17–19, 43, 68

IEEE 802.11a standard *(continued)*
  interference less likely with, 74, 97
  non-overlapping channels with, 46, 112
  performance of, 315
  range of, 319
IEEE 802.11a/b/g standard, 17, 44, 69
IEEE 802.11a/g standard, 306–307
IEEE 802.11b standard
  for audio/video file handling, 247
  channel frequencies for, 112–113
  description of, 17–19, 42–43, 68
  devices causing interference with, 74
  limitations of, 307
  overlapping channels with, 45–46, 112
  used by AirPort Card and Base Station,
    136, 140
IEEE 802.11g standard
  channel frequencies for, 112–113
  description of, 17–19, 44, 68
  devices causing interference with, 74
  mini-PCI card for, 120–122
  overlapping channels with, 112
  used by AirPort Extreme Card and Base
    Station, 136, 140
IEEE 802.11i standard, 198–199
IEEE 802.11x standard, 198
IEEE 802.15.1 standard, 48, 278
iFIT (Icon Fitness), 328–329
iMac computer, 137
industrial, scientific, and medical bands.
    See ISM bands
Industry Standard Architecture adapter.
    See ISA adapter
industry standards. *See* IEEE 802.11
    standards
Infrared Data Association. *See* IrDA
infrared (IR) interface, 272–273
infrastructure mode, 37–38
initialization vector, of WEP key, 191
installation
  wired network, 14–15
  wireless network, 105–111, 118–126,
    129–130, 137–139
Intel Centrino chip. *See* Centrino chip
Intel Web site, 343
interference
  and access point location, 71–72
  cordless phones causing, 323–324

dual-band interference, 317
  measuring, 133
  obstacles affecting, 317–318
  X10 network causing, 324
Intermec Web site, 343
Internet connection
  appliances with, 329–330
  connection sharing for, 164, 175–182
  for handheld computers, 127–128
  router for, 164–165
  security for, 185–186, 192, 309
  sharing, 10–12, 79–83, 163–166, 175–182
  sharing with neighborhood community,
    293, 296
  testing before installing access point, 106
  troubleshooting, 307–308
  wireless standard for, 68
Internet gateway. *See* wireless Internet
    gateway
Internet Service Provider. *See* ISP
interoperability standards, 42
Intrigue Technologies, 272, 273
IP (Internet Protocol) address
  assigned automatically, 167–174
  assigned by access point, 69–70, 114
  definition of, 30
  DHCP assigning, 27, 91, 165
  for gaming, 237–239
  for Internet connection, 107
  local (LAN, private), 114, 311–312
  NAT server converting to multiple IP
    addresses, 165
  subnet portion of, 167
  WAN (public), 114, 311–312
  for wireless network camera, 270
iPAQ Pocket PC H5450 (HP), 54
iPass Web site, 342
iPronto, 272–273
IR (infrared) interface, 272–273
IrDA (Infrared Data Association), Bluetooth
    replacing, 50
iRobot Web site, 332
ISA (Industry Standard Architecture)
    adapter, 24, 124–125. *See also* network
    interface adapters
ISM (industrial, scientific, and medical)
    bands, 44–46

ISP (Internet Service Provider)
  AOL, 139, 141, 156, 166
  definition of, 30
  information required from, 107–108
  IP address assigned by, 114, 168
  restrictions on sharing Internet
    connection, 296
Ivens, Kathy (*Home Networking For
    Dummies*), 186, 203

• *J* •

JABRA FreeSpeak wireless headset, 282
Jacuzzi wireless products, 326
Jaguar operating system. *See* Max OS X
    version 10.2 operating system
J-Allure shower (Jacuzzi), 326
Java games, 226
Jensen Matrix Internet Audio
    Transmitter, 254
jewelry, wireless technologies in, 336

• *K* •

keyboard, Bluetooth-enabled, 48, 284,
    287–288
KX-HCM250/270 Network Cameras
    (Panasonic), 27, 268

• *L* •

La Scala (Jacuzzi), 326
LAN (local area network). *See also* wired
    network; wireless network
  compared with/PAN, 48, 277
  definition of, 26
  subnet mask for, 108
laptop
  Centrino chip for, 19
  connecting to Internet with cell phone
    and, 282
  hot spots for, 292–302
  PC Card for, 23, 32
LEAP (Lightweight Extensible
    Authentication Protocol), 141
Leapfrog Series WaveMaster 20 (Terk), 260
Leviton PowerJack, 322

LGE Internet-capable appliances, 329
link test function, 133
Linksys
  Web site, 22, 59, 236, 255, 318, 343
  WET11, 236
  Wireless Digital Media Adapter, 255
  WSB24 Wireless Signal Booster, 319
Listen Web site, 260
local area network. *See* LAN
local IP address, 114, 311–312
lossless compression, 253
Lucent PC Card, 136
Lyra Wireless Model RD 900W adapter
    (RCA), 254

• *M* •

MAC (Media Access Control) address
  changing, 108
  configuring, 114
  filtering for, 96, 196
Mac OS 9 operating system, 144–152,
    173–174
*Mac OS X All-In-One Desk Reference For
    Dummies* (Chambers, Tejkowski,
    Williams), 203
Mac OS X operating system, 152–159, 174
Mac OS X version 10.2 (Jaguar) operating
    system, 181–182, 223
Macintosh computers, sharing files with
    PCs, 221–223. *See also* computers
Macsense Web site, 343
MacSOHO software, 223
MacStumbler program, 302
Marin Unwired Web site, 343
Martian NetDrive Wireless media
    server, 258
master device in piconet, 51
Matrix Internet Audio Transmitter
    (Jensen), 254
Mbps (megabits per second), 42. *See also*
    data speed
Media Access Control address. *See* MAC
    address
media player, 249, 255–256
media server, 258
MediaManager software, 256

mesh network, with Bluetooth, 49

mice, Bluetooth-enabled, 48, 287–288

Microsoft Smart Personal Objects Technology (SPOT), 335

Microsoft Web site, 343

Microsoft Windows operating system. *See also specific Windows operating systems*

Microsoft Wireless Optical Desktop, 287–288

Microsoft Xbox. *See* Xbox

microwave ovens, interference caused by, 72, 74

Mini Stumbler program, 302

mini-PCI card, 120–122

mobile phones. *See* cell phones

modems. *See also* Internet connection
  cable/DSL, access point combined with, 70
  cable/DSL, router for, 29
  dialup, 80, 139–140, 166, 232, 233
  types of, 10–11
  using cell phones as, 282
  using over a network, 11–12

Motorola Web site, 248

motors, interference caused by, 72, 74

mouse. *See* mice

Movielink Web site, 245, 260

MP3 players, 28. *See also* media player

MP3 servers, 9, 27. *See also* AudioReQuest music server; media server

multi-mode support, for access point standards, 88–89

multipath interference, 56

multi-standard devices, 18

multi-user games, 12

music server, AudioReQuest, 221, 251–253

musical instruments, wirelessly enabled, 330–331

MusicCast (Yamaha), 27, 28, 250–251

MUSICMATCH MX Web site, 260

My Network Places, 26, 205, 207

• *N* •

NAN (neighborhood area network), 331

narrowband connection. *See* dialup connection

NAT (Network Address Translation)
  in access point, 96
  in access point and router, 167
  compared with/firewall, 311
  definition of, 29–30, 91–92, 165
  firewall using, 186
  port forwarding and, 240–242
  router, 79–80, 82

NEC ImageXpress projectors, 250

NetBEUI protocol, 223

NetDrive Wireless media server (Martian), 258

NETGEAR products, 22, 59, 89, 343

Net2Phone Web site, 332

Netstumbler.com, 191, 301–302

network. *See also* equipment for wireless network; wired network; wireless network
  definition of, 26–28, 204–205
  infrastructure for, 28–31
  topology of, 28
  viewing shared resources on, 206–210
  workgroup for, 205–206

Network Adapter, for gaming consoles, 232, 233

network adapters. *See* network interface adapters

network address. *See* IP address

Network Address Translation. *See* NAT

network hub, 28

network ID. *See* SSID

network infrastructure, 28–31

network interface adapters. *See also* wireless adapters
  AirPort Card, 135–139, 161–162
  for audio/video equipment, 248
  CF card, 24, 34–35, 55, 122–124
  configuration, 120
  configuration, modifying, 126–127
  cost of, 85
  definition of, 22, 31
  firmware upgrades for, 118
  form factor for, 90
  for gaming, 228, 233
  installing device drivers and software for, 118–120
  for Internet connection host, 175

ISA adapter, 24, 124–125

PC Card, 23, 32, 90, 120–122

PCI adapter, 24, 33, 124–125

types of, 23–24, 31–35

USB, 24, 33–34, 90, 125–126

WEP, enabling for, 194–195

Wi-Fi, 36

network interface card. *See* NIC

network name. *See* ESSID; SSID

Network Neighborhood, 26, 205, 207

network sniffer program. *See* sniffer program

Network Stumbler program, 301–302

Network World Web site, 341

network-extender devices, 272–273

Nevo (Universal Electronics), 271

NIC (network interface card), 22, 58

Nintendo GameCube, 27, 225, 233

NoCatNet Web site, 343

noise level. *See* interference

nVIDIA Web site, 227

NYCwireless freenet, 294

• *O* •

omnidirectional dipole antenna, 39

online gaming. *See* games, online

operating systems. *See specific operating systems*

Oregon Systems wireless weather station, 328

ORiNOCO products, 113, 126, 343

OS 9 (Mac). *See* Mac OS 9

OS X (Mac). *See* Mac OS X

• *P* •

packets, 29. *See also* SPI

pairing. *See* authentication

Palm devices. *See* handheld computers

PAN (personal area network), 48, 277. *See also* Bluetooth technology

Panasonic cameras, 27, 268

password for access point, 192

PAT (Port Address Translation), 175

PC Card. *See also* network interface adapters

for access point multi-mode support, 89

in audio/video equipment for cars, 267

for Bluetooth, 55

definition of, 23, 32, 90

for HPNA, 58

installing, 120–122

Lucent version of, 136

PC Magazine Web site, 339–340

PC PVR kits, 259

PCI (Peripheral Component Interconnect) adapter. *See also* network interface adapters

definition of, 24, 33

for HPNA, 58

installing, 124–125

mini-PCI card, 120–122

PCMIA (Personal Computer Memory Card International Association). *See* PC Card

PCs. *See also* computers

Bluetooth adapters for, 288–289

gaming PCs, 227

home theater PC, 249, 257–260

sharing files with Macintosh computers, 221–223

PCTV Deluxe (Pinnacle), 259

PDA (personal digital assistant). *See* handheld computers

peer-to-peer networking model, used by Bluetooth, 279

performance. *See also* data speed

access point location affecting, 315–316

access point, number of, affecting, 320–322

antenna location affecting, 316

antennas, number of, affecting, 318

bridge, adding to improve performance, 322–323

channel selection affecting, 316

dual-band interference affecting, 317

of IEEE 802.11 standards, 315

repeater, adding to improve performance, 322–323

signal booster for, 318–320

tracking, 132–133

Peripheral Component Interconnect
   adapter. *See* PCI adapter
peripherals, 9–10, 76–78, 121, 216–221. *See
   also* audio/video equipment;
   Bluetooth-enabled devices; printers
permissions, for file sharing, 214–216
personal area network. *See* PAN
Personal Computer Memory Card
   International Association card. *See*
   PC Card
personal digital assistant (PDA). *See*
   handheld computers
personal firewall, 185
Personal Telco Project Web site, 302, 343
personal video recorder. *See* PVR
Personal Video Station (SnapStream), 259
pets, tracking services for, 331
Philips iPronto, 272–273
Philips ProntoLITE, 271
phoneline network, 58–59
phones
   cell phones, 53–54, 281–282, 283
   cordless phones, 72, 74, 282, 323–324
   HPNA, 57–59
   integrating into wireless network,
      331–332
   making calls over wireless network, 332
photographs, digital. *See* digital
   photographs
physical address. *See* MAC address
piconet, 50–51
pinging, 227
Pinnacle PCTV Deluxe, 259
PlayStation 2 (Sony), 27, 232–233
Pocket PC. *See* handheld computers
Pocket PC h5400 (HP), 35
PoE (Power over Ethernet), 94
Point-to-Point Protocol over Ethernet. *See*
   PPPoE
Port Address Translation. *See* PAT
port forwarding, 92, 239–242, 308, 309
Power Mac G4 computer, 137
power outage, troubleshooting after, 92
Power over Ethernet. *See* PoE
Power Users group, 214
PowerBook computer, 137
PowerJack (Leviton), 322
powerline network, 59–61

PPPoE (Point-to-Point Protocol over
   Ethernet), 114, 143
Practically Networked Web site, 341
print server
   adding printer with, 77
   definition of, 22, 27
   included in access point, 70, 93
   setting up, 216–220
printers
   accessing from networked computers,
      220
   Bluetooth-enabled, 48, 56, 285–286
   connecting to wireless network, 76–78
   installing on networked computers,
      219–220
   print server used to share, 27
   sharing, 9–10, 216–220
PRISMIQ MediaPlayer, 249, 255–256
problems. *See* troubleshooting
programs. *See* software
ProntoLITE (Philips), 271
protocol, 204. *See also specific protocols*
Proxim Web site, 343
PS2. *See* PlayStation 2
public hot spots. *See* hot spots, public
PVR (personal video recorder), home
   theater PC acting as, 258, 259

• R •

radio channel
   changing, to improve performance, 316
   choosing, 37
   configuring, 112–113
   frequencies for, 112–113
   frequencies for, with Bluetooth, 279
   overlapping, 45–46
radio frequency identification. *See* RFID
radio signal
   attenuation, 40
   booster for, 318–320
   interference, 16, 18, 53, 133
   ISM bands for, 44–46
   obstacles affecting, 74–75, 317–318
   range of, 16, 18, 76, 97
   range of, with Bluetooth, 52, 279
   security regarding, 186–187
   shape of, 76

signal booster for, 318–320

SNR (Signal to Noise Ratio), 133

strength of, 39–40, 73–75, 132–133

strength of, limiting, 187

strength of, with Bluetooth, 52, 279

RadioShack Web site, 109

RADIUS (Remote Authentication Dial-In User Service), 141

Rathbone, Andy (*Windows XP For Dummies*), 203

Raylink Web site, 343

RCA jacks, 254

RCA Lyra Wireless Model RD 900W adapter, 254

RCA Web site, 232, 254

RCA wireless phone jacks, 232

receive sensitivity, 40

Reiter's Wireless Data Weblogs Web site, 339

Remote Authentication Dial-In User Service. *See* RADIUS

remote control
  in bathroom, 326
  for car, 327, 328
  for media player, 255–256
  for musical instruments, 330
  for TV, 250
  using PDA as, 271–272

Remote Management function, disabling, 192

repeater, adding to improve performance, 322–323

ReplayTV Web site, 253, 258

RFID (radio frequency identification), 330, 334

risk assessment, 184–187

Robomow robotic lawnmower (Friendly Machines), 333

robots, 275–276, 332–333

Rockford Corporation Web site, 9

rogue access point, 293

Roomba (iRobot) robotic vacuum cleaner, 332

router
  configuring for gaming, 228, 237–242
  definition of, 22, 29–30
  DHCP server built in to, 91
  DMZ for, 243–244

firewall for, 186

HPNA built in to, 58, 59

for Internet connection sharing, 164–165

port forwarding, 239–242

SPI for, 186, 309

testing before installing access point, 106

UPnP-enabled, 242

• S •

Samsung Internet-capable appliances, 329

satellite connection. *See also* broadband connection
  on airplanes, 297
  availability of, 80
  GPS using, 327
  WAN router for, 29

satellite modem, 11. *See also* modems

satellite radio, 263

scatternet, 51

searchNetworking Web site, 342

SeattleWireless Web site, 343

security (home), 268–270, 274, 275

security (wireless network). *See also* firewall; WEP encryption protocol; WPA encryption protocol
  for access point, 95–96
  AES for, 199
  airlink, 86, 186–187
  for AirPort, 141, 143
  antivirus software, 185
  Bluetooth standards for, 52–53
  closed network, creating, 195–196
  crackers, 185
  encryption key for, 37
  hacking, 95
  for HomePlug, 60
  IEEE 802.11i standard, 198–199
  IEEE 802.11x standard, 198
  Internet, 86
  for Internet connection, 185–186, 192, 309
  MAC layer filtering, 196
  NAT providing, 30, 82, 92, 311
  not enabling security features, 184, 293
  permissions, for file sharing, 214–216
  reason for, 16
  risk assessment, 184–187
  sharing and, 212

Bluetooth standards for, 52–53 *(continued)*
  sniffer program, 196, 300–302
  spoofing MAC addresses, 196
  spool attack, 96
  SSID broadcast, disabling, 196
  testing for, 186, 309–310
  VPN providing, 96, 190, 311
  warchalking, 191
  wardrivers, 183, 184, 295
Server Operators group, 214
servers, 27. *See also* DHCP server; media
  server; MP3 servers; print server
service area. *See* SSID
Service Set Identifier. *See* SSID
ShieldsUP!! software (Gibson, Steve), 186,
  310
shopping. *See also* cost
  e-commerce in cars, 328
  price comparison Web sites, 100
Siemens/Efficient Networks Web site, 22,
  59, 70, 343
signal. *See* radio signal
signal processing algorithm, for
  HomePlug, 59
Signal to Noise Ratio. *See* SNR
simplefi (Motorola) digital audio receiver,
  248, 249
slave devices in piconet, 51
Smart Homes For Dummies (Hurley, Briere),
  275
Smart Personal Objects Technology. *See*
  SPOT
smartBridges Web site, 343
SMC Networks Web site, 343
SnapStream Personal Video Station, 259
SneakerNet, 9
sniffer program, 196, 300–302
Snow ABS, 140
SNR (Signal to Noise Ratio), 133
software. *See also* firmware
  access point configuration, 89, 97–99, 109,
  115–116
  adding Mac to Windows network, 162
  AirPort, 141–143
  antivirus, 185
  file sharing between Macs and PCs,
  221–223
  firewall, 30, 82, 96

firewall tests, 186, 309–310
hot spots, locating, 300–302
Internet connection sharing using, 81
MediaManager, 256
network interface adapter configuration,
  118–120, 126–127
performance tracking, 132–133
sniffer program, 196, 300–302
Virtual CD, 221
SONICblue DVD player, 250
Sony
  AIBO robotic dog, 275–276
  DSC-FX77 digital camera, 286
  PlayStation 2, 27, 232–233
  Web site, 27, 225, 289
sound card, gaming requirements for, 228
SoundLink Wireless Audio Delivery
  System, 260
SourceForge Web site, 137
speakers. *See* audio/video equipment
SpectraLink Web site, 332
speed. *See* data speed
SPI (Stateful Packet Inspection), 186, 309
spoofing MAC addresses, 196
spool attack, 96
SPOT (Smart Personal Objects Technology,
  Microsoft), 335
SSID (Service Set Identifier)
  configuring, 111–112
  default, changing, 191–192
  definition of, 36
  specifying for network interface
  adapter, 120
  turning off broadcast for, 196
SST Component Framework (Intrigue
  Technologies), 273
standalone network devices, 208
standards for wireless network. *See* IEEE
  802.11 standards
star-shaped topology, 28
Stateful Packet Inspection. *See* SPI
station. *See* workstation
stereo systems. *See* audio/video
  equipment
storage devices, sharing, 27, 210–216
streaming audio and visual files, 247
subnet, 167
subnet mask, 108, 114, 167

switch, 22, 29, 69, 93
Symbol Technologies Web site, 332, 343
synchronization
  with Bluetooth, 280, 281, 283–285
  definition of, 9
  of handheld computers with PCs,
      127–128, 283–285
  of handheld computers with watches, 336

• T •

TCP/IP (Transmission Control
    Protocol/Internet Protocol), 30, 165
TDK BlueM. *See* BlueM
TDK Systems Europe Web site, 54
technical support for access point, 101
TechWeb Web site, 342
Tejkowski, Erick (*Mac OS X All-In-One Desk
    Reference For Dummies*), 203
telephones. *See* phones
telnetting to access point, 99
Terk Leapfrog Series WaveMaster 20, 260
themes, Windows XP, 205
3Com Web site, 343
throughput, 45. *See also* data speed
Thursby Software Systems Web site, 162
time-gate, 56
TiVo Web site, 258
T-Mobile hot spots, 297, 298
topology of network, 28
touchpanels, home control using, 273–275
Transmission Control Protocol/Internet
    Protocol. *See* TCP/IP
transmission power, 39
Trimble Web site, 285
troubleshooting
  after power outage, 92, 314
  interference from unknown source,
      314–315
  Internet connection not working
      wirelessly, 307–308
  multiple access points set to same
      channel, 113
  orphaning client while reconfiguring
      access point, 116
  performance problems, 314–324
  technical support for access point, 101
  when everything stops working, 312

Turtle Beach Systems AudioTron, 27, 272
TV. *See also* audio/video equipment
  HDTV, 258
  home theater PC, 249, 257–260
  PDA as remote control for, 271–272
2Wire Web site, 59
TX power, 39, 41

• U •

Ultra Wideband. *See* UWB
unconscious connectivity, 50
Universal Electronics Nevo, 271
Universal Plug and Play-enabled router. *See*
    UPnP-enabled router
Universal Serial Bus. *See* USB
Unlicensed National Information
    Infrastructure (U-NII) frequencies, 45
uplink port, for access point, 95
UPnP-enabled router, 242
USB (Universal Serial Bus) adapter. *See
    also* network interface adapters
  for Bluetooth, 55, 288–289
  definition of, 24, 33–34, 90
  HomePlug bridge for, 60
  for HPNA, 58
  installing, 125–126
user groups, for file sharing permissions,
    214–216
Users group, 214
UWB (Ultra Wideband), 56

• V •

VeriChip (Applied Digital Solutions), 335
video cameras
  Bluetooth-enabled, 48, 287
  wireless network-enabled, 13, 27, 268–270
video card, gaming requirements for, 227
video game consoles. *See* gaming console
video games. *See* games
video monitoring, 268–270, 274
video projectors, 250
videoconferencing, 308–309
virtual CD server, 221
Virtual CD software, 221
Virtual Private Network. *See* VPN
virus definition files, 185

viruses, 185
voice-only connection, Bluetooth, 51
VoIP telephone companies, 332
Vonage Web site, 332
VPN (Virtual Private Network)
  ABS compatible with, 142
  Boingo Wireless providing, 300
  definition of, 96, 190, 311

• W •

WAG511 Dual Band Wireless PC Card
    (NETGEAR), 89
WAN router, 29–30
WAN (wide area network), 26, 114, 311–312
warchalking, 191
wardrivers, 86, 183, 184, 295
warranties for access point, 100–101
watches, wireless technologies in, 334–336
WAV lossless compression, 253
Wayport hot spots, 299
weather station, wireless, 328
Web server, mapping on ABS for, 142
Web sites. *See also specific Web sites*
  AC adapters, product for hiding, 322
  access point vendors, 22
  access points with HomePlug, 70
  AirPort software, 144, 152
  antenna information, 318
  AudioReQuest music server, 221
  BlueM device for PDAs, 54
  Bluetooth adapters, 289
  Bluetooth technology, 48, 278
  Bluetooth-enabled devices, 53, 278,
    282–283, 285–287
  Boingo Wireless hot spots, 299
  broadband discussions, 81
  car remote controls, 328
  cars, wireless products for, 264
  CF cards, 35
  clothing with cell phone headset
    wires, 283
  digital audio receiver, 248
  DVD players, 250
  entertainment devices, 253
  Ethernet bridge, 253
  Ethernet cables, 109
  exercise equipment, 328–329
  file servers, 27

firewall tests, 186
firewalls, personal, 185
freenets, 294
gaming consoles, 27, 225
HomePlug devices, 70
HomePlug standard, 59
HPNA, 58
industry standards, 342
Internet-capable appliances, 329
iPAQ Pocket PC H5450, 54
IR interfaces, 272
ISPs, wireless-friendly, 296
Java games, 226
list of, 338–343
Mac, adding to Windows network, 162
media players, 249, 256
media server, 258
movies, 245, 259–260
MP3 players, 28, 264
MP3 servers, 9
music, online, 259–260
music servers, 252
network interface adapter software, 126
network interface adapters, 36
online gaming, 227, 231, 233, 235, 236
open source driver project, 137
PC Card, dual-band, 89
PC PVR kits, 259
PDA remote control products, 271–272
pet tracking service, 331
phone headsets, 282
phone jacks, wireless, 232
phone service over wireless network, 332
phone synchronization software, 281
phones supporting 802.11 standard, 332
port forwarding, 242
powerline network products, 59
price comparisons of equipment, 100
roaming services, 342
robots, 276, 332–333
routers with HPNA, 59
sniffer programs, 301–302
for this book, 4, 262, 337
T-Mobile hot spots, 298
touchpanels, 273, 274, 275
UWB, 56
vehicle monitoring systems, 327
video cards, 227
virtual CD software, 221

watches, wirelessly enabled, 335–336
Wayport hot spots, 299
weather station, wireless, 328
wireless adapters for audio/video
    equipment, 254–255
wireless Internet gateways, 30
wireless network video cameras, 27, 269,
    270
wireless networking, list of Web sites for,
    338–343
Web-based configuration software, 98, 115
WEP (Wired Equivalent Privacy)
    encryption protocol
    configuring, 113–114
    definition of, 37, 95–96, 187–188
    enabling, 190–195
    how it works, 188–189
    key for, creating, 193–194
    key for, format of, 195
    key length for, 188–189, 191
    limitations of, 189–190
Wherify Web site, 335
whole home audio/video network, 246. *See
    also* audio/video equipment
wide area network. *See* WAN
Wi-Fi Alliance
    compared with/Bluetooth, 49–50
    data speed standards, 45
    definition of, 17
    encryption protocols used by, 37
    interoperability standards, 17, 42, 88
    network interface adapters, 36
    Web site for, 342
Wi-Fi Protected Access encryption
    protocol. *See* WPA encryption protocol
Williams, Michael L. (*Mac OS X All-In-One
    Desk Reference For Dummies*), 203
Windows 95/98 operating system
    assigning IP addresses automatically,
        169–170
    Network Neighborhood for, 205
    setting up workgroup in, 206
    sharing files on, 211–213
    sharing printers on, 218
    viewing shared resources on, 207
Windows 98 SE operating system, Internet
    connection sharing using, 176–178
Windows 2000 operating system

assigning IP addresses automatically,
    170–172
Internet connection sharing using,
    178–179
setting permissions for, 214–216
setting up workgroup in, 206
sharing files on, 213–214
sharing printers on, 218–219
viewing shared resources on, 207
Windows 2000 Professional operating
    system, My Network Places for, 205
Windows Explorer, viewing shared
    resources with, 209
Windows Me operating system
    Internet connection sharing using,
        176–178
    Network Neighborhood for, 205
    setting up workgroup in, 206
    sharing files on, 211–213
    sharing printers on, 218
    viewing shared resources on, 207
Windows Pocket PC. *See* handheld
    computers
Windows XP For Dummies (Rathbone), 203
Windows XP Media Center Edition, 245
Windows XP operating system
    assigning IP addresses automatically,
        172–173
    automatic network connections, 130–132
    installing and configuring network
        interface adapter, 129–130
    Internet connection sharing using,
        180–181
    modifying configuration for network
        interface adapter, 127
    My Network Places for, 205
    setting permissions for, 214–216
    setting up workgroup in, 206
    sharing files on, 213–214
    sharing printers on, 218–219
    themes in, 205
    viewing shared resources on, 207
Wired Equivalent Privacy encryption
    protocol. *See* WEP encryption protocol
wired network. *See also* network
    benefits of, 14
    book about, 186
    combining with wireless network, 67

wired network. *See also* network *(continued)*
compared with/wireless network, 13–16
  installing, 14–15
wireless adapters, 248, 251–255. *See also*
  network interface adapters
Wireless Audio Delivery System
  (SoundLink), 260
Wireless Digital Media Adapter
  (Linksys), 255
wireless Ethernet. *See* IEEE 802.11
  standards
wireless Ethernet bridge. *See* Ethernet
  bridge
wireless fidelity, 17. *See also* Wi-Fi Alliance
wireless gateway, 31, 84
wireless Internet gateway
  connecting printer to, 78
  cost of, 84
  definition of, 30–31, 70, 91–93, 164–165
Wireless LAN Association Web site, 342
wireless media player. *See* media player
wireless network. *See also* network
  benefits of, 7–13, 15
  choosing devices to connect to, 66
  choosing standard for, 16–19, 68–69
  closing, 195–196
  compared with/wired network, 13–16
  connecting automatically, with Windows
    XP, 130–132
  connecting Mac to non-Apple network,
    161–162
  cost of, 84–85
  drawbacks of, 15–16
  equipment required for, 20–24
  HomePlug used with, 57, 59–61
  HPNA used with, 57–59
  installing components of, 105–111,
    118–126, 129–130, 137–139
  performance tracking for, 132–133
  planning for, 20
  Web sites about, 338–343
  wired connections in, 67
wireless networking adapter. *See* network
  interface adapters

Wireless Node Database Project
  freenet, 294
Wireless Optical Desktop (Microsoft),
  287–288
wireless personal area network. *See* WPAN
Wireless Zero Configuration (Microsoft),
  129–130
workgroup, 26, 205–206
workstation, 26. *See also* computers
WPA (Wi-Fi Protected Access) encryption
  protocol, 37, 96, 197–198
WPAN (wireless personal area network),
  48. *See also* piconet
WQV10D-2 Color Wrist Camera (Casio), 336
WSB24 Wireless Signal Booster (Linksys),
  319

X10
  Entertainment Anywhere, 254
  FloodCam camera, 270
  networks, interference caused by, 324
  Web site, 254, 270
Xbox Live (Microsoft) Web site, 231
Xbox (Microsoft)
  Ethernet bridge for, 253
  online gaming with, 231–232
  Web site for, 27, 225, 253
Xircom products, 36, 343

• *Y* •

Yahoo! Web site, 100, 259
Yamaha MusicCast. *See* MusicCast
Yamaha Web site, 27, 28

• *Z* •

Zandiant Technologies Web site, 264
ZDNet Web site, 342
ZoneAlarm personal firewall, 185

FOR DUMMIES®

The easy way to get more done and have more fun

FOR DUMMIES®

A world of resources to help you grow

TRAVEL

0-7645-5453-0

0-7645-5438-7

0-7645-5444-1

Also available:

America's National Parks For Dummies
(0-7645-6204-5)

Caribbean For Dummies
(0-7645-5445-X)

Cruise Vacations For Dummies 2003
(0-7645-5459-X)

Europe For Dummies
(0-7645-5456-5)

Ireland For Dummies
(0-7645-6199-5)

France For Dummies
(0-7645-6292-4)

Las Vegas For Dummies
(0-7645-5448-4)

London For Dummies
(0-7645-5416-6)

Mexico's Beach Resorts For Dummies
(0-7645-6262-2)

Paris For Dummies
(0-7645-5494-8)

RV Vacations For Dummies
(0-7645-5443-3)

EDUCATION & TEST PREPARATION

0-7645-5194-9

0-7645-5325-9

0-7645-5249-X

Also available:

The ACT For Dummies
(0-7645-5210-4)

Chemistry For Dummies
(0-7645-5430-1)

English Grammar For Dummies
(0-7645-5322-4)

French For Dummies
(0-7645-5193-0)

GMAT For Dummies
(0-7645-5251-1)

Inglés Para Dummies
(0-7645-5427-1)

Italian For Dummies
(0-7645-5196-5)

Research Papers For Dummies
(0-7645-5426-3)

SAT I For Dummies
(0-7645-5472-7)

U.S. History For Dummies
(0-7645-5249-X)

World History For Dummies
(0-7645-5242-2)

HEALTH, SELF-HELP & SPIRITUALITY

0-7645-5154-X

0-7645-5302-X

0-7645-5418-2

Also available:

The Bible For Dummies
(0-7645-5296-1)

Controlling Cholesterol For Dummies
(0-7645-5440-9)

Dating For Dummies
(0-7645-5072-1)

Dieting For Dummies
(0-7645-5126-4)

High Blood Pressure For Dummies
(0-7645-5424-7)

Judaism For Dummies
(0-7645-5299-6)

Menopause For Dummies
(0-7645-5458-1)

Nutrition For Dummies
(0-7645-5180-9)

Potty Training For Dummies
(0-7645-5417-4)

Pregnancy For Dummies
(0-7645-5074-8)

Rekindling Romance For Dummies
(0-7645-5303-8)

Religion For Dummies
(0-7645-5264-3)

Available wherever books are sold. Go to www.dummies.com or call 1-877-762-2974 to order direct